W9-DBD-824

HOW TO SURVIVE IN THE NORTH

Luke Healy

Nobrow

London | *New York*

Introduction

In 1912, after returning from his second Arctic expedition, explorer Vilhjalmur Stefansson set about attempting to prove his theory of "The Friendly Arctic". Stefansson believed that survival in the far north – farther north than even the Inuit villages he had visited – was not only possible, but easy.

Stefansson believed that all the food and fuel a person could need for their indefinite survival were simply hidden beneath the Arctic ice, and could be retrieved with the right knowledge and techniques.

In his 1922 book The Friendly Arctic, he wrote:

"…if it could be demonstrated that food suitable to sustain indefinitely both men and dogs could be secured anywhere on the polar sea, then obviously journeys over the ice would cease to be limited either in time or distance. Any part of the polar sea would then become accessible to whoever was willing to undergo the supposed hardships of living on meat exclusively, using nothing but blubber for fuel, and remaining separated from other human beings than his own traveling companions for a period of years.

To demonstrate the feasibility of this and thereby to bring in the fourth stage of polar exploration, was the main task of our expedition. From my point of view, at least, any discoveries which might be made through the application of this method were secondary to the establishment of the method itself. For, with the method once established, anyone could go out and make the discoveries. When the world was once known to be round, there was no difficulty in finding many navigators to sail around it. When the polar regions are once understood to be friendly and fruitful, men will quickly and easily penetrate their deepest recesses."

Over the next decade, Stefansson launched a pair of expeditions, under other pretences, to prove that anyone with the right knowledge could survive in the Arctic, no matter how ill-equipped or inexperienced.

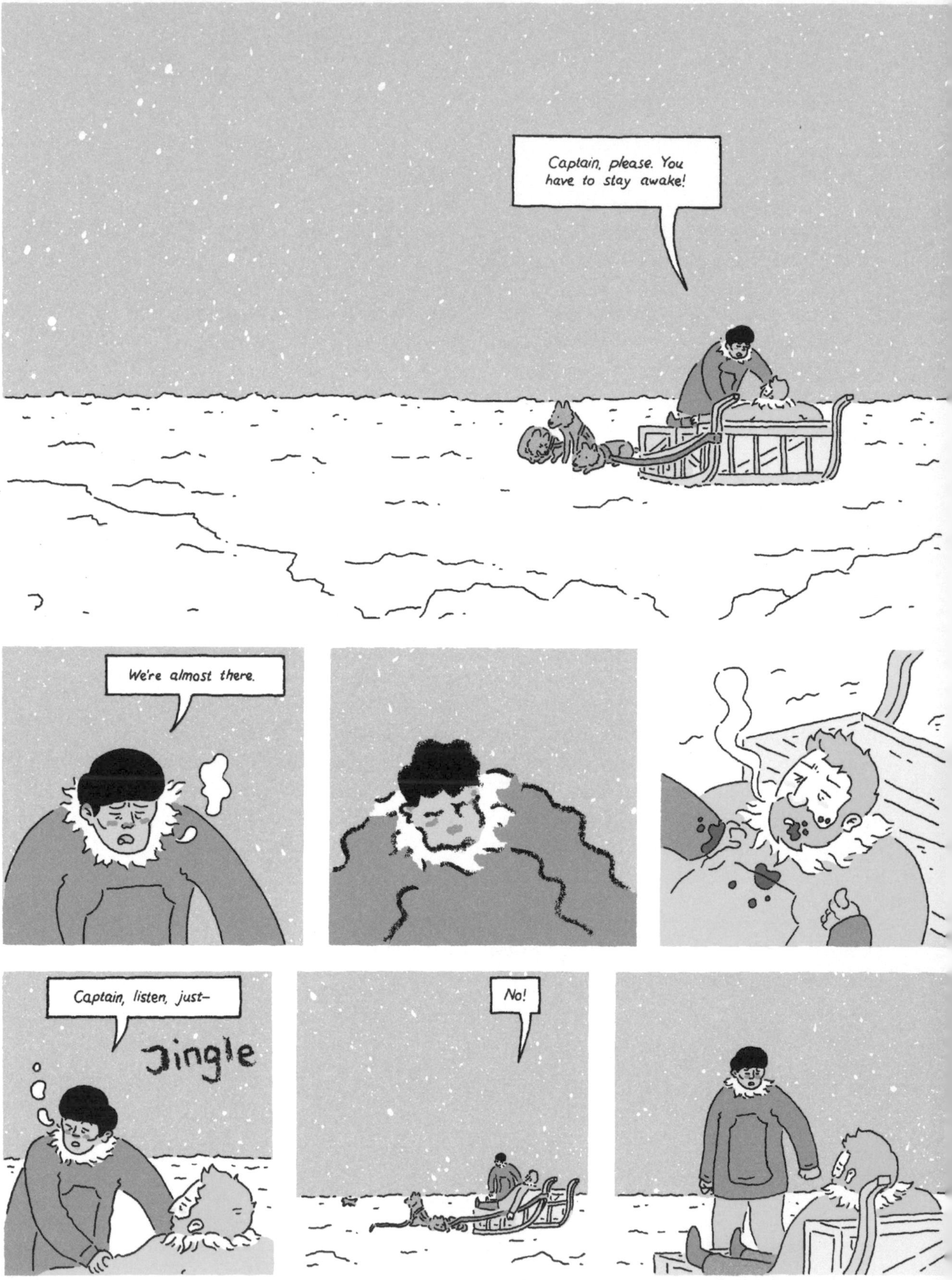
Captain, please. You have to stay awake!
We're almost there.
Captain, listen, just-
Jingle
No!

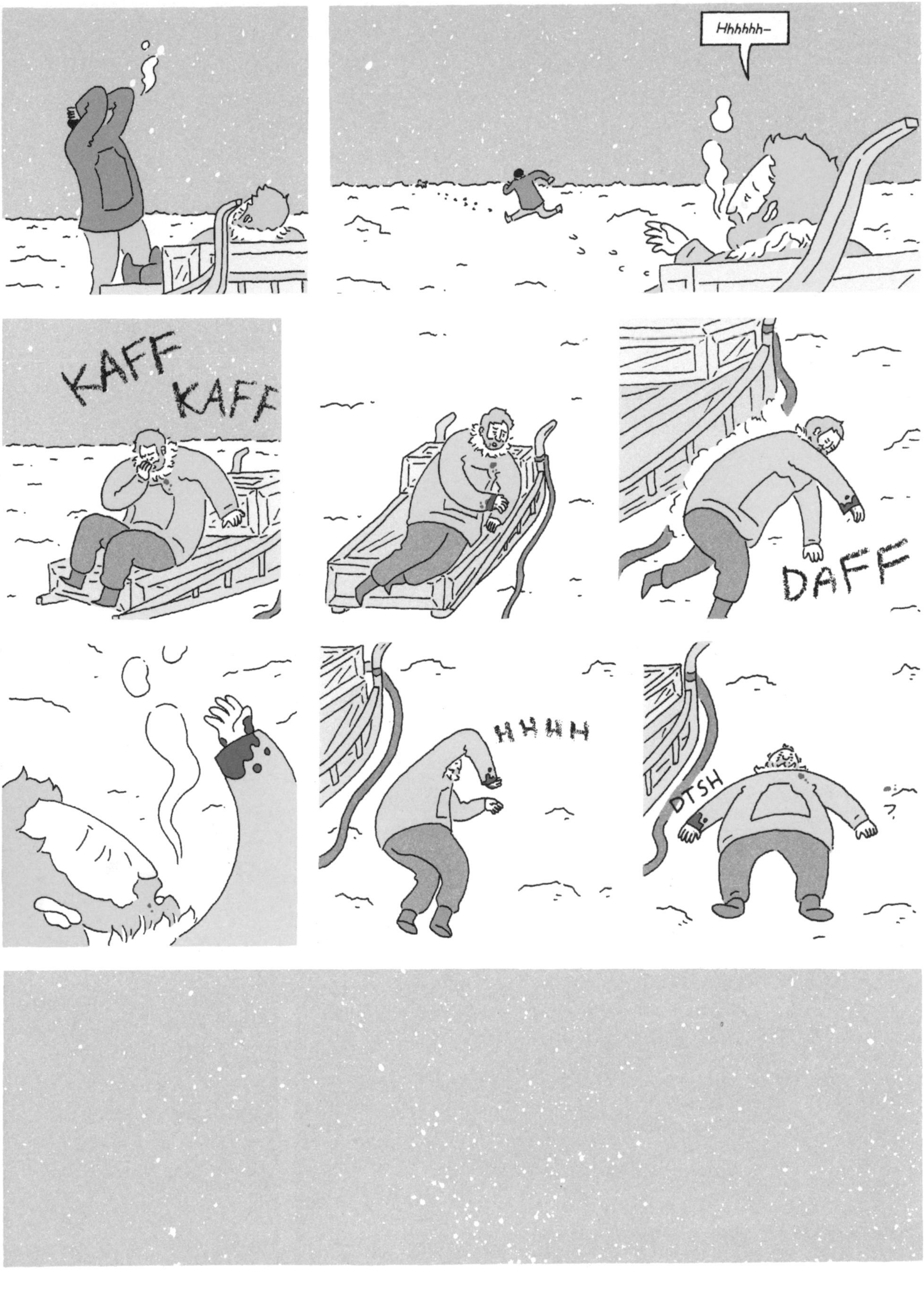
Hhhhhh-
KAFF KAFF
DAFF
HHHH
DTSH

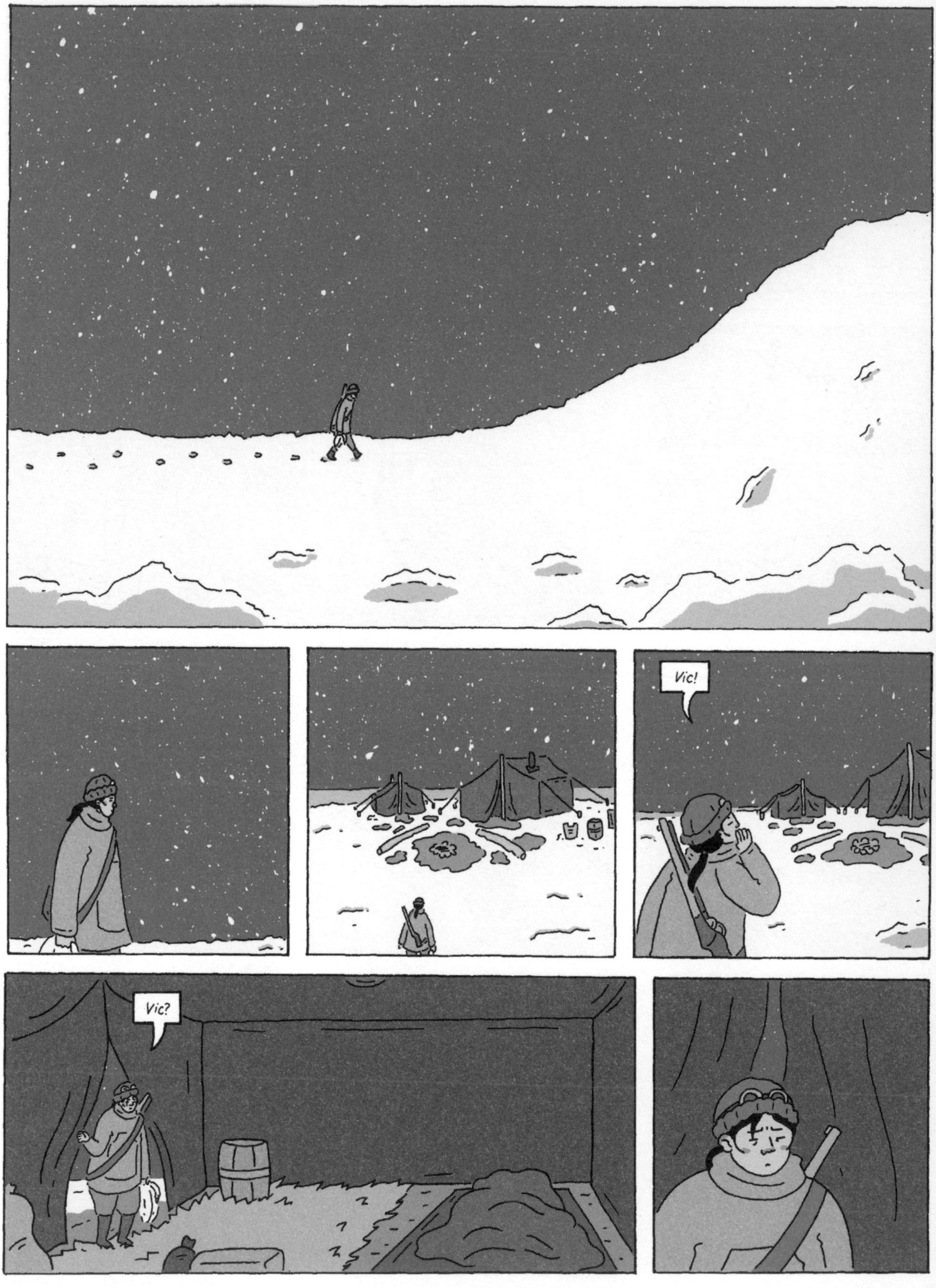
Vic!
Vic?

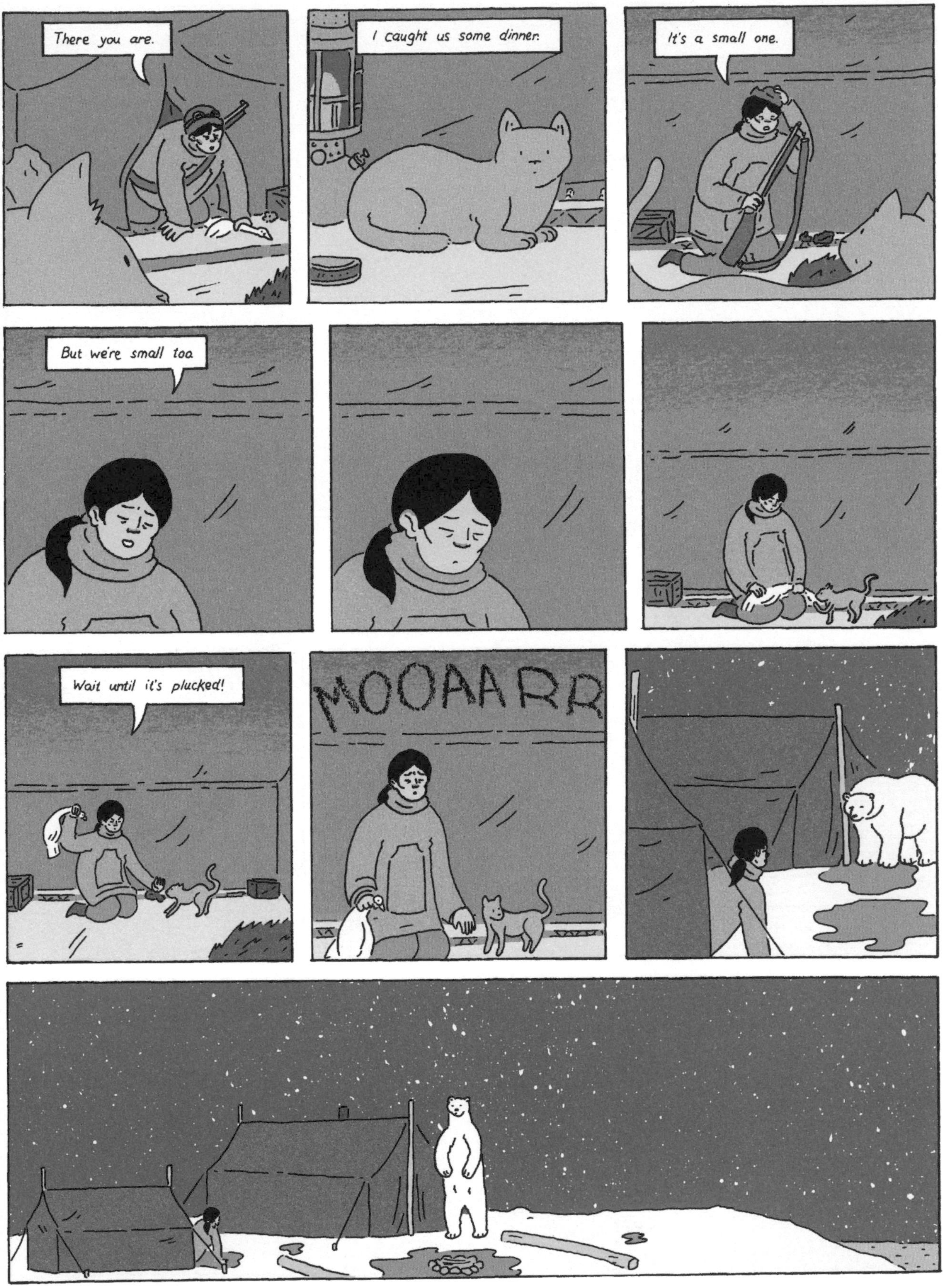
There you are.
I caught us some dinner.
It's a small one.
But we're small too.
Wait until it's plucked!
MOOAARR

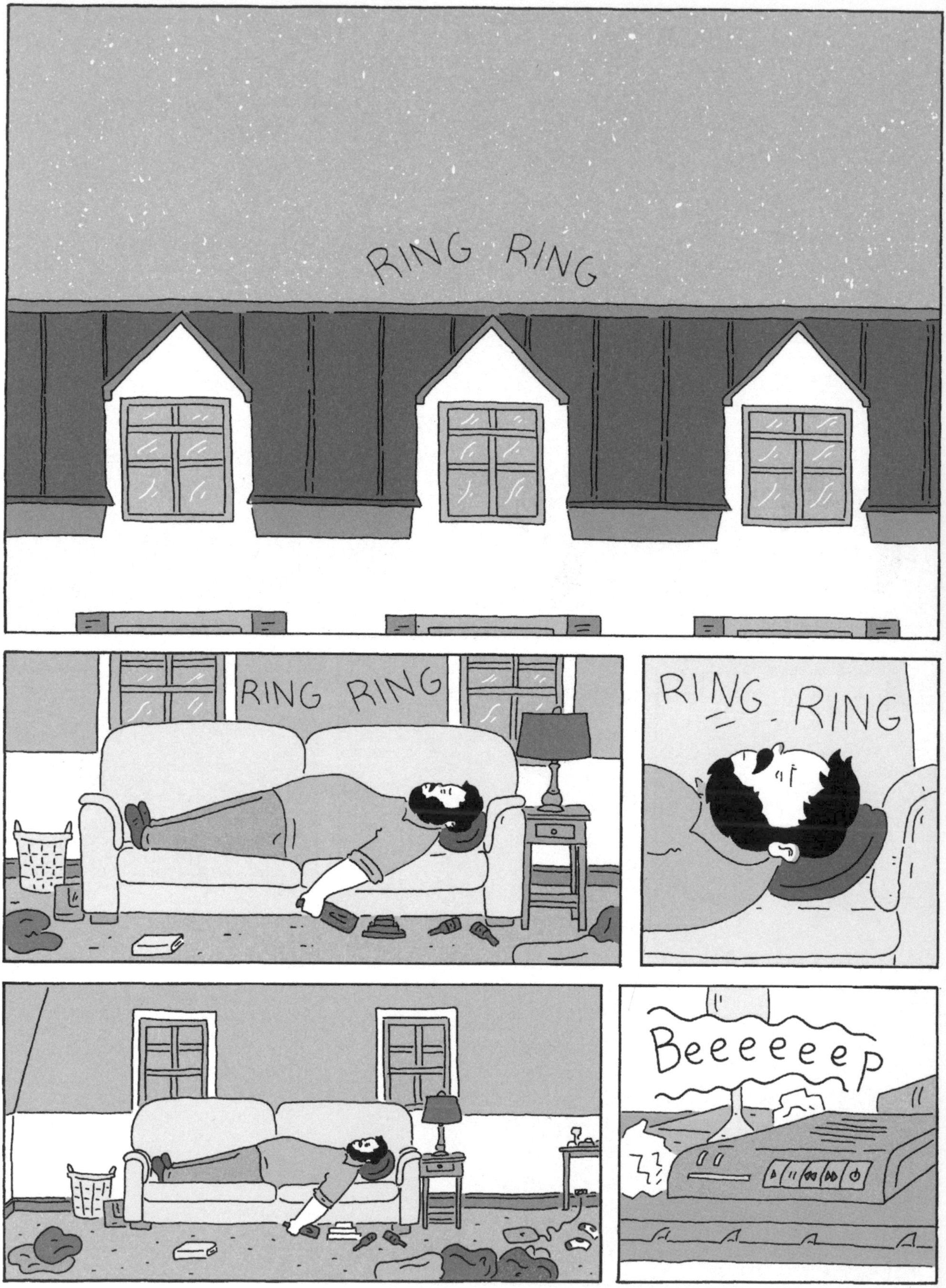
RING RING
RING RING
RING RING
Beeeeeep

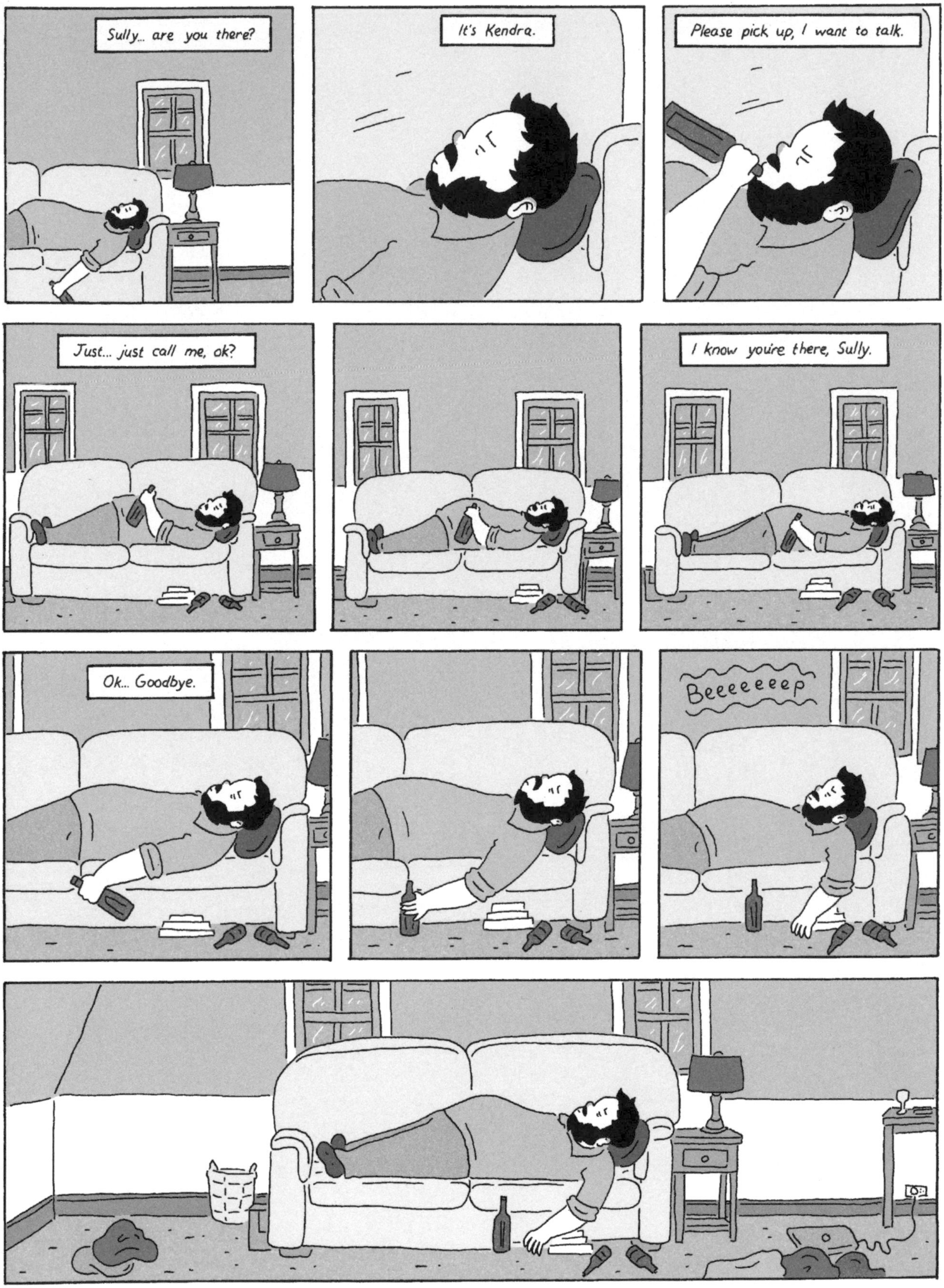
Sully... are you there?
It's Kendra.
Please pick up, I want to talk.
Just... just call me, ok?
I know you're there, Sully.
Ok... Goodbye.
Beeeeeeep

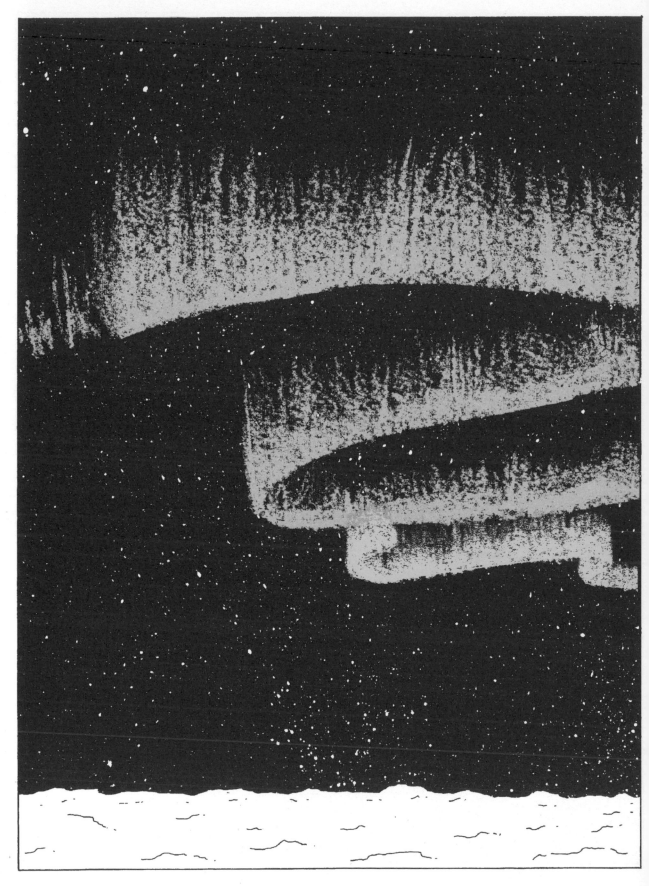

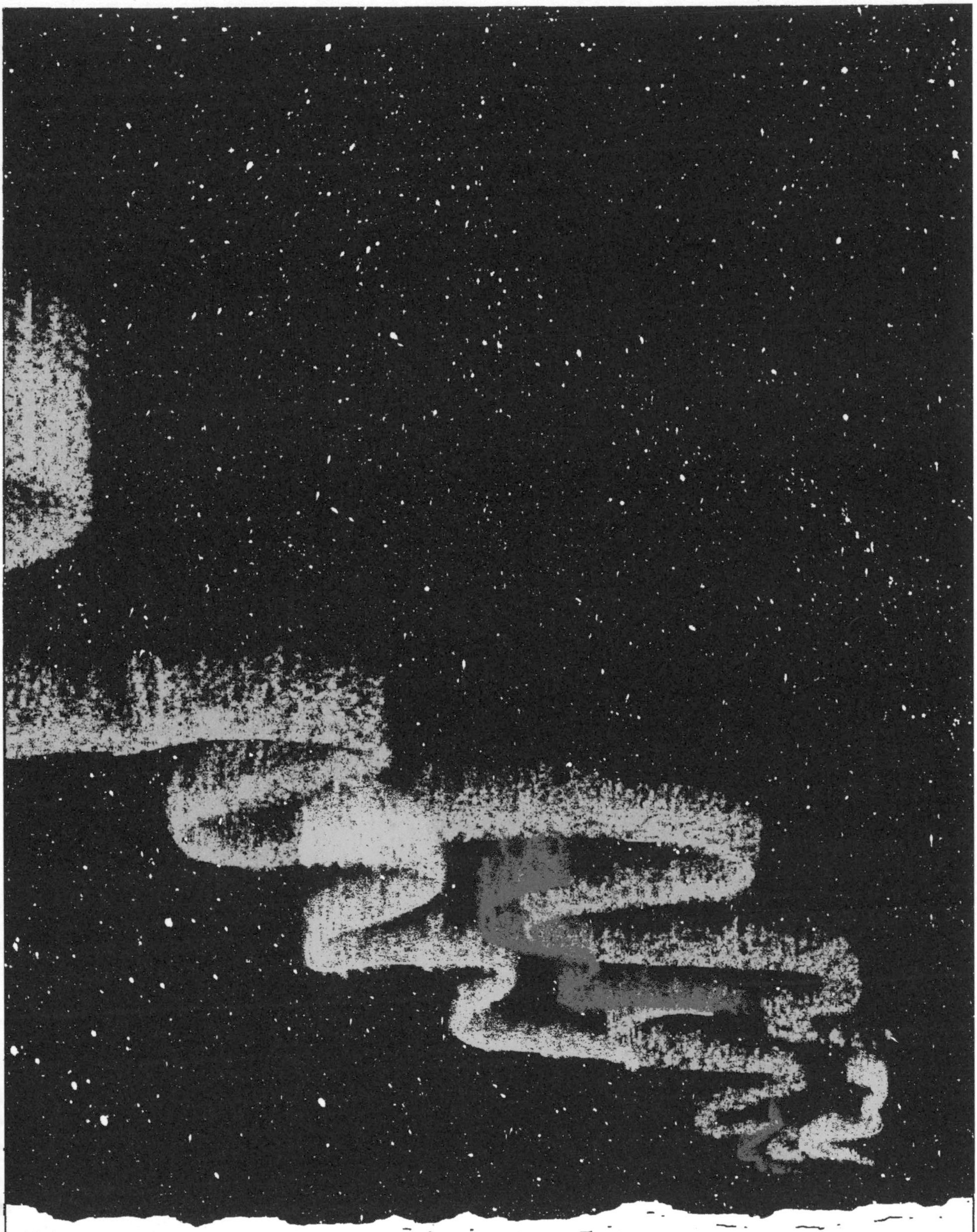

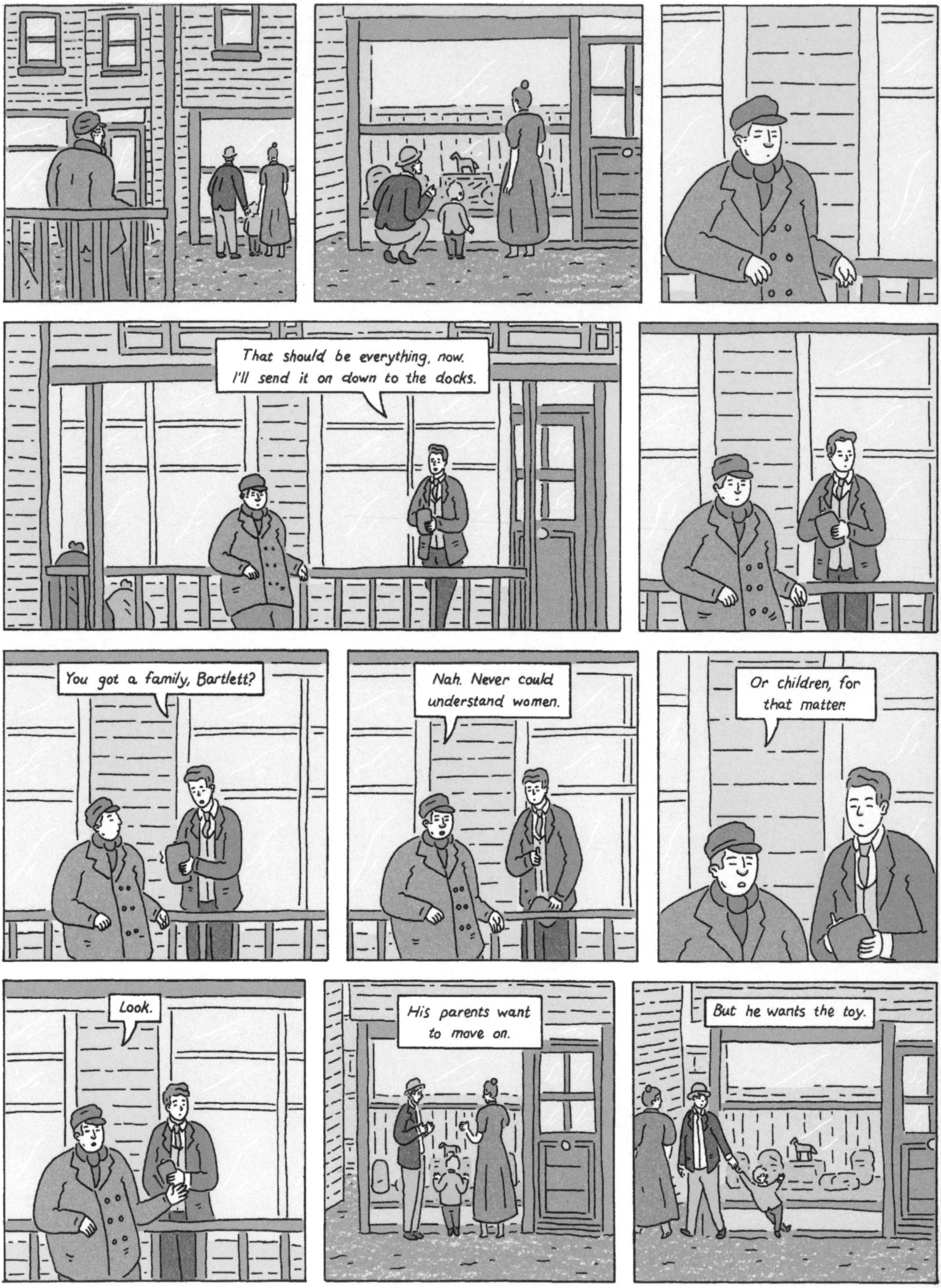
That should be everything, now. I'll send it on down to the docks.
You got a family, Bartlett?
Nah. Never could understand women.
Or children, for that matter.
Look.
His parents want to move on.
But he wants the toy.

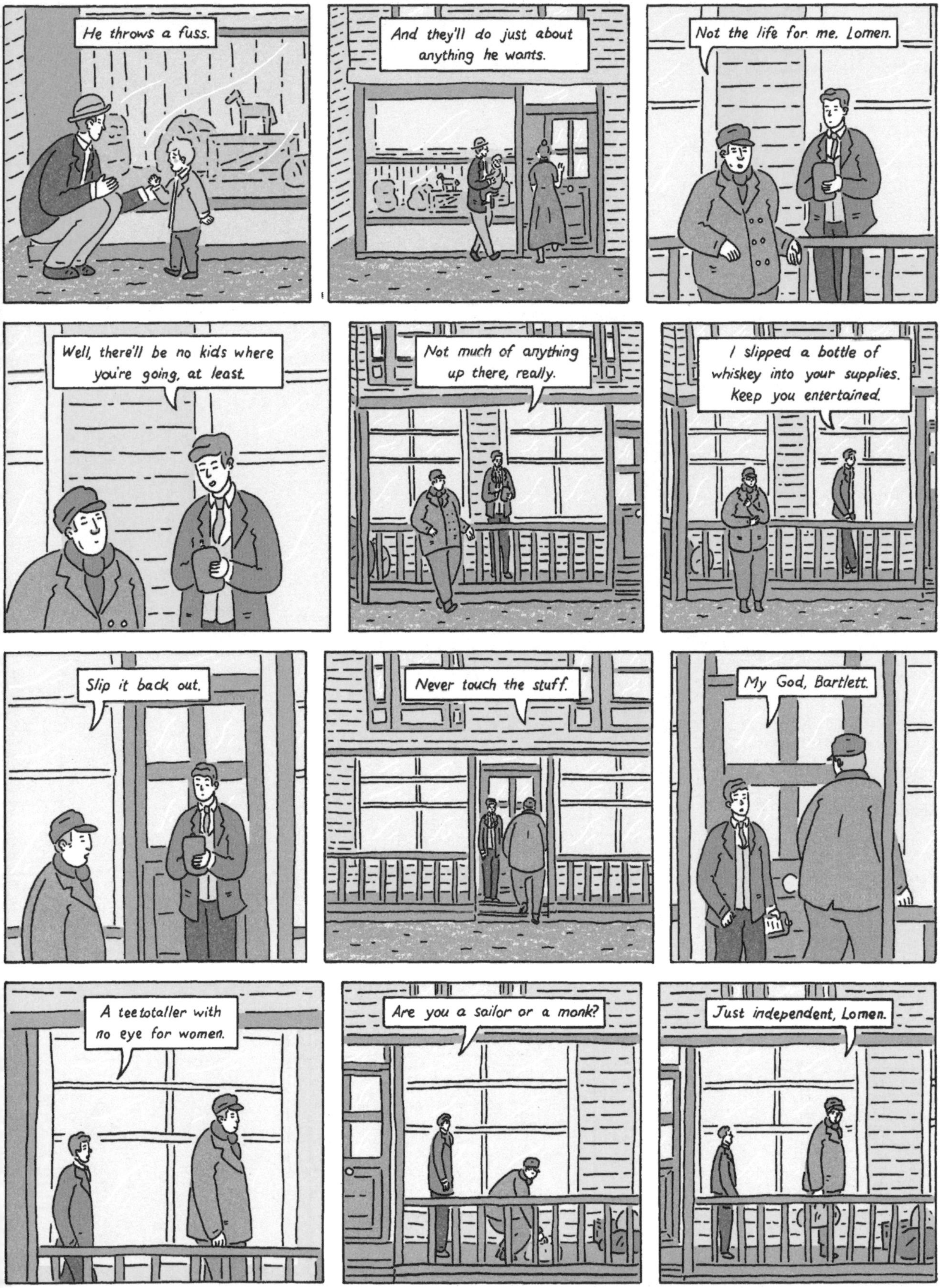
He throws a fuss.
And they'll do just about anything he wants.
Not the life for me, Lomen.
Well, there'll be no kids where you're going, at least.
Not much of anything up there, really.
I slipped a bottle of whiskey into your supplies. Keep you entertained.
Slip it back out.
Never touch the stuff.
My God, Bartlett.
A teetotaller with no eye for women.
Are you a sailor or a monk?
Just independent, Lomen.

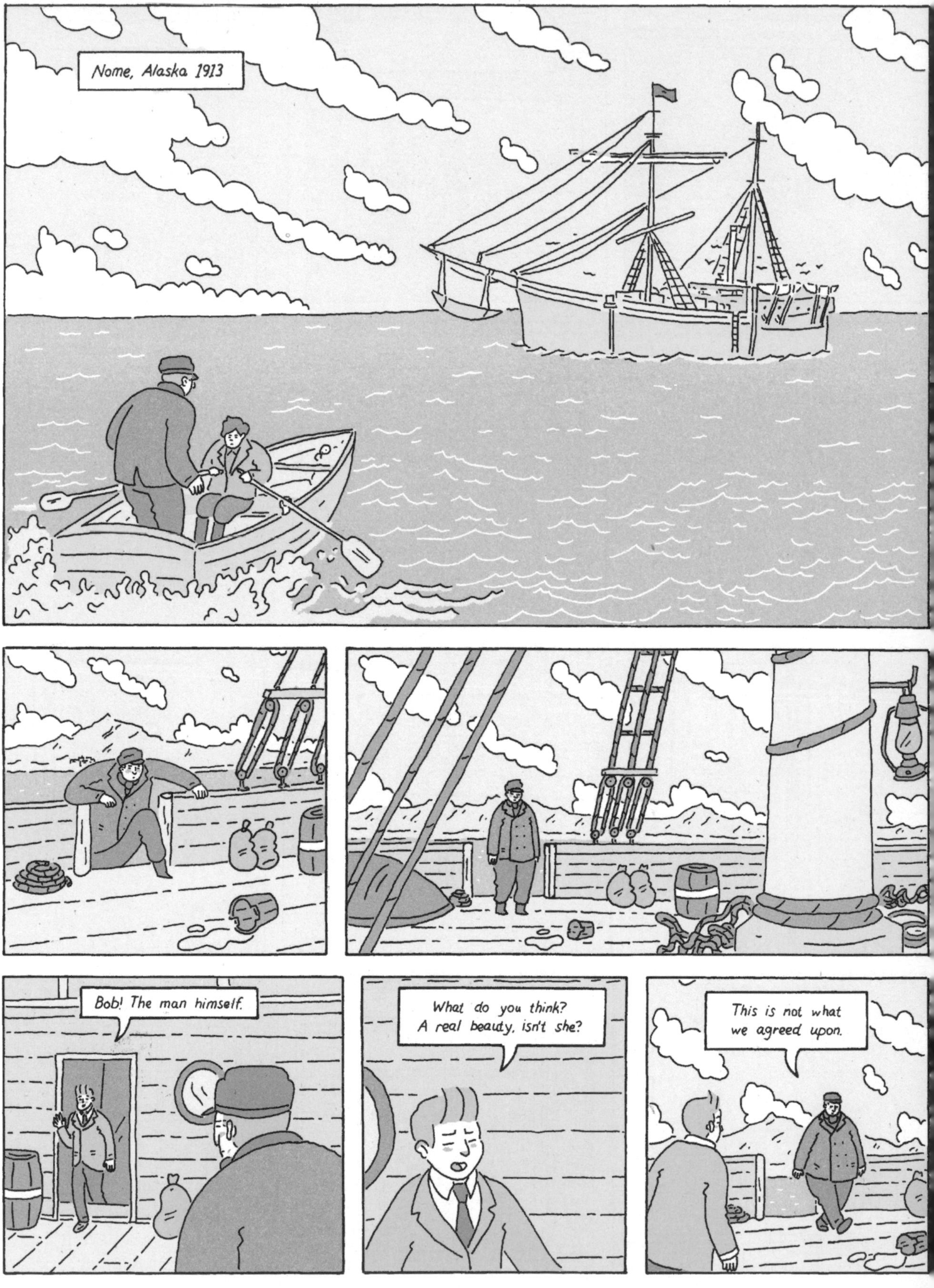
Nome, Alaska 1913
Bob! The man himself.
What do you think? A real beauty, isn't she?
This is not what we agreed upon.

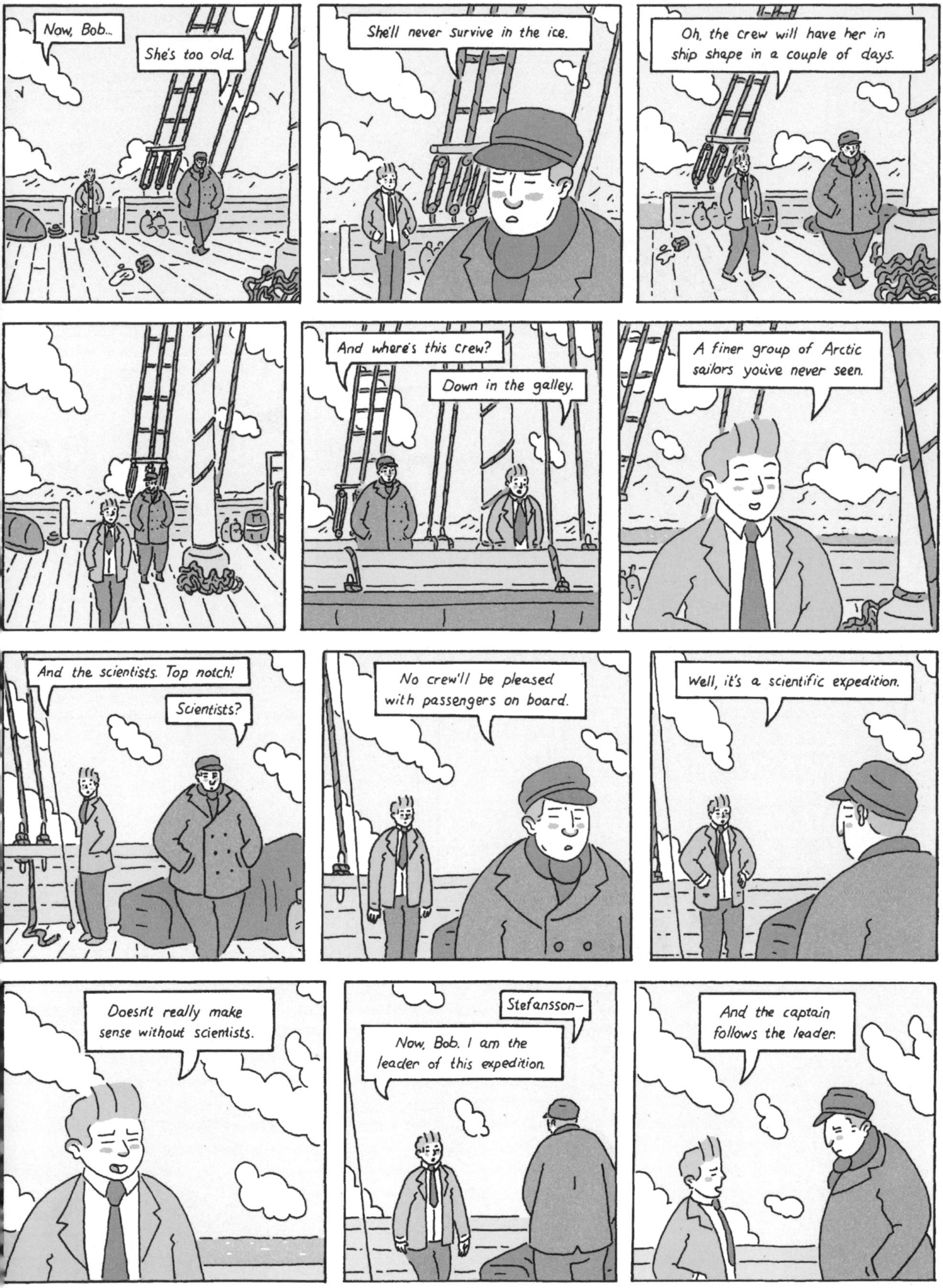
Now, Bob...
She's too old.
She'll never survive in the ice.
Oh, the crew will have her in ship shape in a couple of days.
And where's this crew?
Down in the galley.
A finer group of Arctic sailors you've never seen.
And the scientists. Top notch!
Scientists?
No crew'll be pleased with passengers on board.
Well, it's a scientific expedition.
Doesn't really make sense without scientists.
Stefansson—
Now, Bob. I am the leader of this expedition.
And the captain follows the leader.

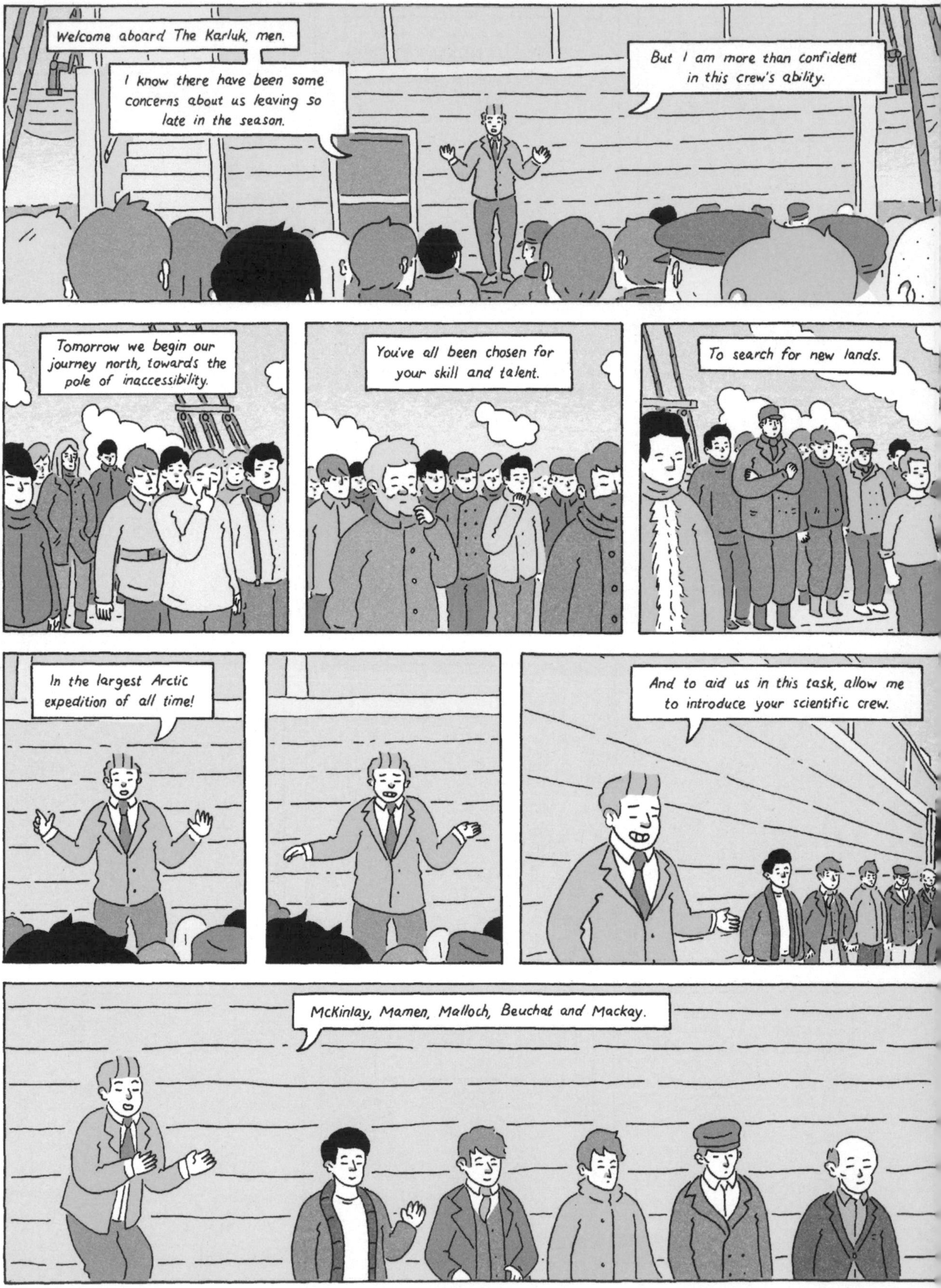
Welcome aboard The Karluk, men.
I know there have been some concerns about us leaving so late in the season.
But I am more than confident in this crew's ability.
Tomorrow we begin our journey north, towards the pole of inaccessibility.
You've all been chosen for your skill and talent.
To search for new lands.
In the largest Arctic expedition of all time!
And to aid us in this task, allow me to introduce your scientific crew.
McKinlay, Mamen, Malloch, Beuchat and Mackay.

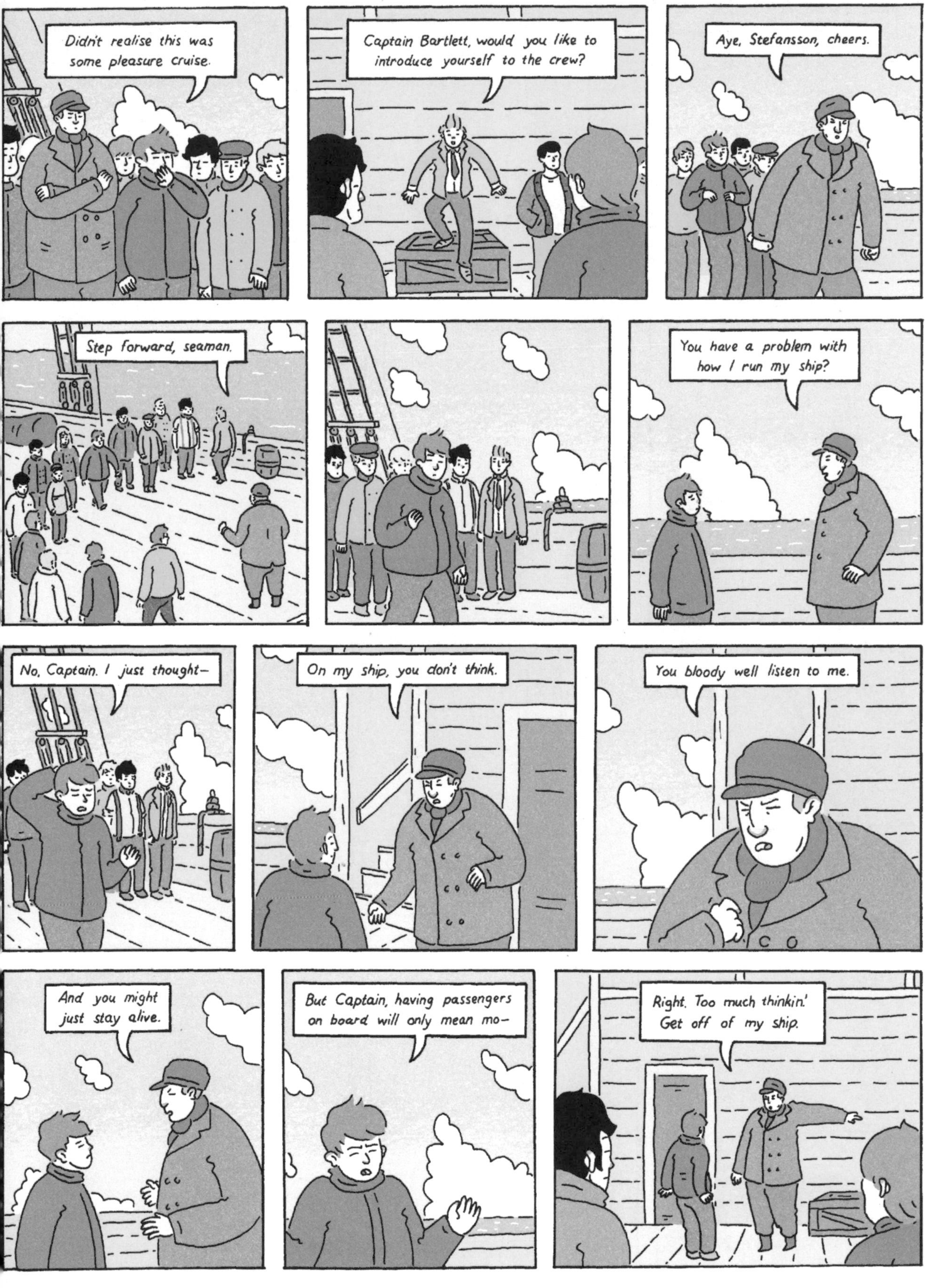
Didn't realise this was some pleasure cruise.
Captain Bartlett, would you like to introduce yourself to the crew?
Aye, Stefansson, cheers.
Step forward, seaman.
You have a problem with how I run my ship?
No, Captain. I just thought–
On my ship, you don't think.
You bloody well listen to me.
And you might just stay alive.
But Captain, having passengers on board will only mean mo–
Right. Too much thinkin'. Get off of my ship.

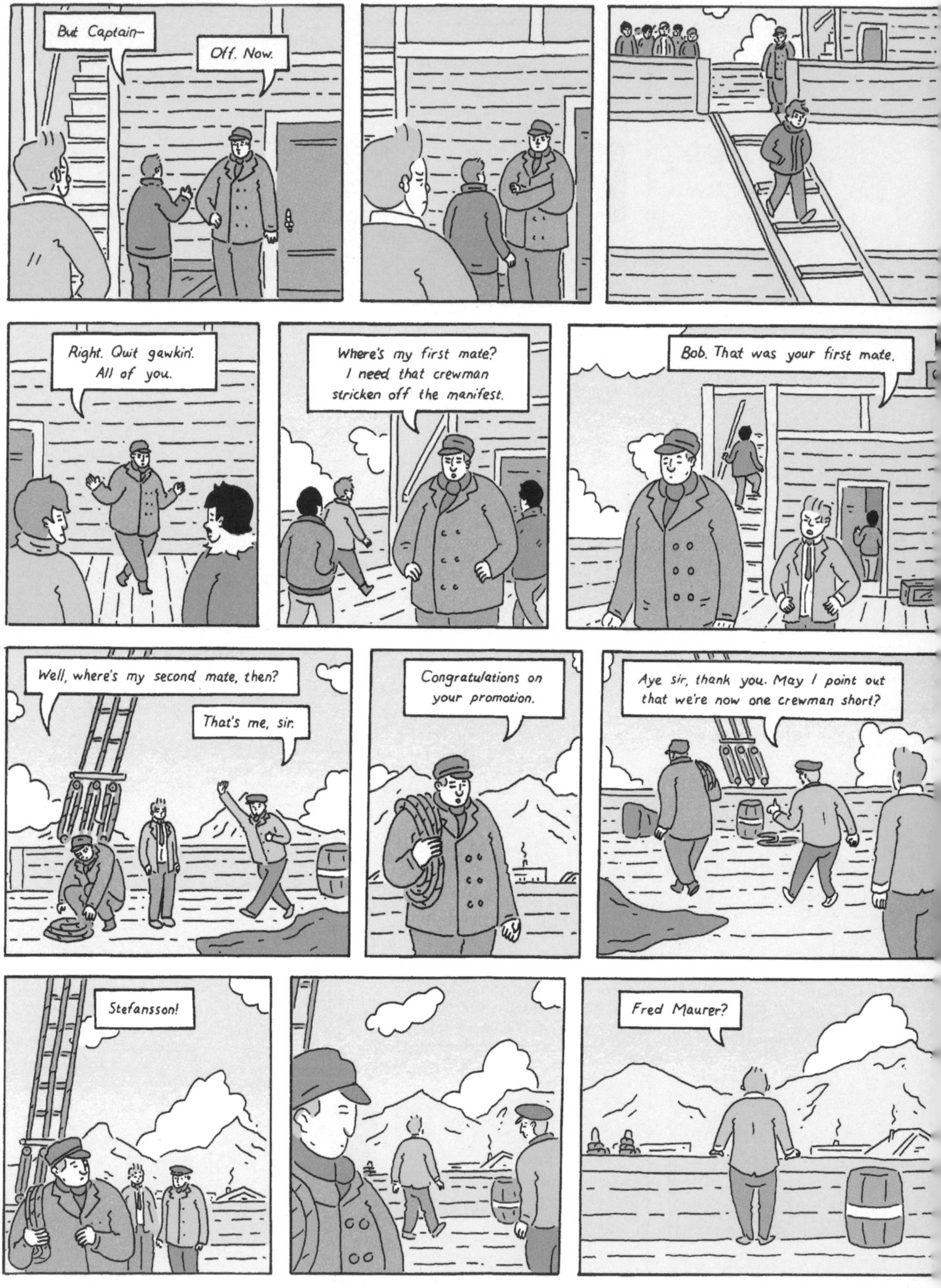
But Captain–
Off. Now.
Right. Quit gawkin'. All of you.
Where's my first mate? I need that crewman stricken off the manifest.
Bob. That was your first mate.
Well, where's my second mate, then?
That's me, sir.
Congratulations on your promotion.
Aye sir, thank you. May I point out that we're now one crewman short?
Stefansson!
Fred Maurer?

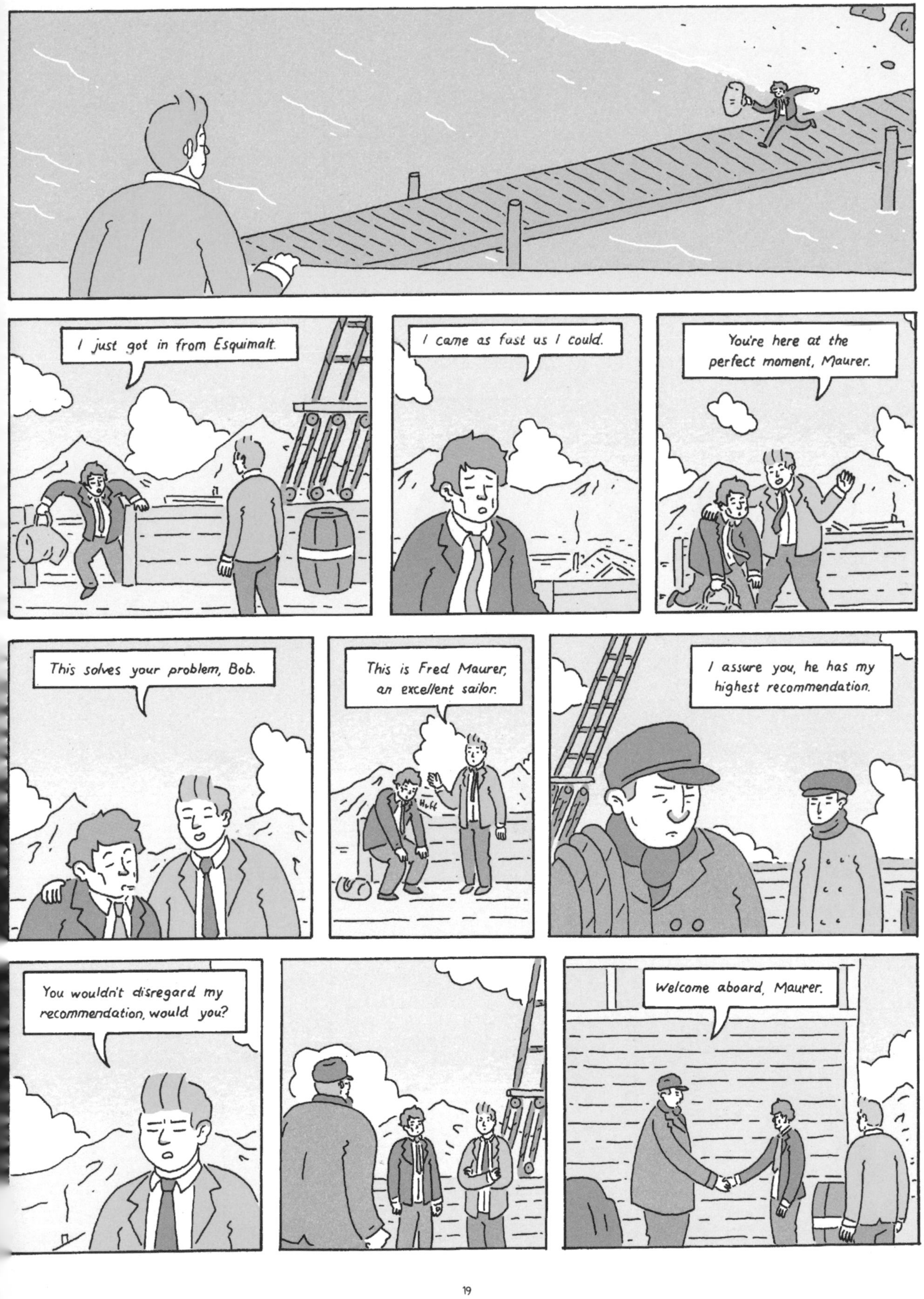
I just got in from Esquimalt.
I came as fast us I could.
You're here at the perfect moment, Maurer.
This solves your problem, Bob.
This is Fred Maurer, an excellent sailor.
Huff
I assure you, he has my highest recommendation.
You wouldn't disregard my recommendation, would you?
Welcome aboard, Maurer.

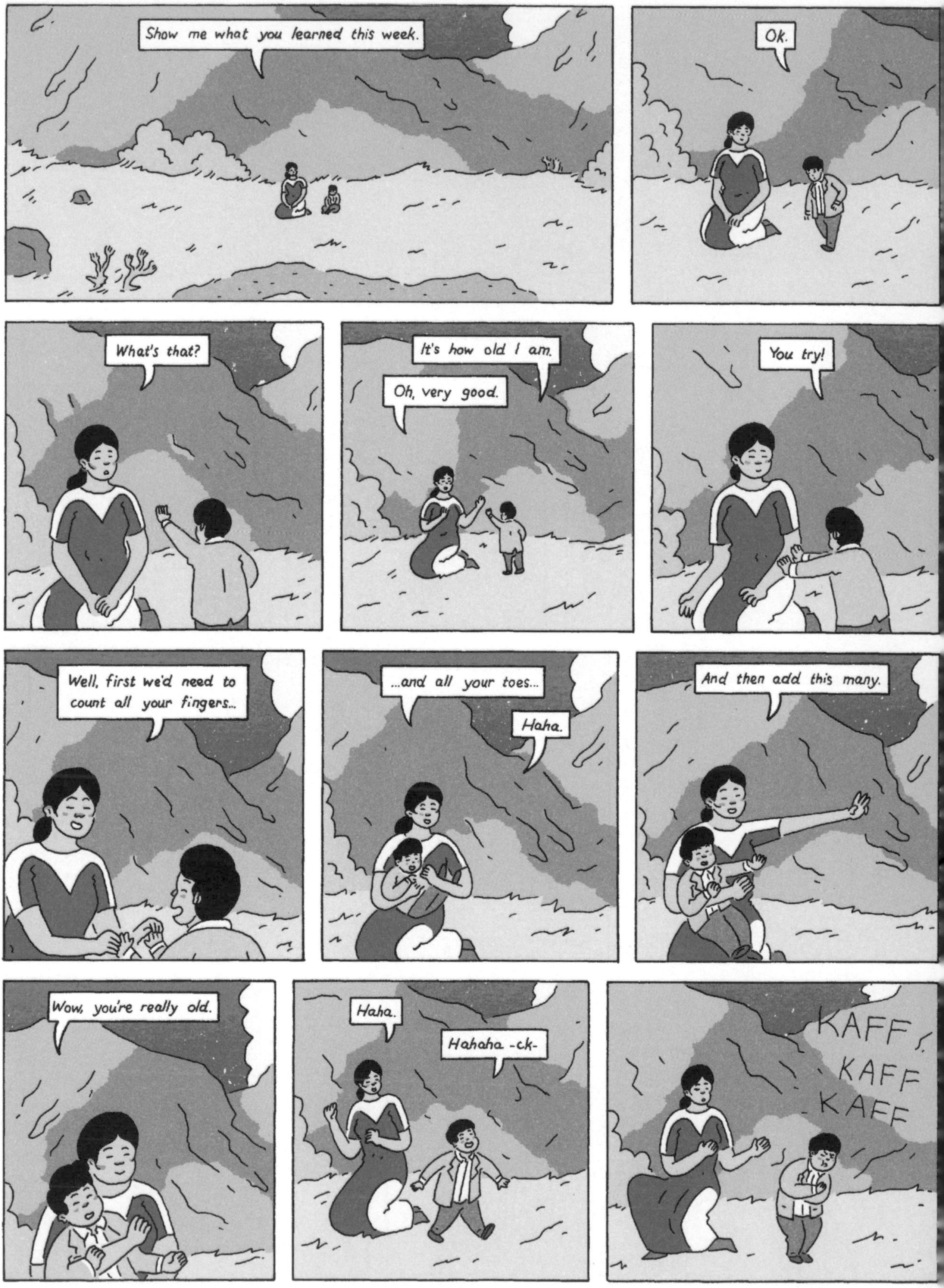
Show me what you learned this week.
Ok.
What's that?
It's how old I am.
Oh, very good.
You try!
Well, first we'd need to count all your fingers...
...and all your toes...
Haha.
And then add this many.
Wow, you're really old.
Haha.
Hahaha -ck-
KAFF
KAFF
KAFF

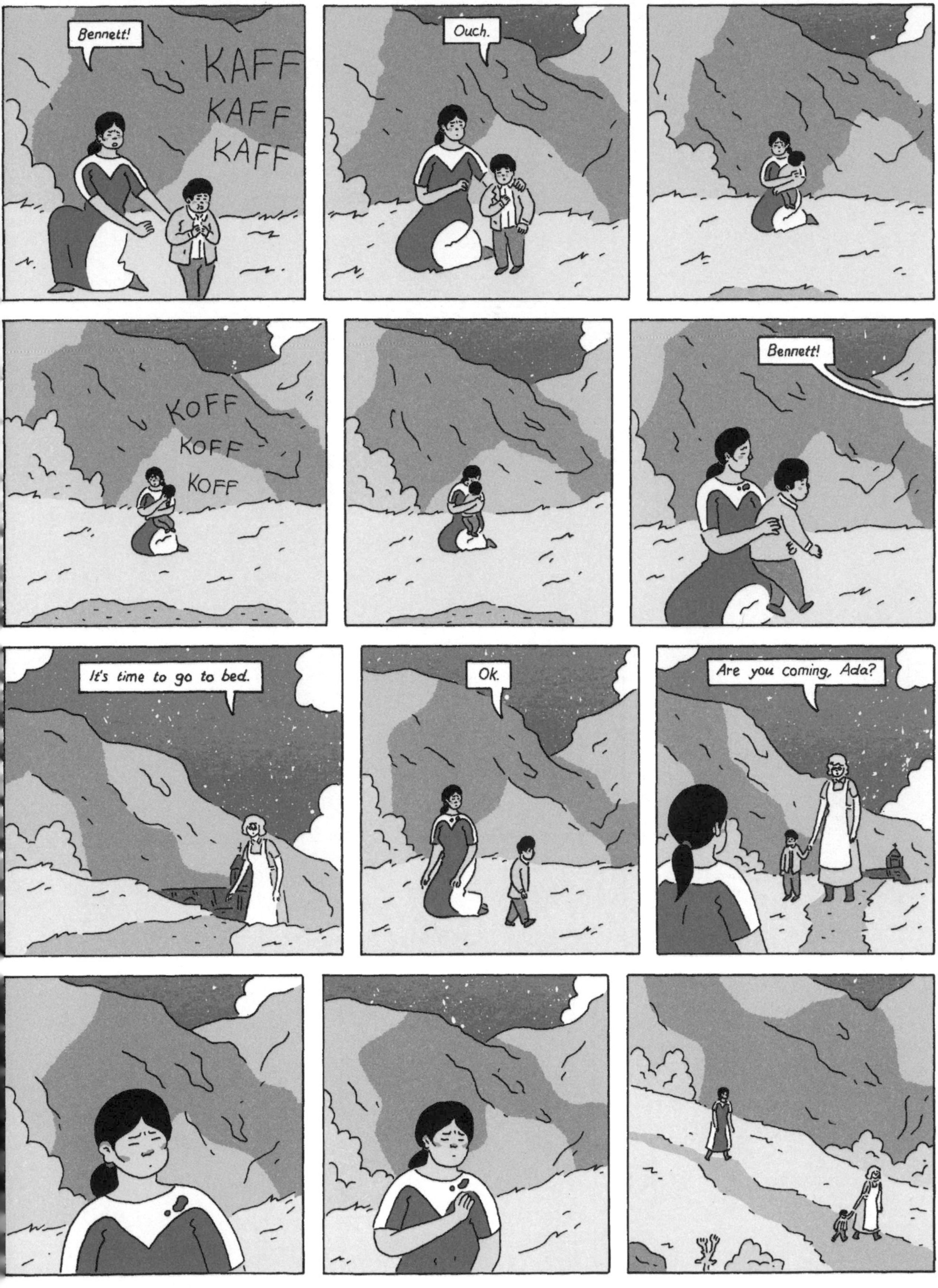
Bennett!
KAFF
KAFF
KAFF
Ouch.
KOFF
KOFF
KOFF
Bennett!
It's time to go to bed.
Ok.
Are you coming, Ada?

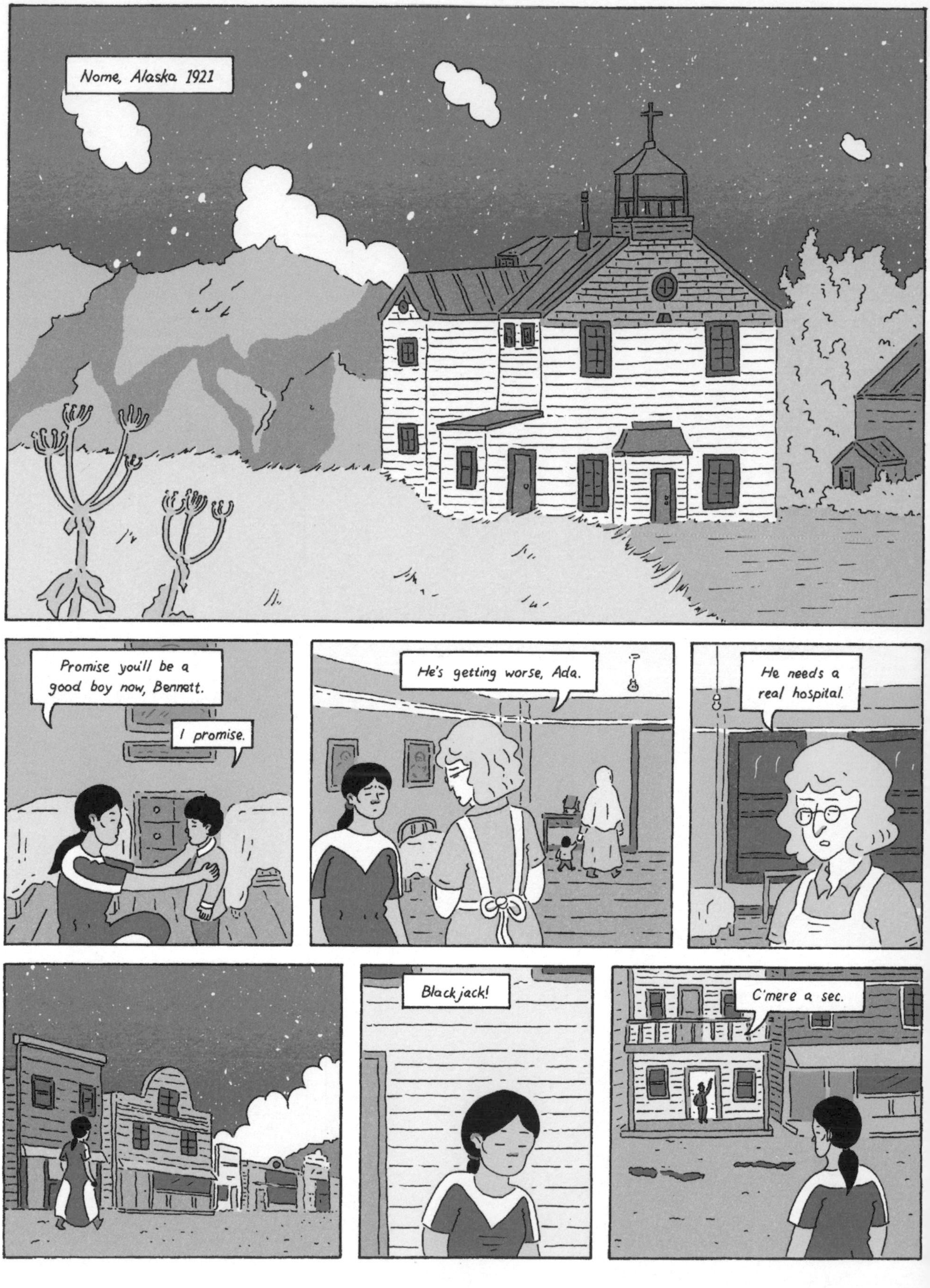
Nome, Alaska 1921
Promise you'll be a good boy now, Bennett.
I promise.
He's getting worse, Ada.
He needs a real hospital.
Blackjack!
C'mere a sec.

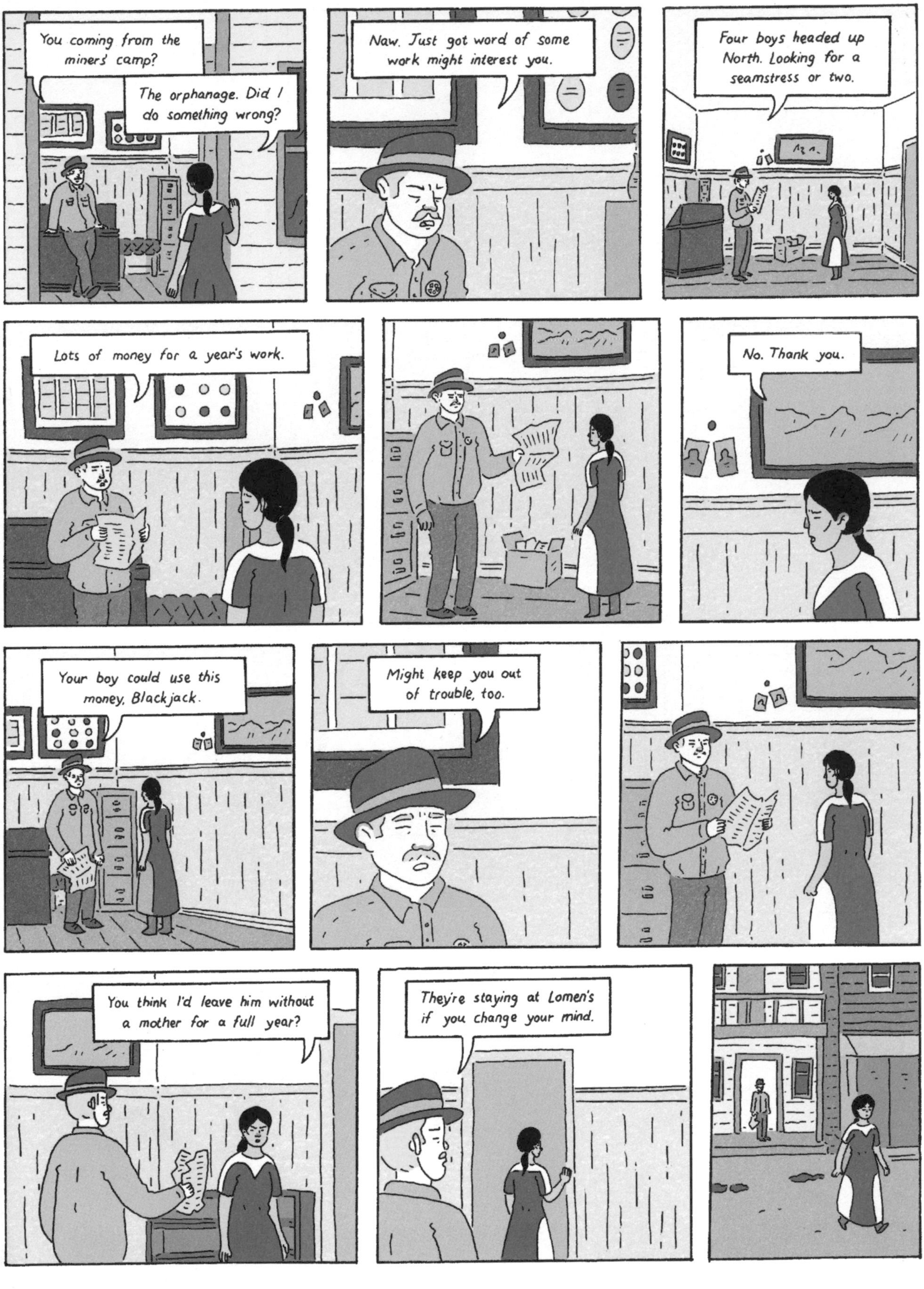
You coming from the miners' camp?
The orphanage. Did I do something wrong?
Naw. Just got word of some work might interest you.
Four boys headed up North. Looking for a seamstress or two.
Lots of money for a year's work.
No. Thank you.
Your boy could use this money, Blackjack.
Might keep you out of trouble, too.
You think I'd leave him without a mother for a full year?
They're staying at Lomen's if you change your mind.

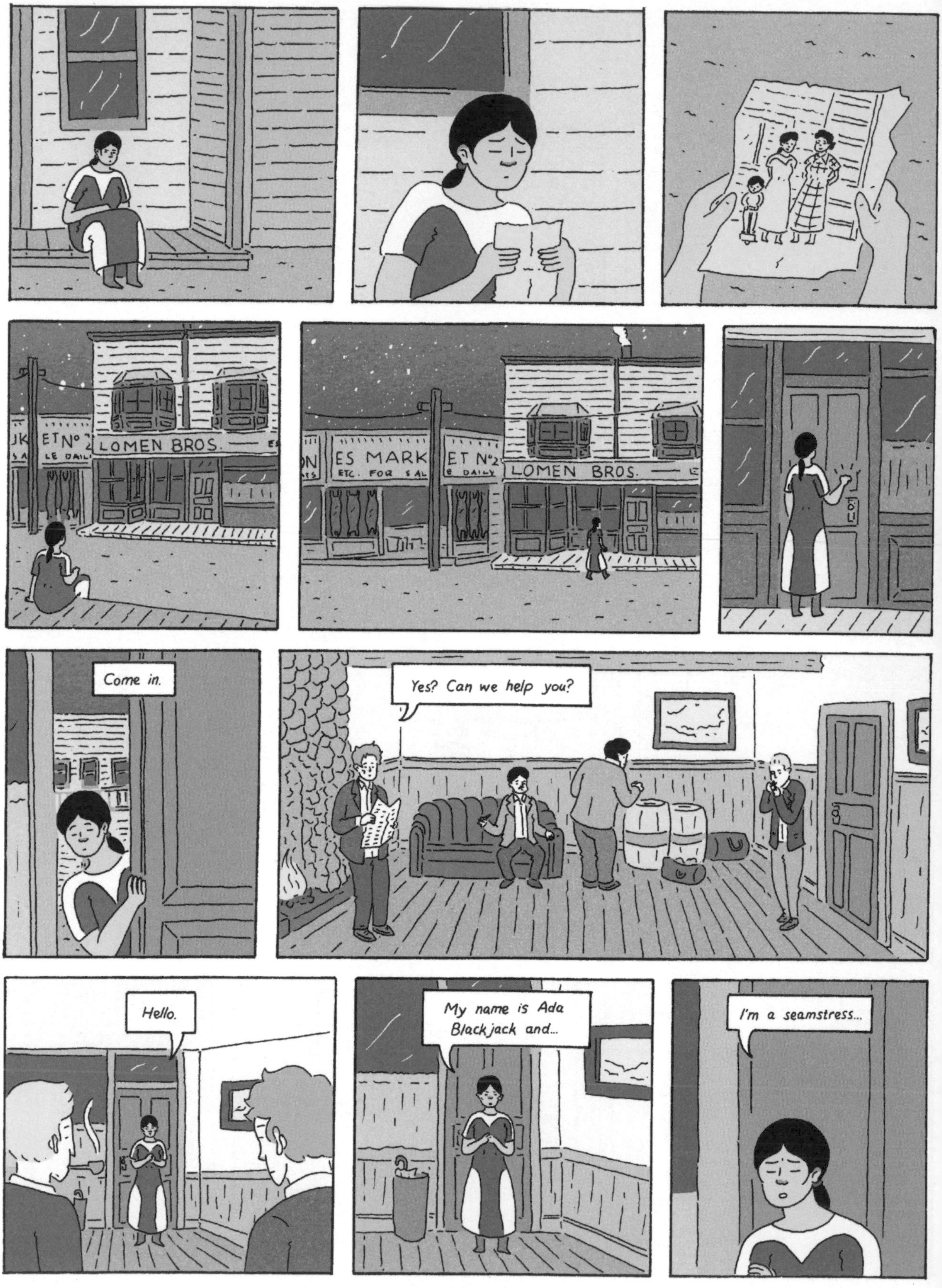
ET Nº 2
LE DAIL
LOMEN BROS.
ES MARK
ET Nº 2
ETC. FOR SAL
E DAILY
LOMEN BROS.
Come in.
Yes? Can we help you?
Hello.
My name is Ada Blackjack and...
I'm a seamstress...

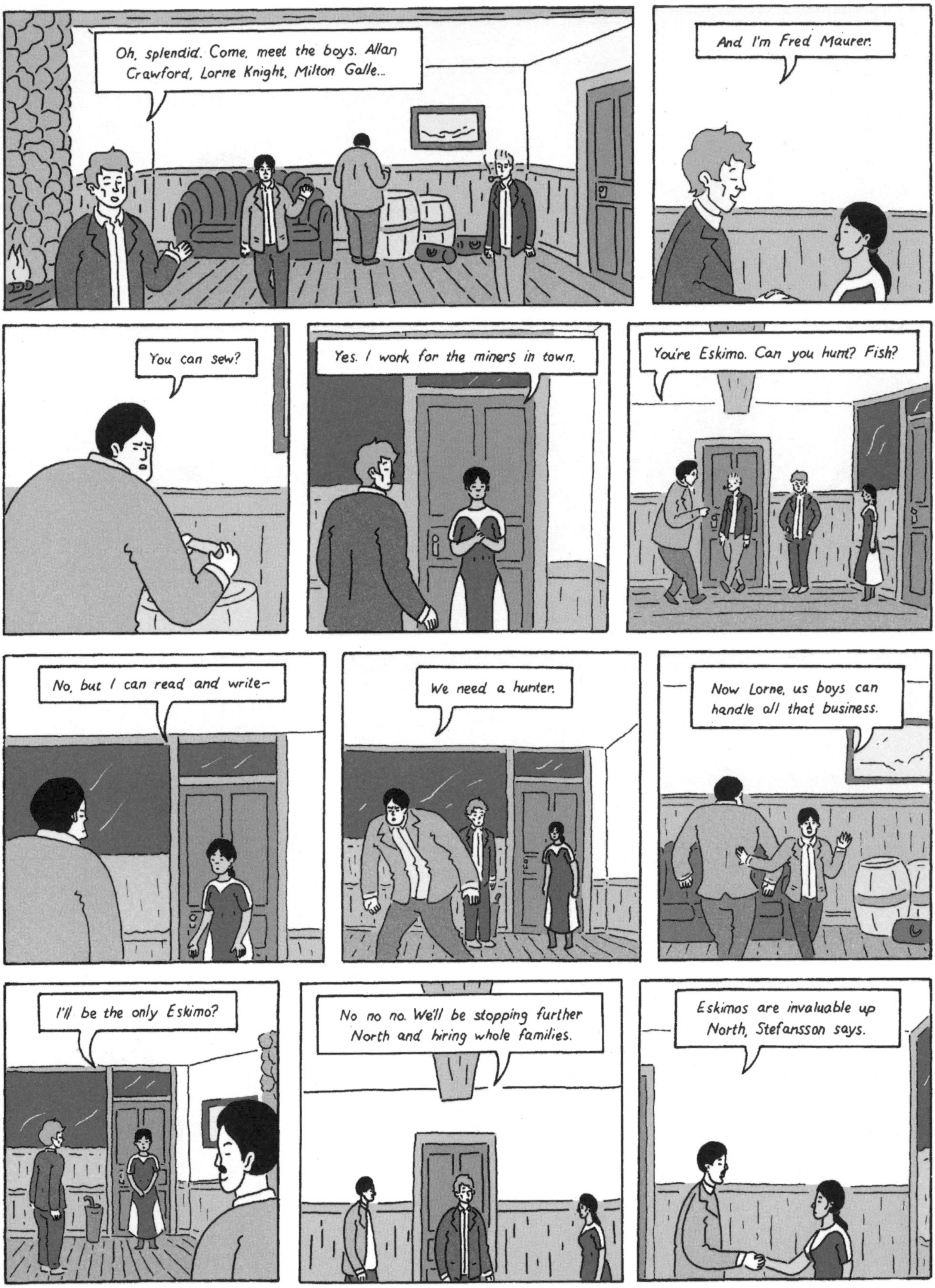
Oh, splendid. Come, meet the boys. Allan Crawford, Lorne Knight, Milton Galle...
And I'm Fred Maurer.
You can sew?
Yes. I work for the miners in town.
You're Eskimo. Can you hunt? Fish?
No, but I can read and write–
We need a hunter.
Now Lorne, us boys can handle all that business.
I'll be the only Eskimo?
No no no. We'll be stopping further North and hiring whole families.
Eskimos are invaluable up North, Stefansson says.

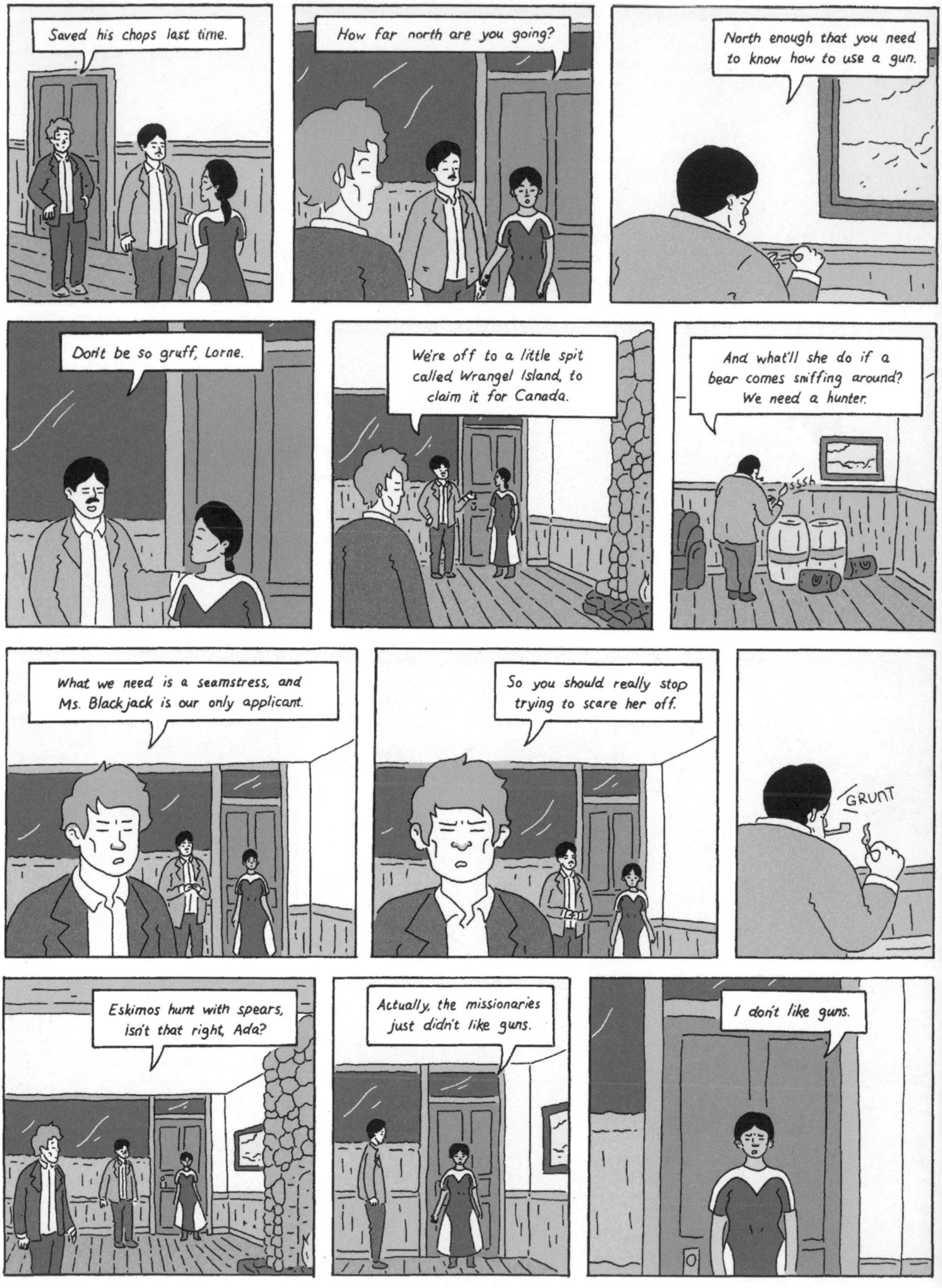

Saved his chops last time.
How far north are you going?
North enough that you need to know how to use a gun.
Don't be so gruff, Lorne.
We're off to a little spit called Wrangel Island, to claim it for Canada.
And what'll she do if a bear comes sniffing around? We need a hunter.
SSSh
What we need is a seamstress, and Ms. Blackjack is our only applicant.
So you should really stop trying to scare her off.
GRUNT
Eskimos hunt with spears, isn't that right, Ada?
Actually, the missionaries just didn't like guns.
I don't like guns.

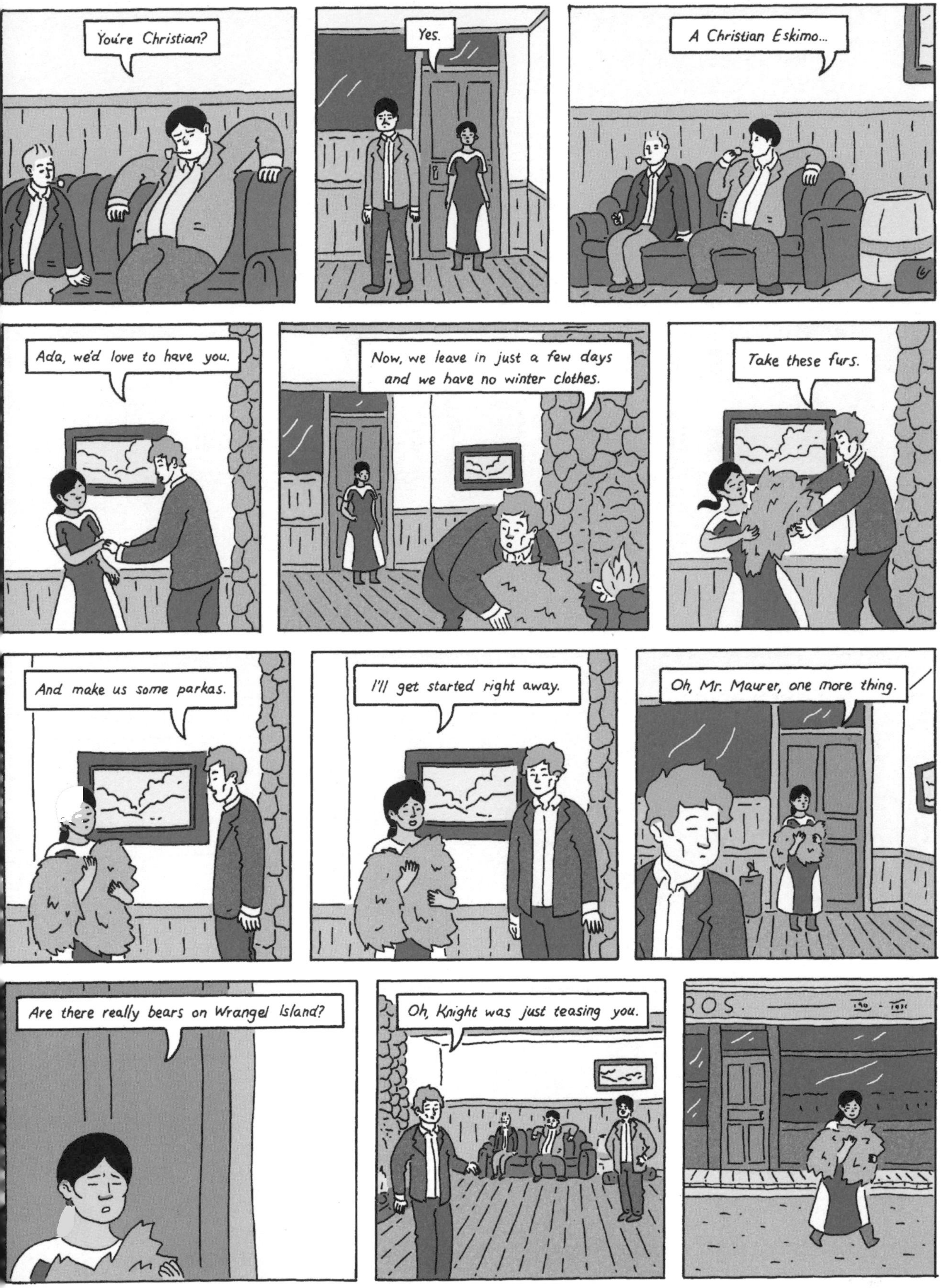
You're Christian?
Yes.
A Christian Eskimo...
Ada, we'd love to have you.
Now, we leave in just a few days and we have no winter clothes.
Take these furs.
And make us some parkas.
I'll get started right away.
Oh, Mr. Maurer, one more thing.
Are there really bears on Wrangel Island?
Oh, Knight was just teasing you.
ROS.

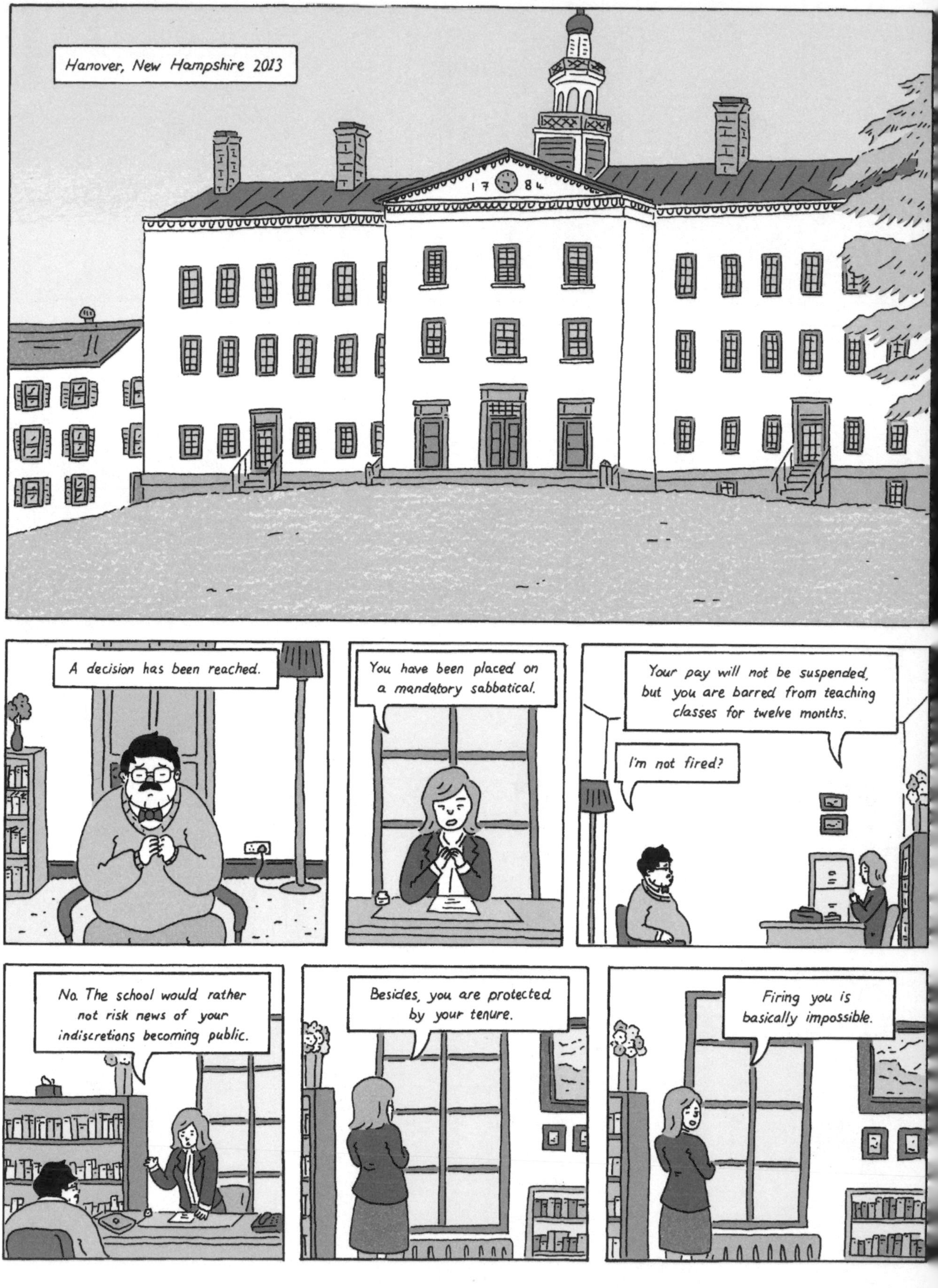
Hanover, New Hampshire 2013
1784
A decision has been reached.
You have been placed on a mandatory sabbatical.
Your pay will not be suspended, but you are barred from teaching classes for twelve months.
I'm not fired?
No. The school would rather not risk news of your indiscretions becoming public.
Besides, you are protected by your tenure.
Firing you is basically impossible.

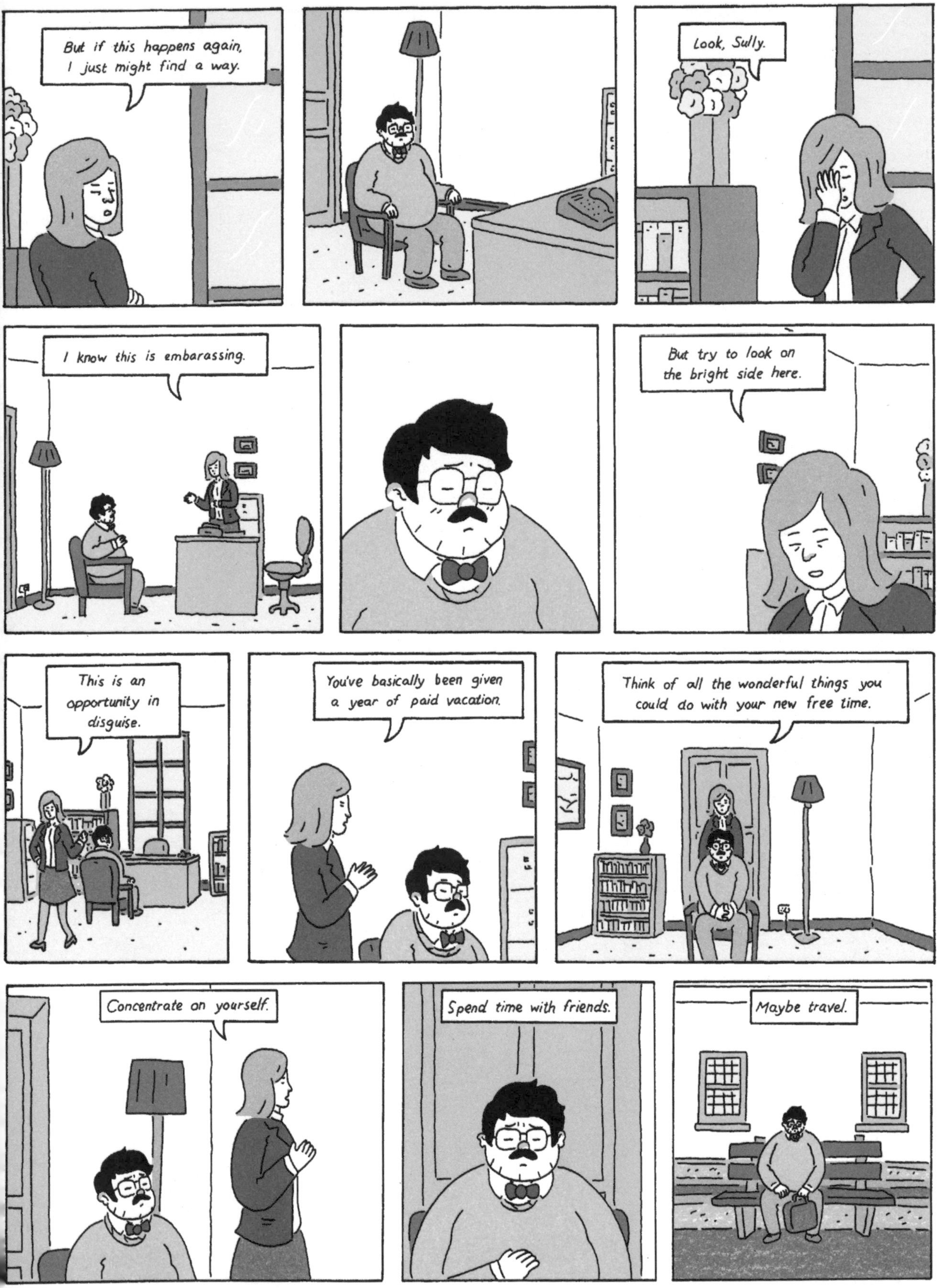
But if this happens again, I just might find a way.
Look, Sully.
I know this is embarassing.
But try to look on the bright side here.
This is an opportunity in disguise.
You've basically been given a year of paid vacation.
Think of all the wonderful things you could do with your new free time.
Concentrate on yourself.
Spend time with friends.
Maybe travel.

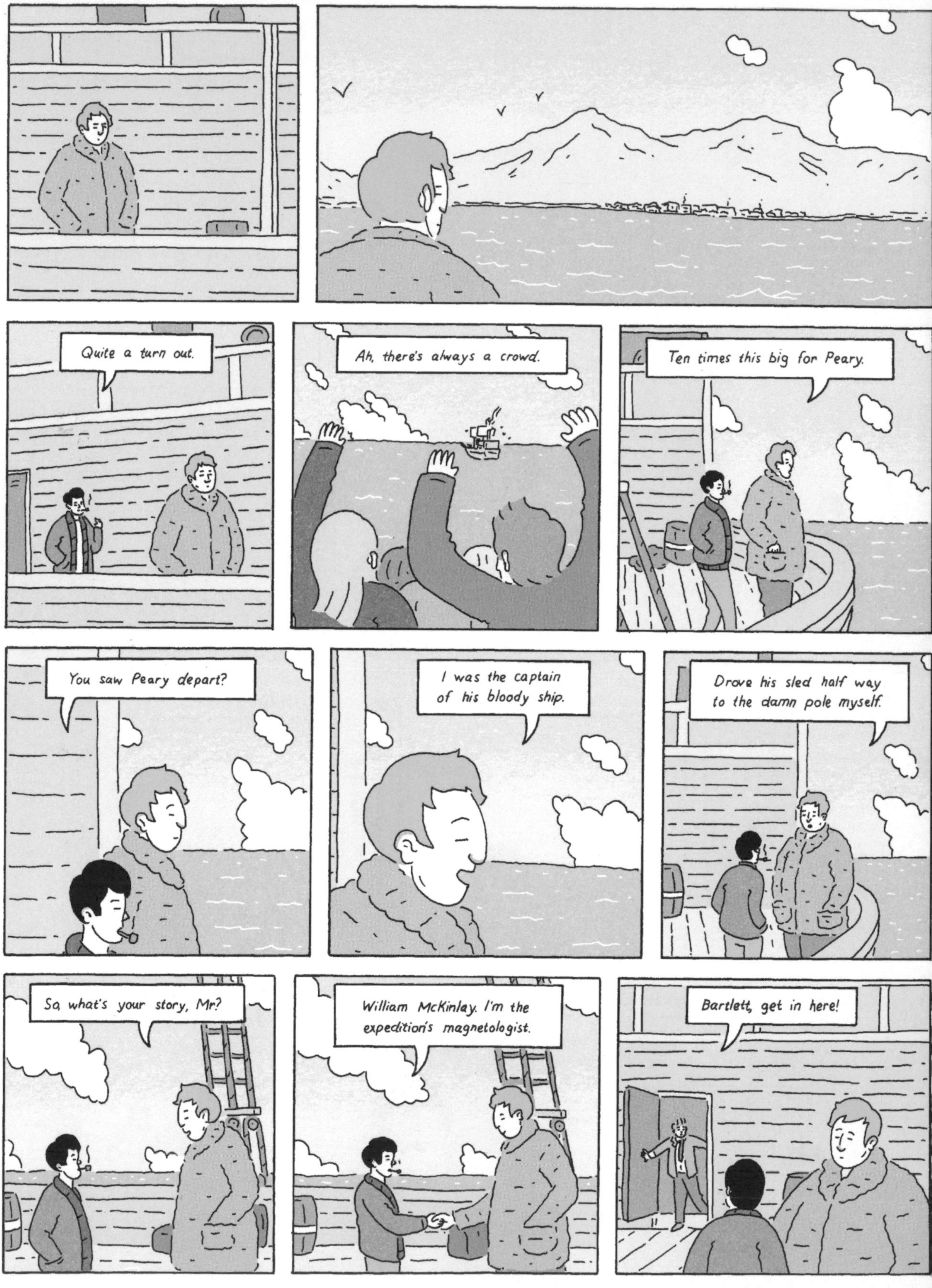
Quite a turn out.
Ah, there's always a crowd.
Ten times this big for Peary.
You saw Peary depart?
I was the captain of his bloody ship.
Drove his sled half way to the damn pole myself.
So, what's your story, Mr?
William McKinlay. I'm the expedition's magnetologist.
Bartlett, get in here!

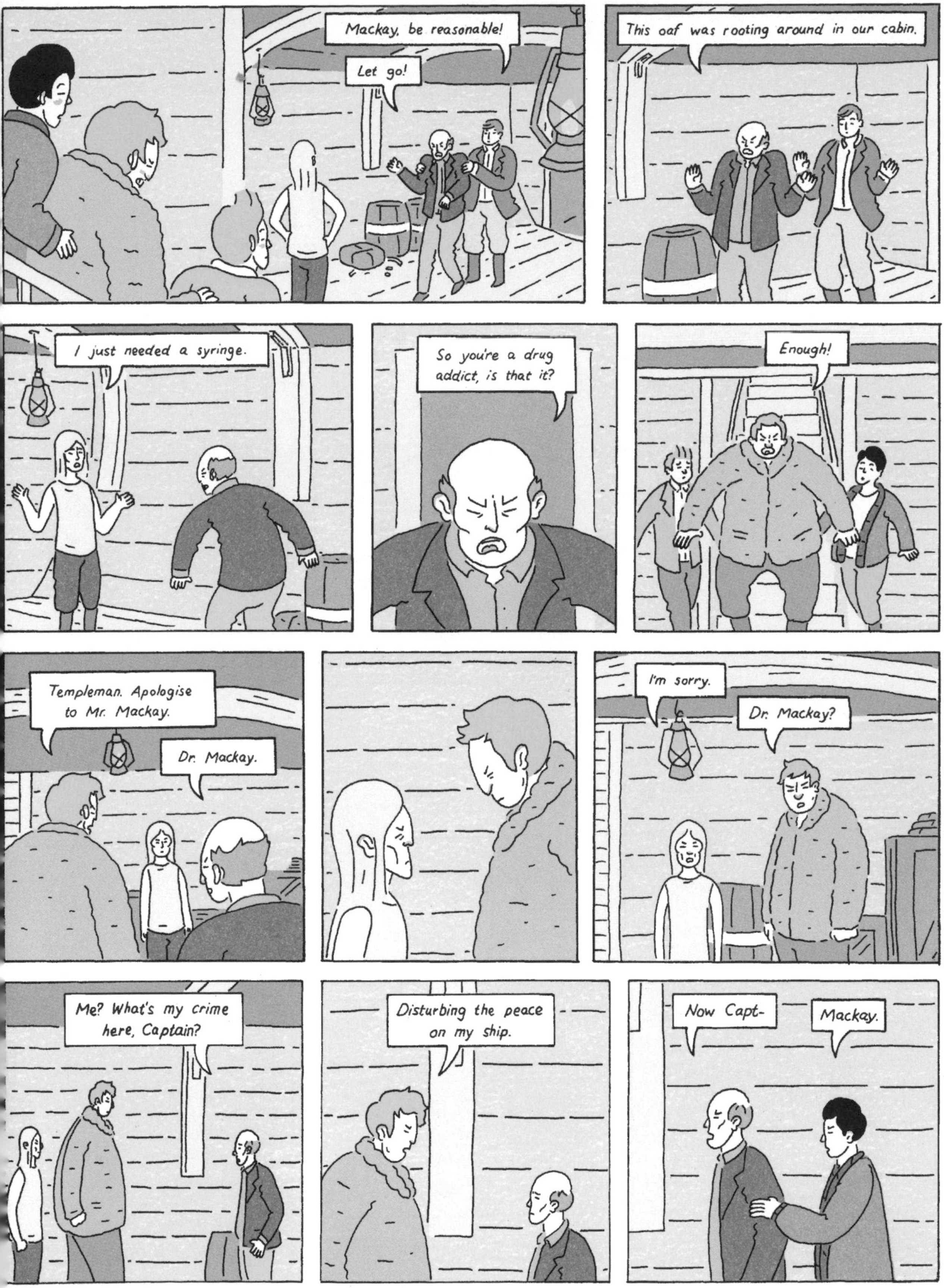
Mackay, be reasonable!
Let go!
This oaf was rooting around in our cabin.
I just needed a syringe.
So you're a drug addict, is that it?
Enough!
Templeman. Apologise to Mr. Mackay.
Dr. Mackay.
I'm sorry.
Dr. Mackay?
Me? What's my crime here, Captain?
Disturbing the peace on my ship.
Now Capt-
Mackay.

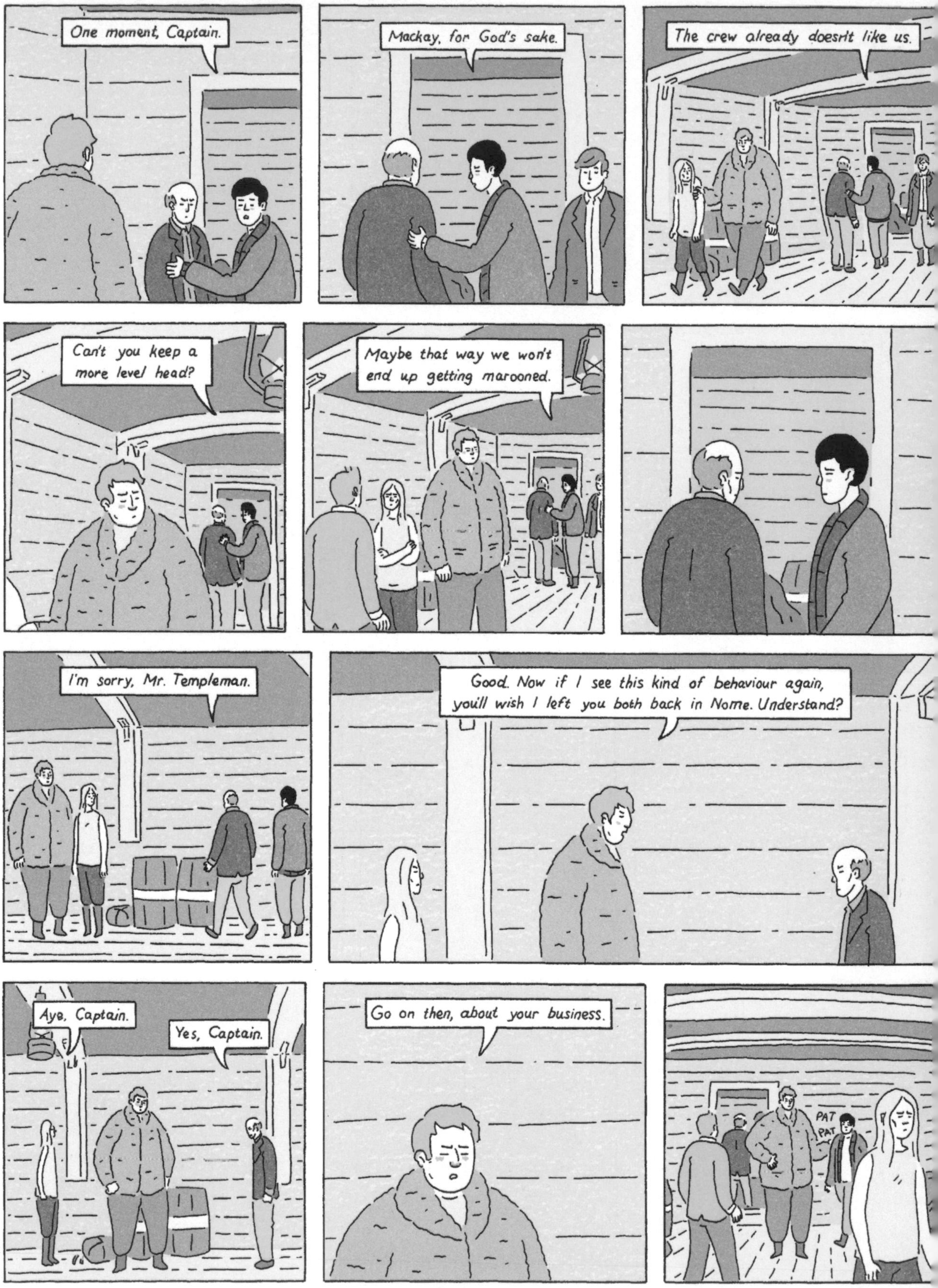
One moment, Captain.
Mackay, for God's sake.
The crew already doesn't like us.
Can't you keep a more level head?
Maybe that way we won't end up getting marooned.
I'm sorry, Mr. Templeman.
Good. Now if I see this kind of behaviour again, you'll wish I left you both back in Nome. Understand?
Aye, Captain.
Yes, Captain.
Go on then, about your business.
PAT PAT

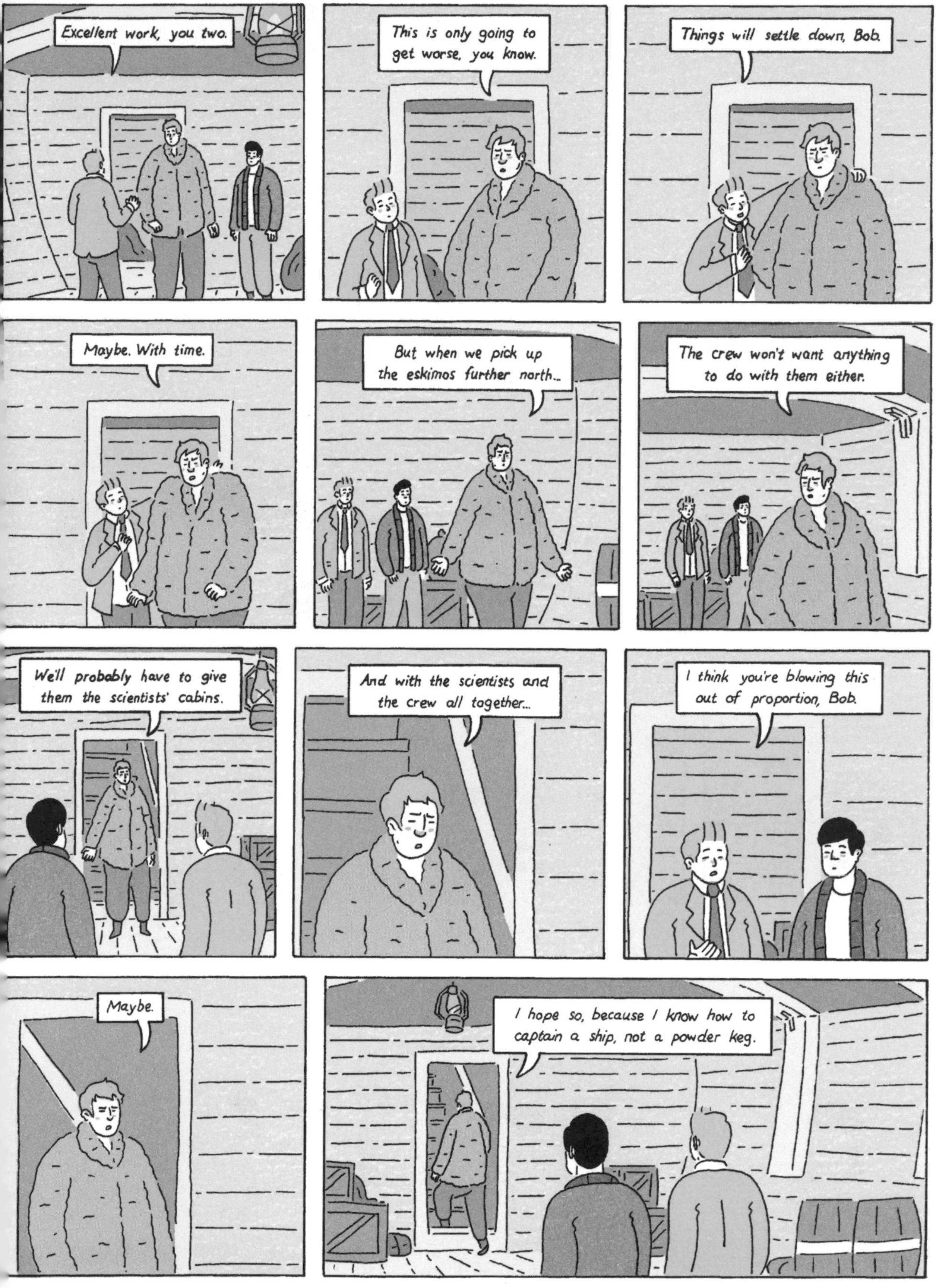
Excellent work, you two.
This is only going to get worse, you know.
Things will settle down, Bob.
Maybe. With time.
But when we pick up the eskimos further north...
The crew won't want anything to do with them either.
We'll probably have to give them the scientists' cabins.
And with the scientists and the crew all together...
I think you're blowing this out of proportion, Bob.
Maybe.
I hope so, because I know how to captain a ship, not a powder keg.

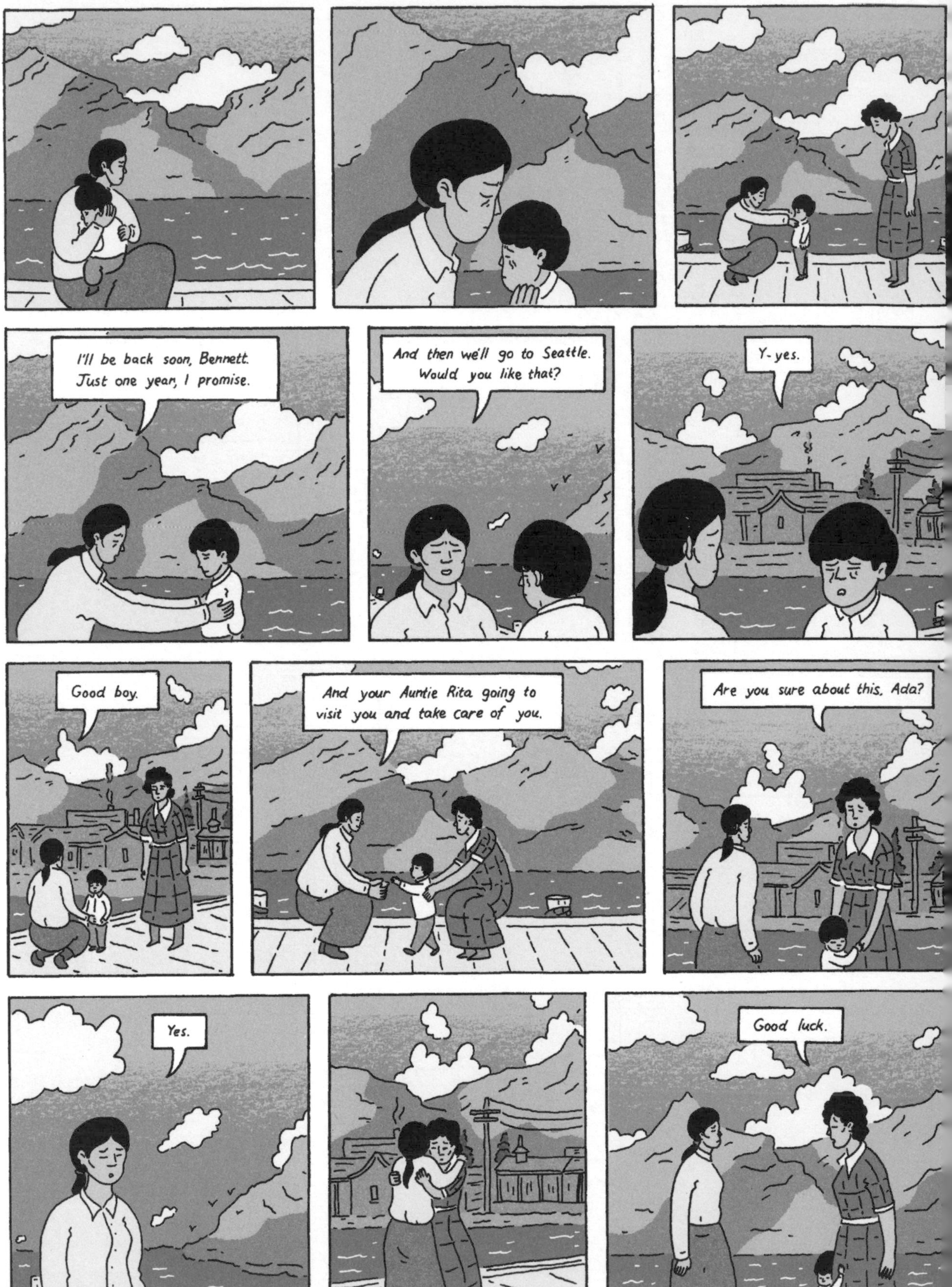

I'll be back soon, Bennett. Just one year, I promise.
And then we'll go to Seattle. Would you like that?
Y-yes.
Good boy.
And your Auntie Rita going to visit you and take care of you.
Are you sure about this, Ada?
Yes.
Good luck.

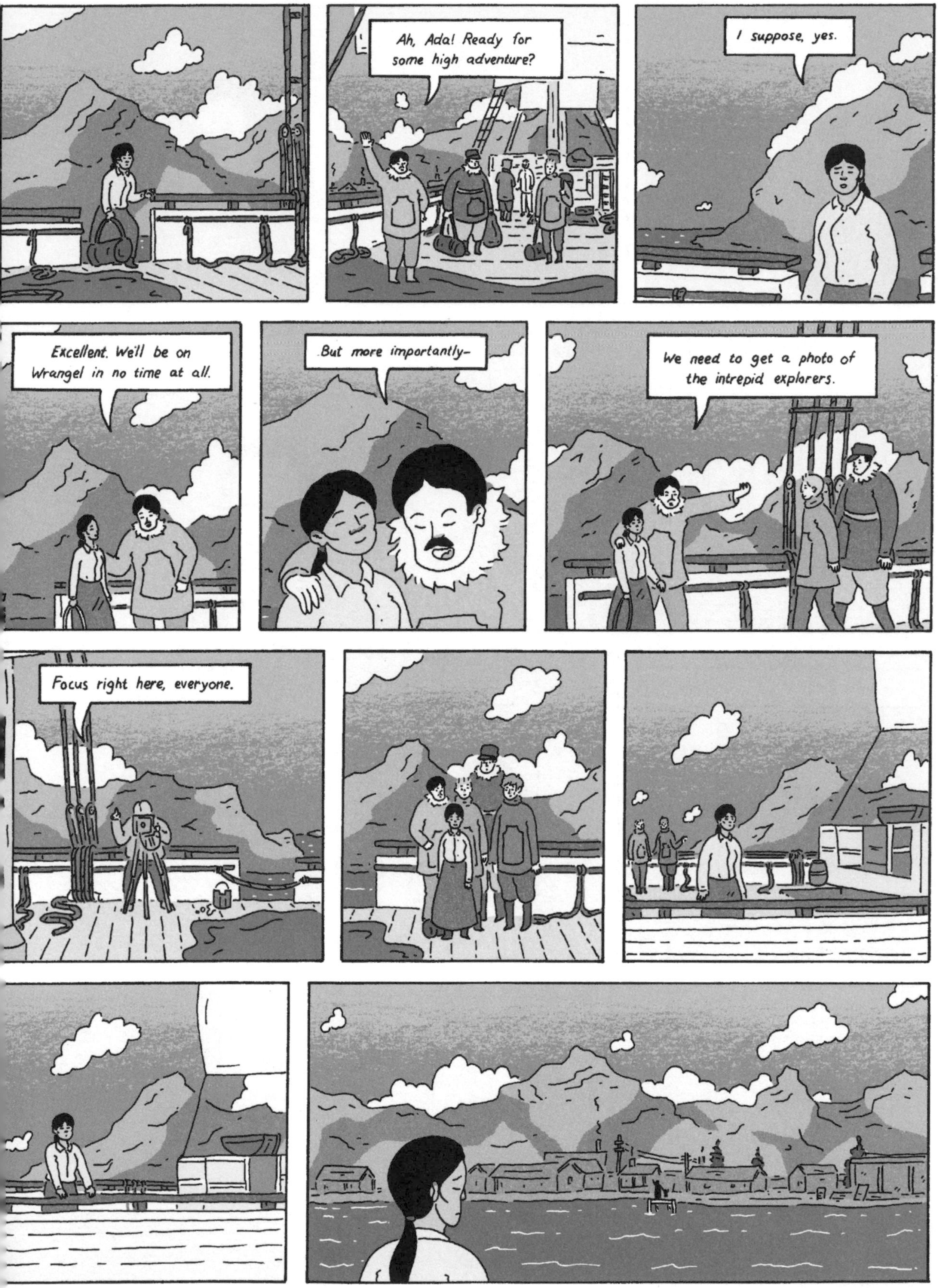
Ah, Ada! Ready for some high adventure?
I suppose, yes.
Excellent. We'll be on Wrangel in no time at all.
But more importantly-
We need to get a photo of the intrepid explorers.
Focus right here, everyone.

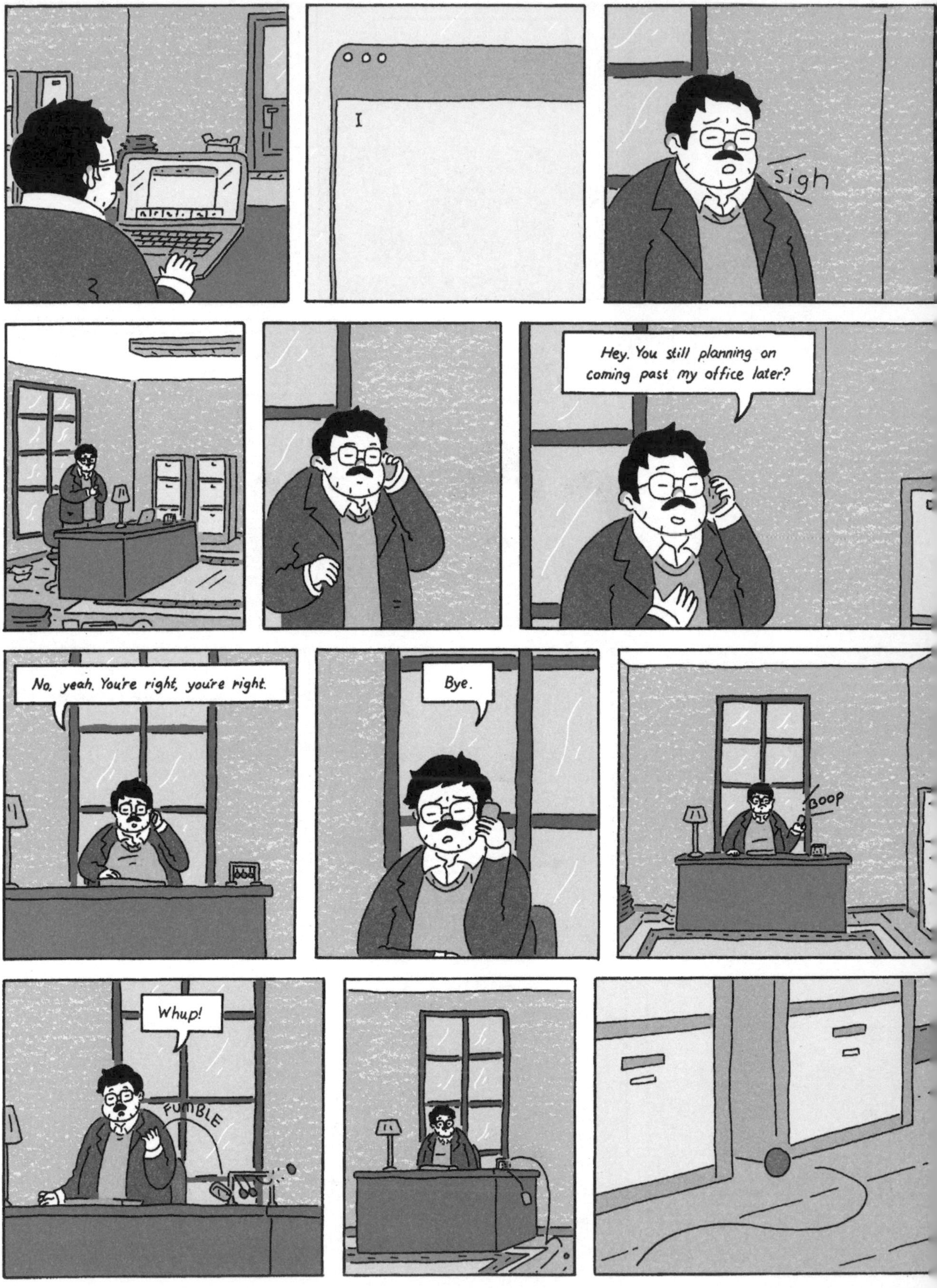
sigh
Hey. You still planning on coming past my office later?
No, yeah. You're right, you're right.
Bye.
BOOP
Whup!
FUMBLE

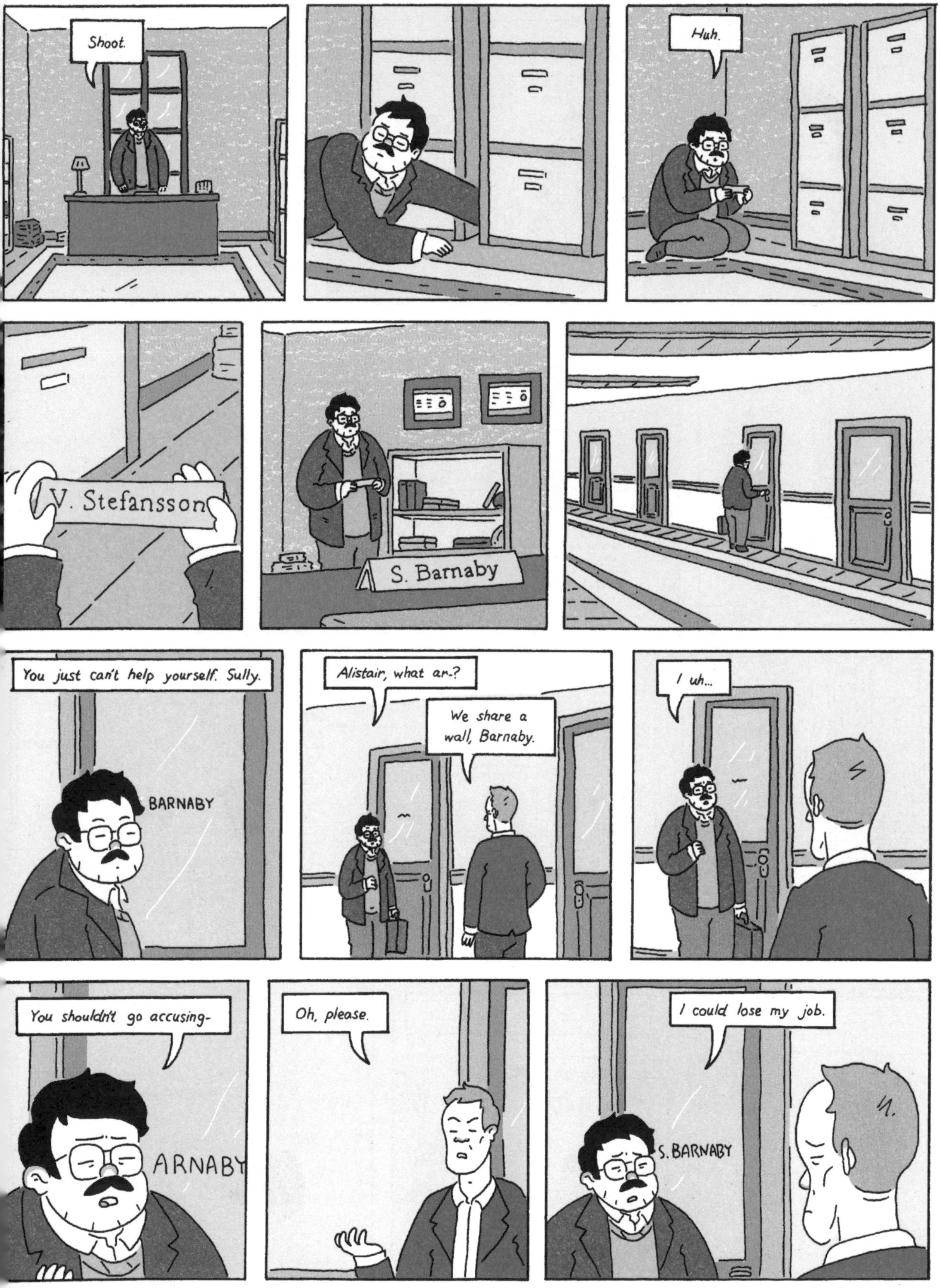
Shoot.
Huh.
V. Stefansson
S. Barnaby
You just can't help yourself. Sully.
BARNABY
Alistair, what ar-?
We share a wall, Barnaby.
I uh...
You shouldn't go accusing-
ARNABY
Oh, please.
I could lose my job.
S. BARNABY

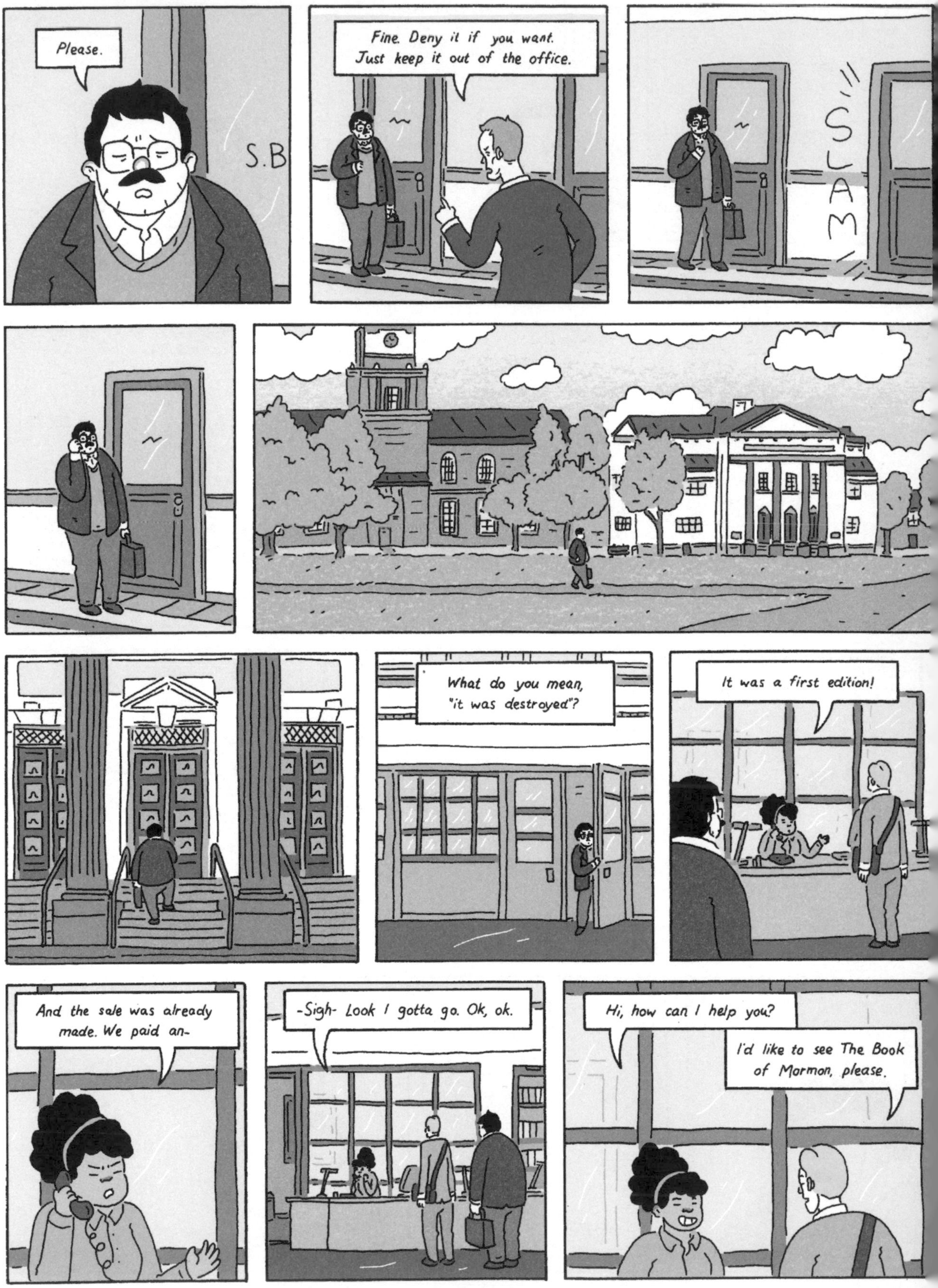
Please.
S.B
Fine. Deny it if you want. Just keep it out of the office.
SLAM
What do you mean, "it was destroyed"?
It was a first edition!
And the sale was already made. We paid an-
-Sigh- Look I gotta go. Ok, ok.
Hi, how can I help you?
I'd like to see The Book of Mormon, please.

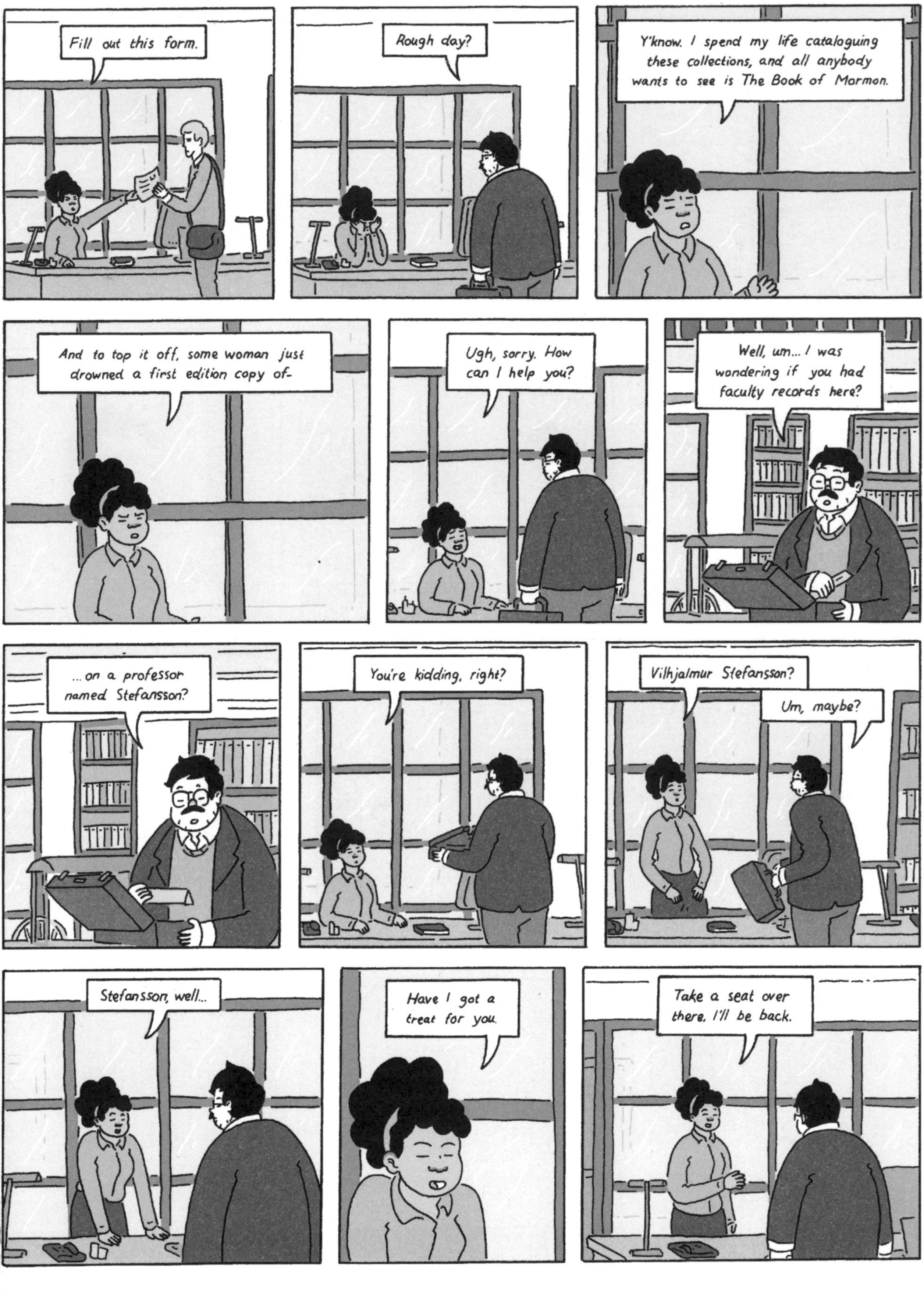
Fill out this form.
Rough day?
Y'know. I spend my life cataloguing these collections, and all anybody wants to see is The Book of Mormon.
And to top it off, some woman just drowned a first edition copy of-
Ugh, sorry. How can I help you?
Well, um... I was wondering if you had faculty records here?
...on a professor named Stefansson?
You're kidding, right?
Vilhjalmur Stefansson?
Um, maybe?
Stefansson, well...
Have I got a treat for you.
Take a seat over there. I'll be back.

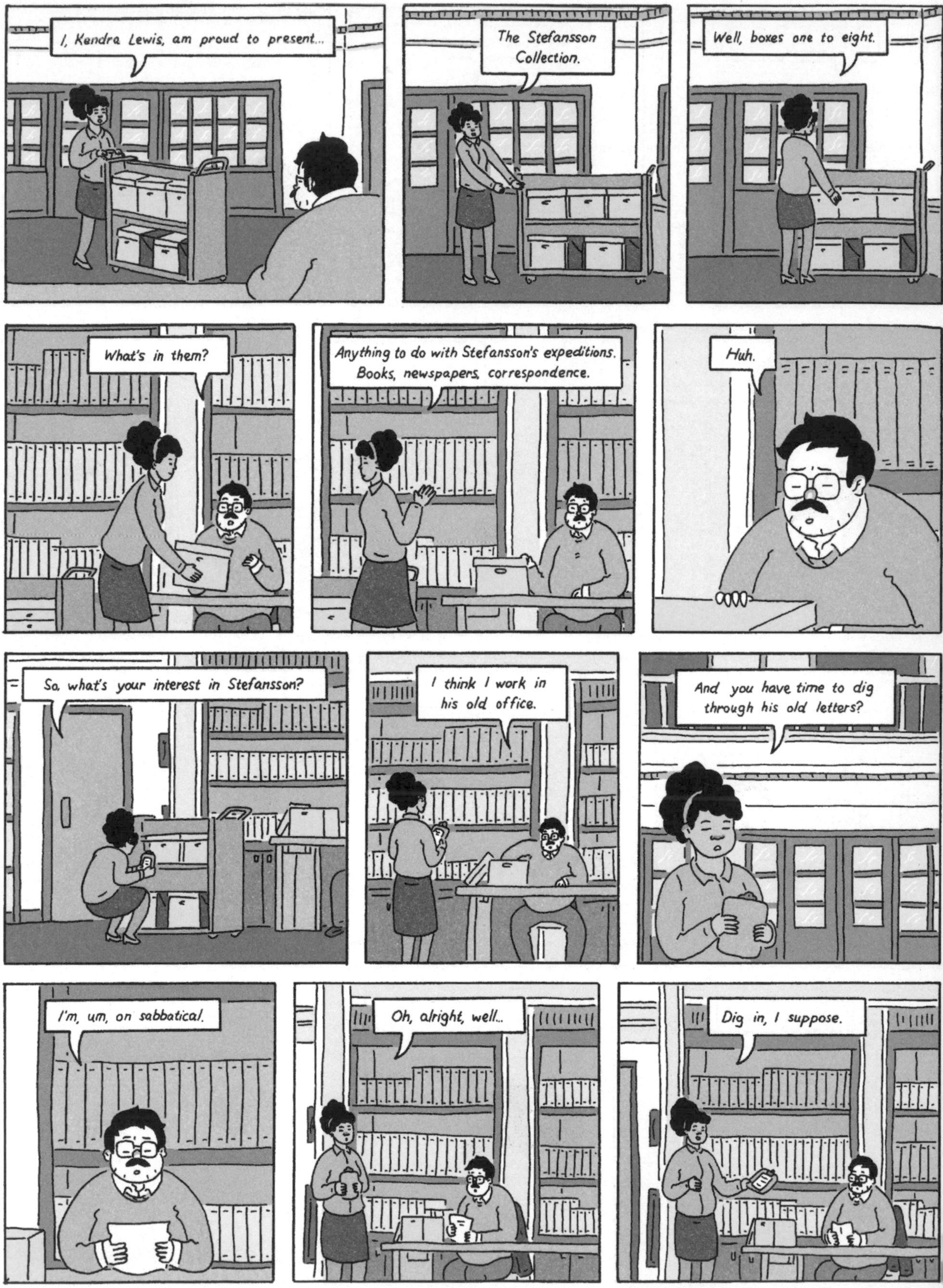
I, Kendra Lewis, am proud to present...
The Stefansson Collection.
Well, boxes one to eight.
What's in them?
Anything to do with Stefansson's expeditions. Books, newspapers, correspondence.
Huh.
So, what's your interest in Stefansson?
I think I work in his old office.
And you have time to dig through his old letters?
I'm, um, on sabbatical.
Oh, alright, well...
Dig in, I suppose.

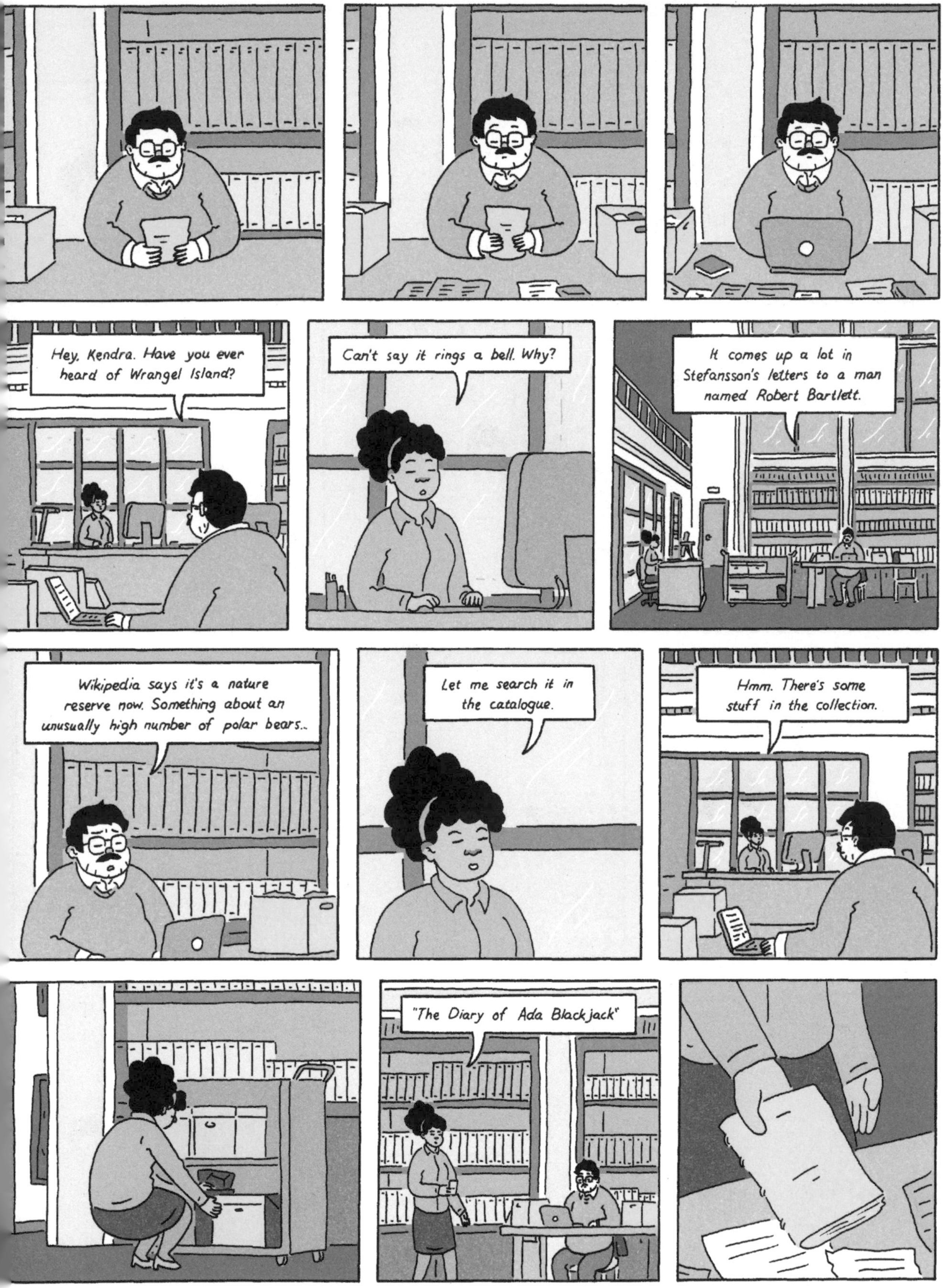
Hey, Kendra. Have you ever heard of Wrangel Island?
Can't say it rings a bell. Why?
It comes up a lot in Stefansson's letters to a man named Robert Bartlett.
Wikipedia says it's a nature reserve now. Something about an unusually high number of polar bears..
Let me search it in the catalogue.
Hmm. There's some stuff in the collection.
"The Diary of Ada Blackjack"

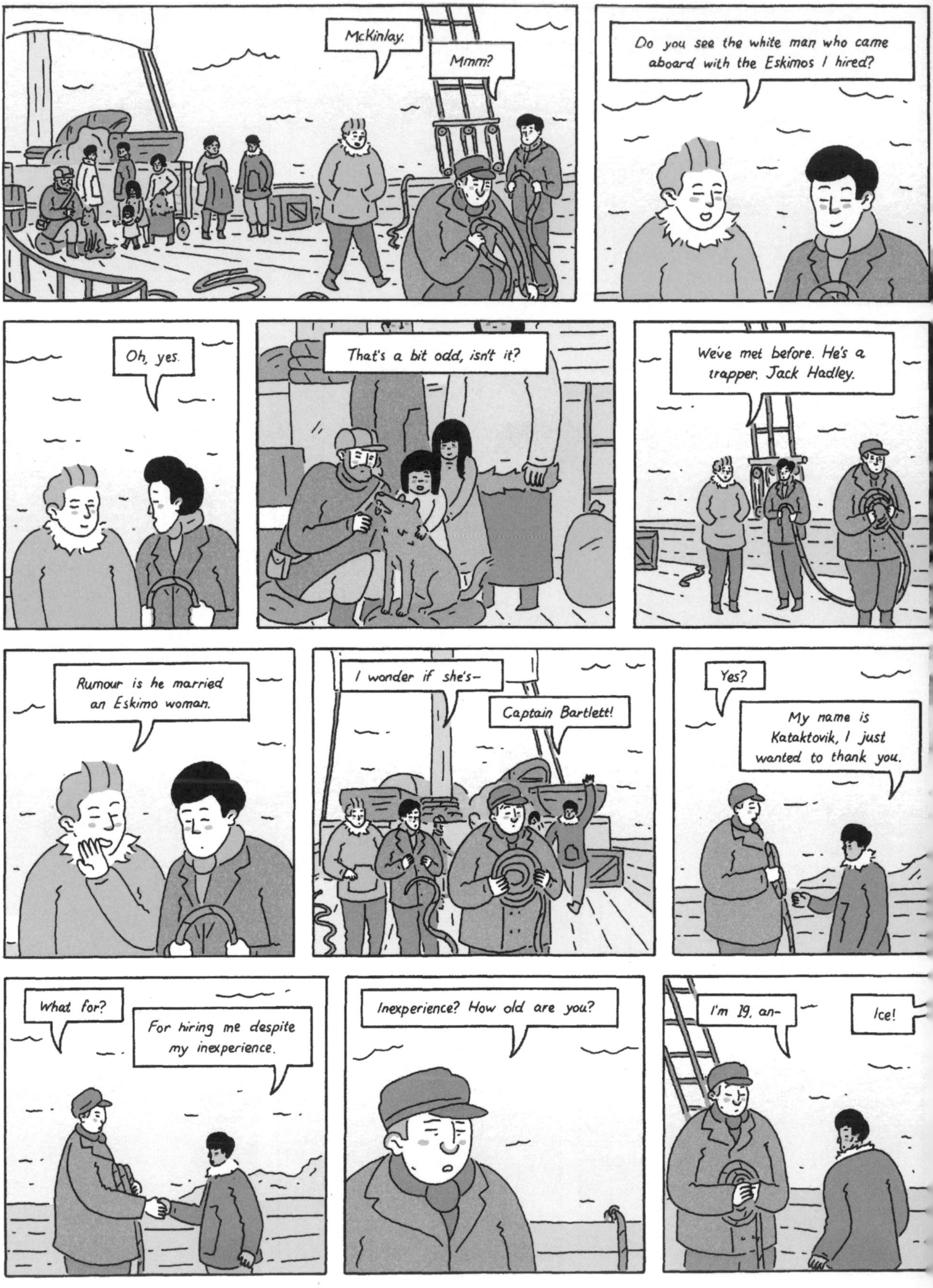
McKinlay.
Mmm?
Do you see the white man who came aboard with the Eskimos I hired?
Oh, yes.
That's a bit odd, isn't it?
We've met before. He's a trapper. Jack Hadley.
Rumour is he married an Eskimo woman.
I wonder if she's–
Captain Bartlett!
Yes?
My name is Kataktovik, I just wanted to thank you.
What for?
For hiring me despite my inexperience.
Inexperience? How old are you?
I'm 19, an–
Ice!

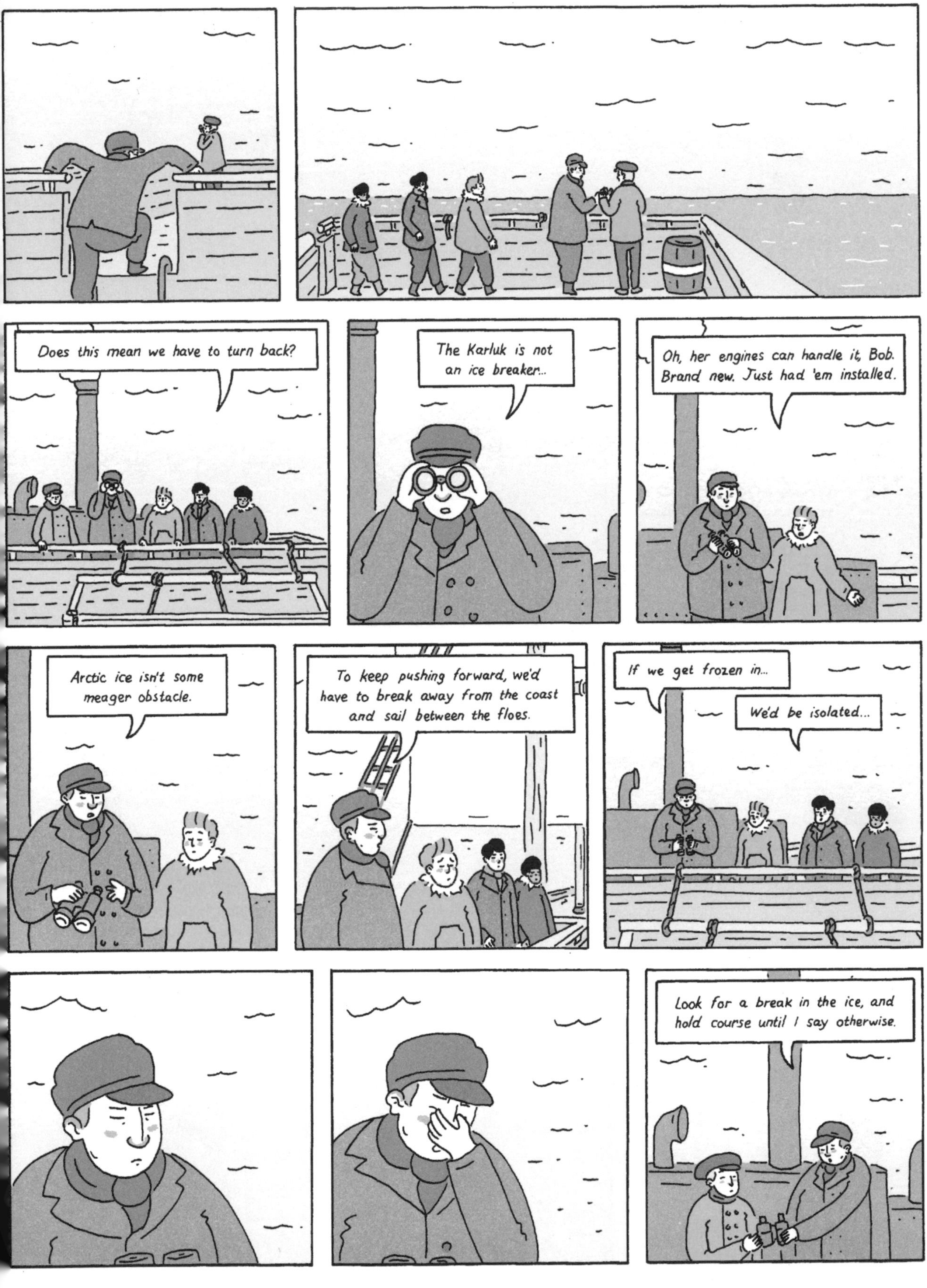
Does this mean we have to turn back?
The Karluk is not an ice breaker...
Oh, her engines can handle it, Bob. Brand new. Just had 'em installed.
Arctic ice isn't some meager obstacle.
To keep pushing forward, we'd have to break away from the coast and sail between the floes.
If we get frozen in...
We'd be isolated...
Look for a break in the ice, and hold course until I say otherwise.

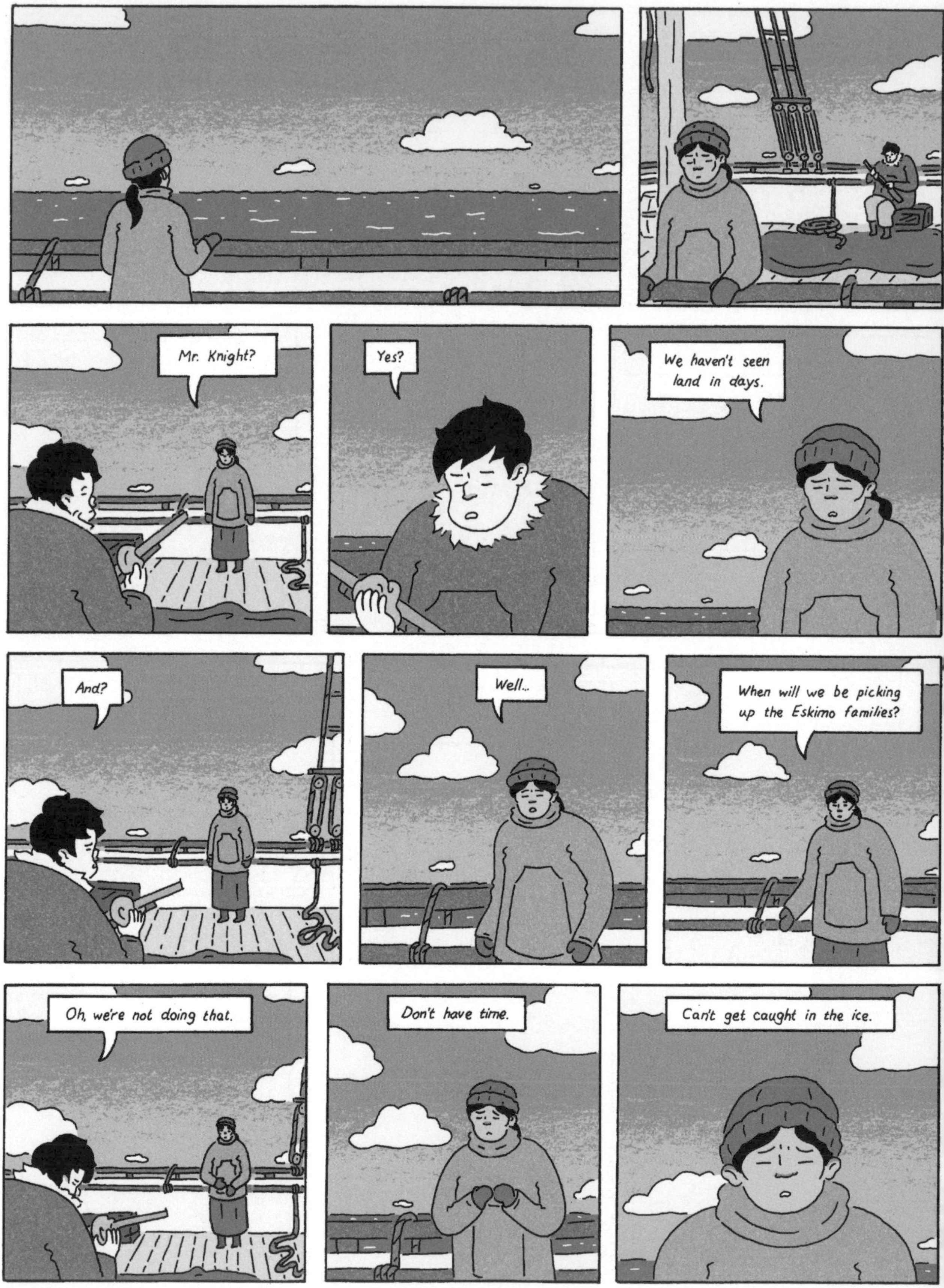
Mr. Knight?
Yes?
We haven't seen land in days.
And?
Well..
When will we be picking up the Eskimo families?
Oh, we're not doing that.
Don't have time.
Can't get caught in the ice.

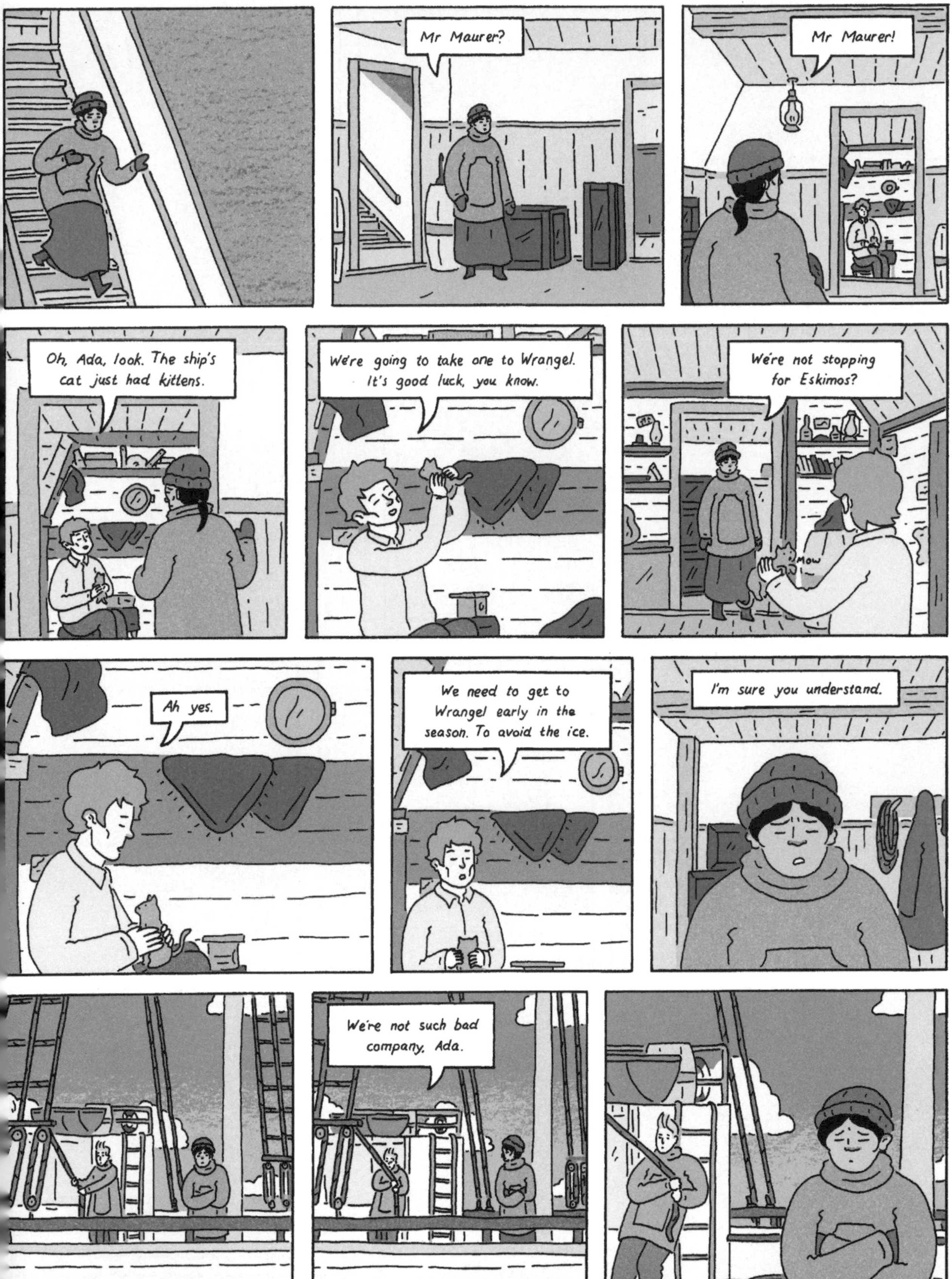
Mr Maurer?
Mr Maurer!
Oh, Ada, look. The ship's cat just had kittens.
We're going to take one to Wrangel. It's good luck, you know.
We're not stopping for Eskimos?
Mow
Ah yes.
We need to get to Wrangel early in the season. To avoid the ice.
I'm sure you understand.
We're not such bad company, Ada.

THUNK

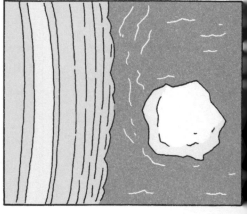

Would you like a drink, Captain?

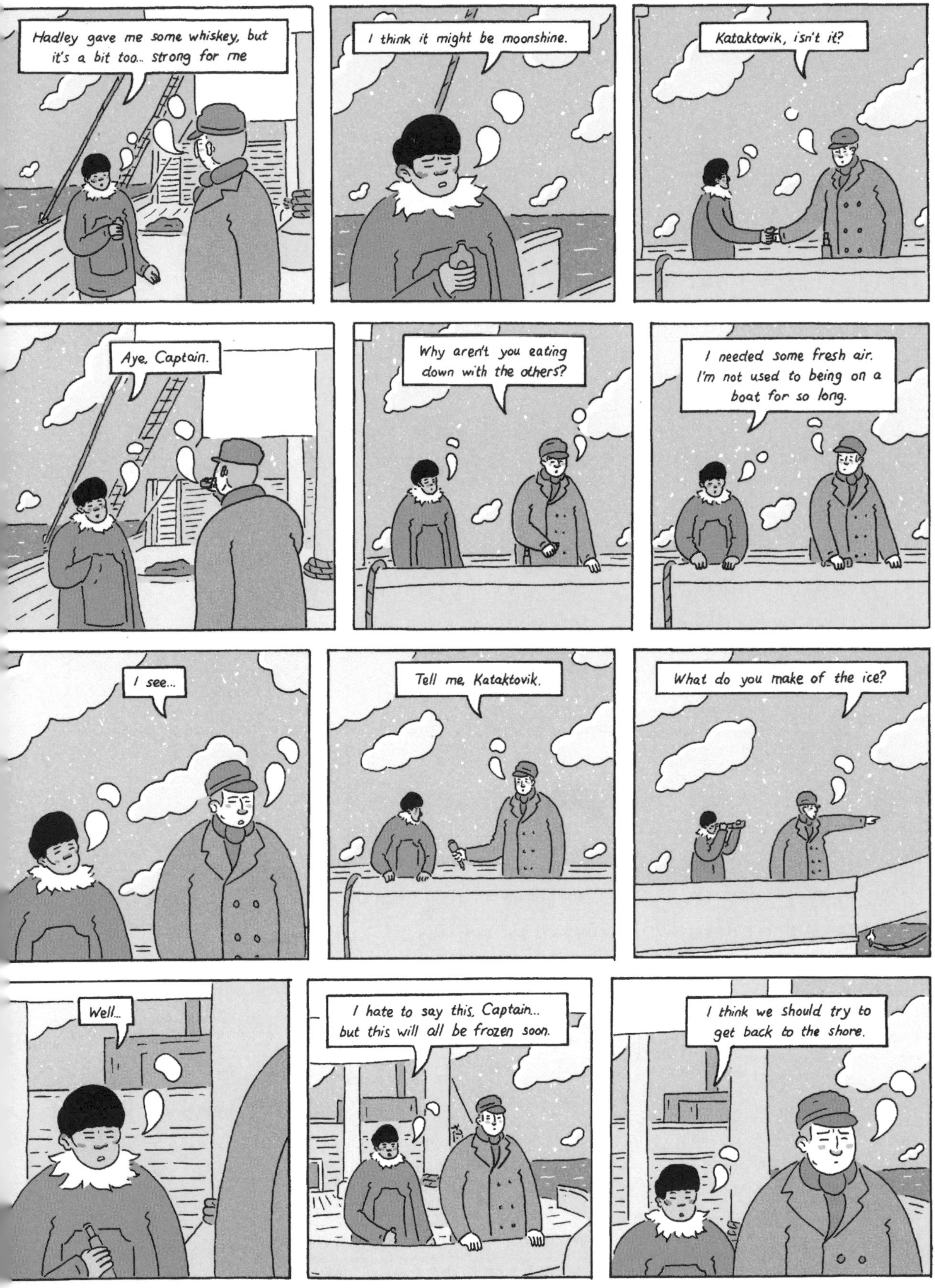

Hadley gave me some whiskey, but it's a bit too... strong for me
I think it might be moonshine.
Kataktovik, isn't it?
Aye, Captain.
Why aren't you eating down with the others?
I needed some fresh air. I'm not used to being on a boat for so long.
I see...
Tell me, Kataktovik.
What do you make of the ice?
Well...
I hate to say this, Captain... but this will all be frozen soon.
I think we should try to get back to the shore.

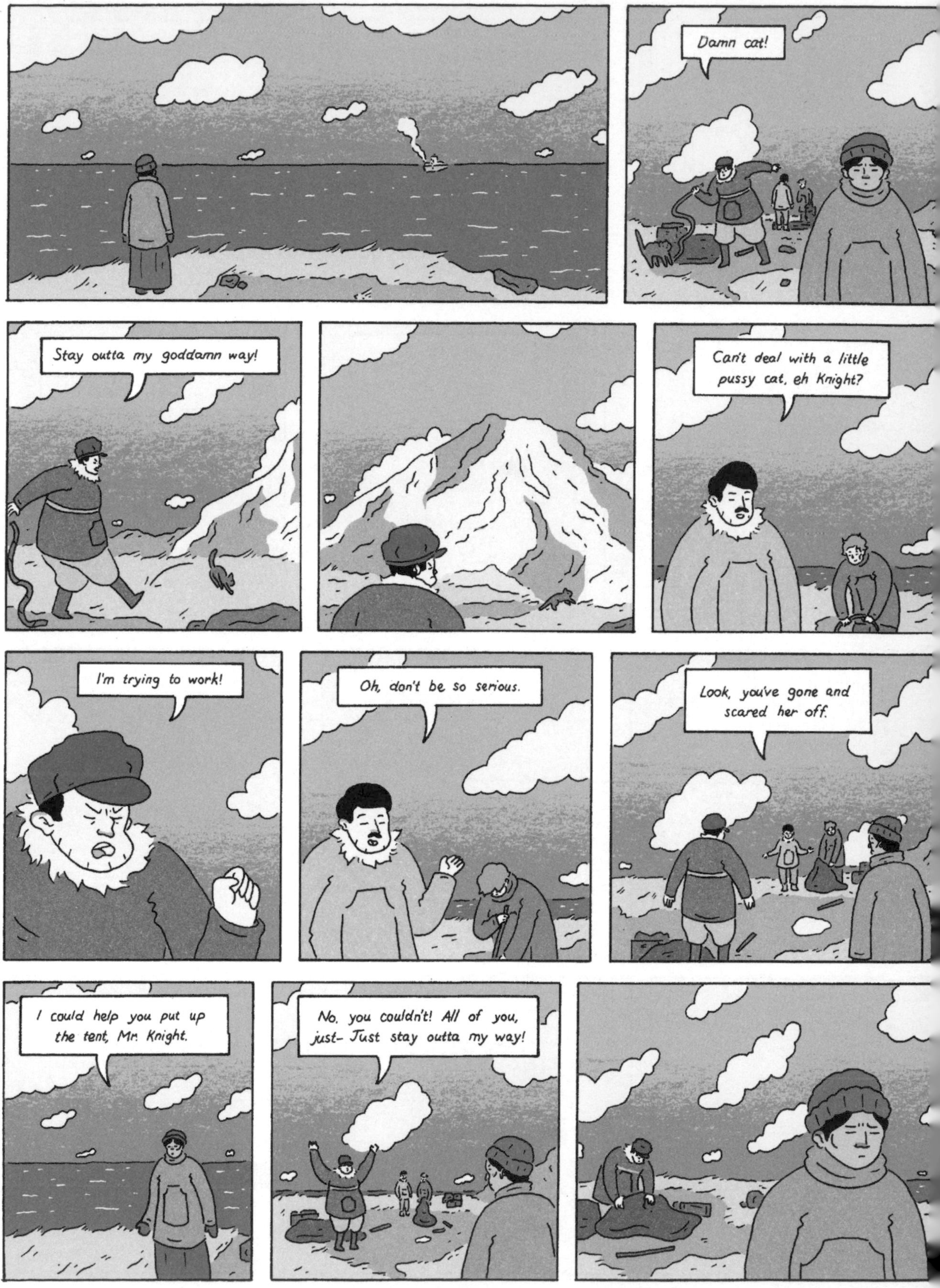
Damn cat!
Stay outta my goddamn way!
Can't deal with a little pussy cat, eh Knight?
I'm trying to work!
Oh, don't be so serious.
Look, you've gone and scared her off.
I could help you put up the tent, Mr. Knight.
No, you couldn't! All of you, just- Just stay outta my way!

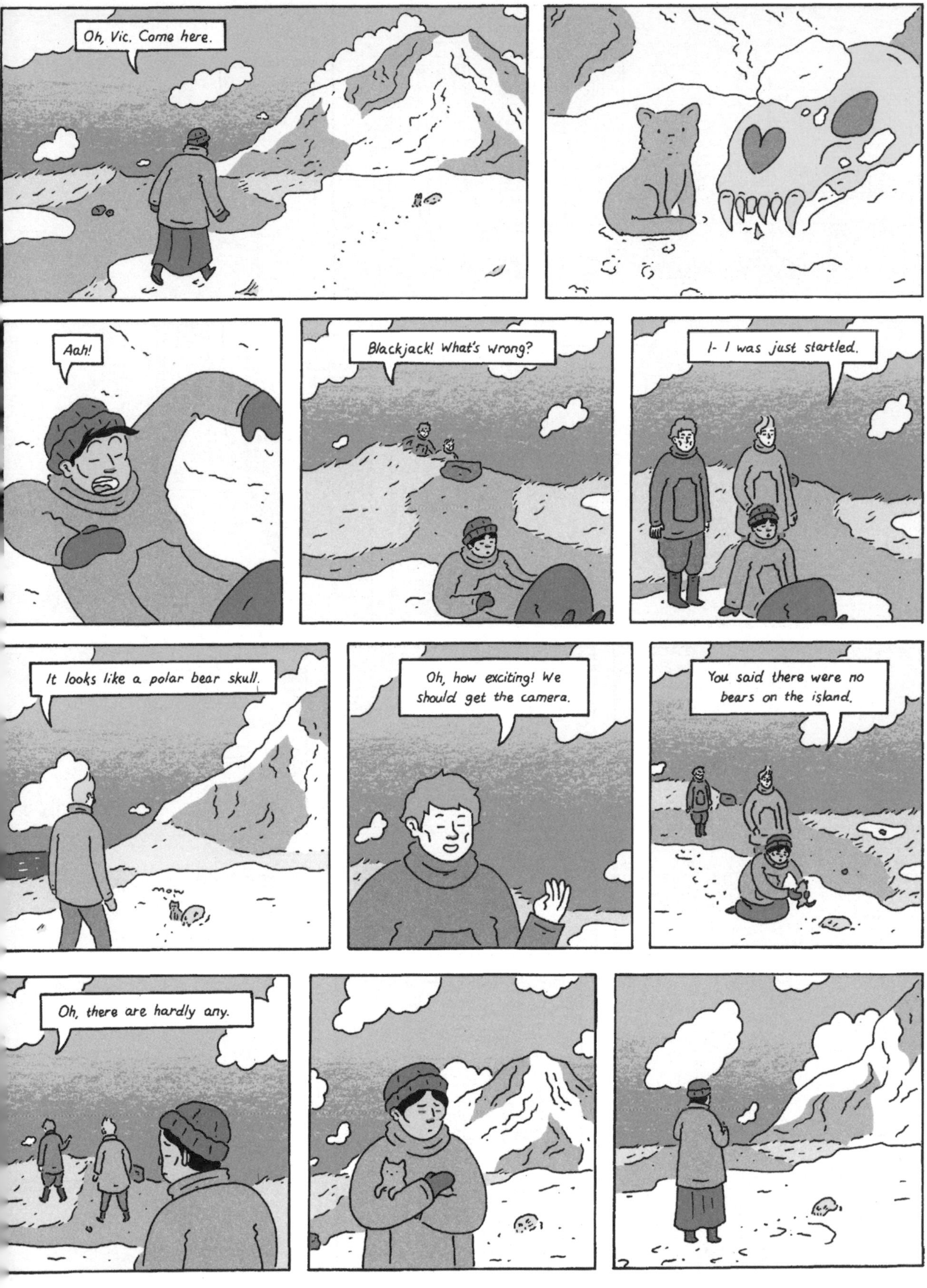
Oh, Vic. Come here.
Aah!
Blackjack! What's wrong?
I- I was just startled.
It looks like a polar bear skull.
mow
Oh, how exciting! We should get the camera.
You said there were no bears on the island.
Oh, there are hardly any.

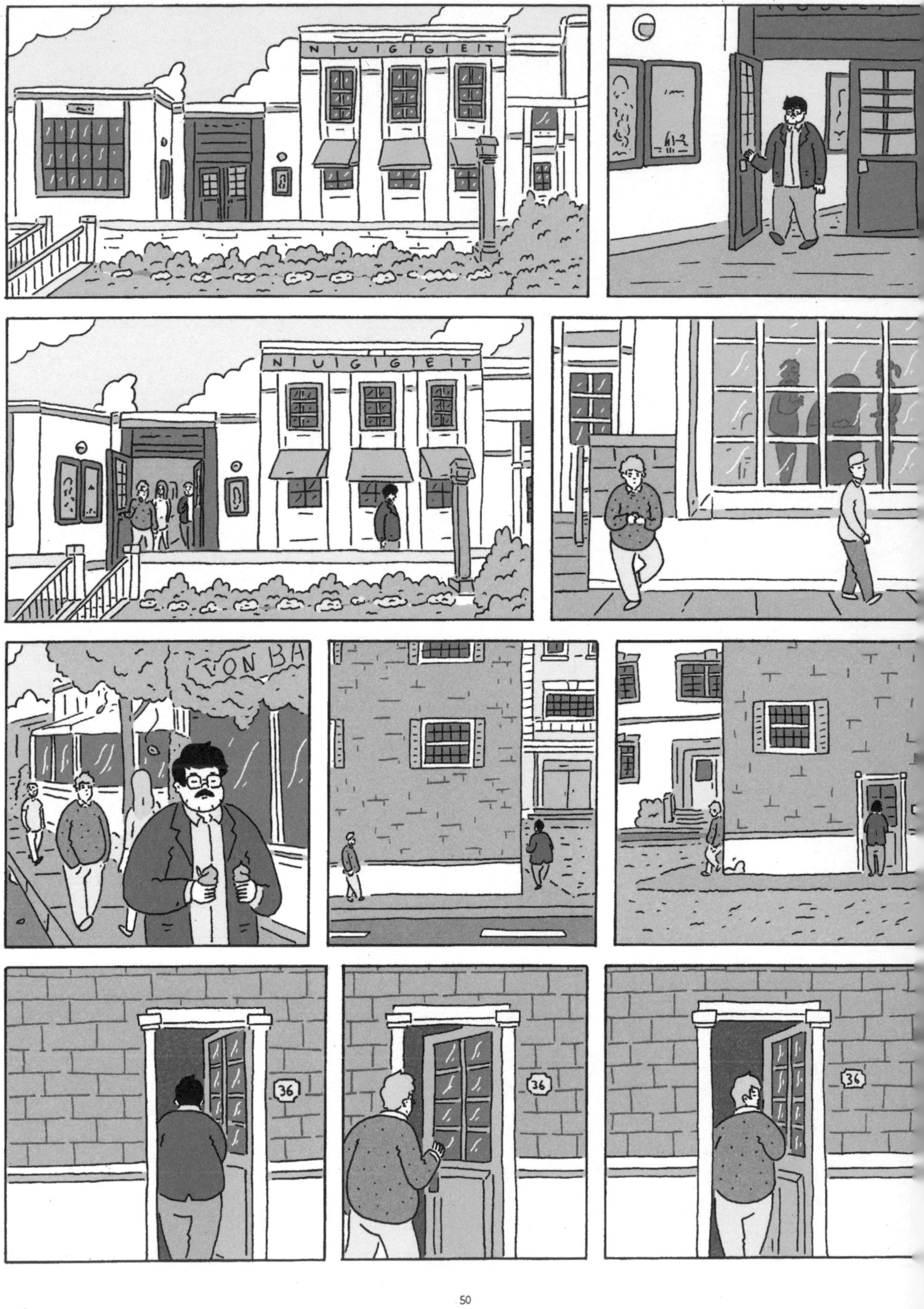
NUGGET
VON BA
36

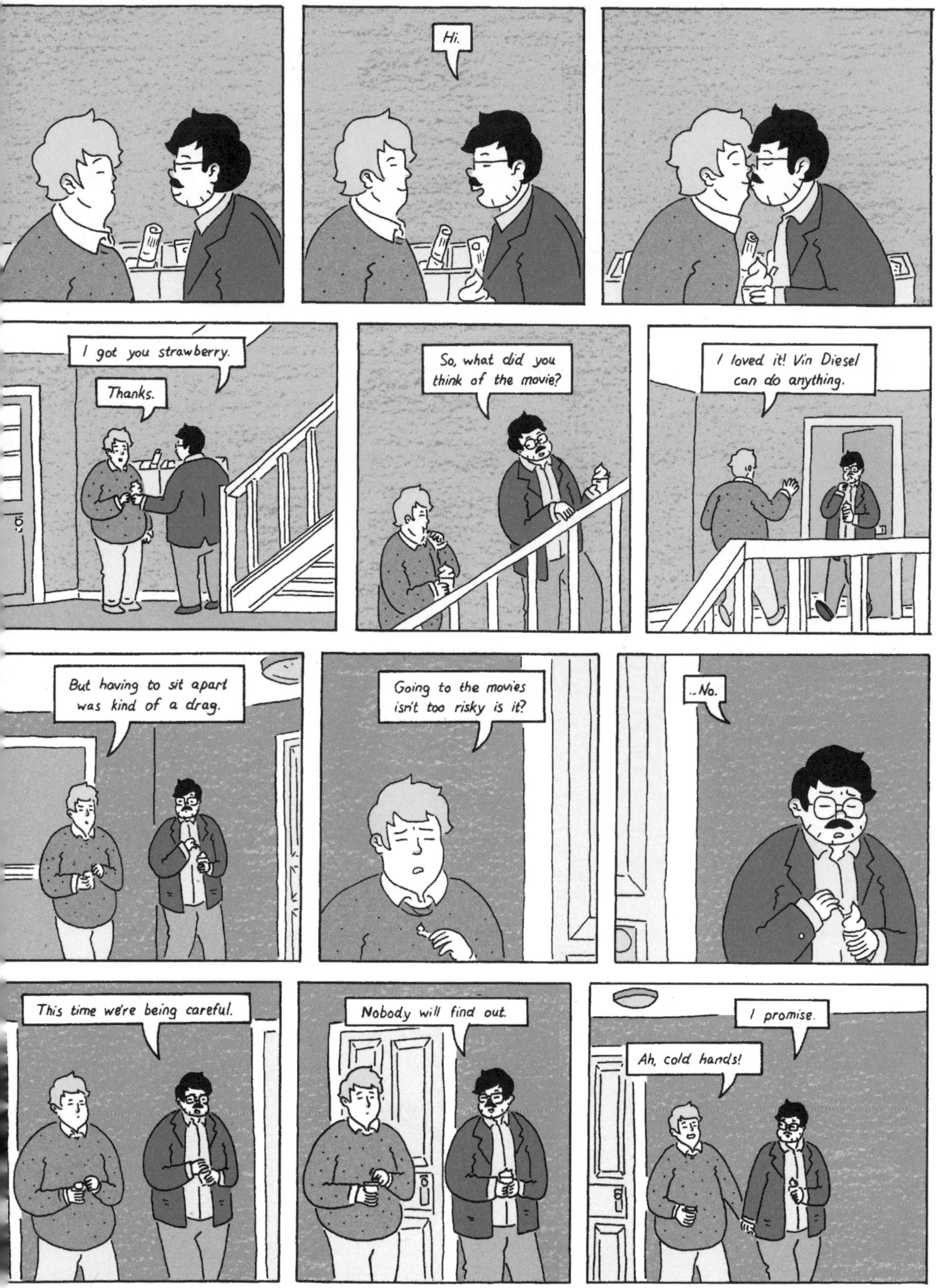
Hi.
I got you strawberry.
Thanks.
So, what did you think of the movie?
I loved it! Vin Diesel can do anything.
But having to sit apart was kind of a drag.
Going to the movies isn't too risky is it?
..No.
This time we're being careful.
Nobody will find out.
I promise.
Ah, cold hands!

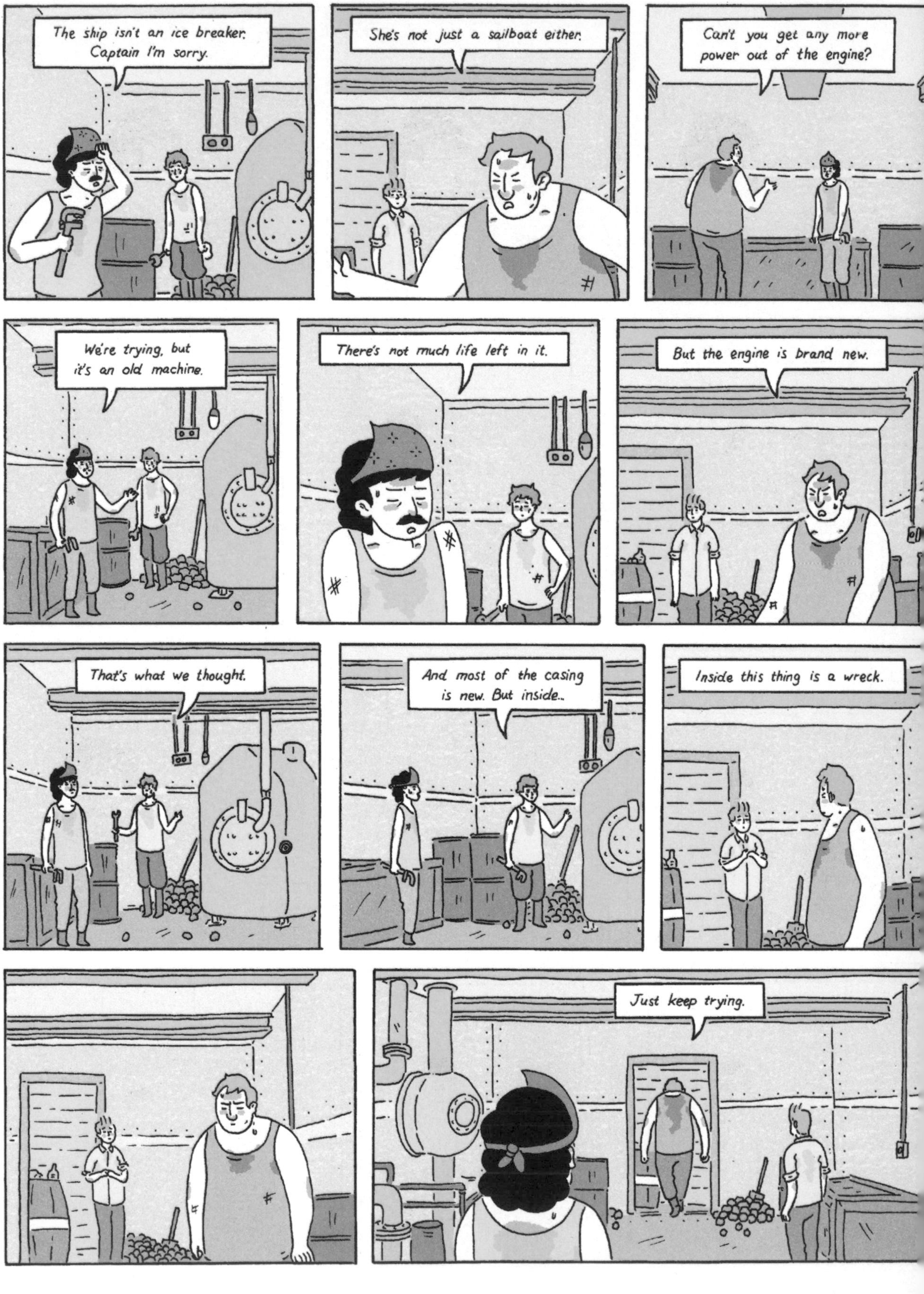
The ship isn't an ice breaker. Captain I'm sorry.
She's not just a sailboat either.
Can't you get any more power out of the engine?
We're trying, but it's an old machine.
There's not much life left in it.
But the engine is brand new.
That's what we thought.
And most of the casing is new. But inside..
Inside this thing is a wreck.
Just keep trying.

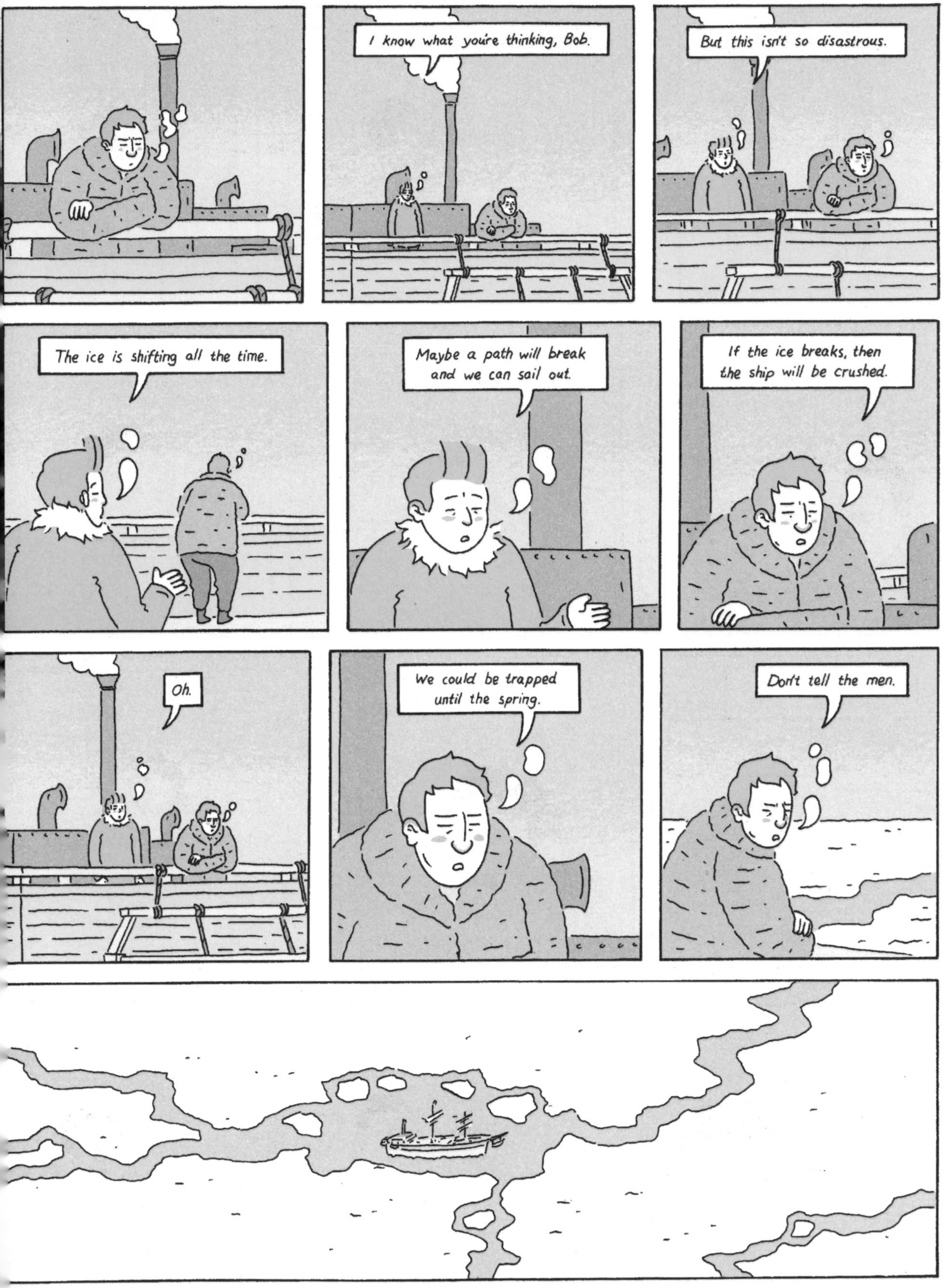
I know what you're thinking, Bob.
But this isn't so disastrous.
The ice is shifting all the time.
Maybe a path will break and we can sail out.
If the ice breaks, then the ship will be crushed.
Oh.
We could be trapped until the spring.
Don't tell the men.

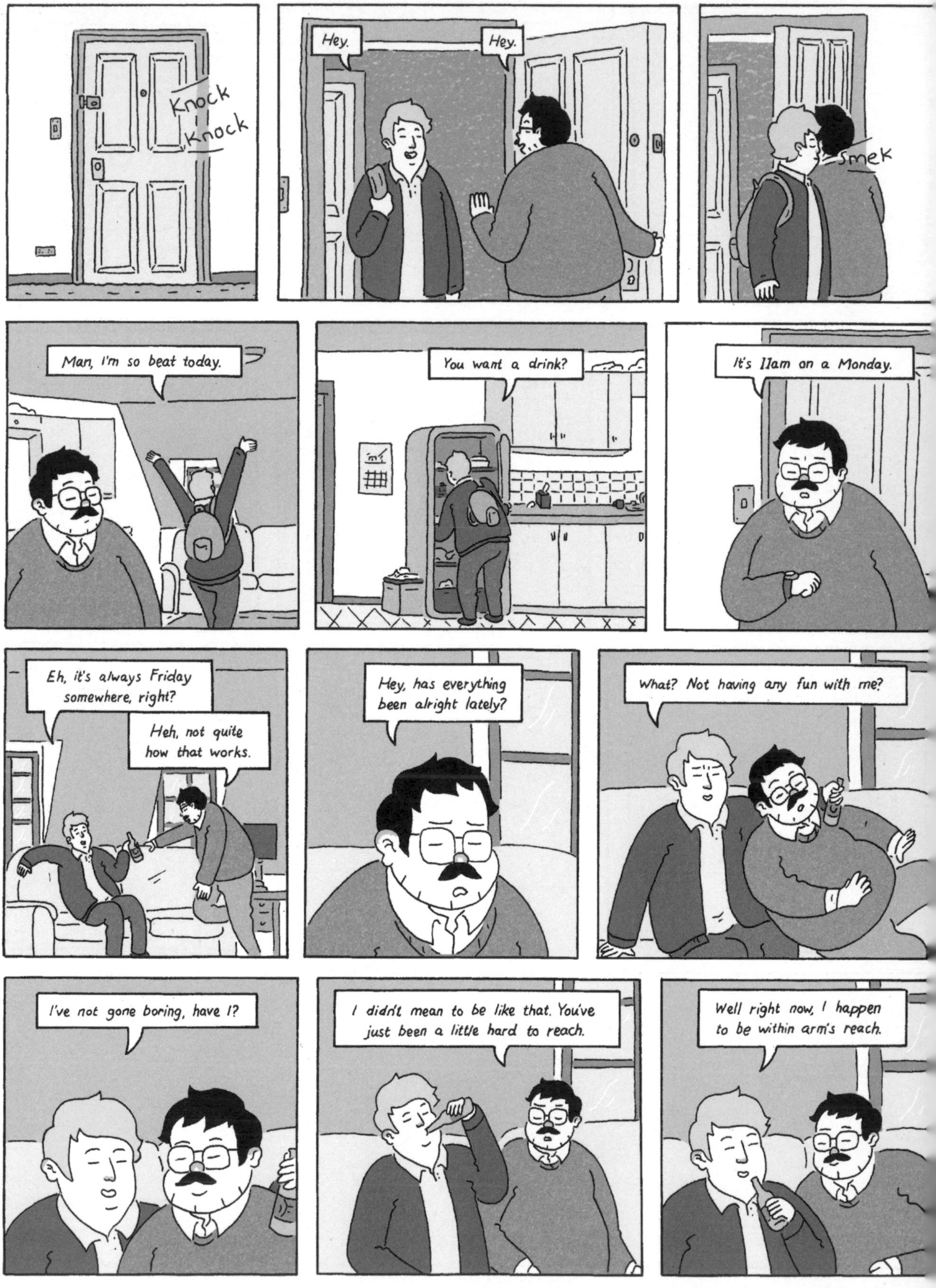

Knock
Knock
Hey.
Hey.
Smek
Man, I'm so beat today.
You want a drink?
It's 11am on a Monday.
Eh, it's always Friday somewhere, right?
Heh, not quite how that works.
Hey, has everything been alright lately?
What? Not having any fun with me?
I've not gone boring, have I?
I didn't mean to be like that. You've just been a little hard to reach.
Well right now, I happen to be within arm's reach.

Beep Boop
Alright, I gotta go.
Oh, I thought we could spend the day together.
Sorry, Sully.
I've got class.
Can't you skip? Please, being on sabbatical is so boring.
Sorry, I can't. Why don't you go meet some friends or something?

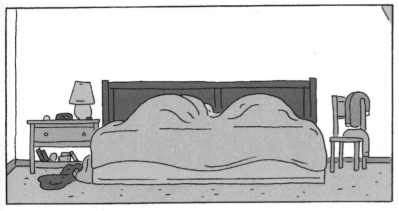

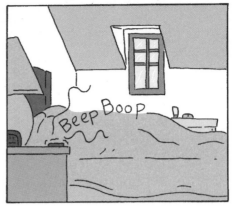

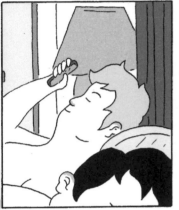

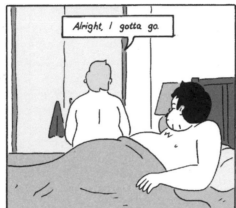

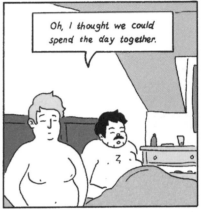

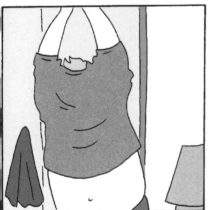

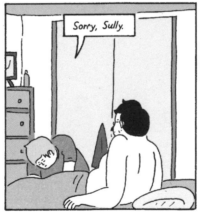

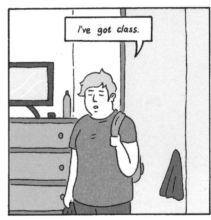

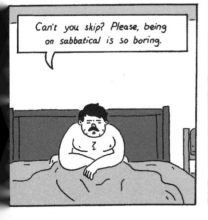

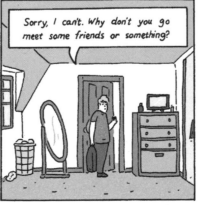

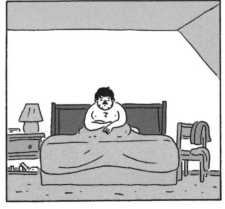

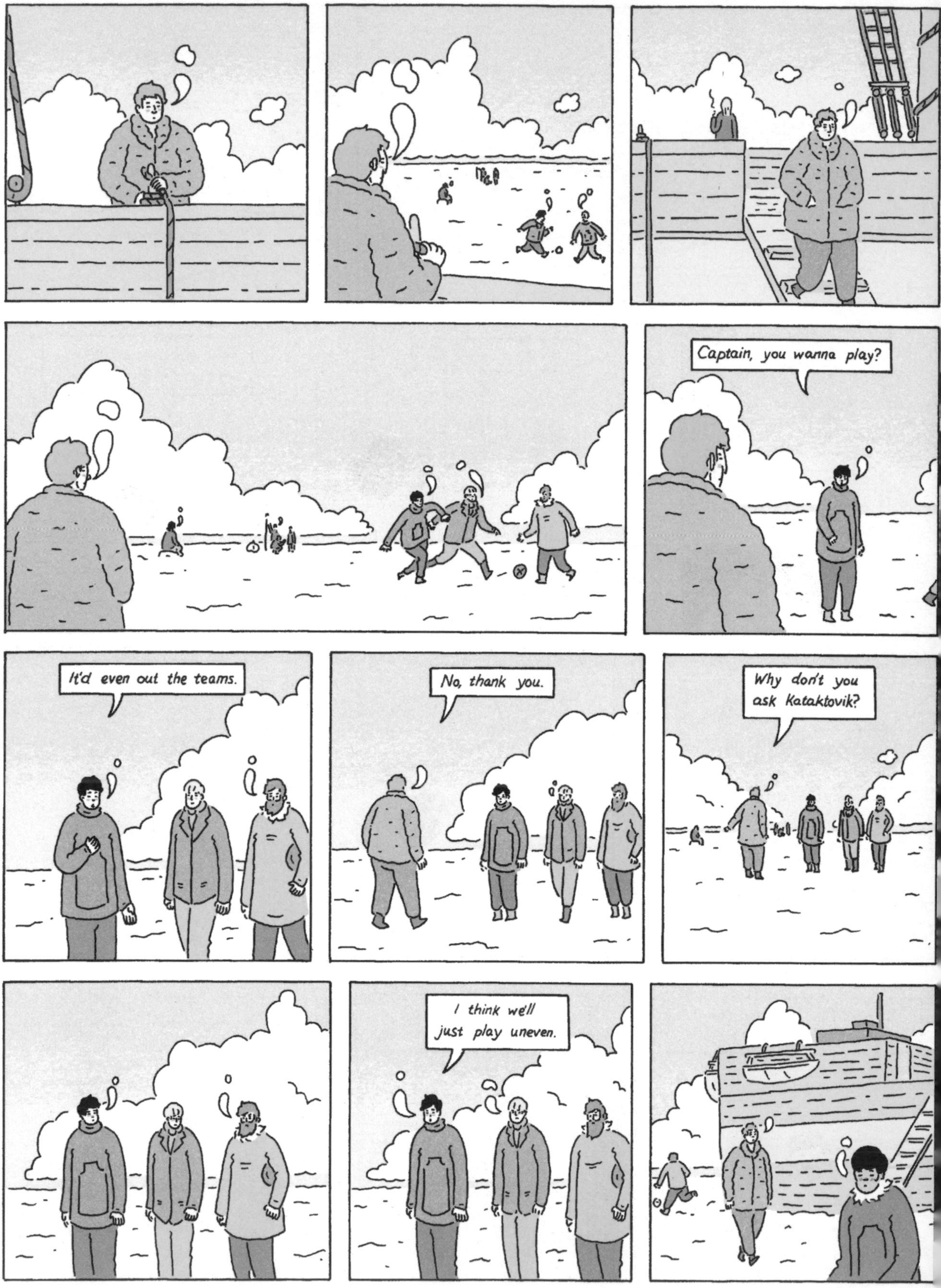

Captain, you wanna play?
It'd even out the teams.
No, thank you.
Why don't you ask Kataktovik?
I think we'll just play uneven.

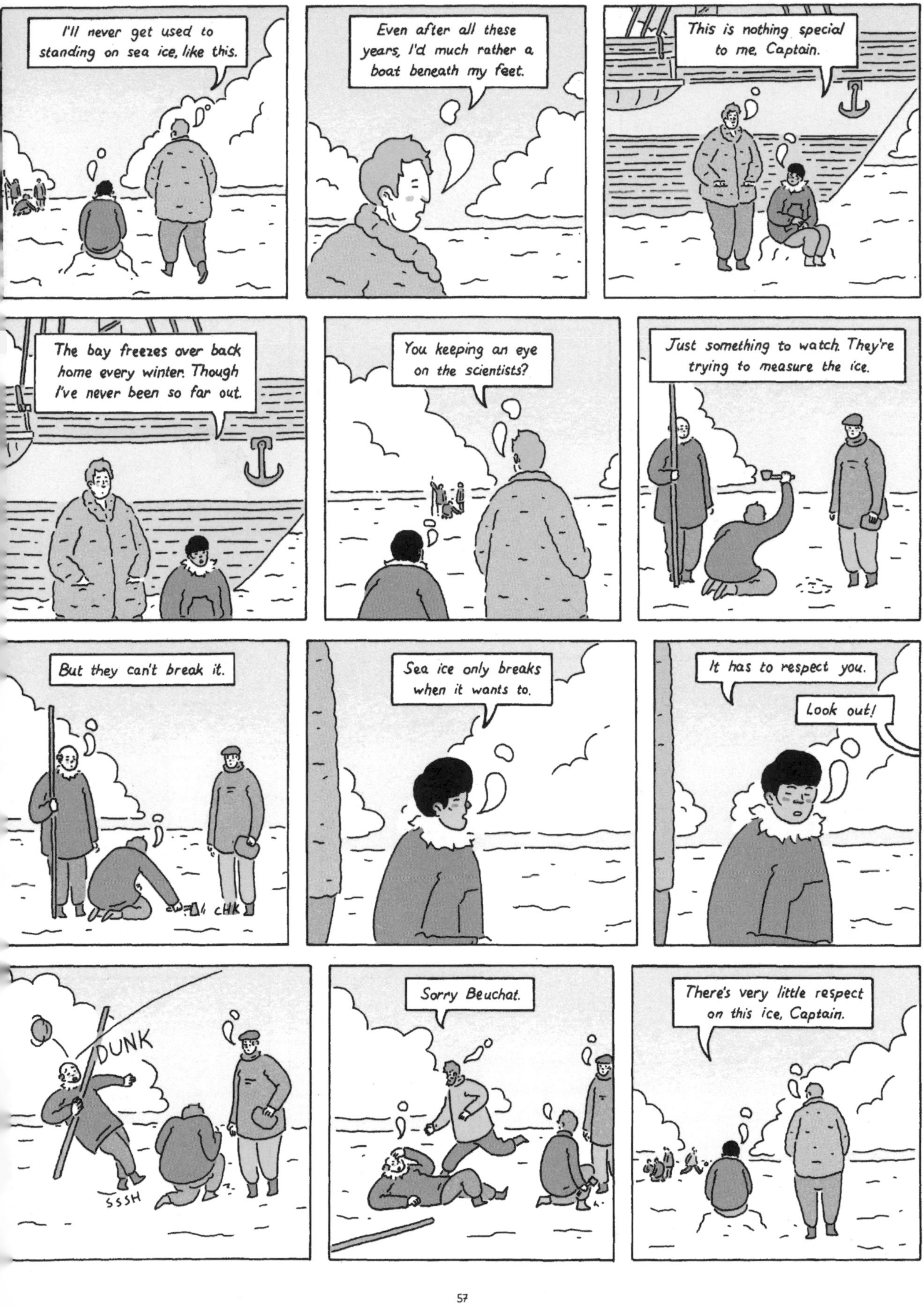
I'll never get used to standing on sea ice, like this.
Even after all these years, I'd much rather a boat beneath my feet.
This is nothing special to me, Captain.
The bay freezes over back home every winter. Though I've never been so far out.
You keeping an eye on the scientists?
Just something to watch. They're trying to measure the ice.
But they can't break it.
CHK
Sea ice only breaks when it wants to.
It has to respect you.
Look out!
DUNK
SSSH
Sorry Beuchat.
There's very little respect on this ice, Captain.

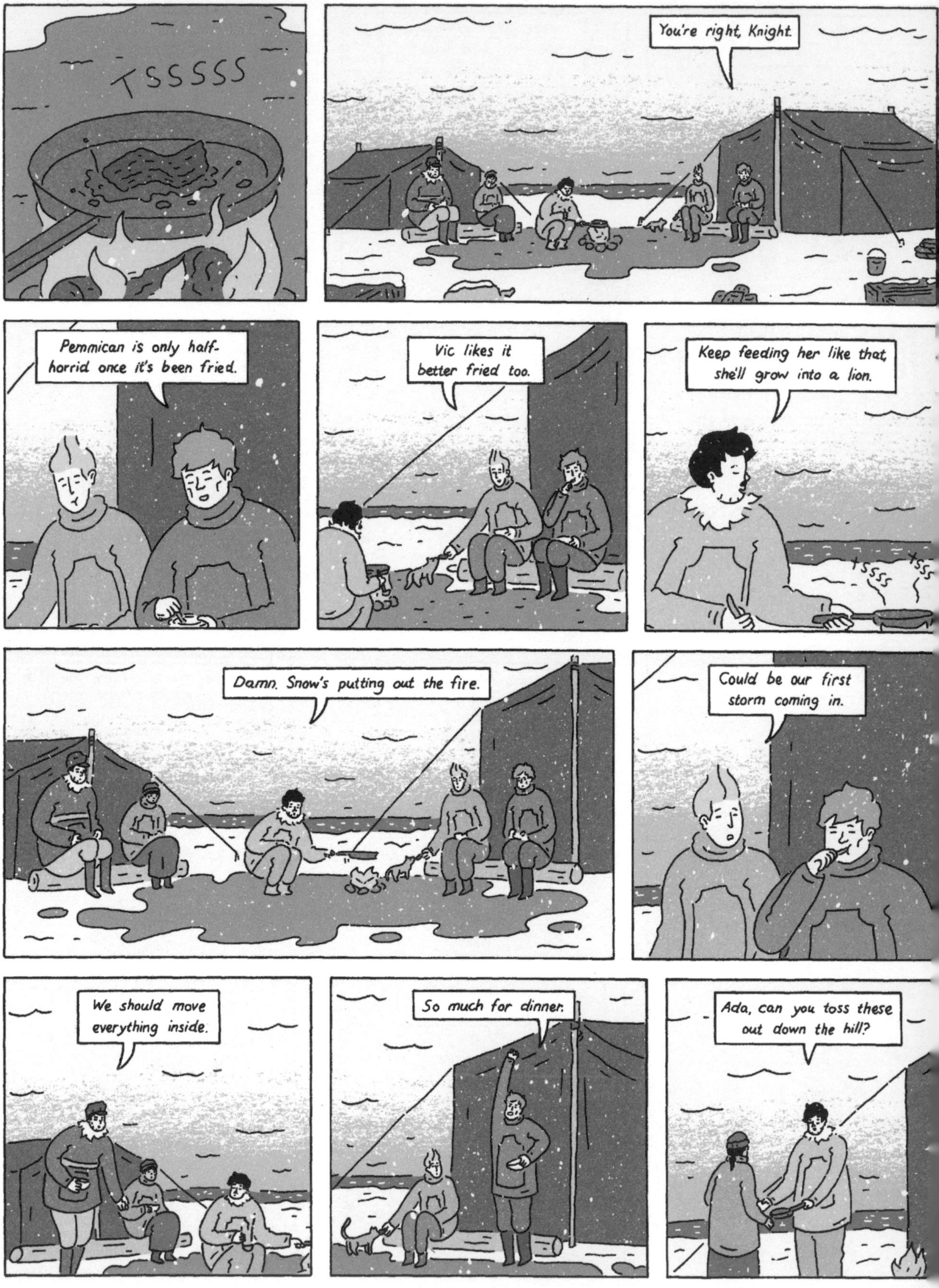
TSSSSS
You're right, Knight.
Pemmican is only half-horrid once it's been fried.
Vic likes it better fried too.
Keep feeding her like that, she'll grow into a lion.
TSSSS
TSSS
Damn. Snow's putting out the fire.
Could be our first storm coming in.
We should move everything inside.
So much for dinner.
Ada, can you toss these out down the hill?

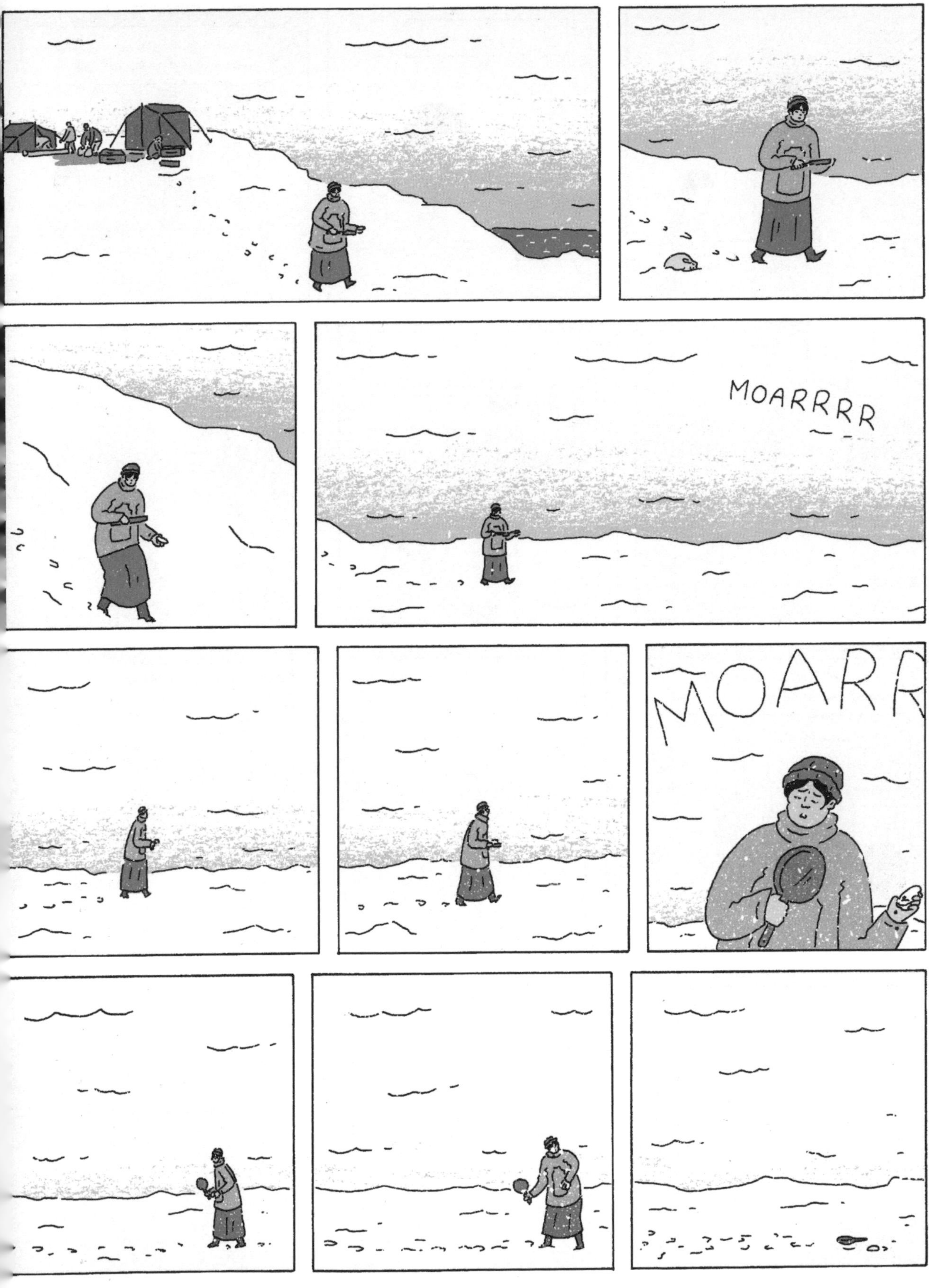
MOARRRR
MOARR

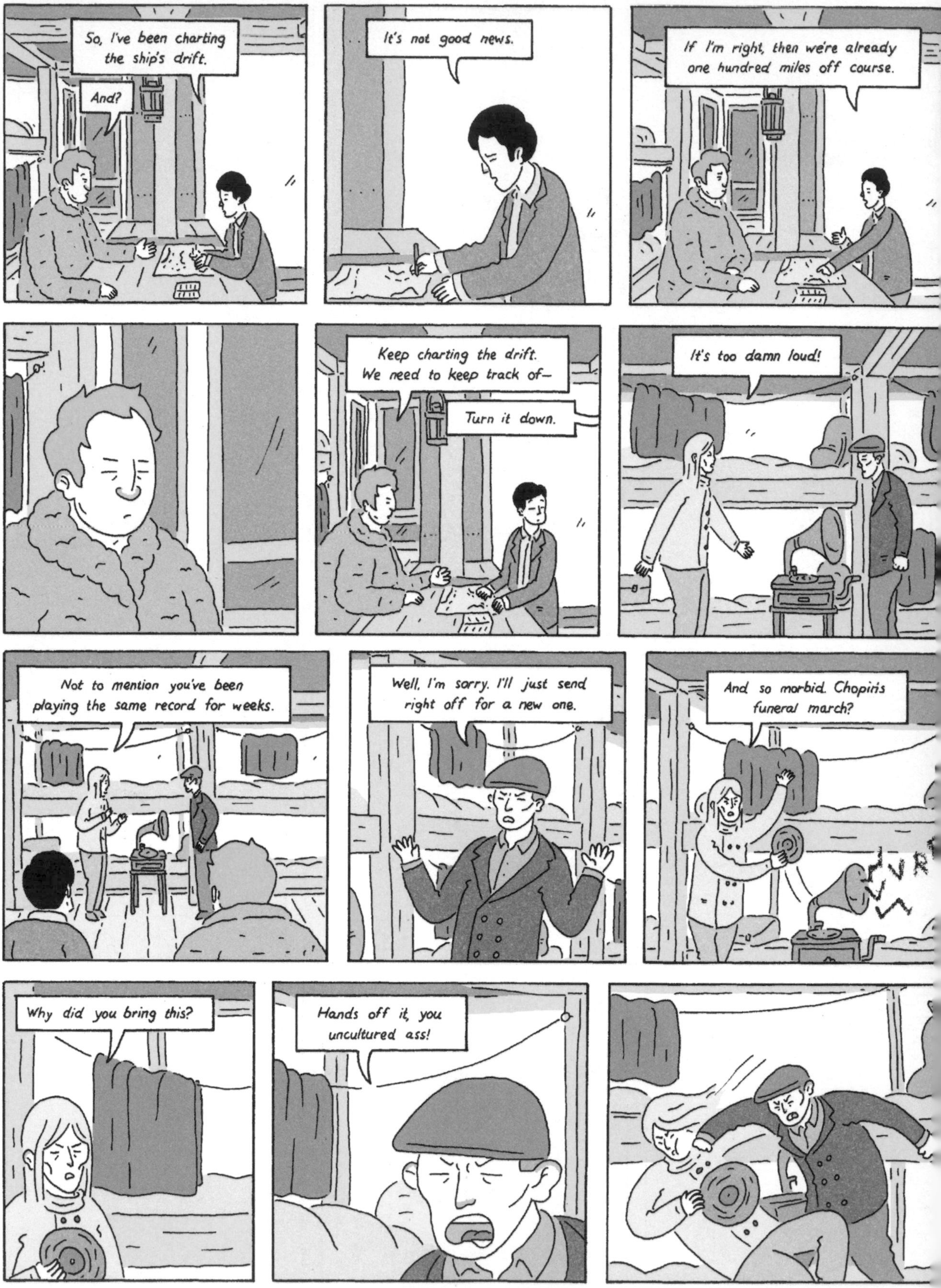
So, I've been charting the ship's drift.
And?
It's not good news.
If I'm right, then we're already one hundred miles off course.
Keep charting the drift. We need to keep track of—
Turn it down.
It's too damn loud!
Not to mention you've been playing the same record for weeks.
Well, I'm sorry. I'll just send right off for a new one.
And so morbid. Chopin's funeral march?
Why did you bring this?
Hands off it, you uncultured ass!

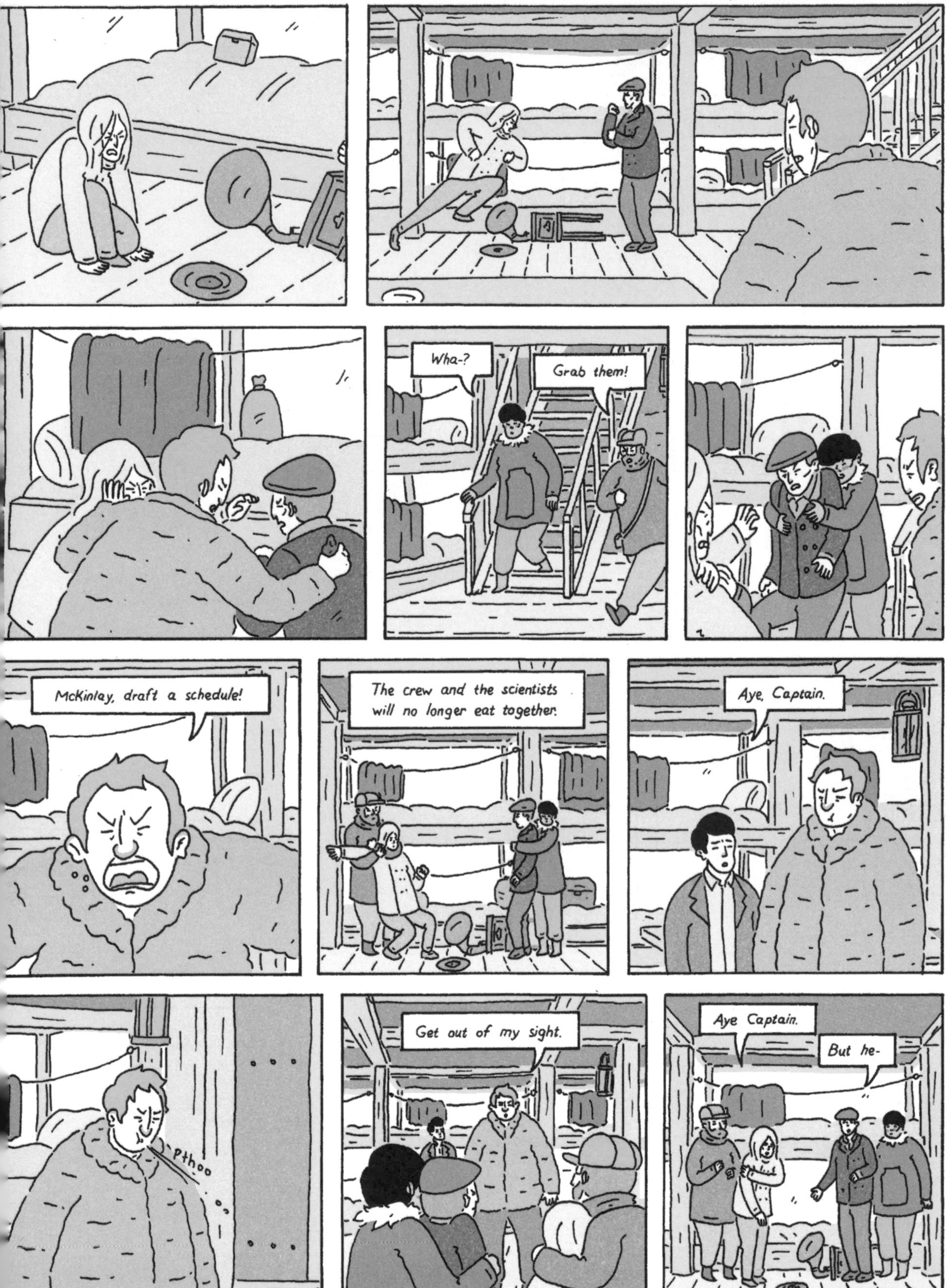
Wha-?
Grab them!
McKinlay, draft a schedule!
The crew and the scientists will no longer eat together.
Aye, Captain.
pthoo
Get out of my sight.
Aye Captain.
But he-

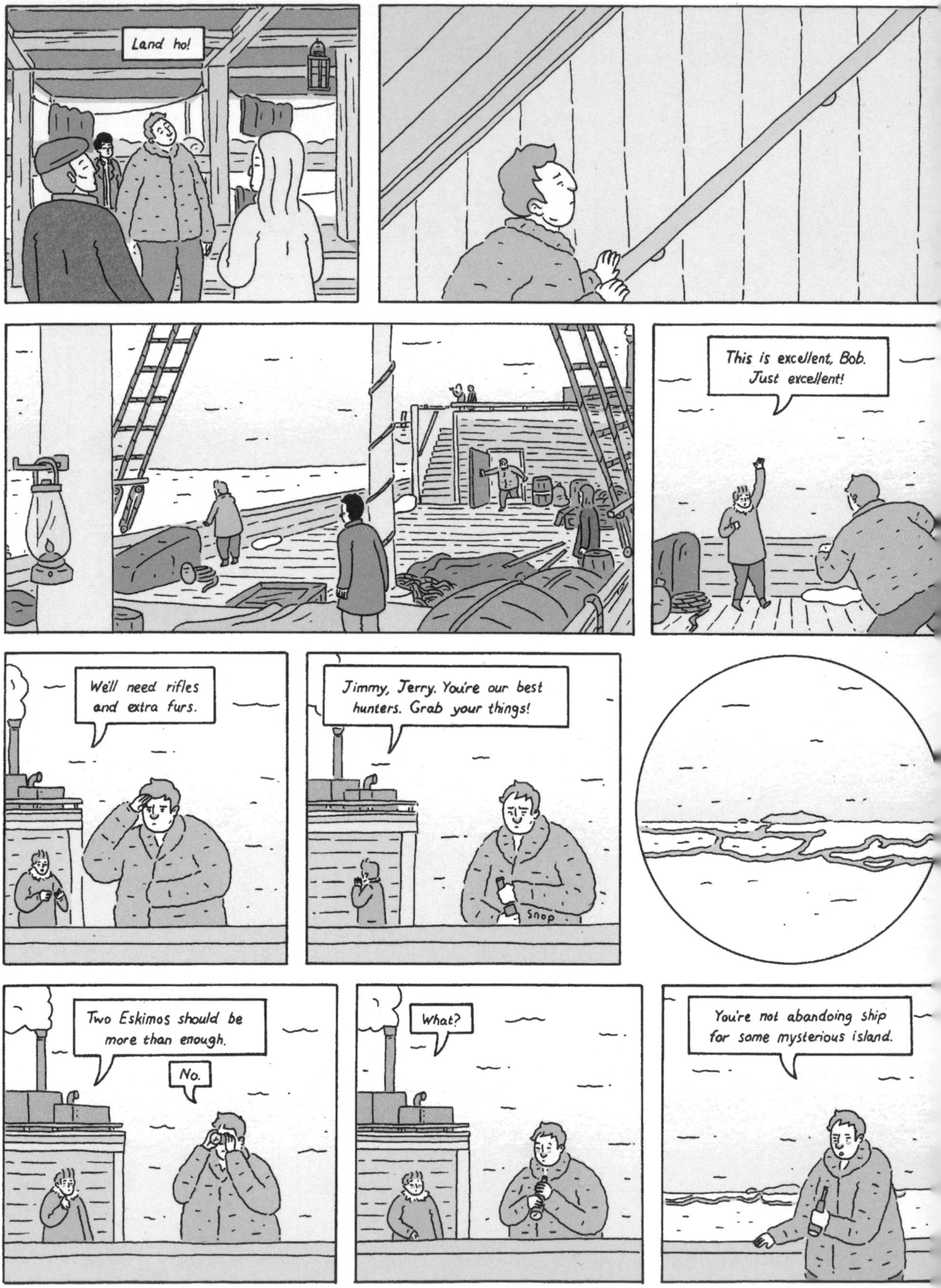
Land ho!
This is excellent, Bob. Just excellent!
We'll need rifles and extra furs.
Jimmy, Jerry. You're our best hunters. Grab your things!
Snop
Two Eskimos should be more than enough.
No.
What?
You're not abandoing ship for some mysterious island.

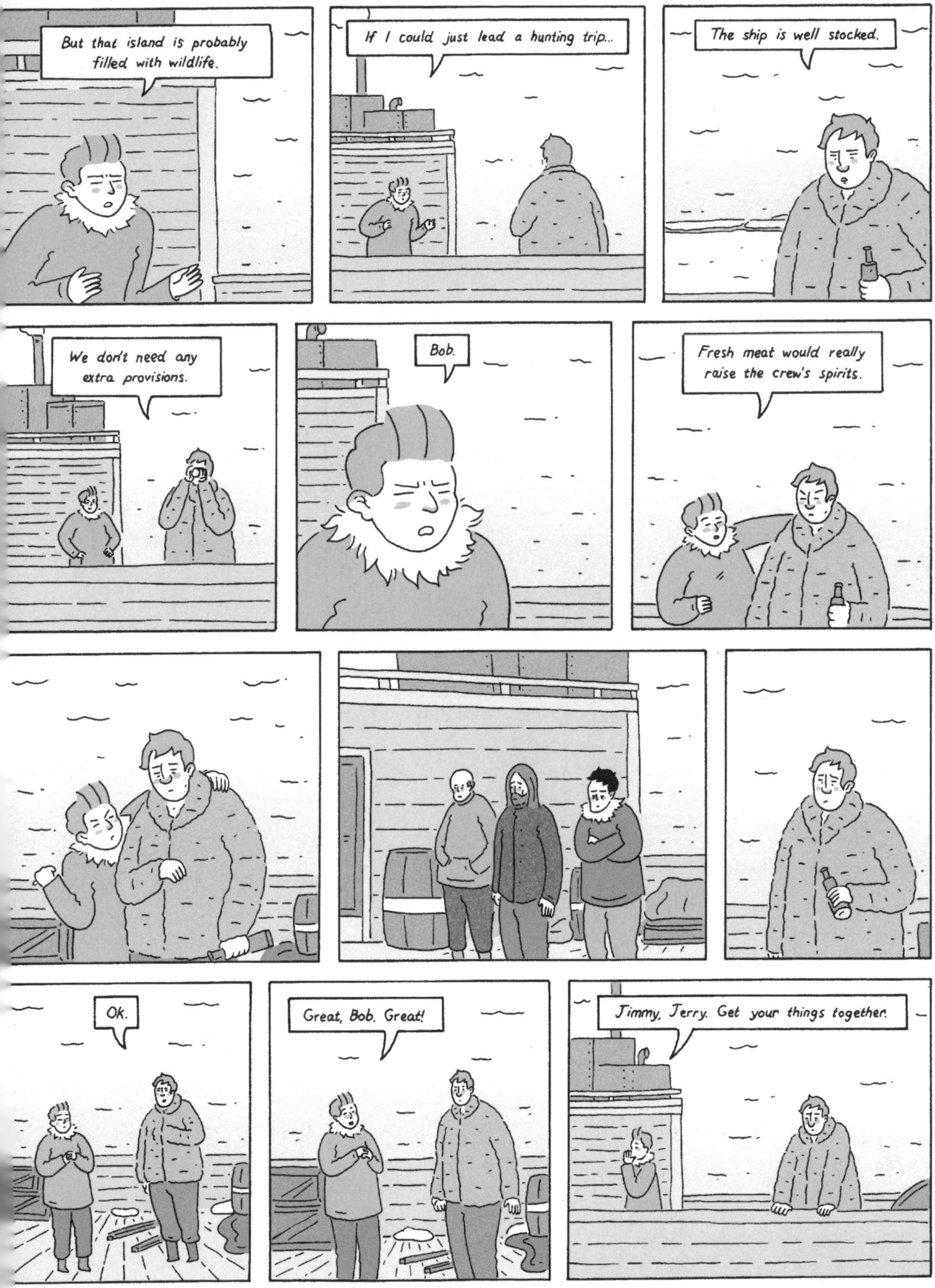
But that island is probably filled with wildlife.
If I could just lead a hunting trip...
The ship is well stocked.
We don't need any extra provisions.
Bob.
Fresh meat would really raise the crew's spirits.
Ok.
Great, Bob. Great!
Jimmy, Jerry. Get your things together.

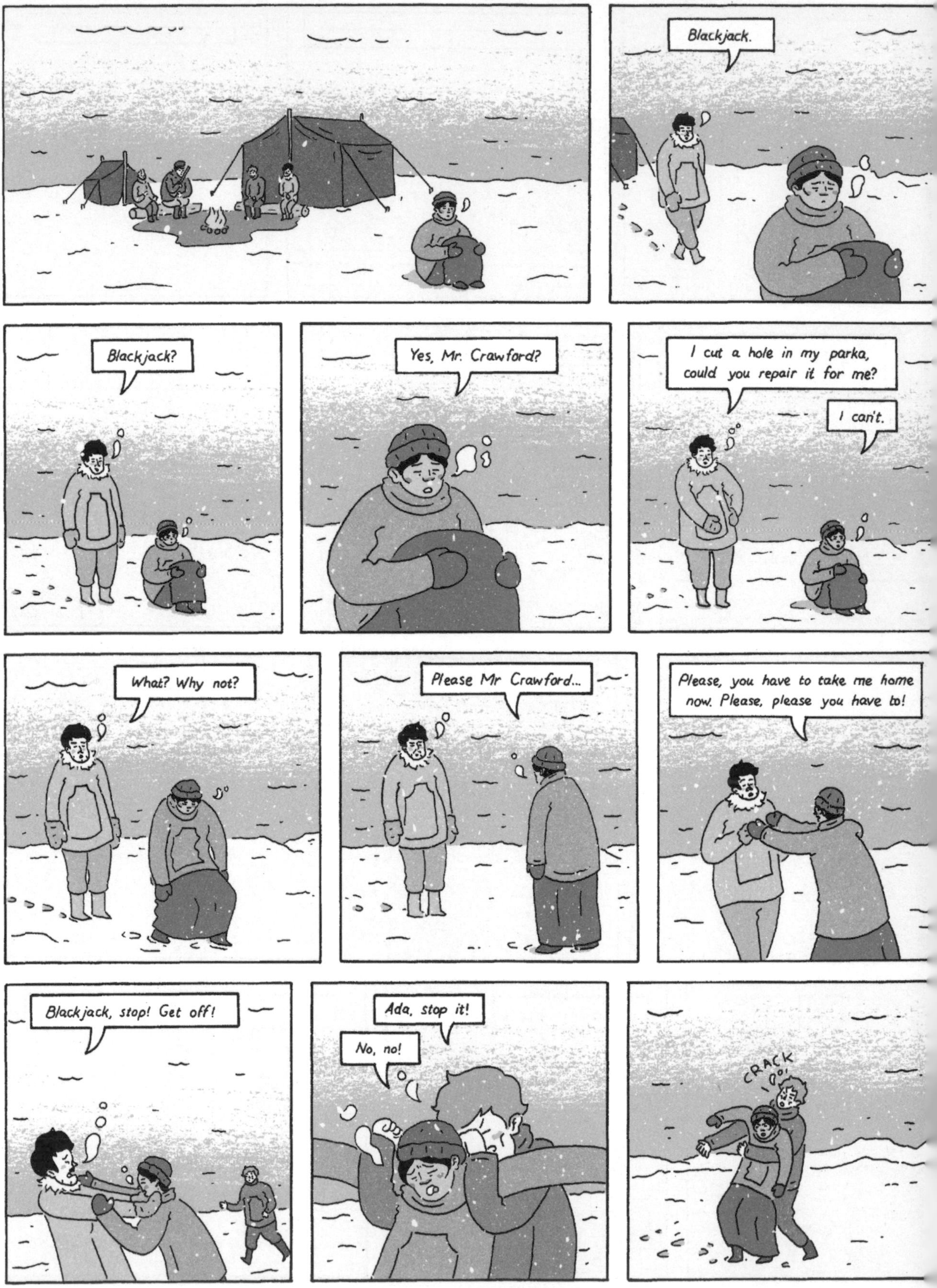
Blackjack.
Blackjack?
Yes, Mr. Crawford?
I cut a hole in my parka, could you repair it for me?
I can't.
What? Why not?
Please Mr Crawford...
Please, you have to take me home now. Please, please you have to!
Blackjack, stop! Get off!
Ada, stop it!
No, no!
CRACK

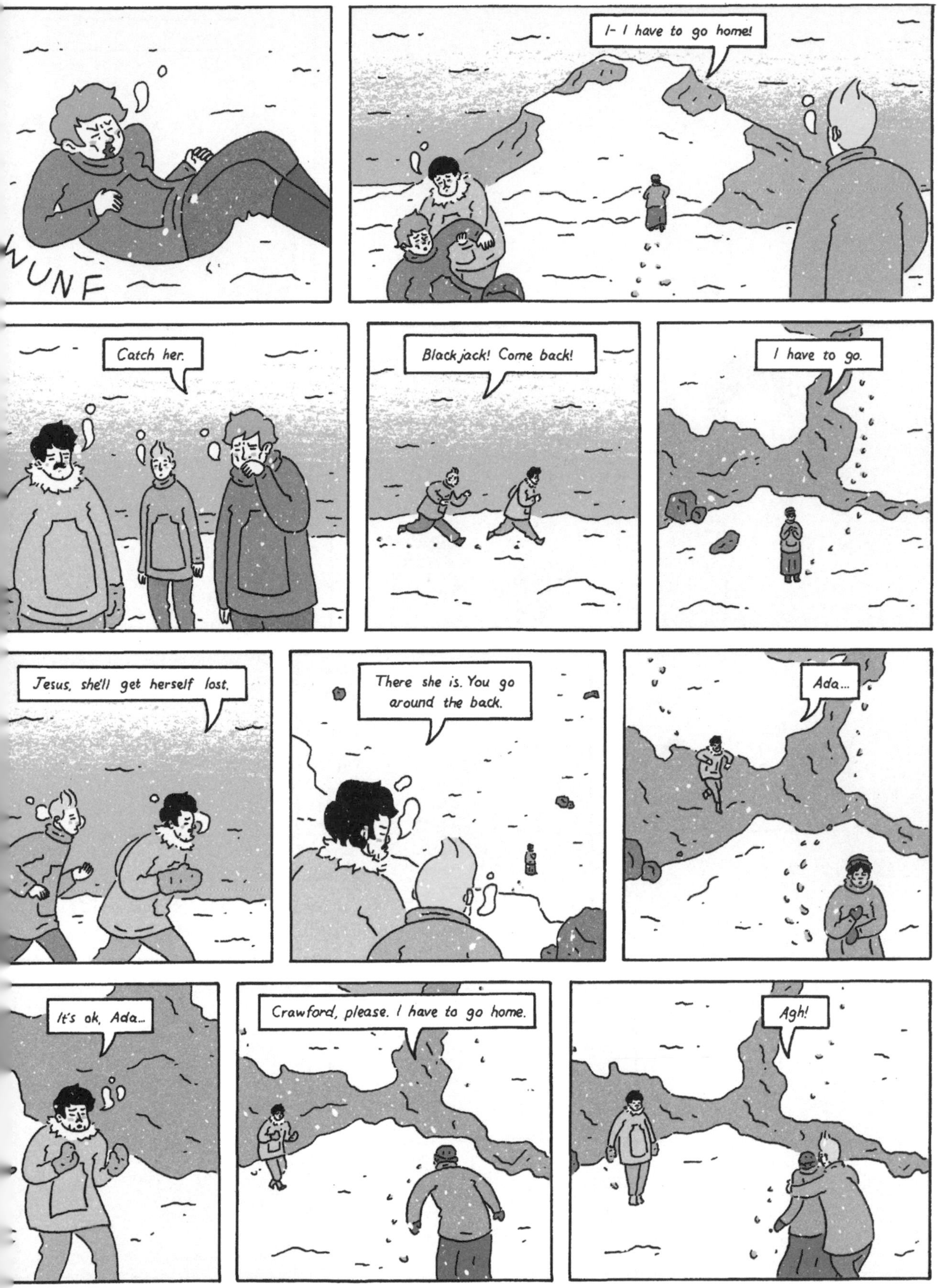
WUNF
I- I have to go home!
Catch her.
Blackjack! Come back!
I have to go.
Jesus, she'll get herself lost.
There she is. You go around the back.
Ada...
It's ok, Ada...
Crawford, please. I have to go home.
Agh!

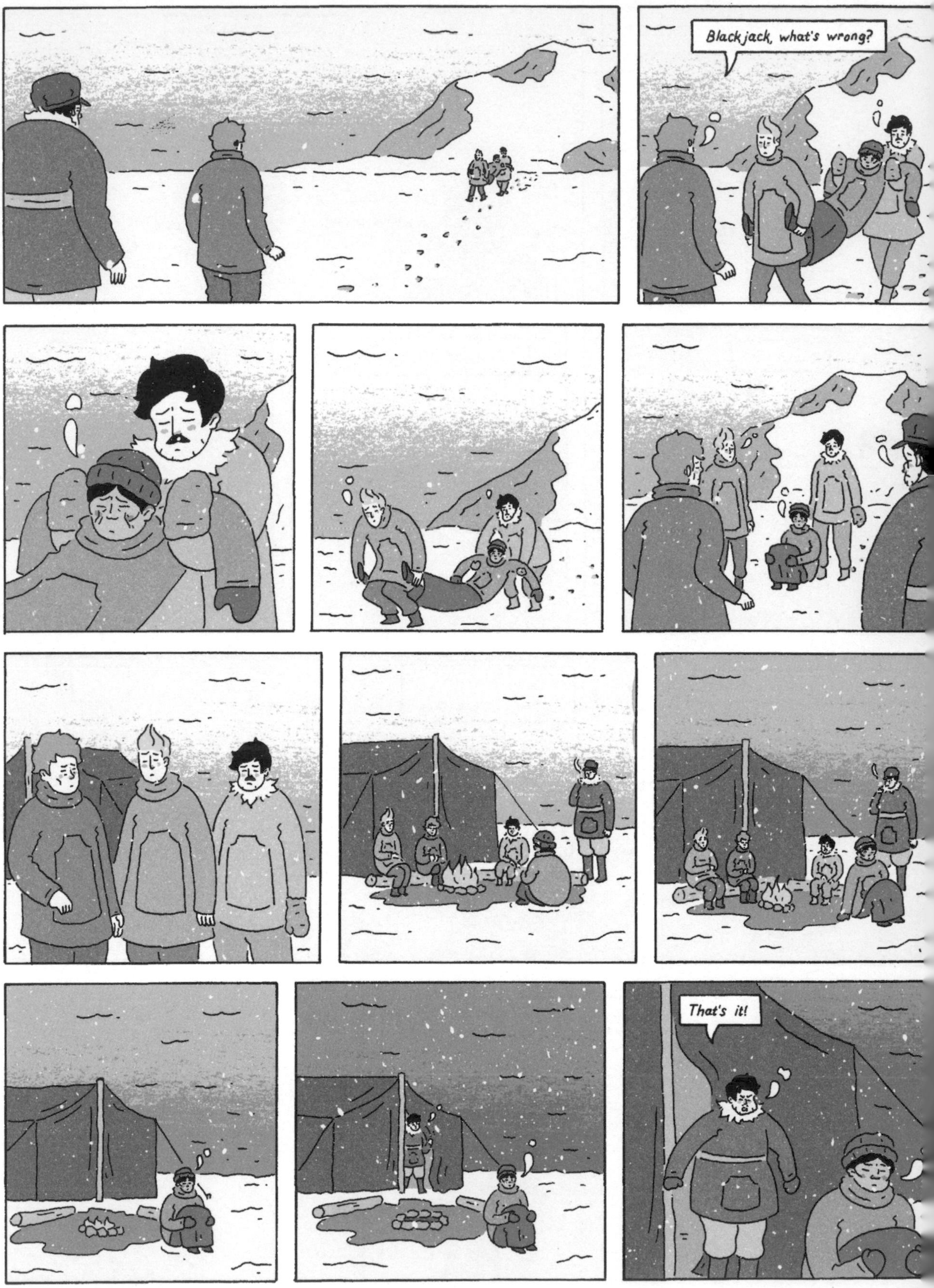
Blackjack, what's wrong?
That's it!

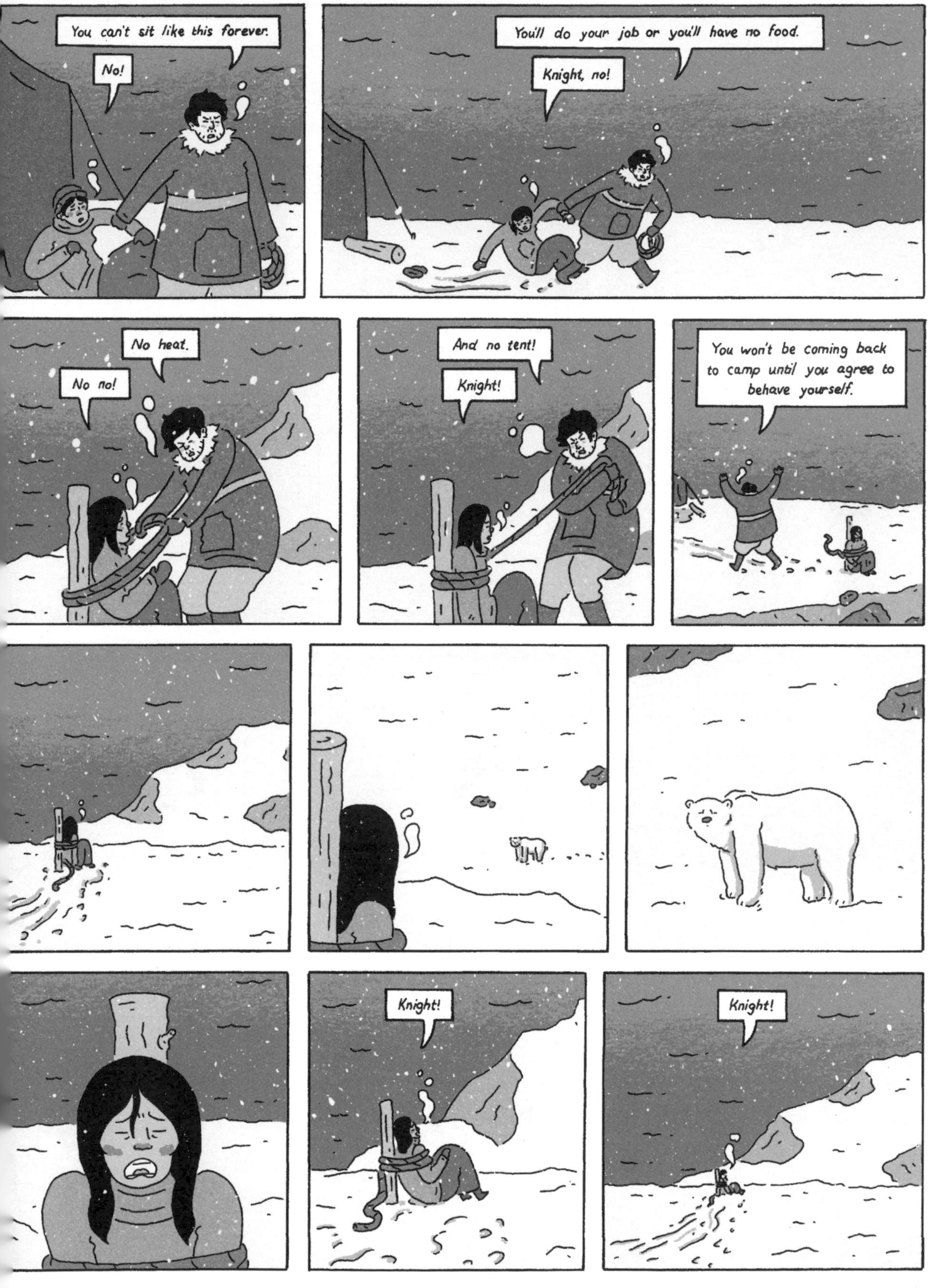
You can't sit like this forever.
No!
You'll do your job or you'll have no food.
Knight, no!
No heat.
No no!
And no tent!
Knight!
You won't be coming back to camp until you agree to behave yourself.
Knight!
Knight!

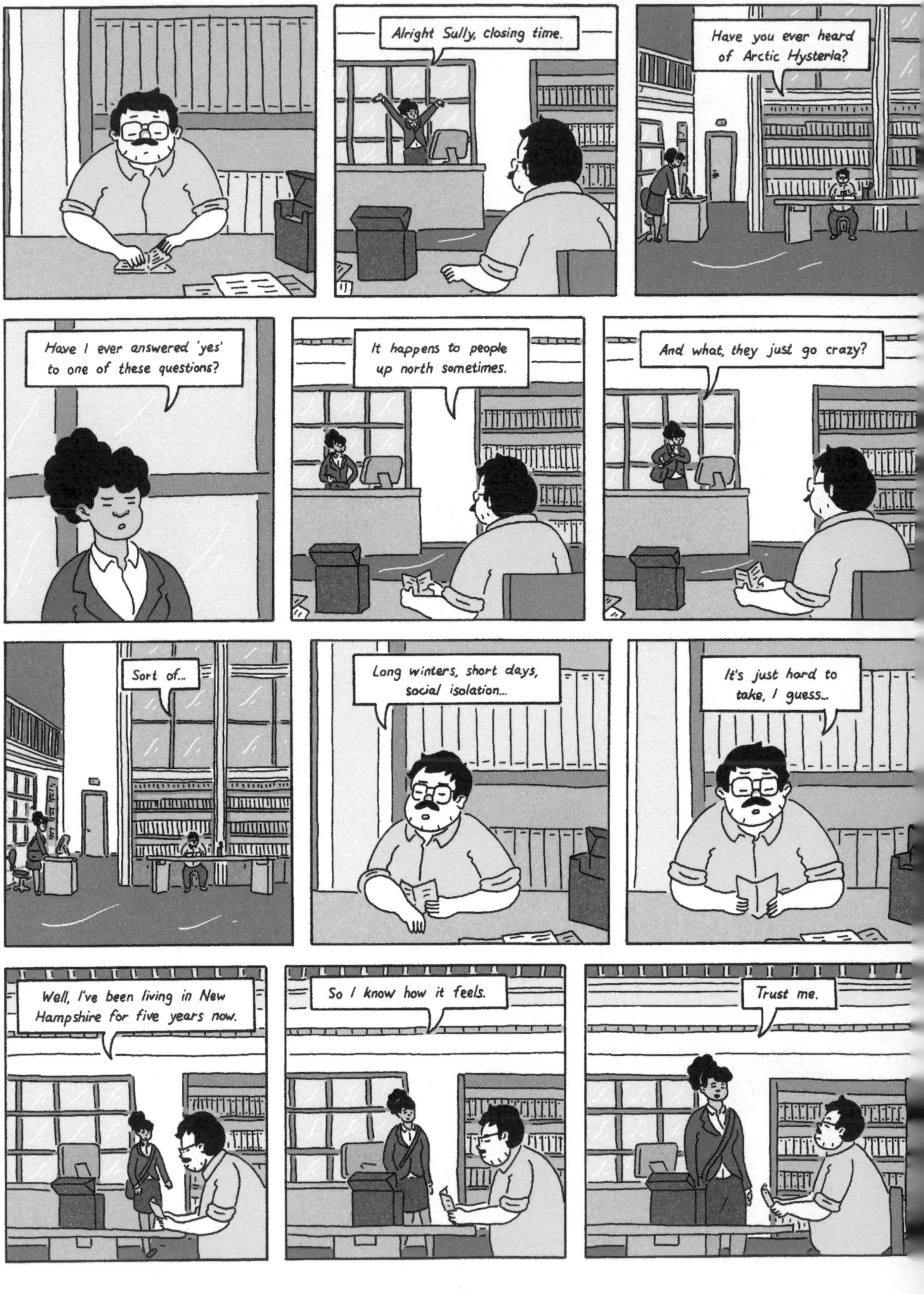
Alright Sully, closing time.
Have you ever heard of Arctic Hysteria?
Have I ever answered 'yes' to one of these questions?
It happens to people up north sometimes.
And what, they just go crazy?
Sort of...
Long winters, short days, social isolation...
It's just hard to take, I guess...
Well, I've been living in New Hampshire for five years now.
So I know how it feels.
Trust me.

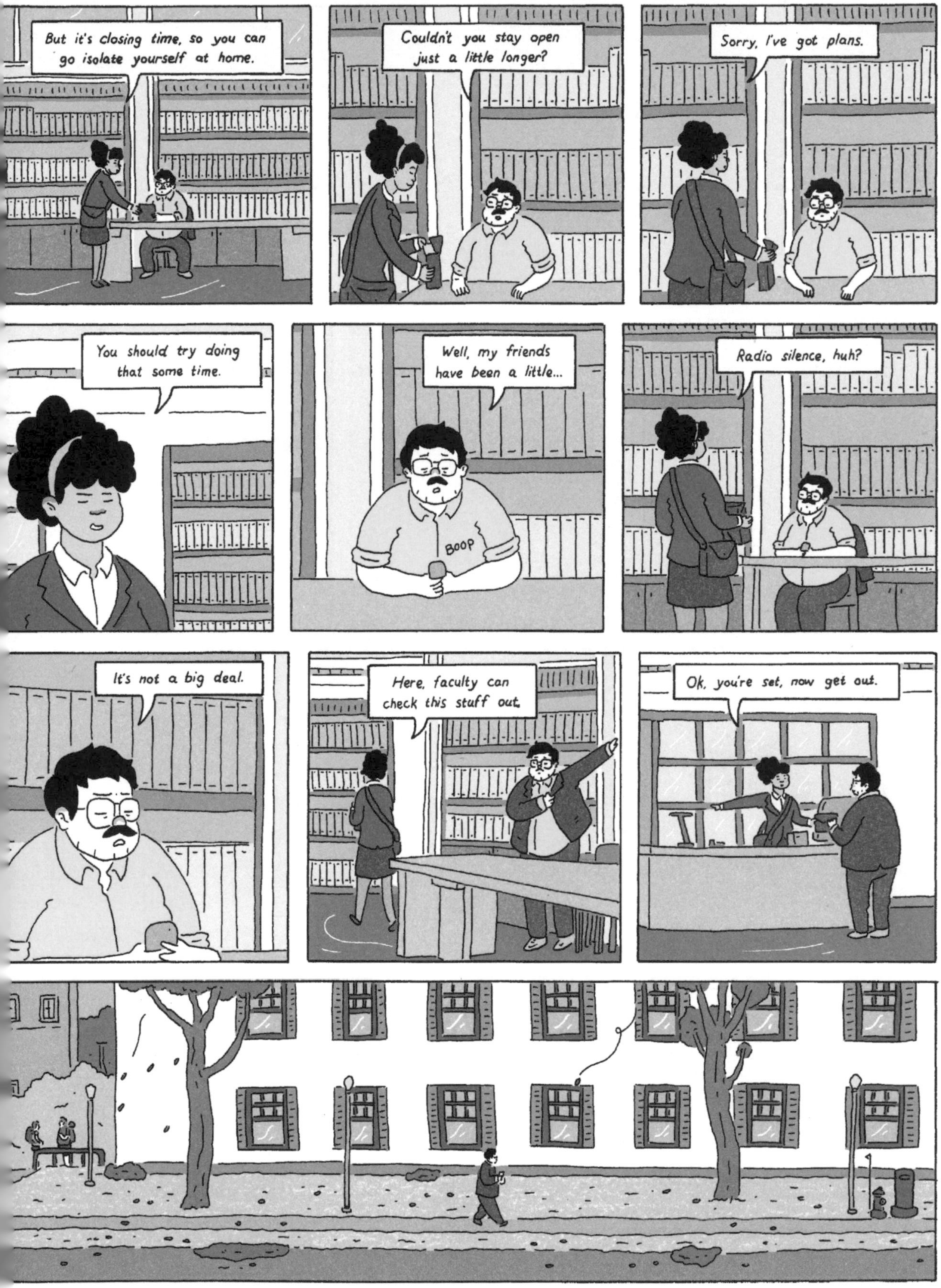
But it's closing time, so you can go isolate yourself at home.
Couldn't you stay open just a little longer?
Sorry, I've got plans.
You should try doing that some time.
Well, my friends have been a little...
BOOP
Radio silence, huh?
It's not a big deal.
Here, faculty can check this stuff out.
Ok, you're set, now get out.

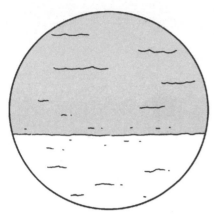

The island is out of sight.

Stefansson's not coming back.

He's been itching to abandon ship for weeks.

Agreed.

I am ashamed.

Ashamed? Why?

That Jimmy and Jerry left with him.

My own friends.

Cowards, both of them!

Well, you still have me, Captain.

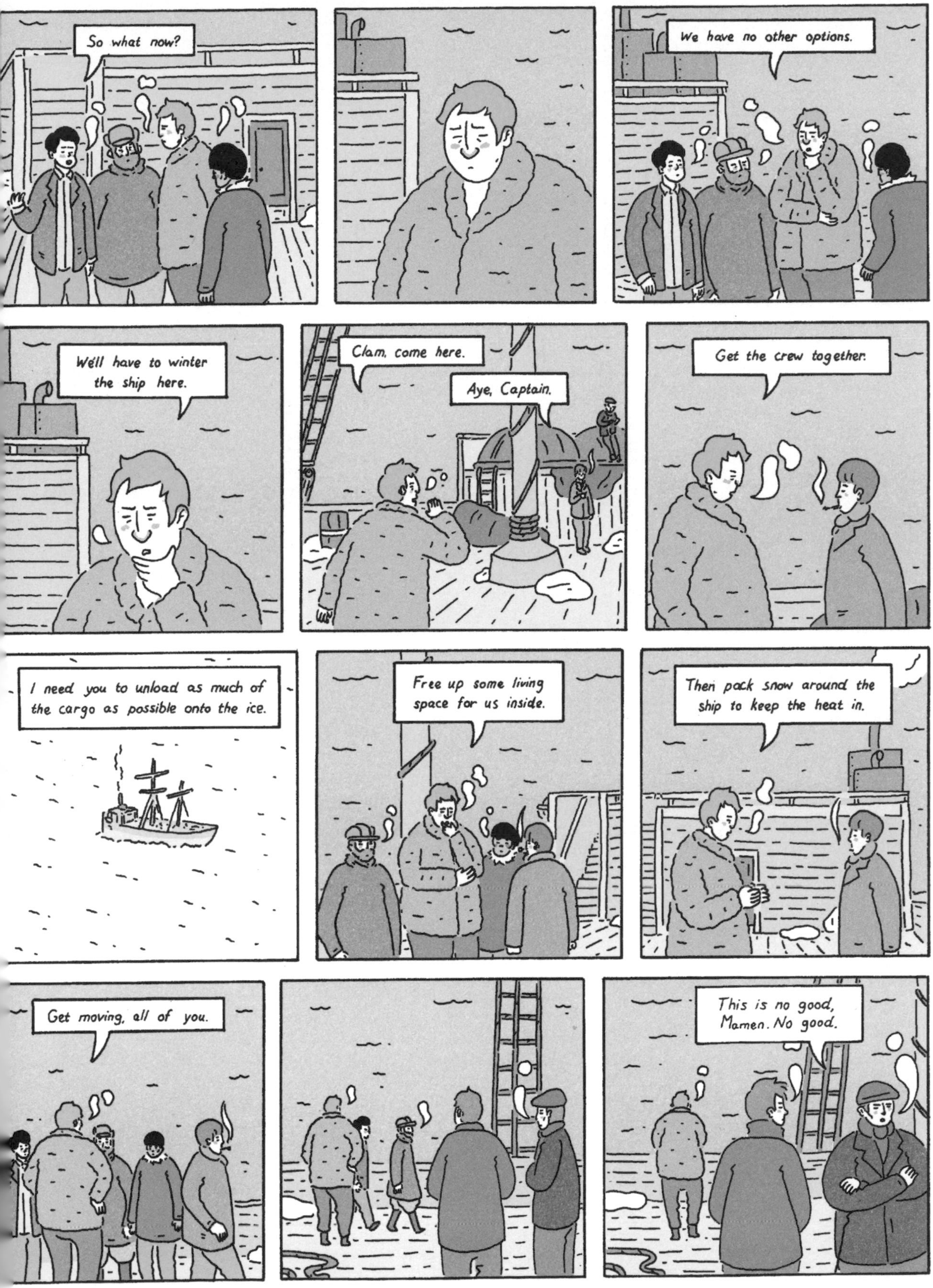
So what now?
We have no other options.
We'll have to winter the ship here.
Clam, come here.
Aye, Captain.
Get the crew together.
I need you to unload as much of the cargo as possible onto the ice.
Free up some living space for us inside.
Then pack snow around the ship to keep the heat in.
Get moving, all of you.
This is no good, Mamen. No good.

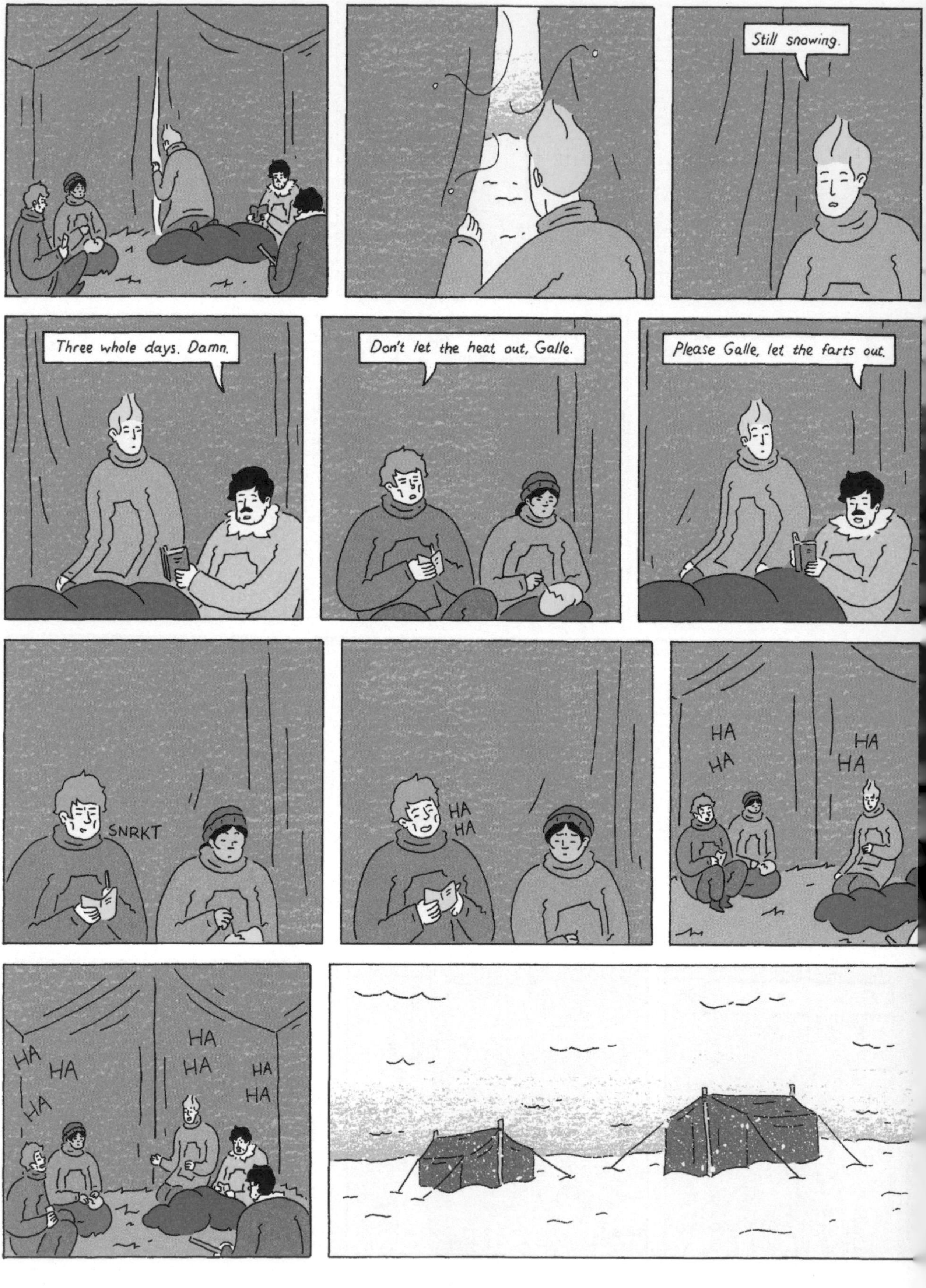
Still snowing.
Three whole days. Damn.
Don't let the heat out, Galle.
Please Galle, let the farts out.
SNRKT
HA HA
HA HA
HA HA
HA HA HA
HA HA
HA HA

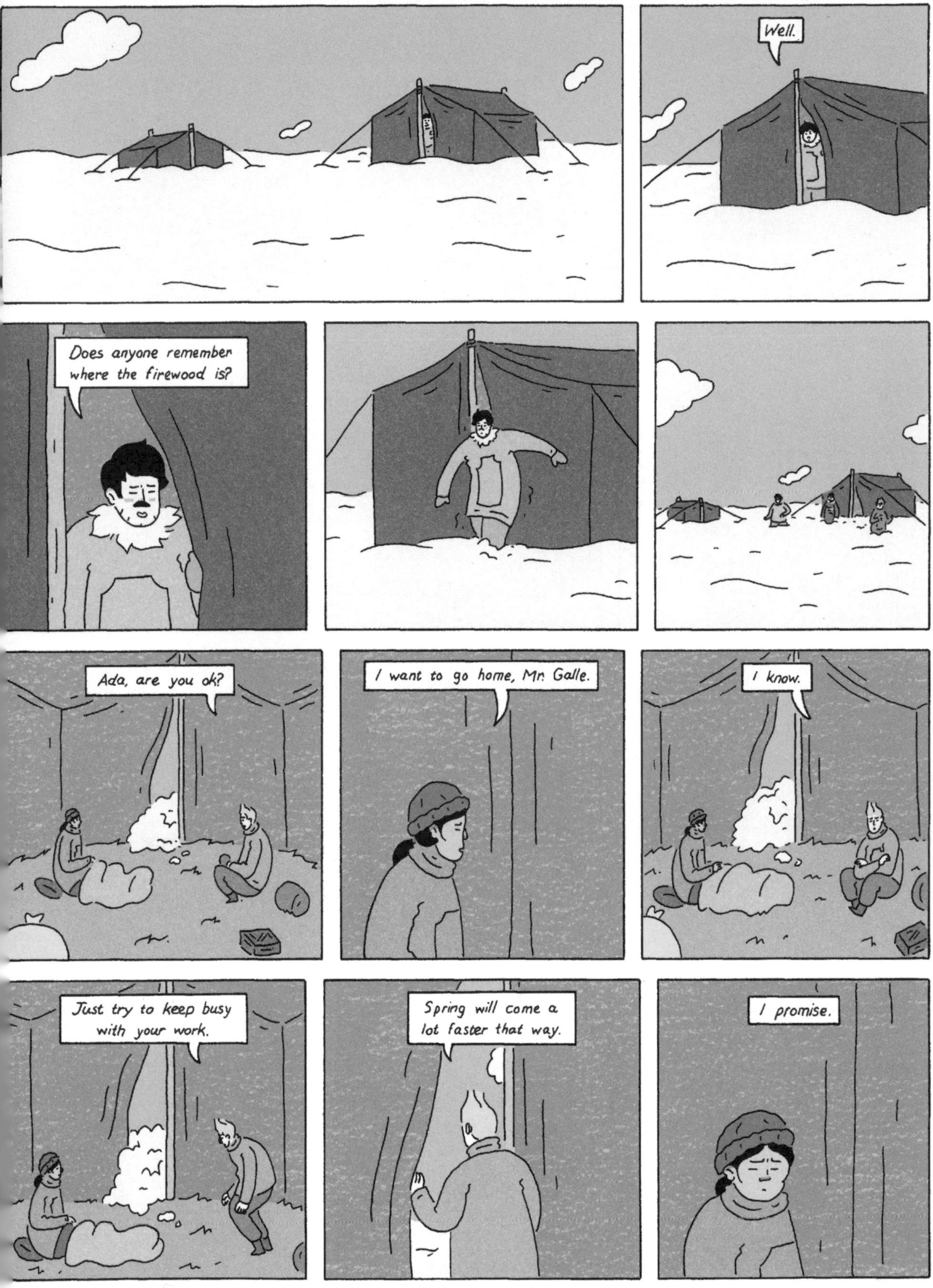
Well.
Does anyone remember where the firewood is?
Ada, are you ok?
I want to go home, Mr. Galle.
I know.
Just try to keep busy with your work.
Spring will come a lot faster that way.
I promise.

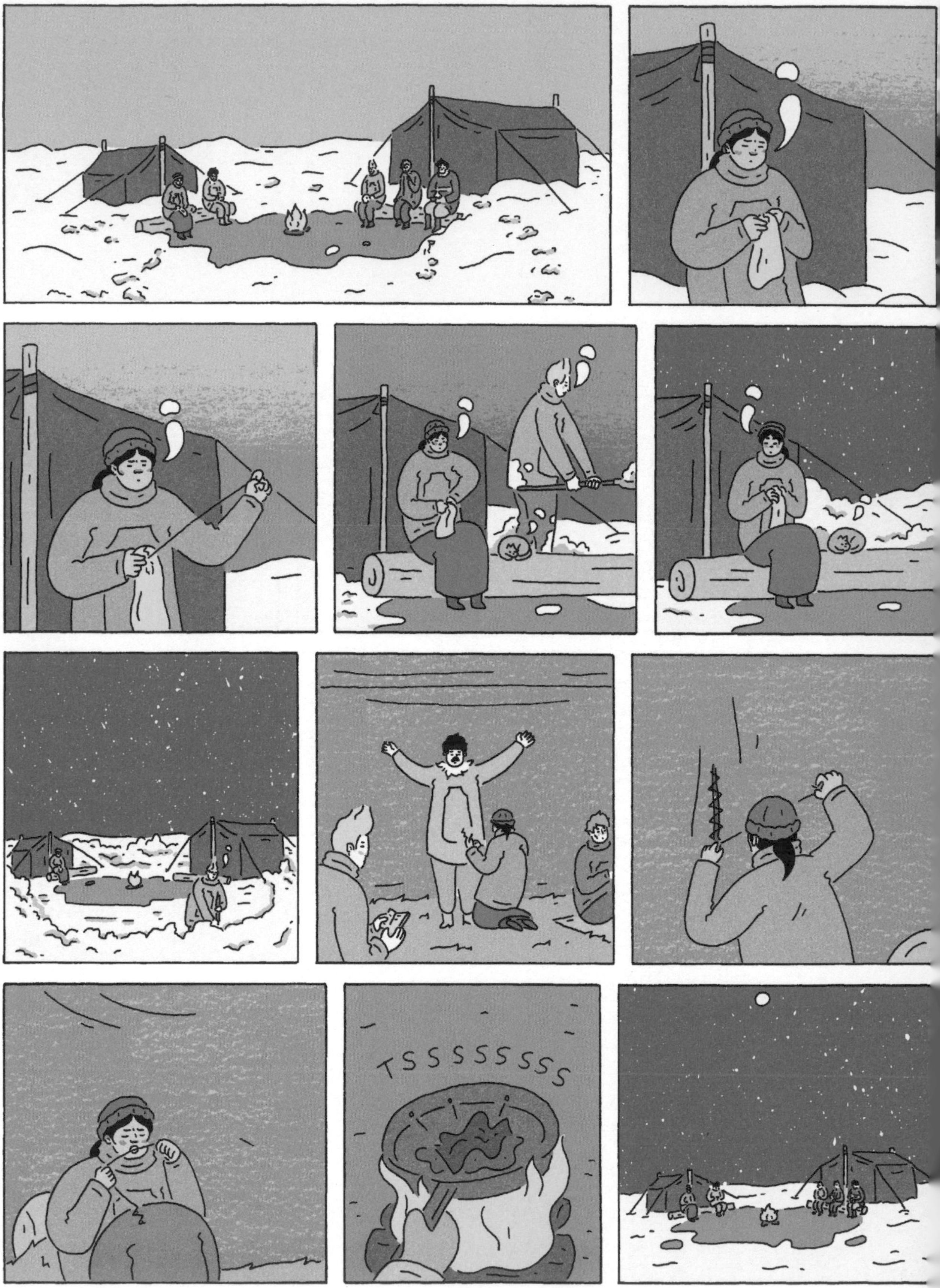
TSSSSSSSS

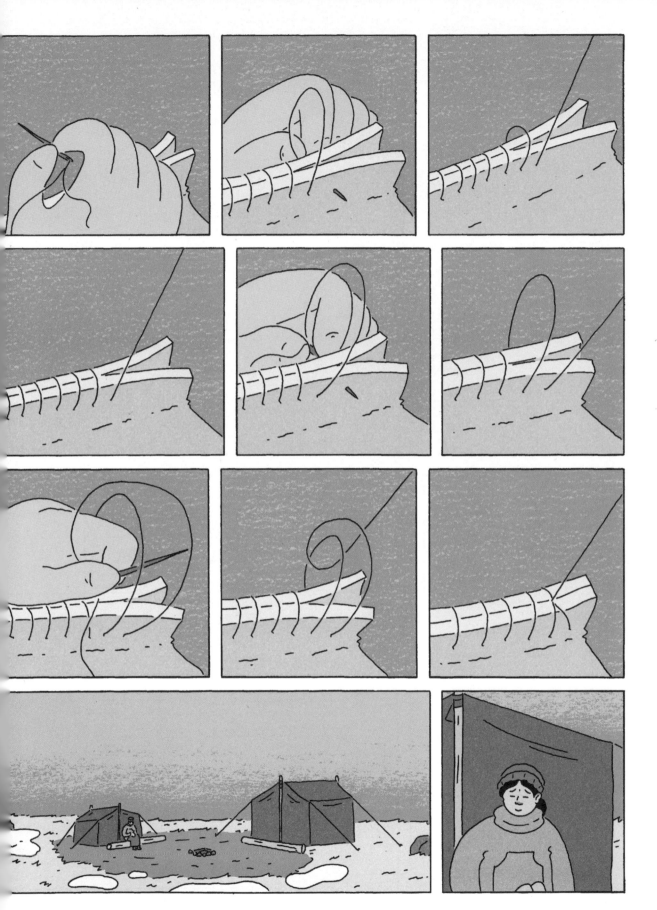

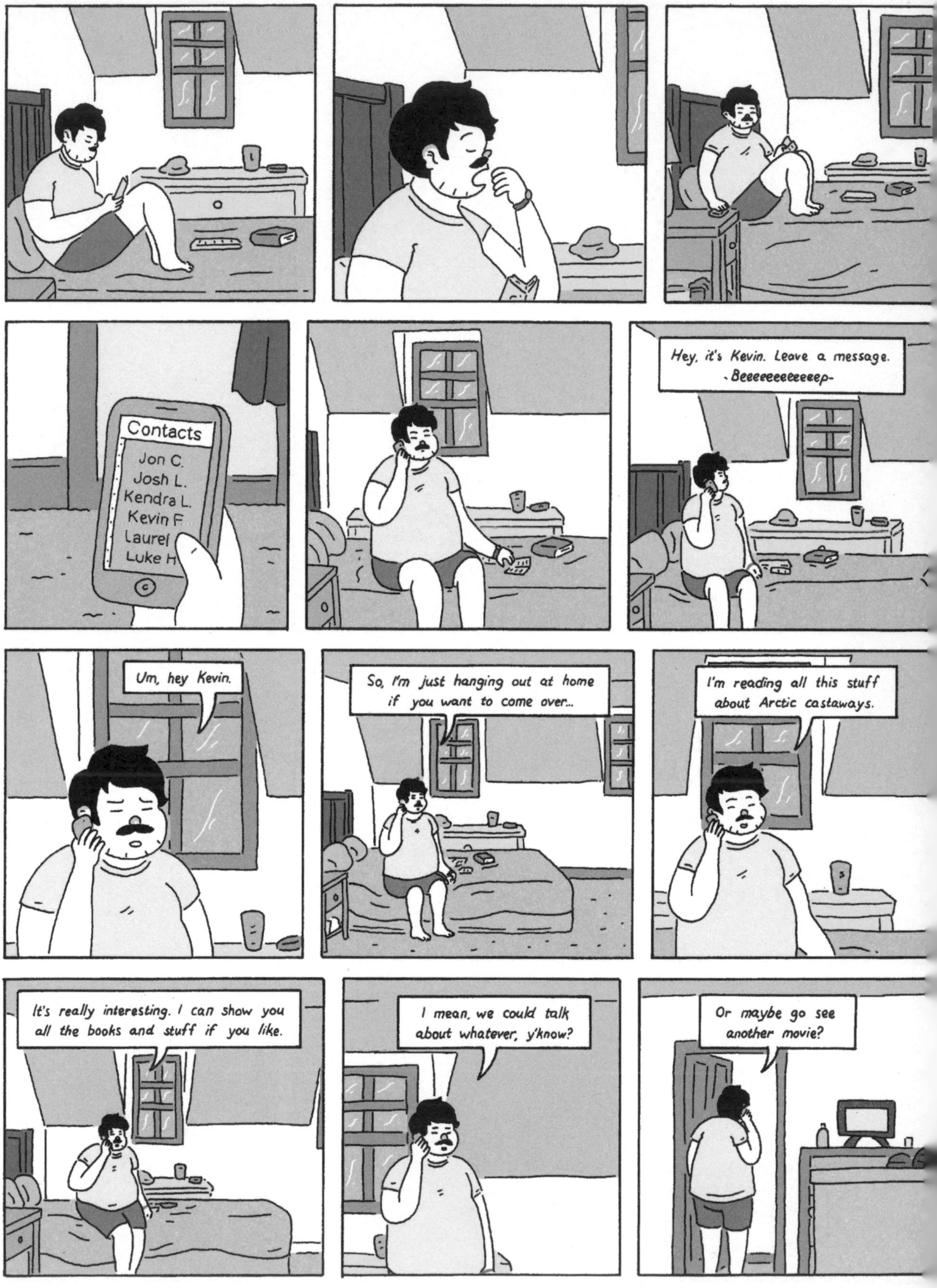
Contacts
Jon C.
Josh L.
Kendra L.
Kevin F.
Laurel
Luke H
Hey, it's Kevin. Leave a message.
-Beeeeeeeeeeeep-
Um, hey Kevin.
So, I'm just hanging out at home if you want to come over...
I'm reading all this stuff about Arctic castaways.
It's really interesting. I can show you all the books and stuff if you like.
I mean, we could talk about whatever, y'know?
Or maybe go see another movie?

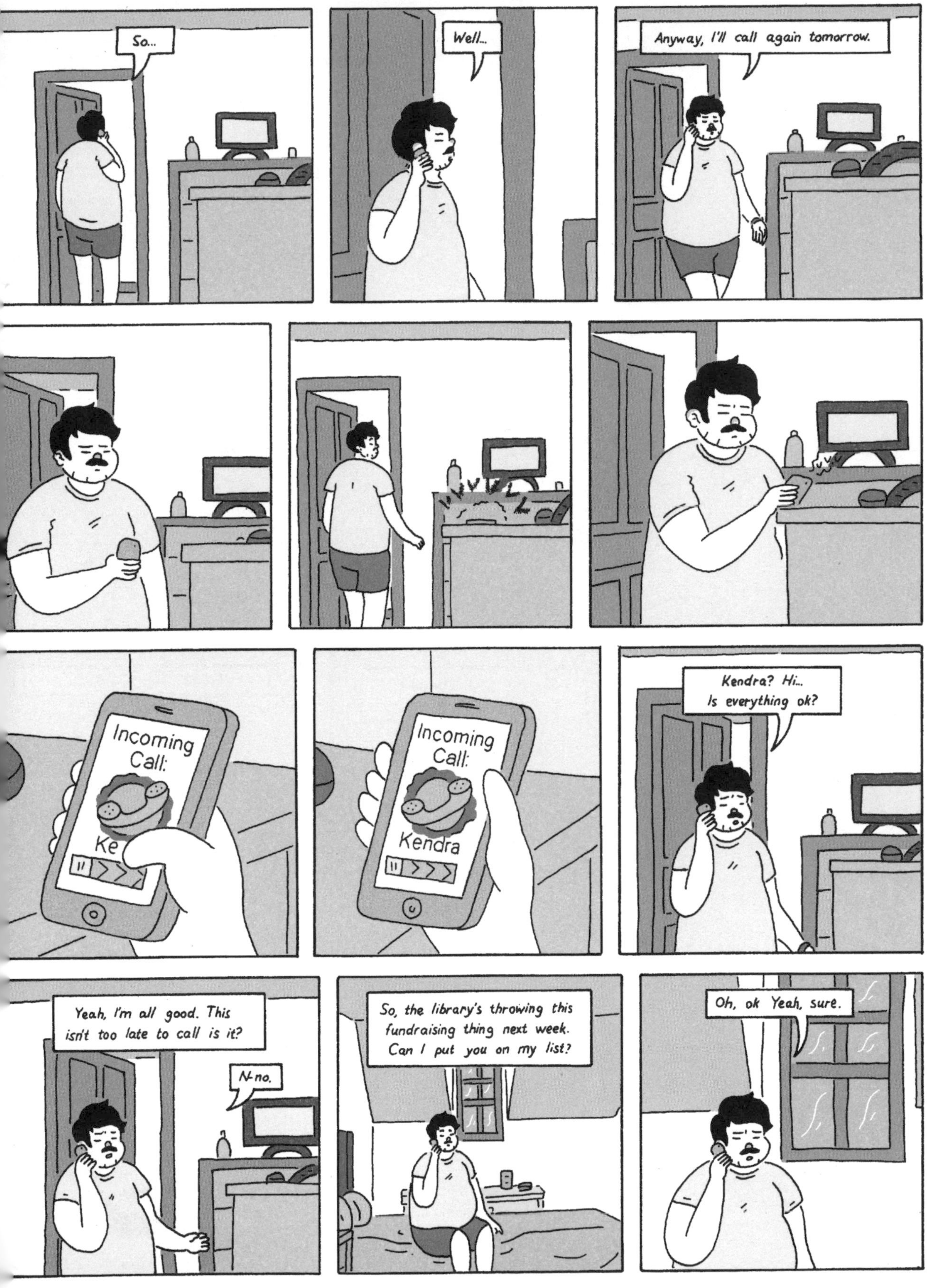
So...
Well...
Anyway, I'll call again tomorrow.
Incoming Call:
Ke
Incoming Call:
Kendra
Kendra? Hi...
Is everything ok?
Yeah, I'm all good. This isn't too late to call is it?
N-no.
So, the library's throwing this fundraising thing next week. Can I put you on my list?
Oh, ok Yeah, sure.

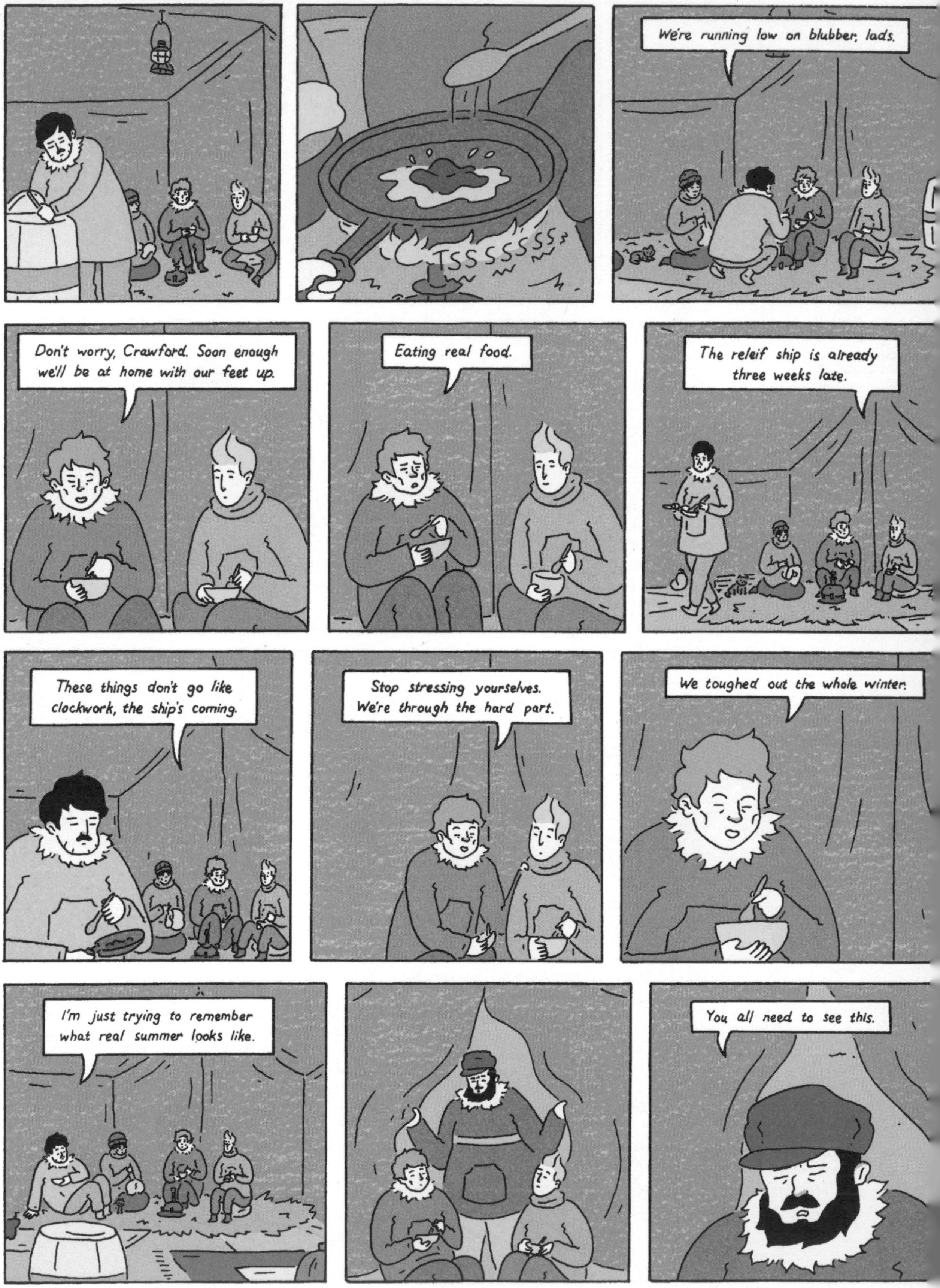
TSSSSSSSS
We're running low on blubber, lads.
Don't worry, Crawford. Soon enough we'll be at home with our feet up.
Eating real food.
The releif ship is already three weeks late.
These things don't go like clockwork, the ship's coming.
Stop stressing yourselves. We're through the hard part.
We toughed out the whole winter.
I'm just trying to remember what real summer looks like.
You all need to see this.

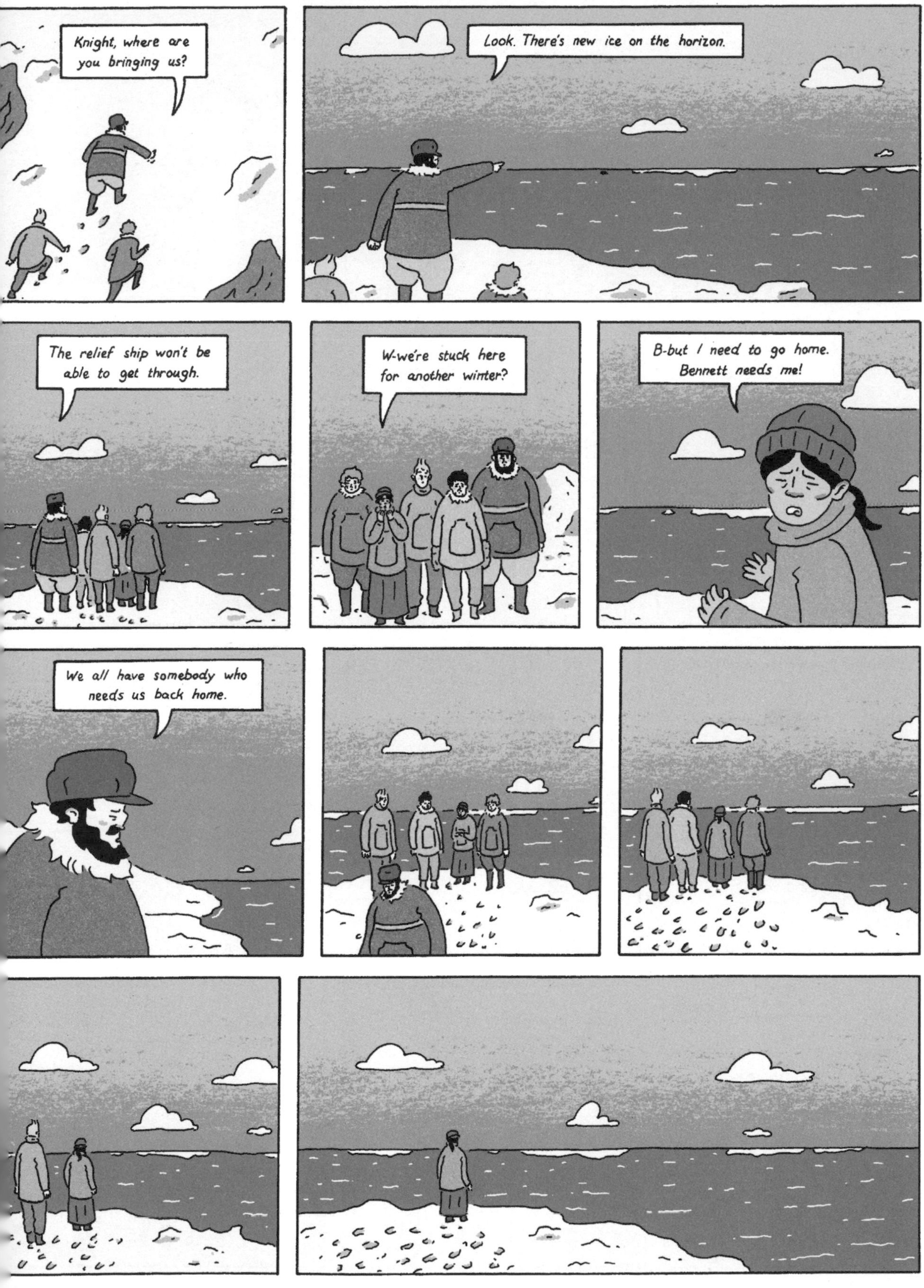
Knight, where are you bringing us?
Look. There's new ice on the horizon.
The relief ship won't be able to get through.
W-we're stuck here for another winter?
B-but I need to go home. Bennett needs me!
We all have somebody who needs us back home.

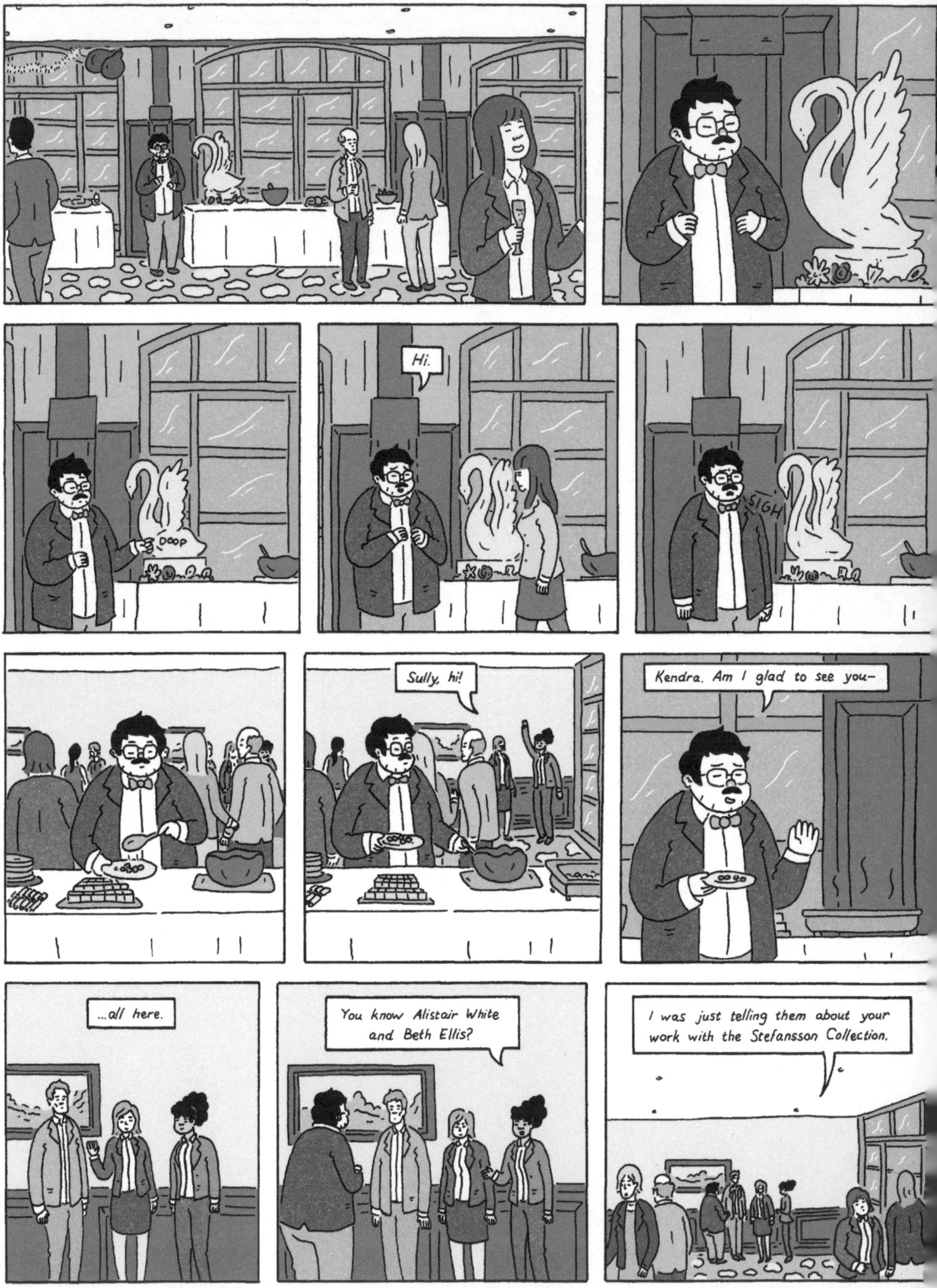
DOOP
Hi.
SIGH
Sully, hi!
Kendra. Am I glad to see you—
...all here.
You know Alistair White and Beth Ellis?
I was just telling them about your work with the Stefansson Collection.

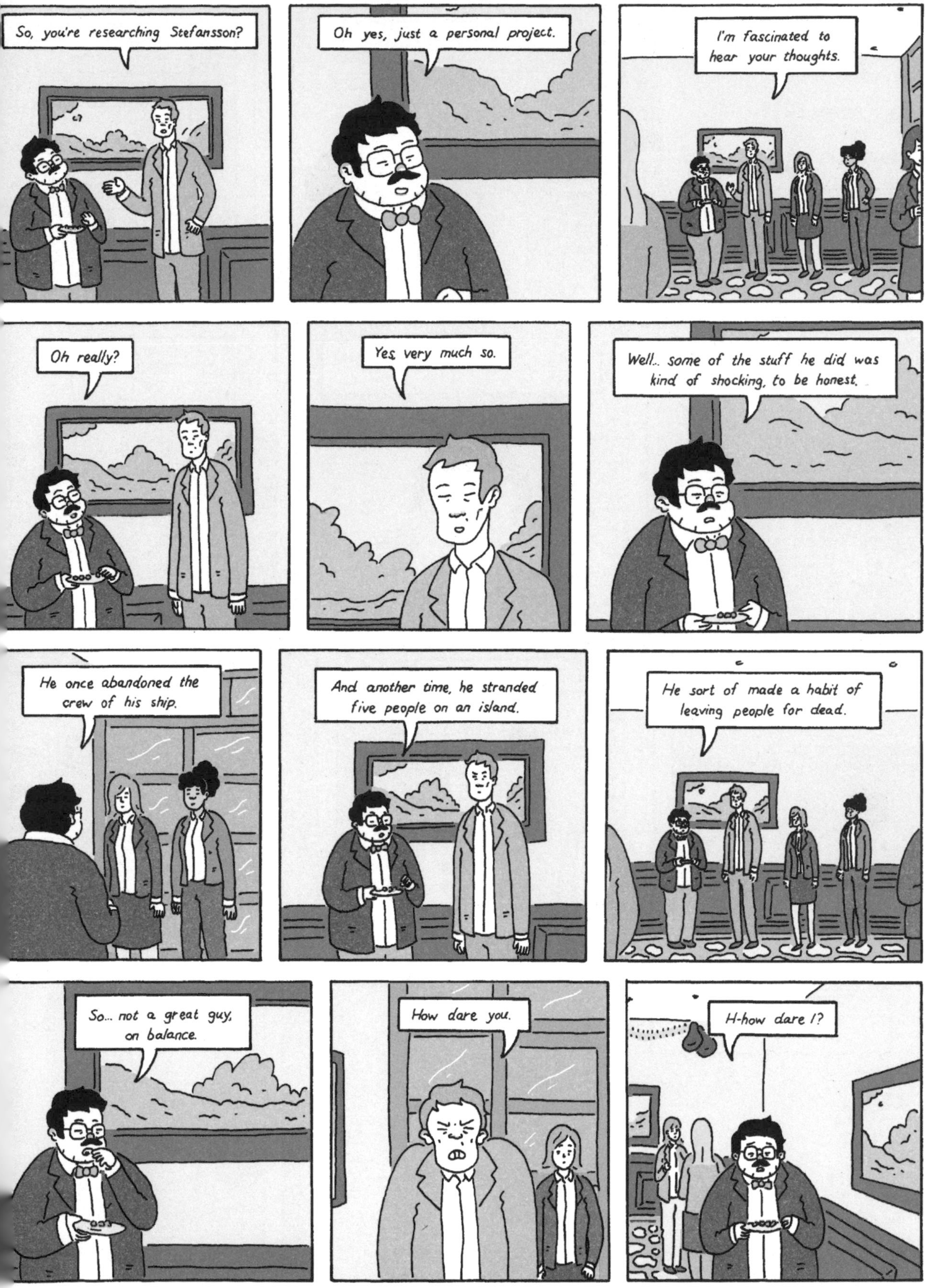
So, you're researching Stefansson?
Oh yes, just a personal project.
I'm fascinated to hear your thoughts.
Oh really?
Yes, very much so.
Well... some of the stuff he did was kind of shocking, to be honest.
He once abandoned the crew of his ship.
And another time, he stranded five people on an island.
He sort of made a habit of leaving people for dead.
So... not a great guy, on balance.
How dare you.
H-how dare I?

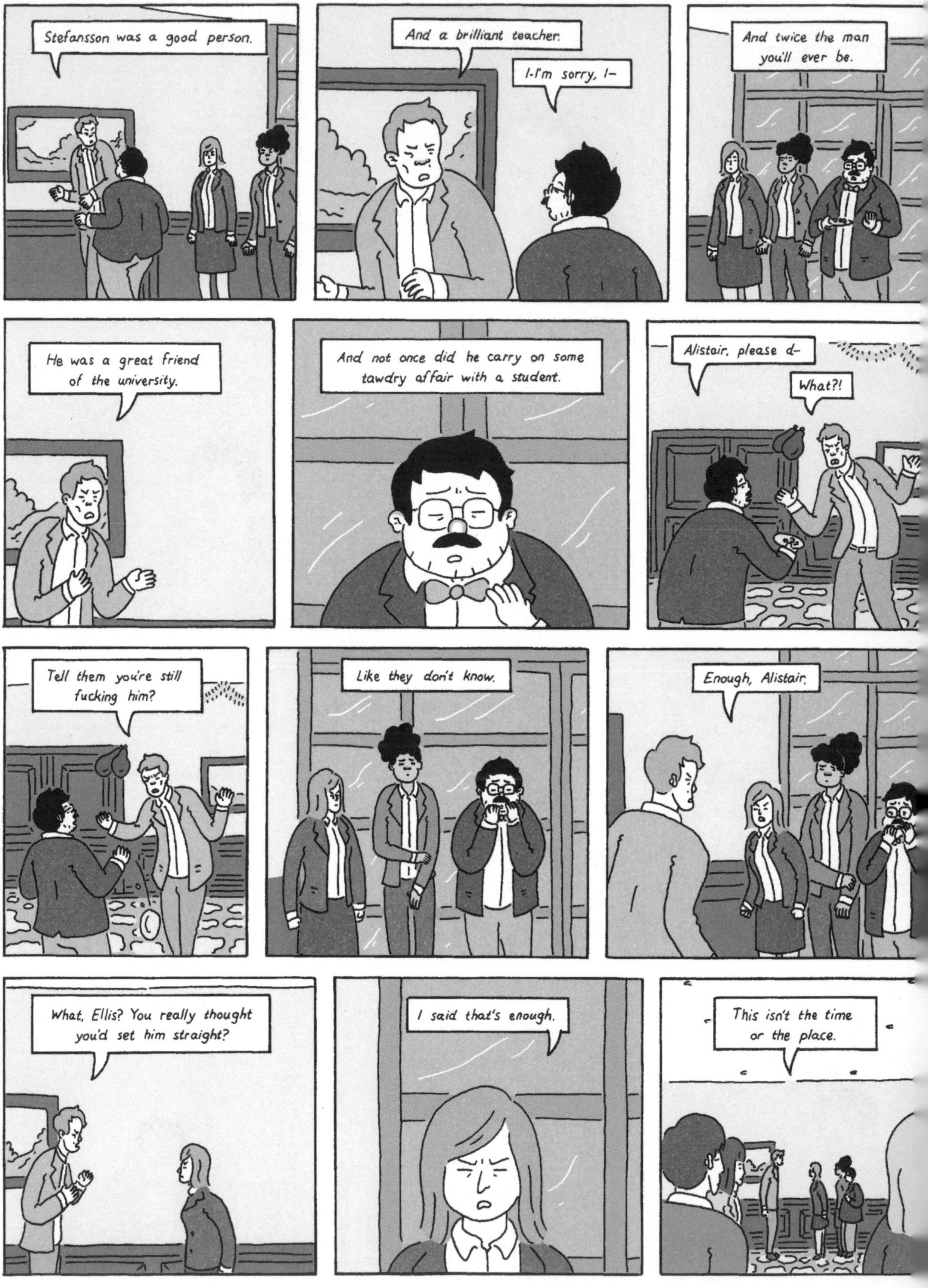
Stefansson was a good person.
And a brilliant teacher.
I-I'm sorry, I-
And twice the man you'll ever be.
He was a great friend of the university.
And not once did he carry on some tawdry affair with a student.
Alistair, please d-
What?!
Tell them you're still fucking him?
Like they don't know.
Enough, Alistair.
What, Ellis? You really thought you'd set him straight?
I said that's enough.
This isn't the time or the place.

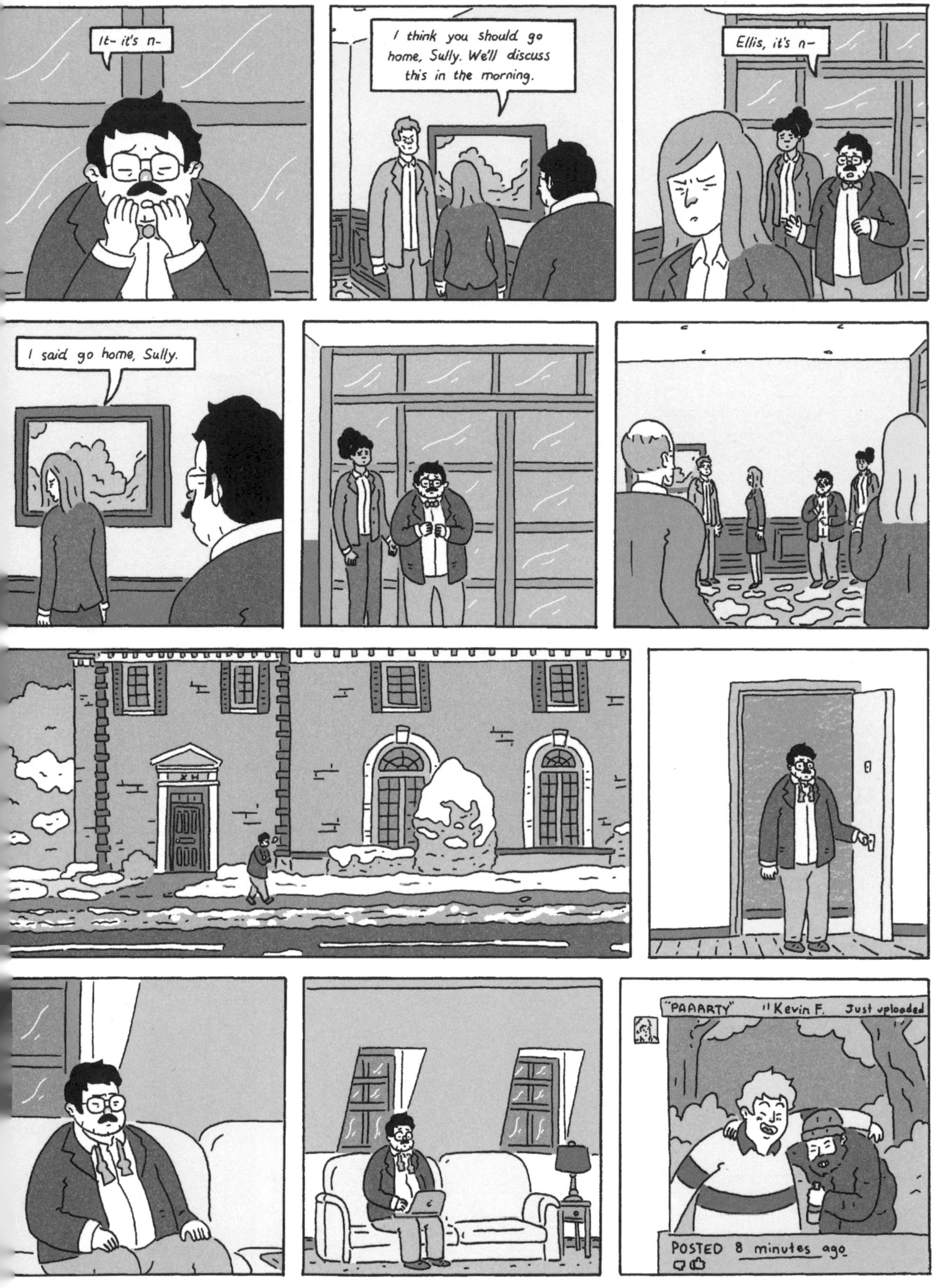
It- it's n-
I think you should go home, Sully. We'll discuss this in the morning.
Ellis, it's n-
I said go home, Sully.
"PAAARTY"
Kevin F.
Just uploaded
POSTED 8 minutes ago

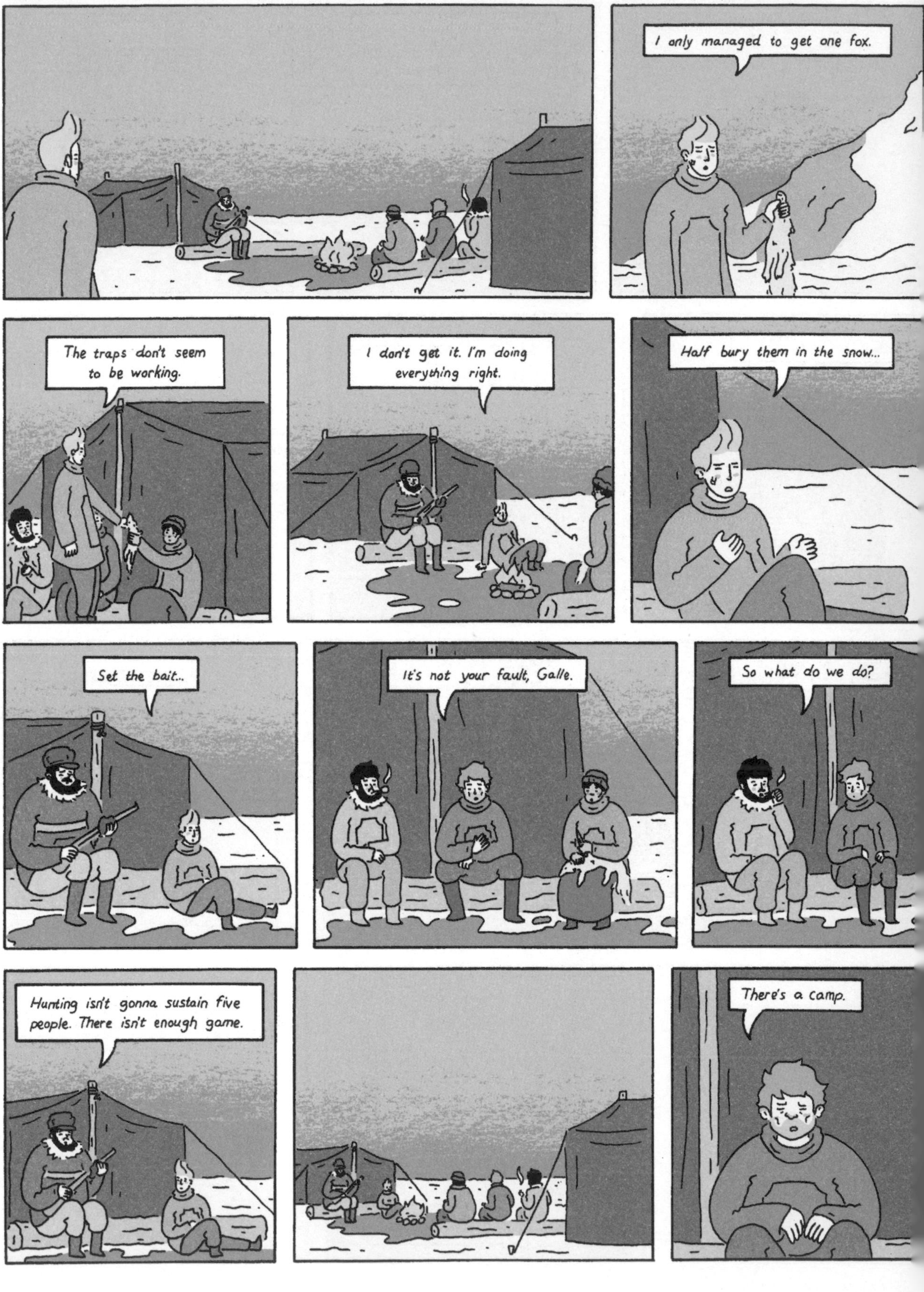
I only managed to get one fox.
The traps don't seem to be working.
I don't get it. I'm doing everything right.
Half bury them in the snow...
Set the bait...
It's not your fault, Galle.
So what do we do?
Hunting isn't gonna sustain five people. There isn't enough game.
There's a camp.

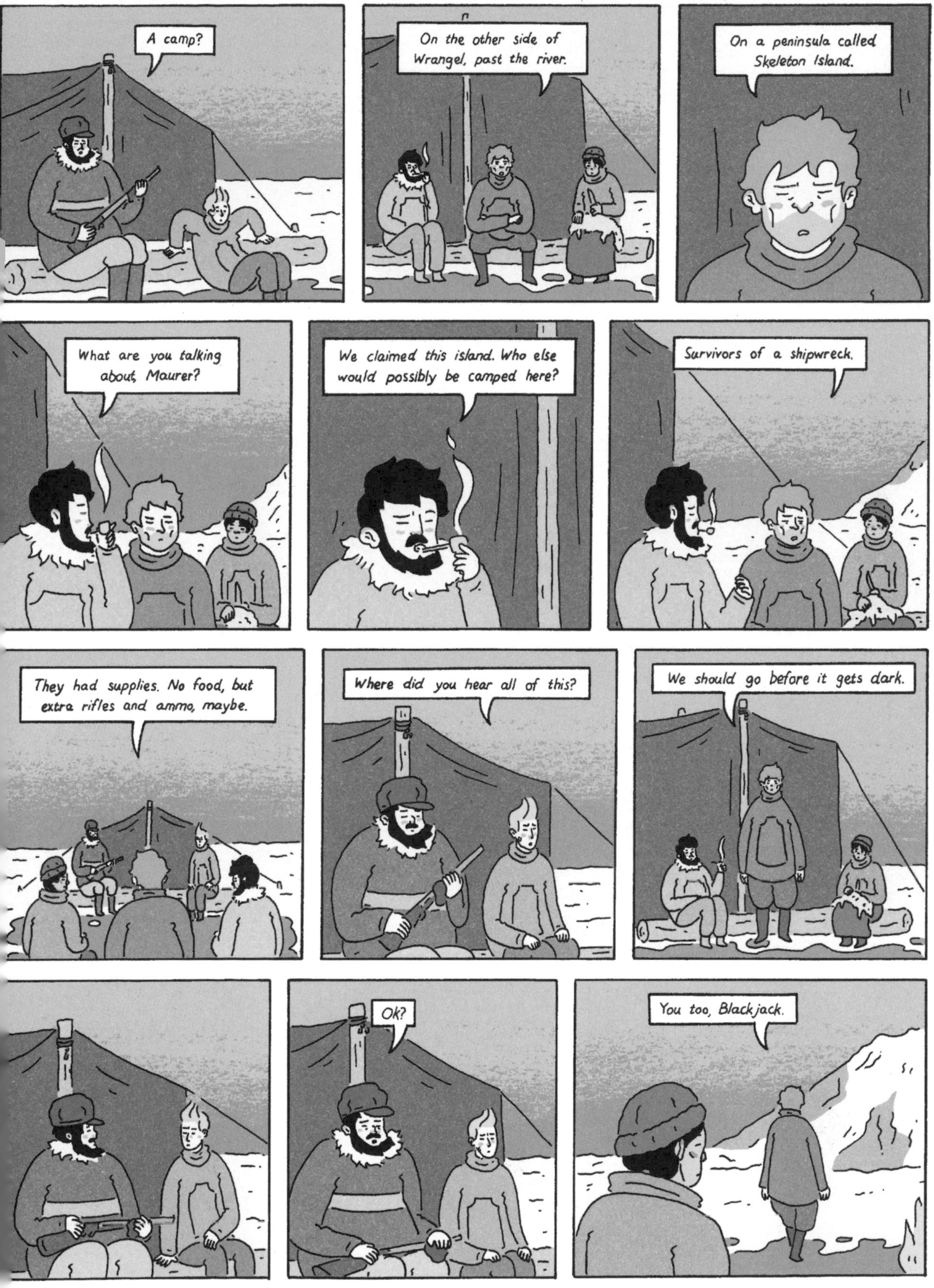
A camp?
On the other side of Wrangel, past the river.
On a peninsula called Skeleton Island.
What are you talking about, Maurer?
We claimed this island. Who else would possibly be camped here?
Survivors of a shipwreck.
They had supplies. No food, but extra rifles and ammo, maybe.
Where did you hear all of this?
We should go before it gets dark.
Ok?
You too, Blackjack.

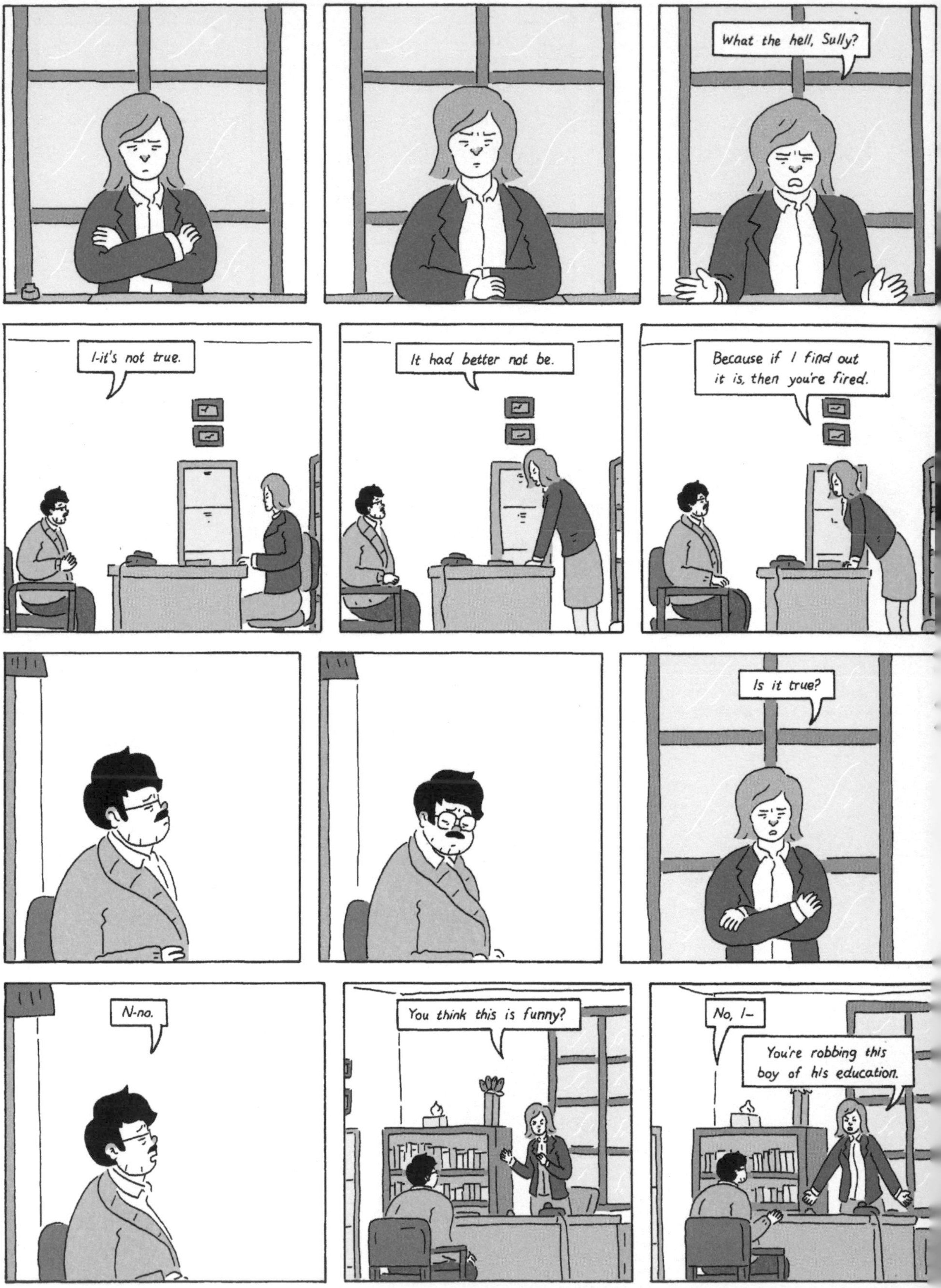

What the hell, Sully?
I-it's not true.
It had better not be.
Because if I find out it is, then you're fired.
Is it true?
N-no.
You think this is funny?
No, I–
You're robbing this boy of his education.

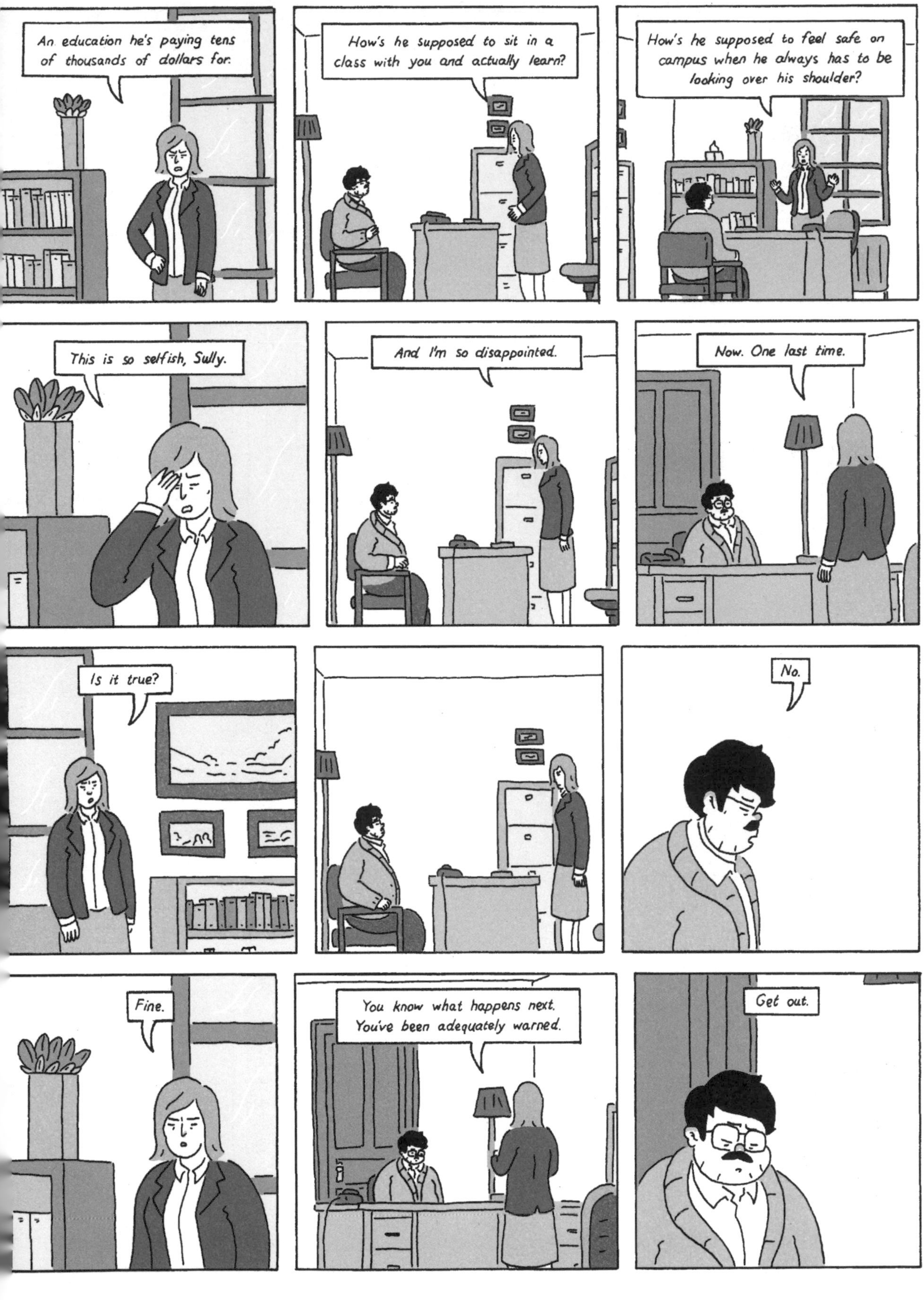
An education he's paying tens of thousands of dollars for.
How's he supposed to sit in a class with you and actually learn?
How's he supposed to feel safe on campus when he always has to be looking over his shoulder?
This is so selfish, Sully.
And I'm so disappointed.
Now. One last time.
Is it true?
No.
Fine.
You know what happens next. You've been adequately warned.
Get out.

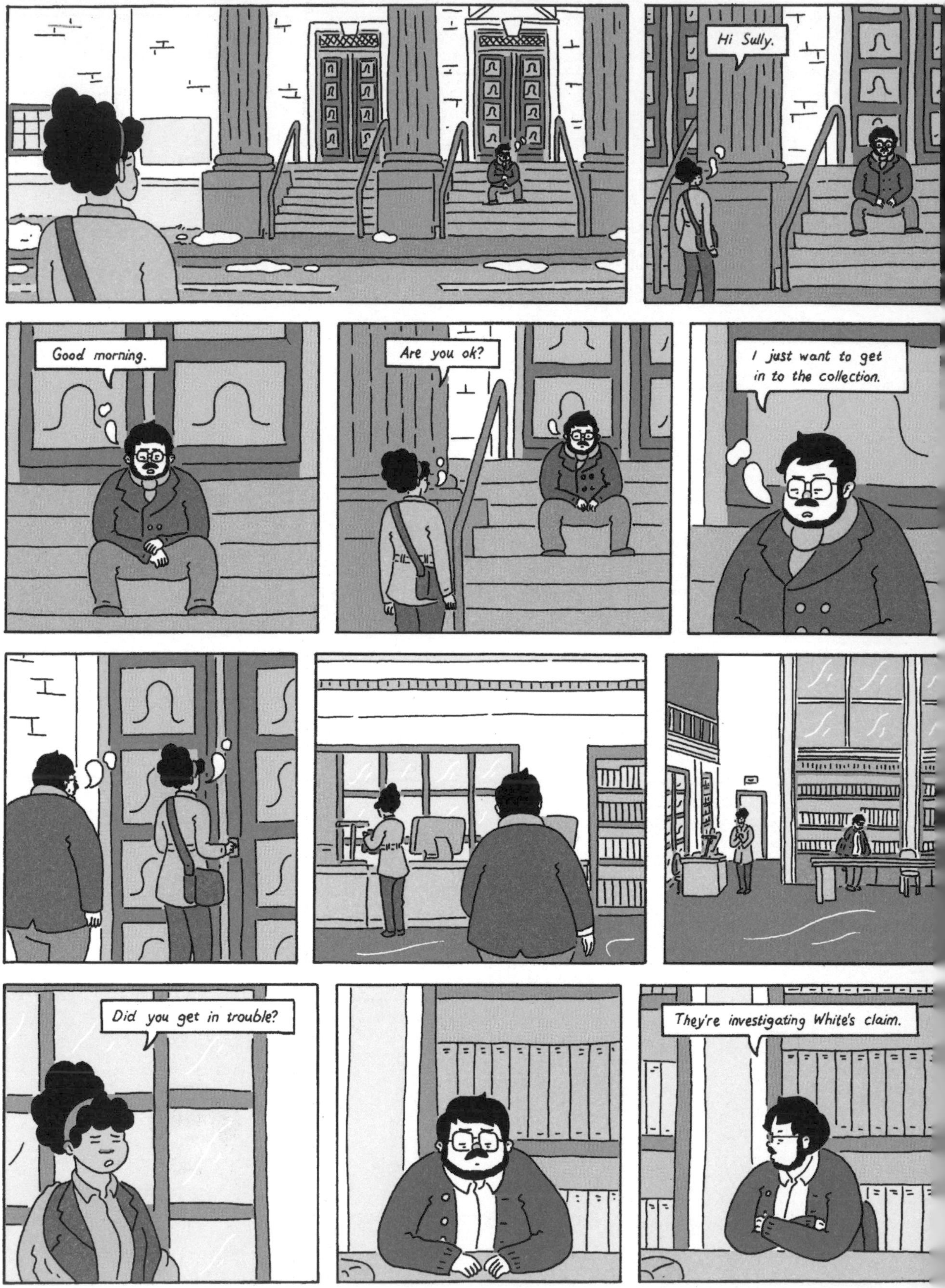
Hi Sully.
Good morning.
Are you ok?
I just want to get in to the collection.
Did you get in trouble?
They're investigating White's claim.

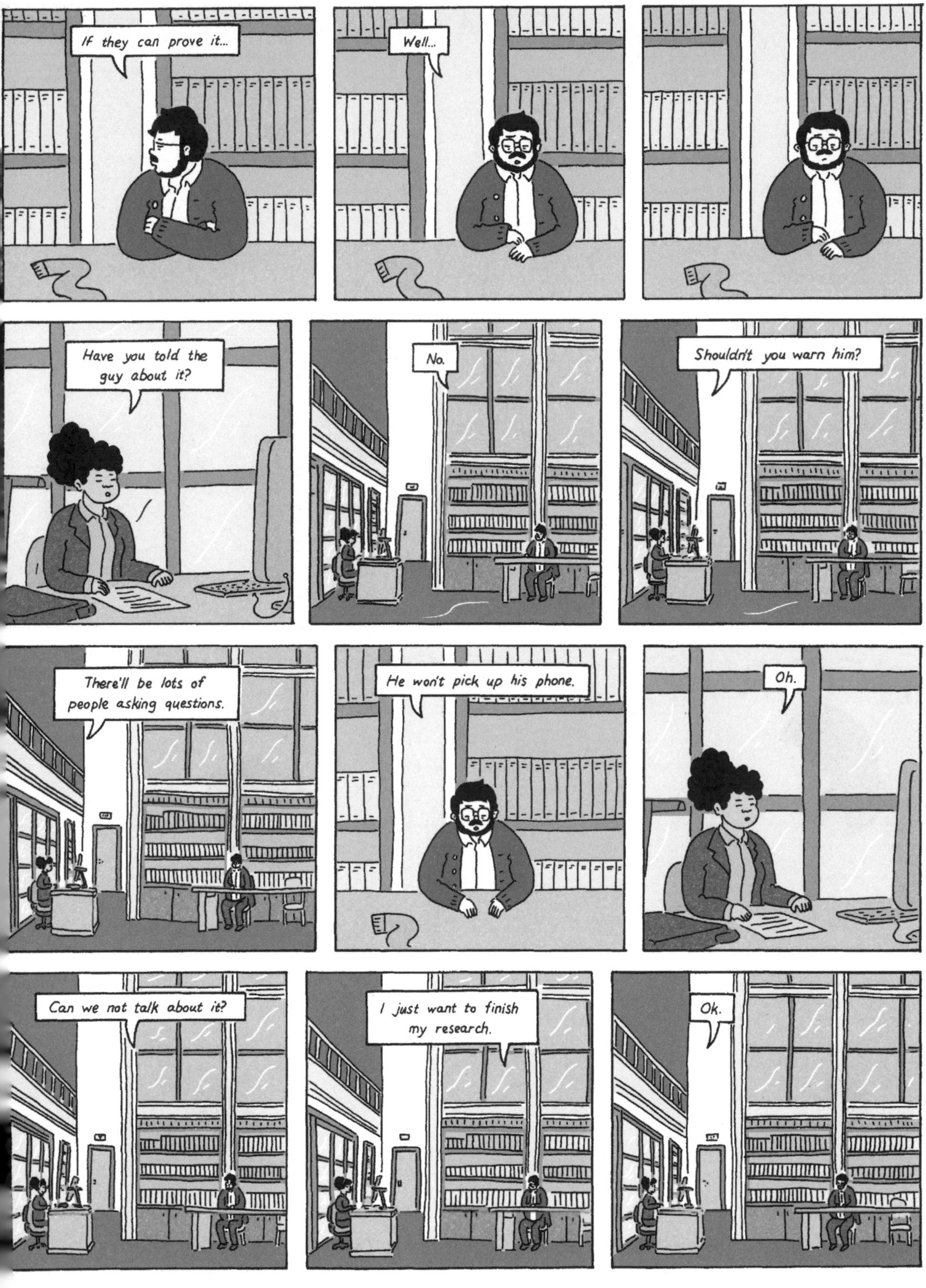
If they can prove it...
Well...
Have you told the guy about it?
No.
Shouldn't you warn him?
There'll be lots of people asking questions.
He won't pick up his phone.
Oh.
Can we not talk about it?
I just want to finish my research.
Ok.

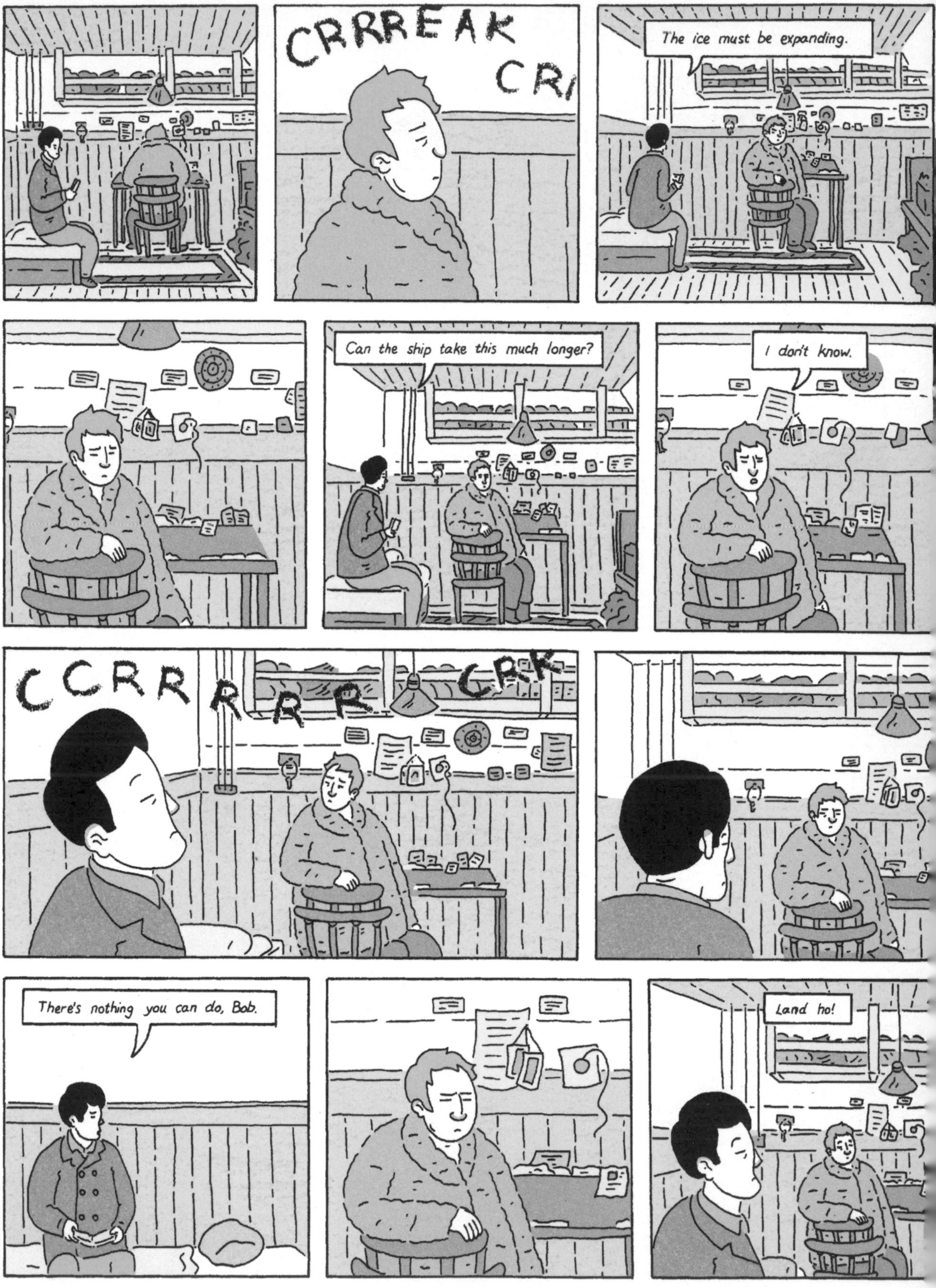
CRRREAK
CRI
The ice must be expanding.
Can the ship take this much longer?
I don't know.
CCRRRRRR
CRK
There's nothing you can do, Bob.
Land ho!

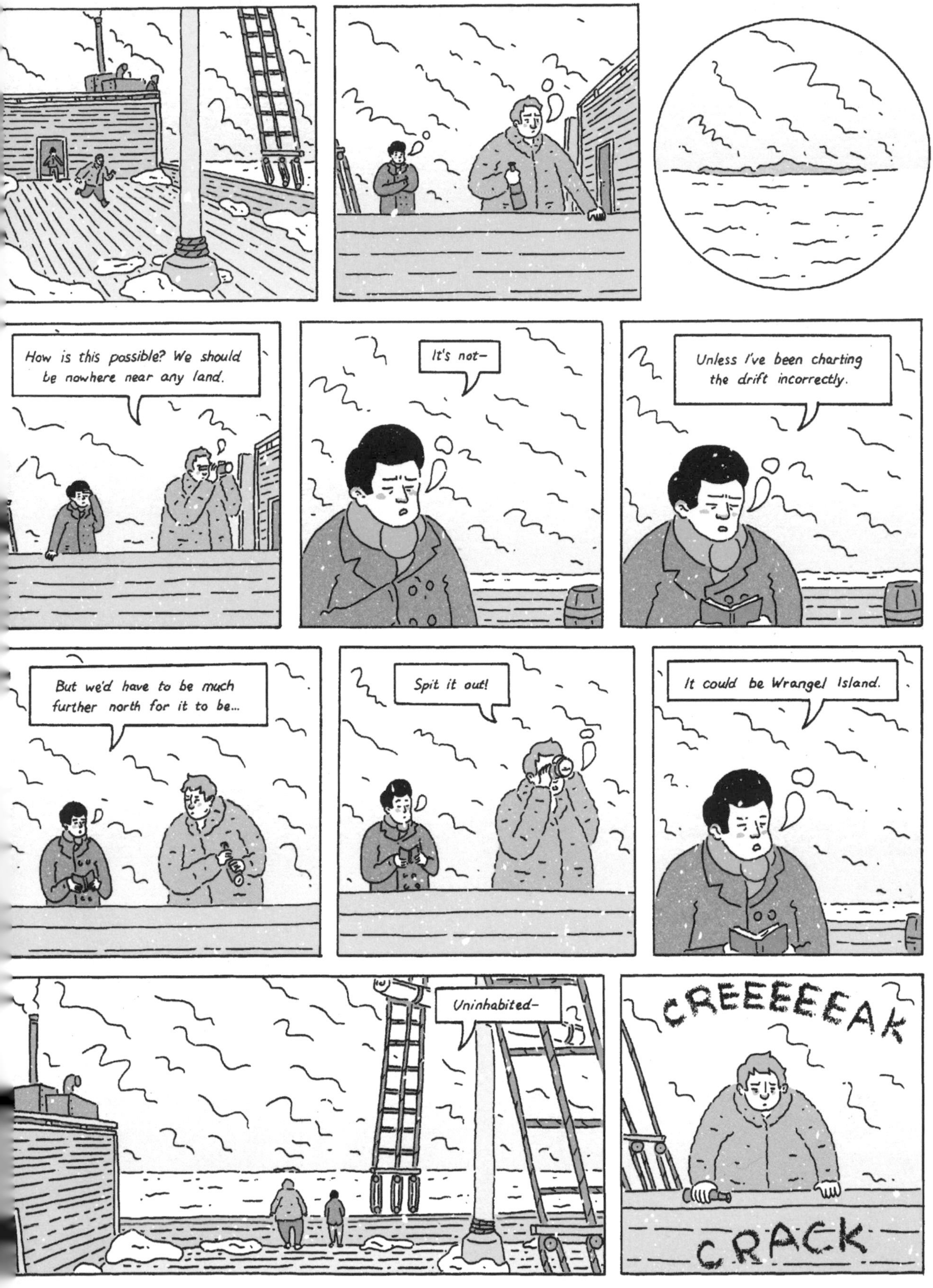
How is this possible? We should be nowhere near any land.
It's not-
Unless I've been charting the drift incorrectly.
But we'd have to be much further north for it to be...
Spit it out!
It could be Wrangel Island.
Uninhabited-
CREEEEEAK
CRACK

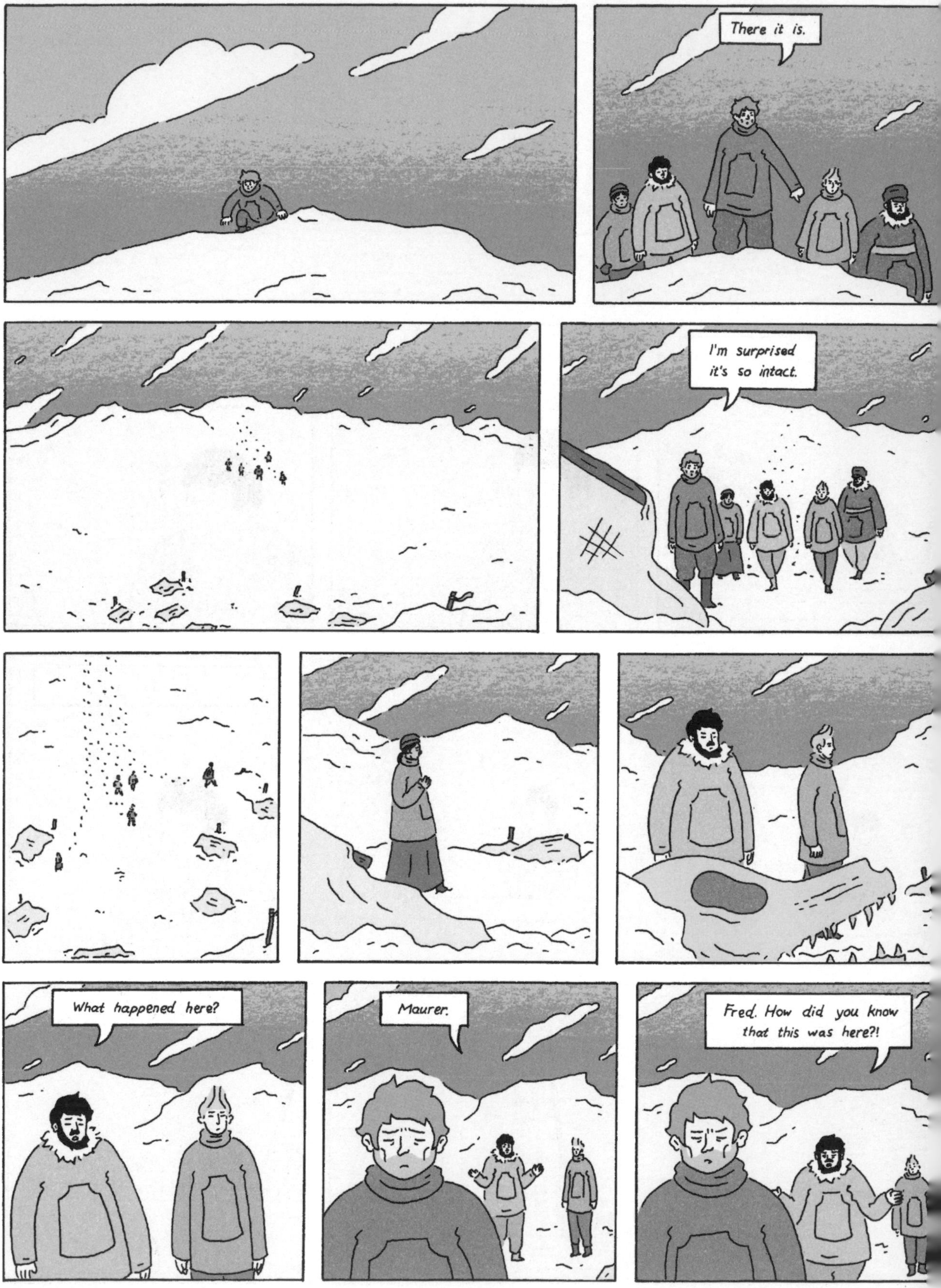

There it is.
I'm surprised it's so intact.
What happened here?
Maurer.
Fred. How did you know that this was here?!

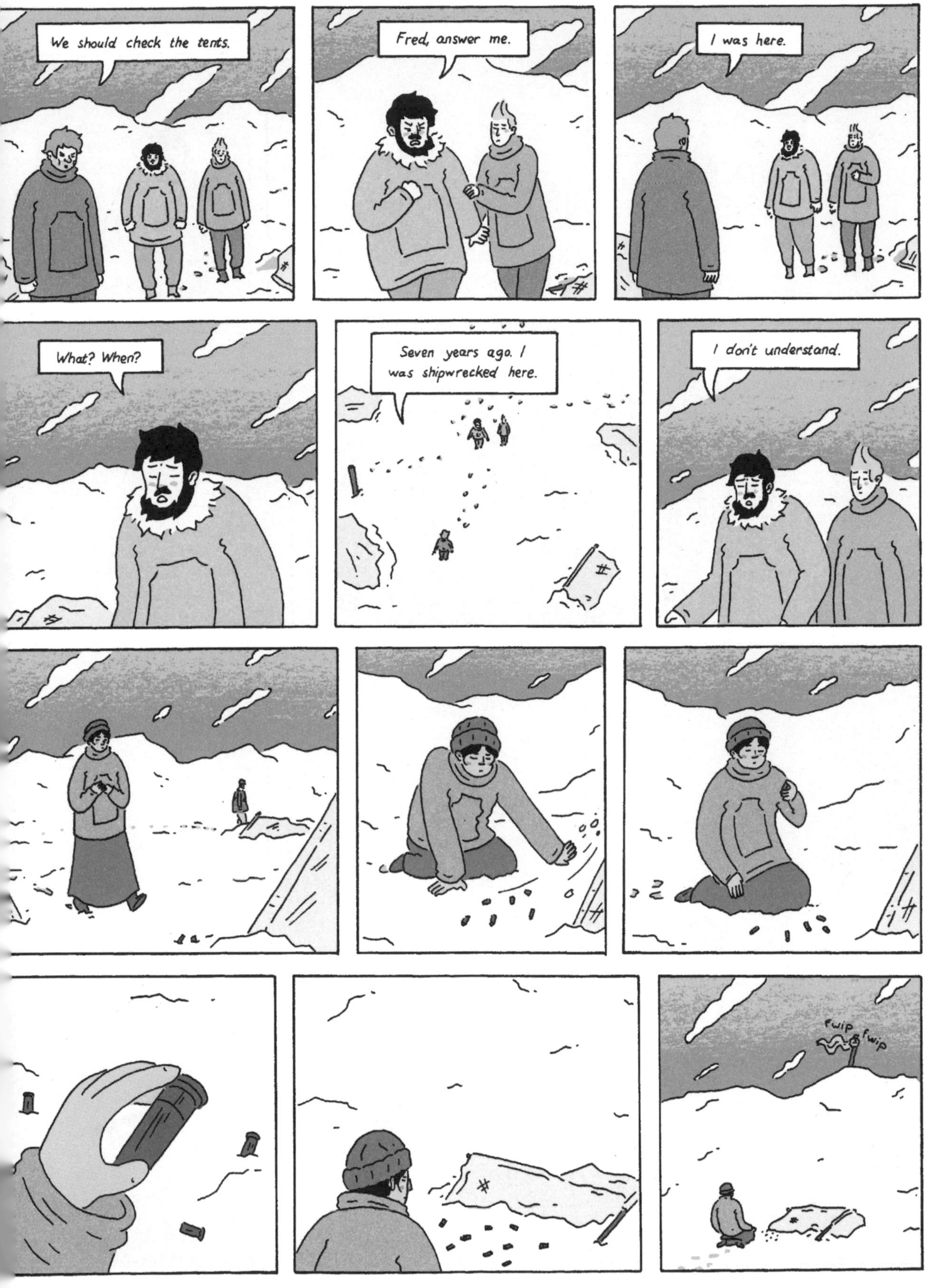
We should check the tents.
Fred, answer me.
I was here.
What? When?
Seven years ago. I was shipwrecked here.
I don't understand.
Fwip
Fwip

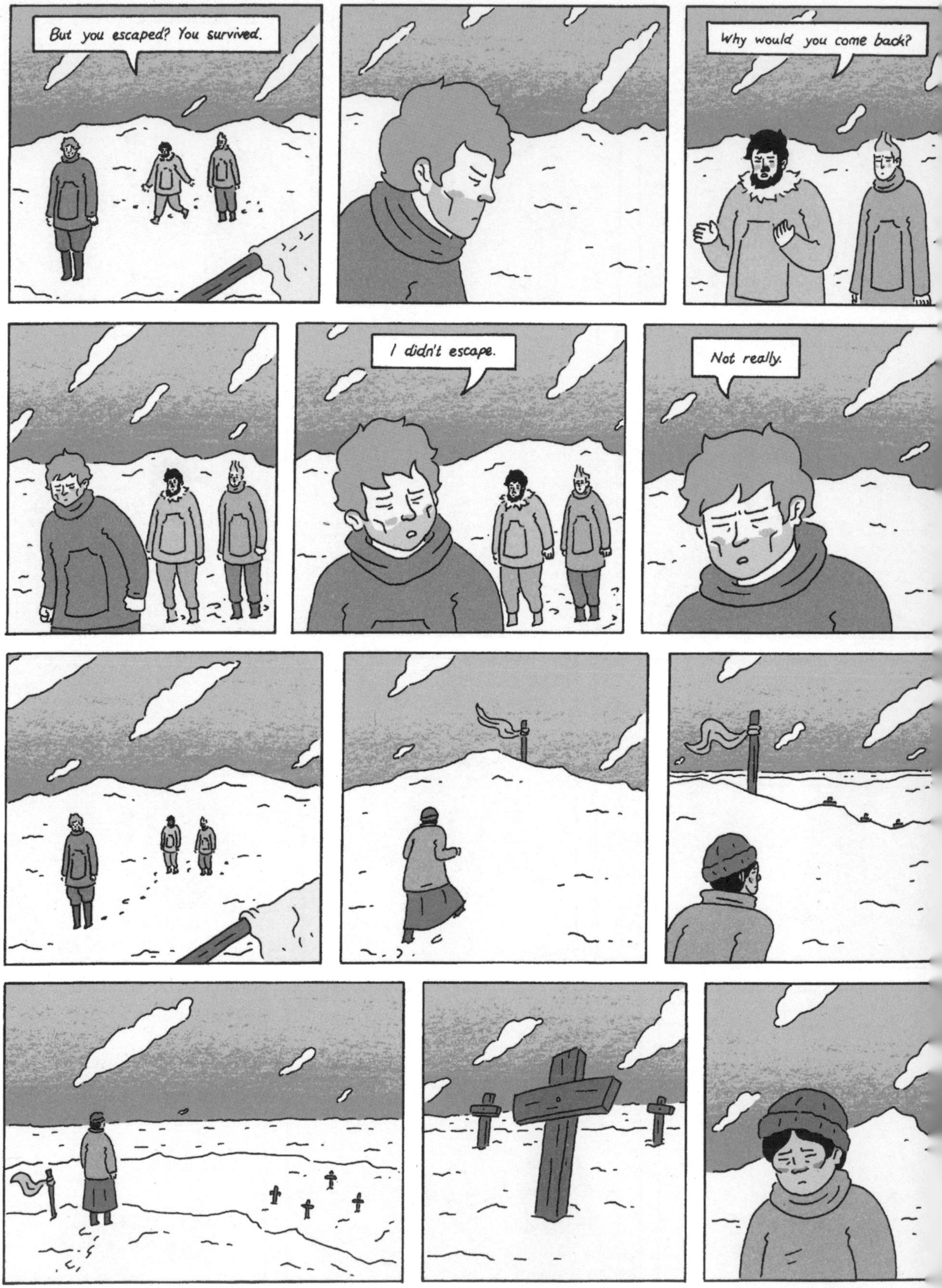
But you escaped? You survived.
Why would you come back?
I didn't escape.
Not really.

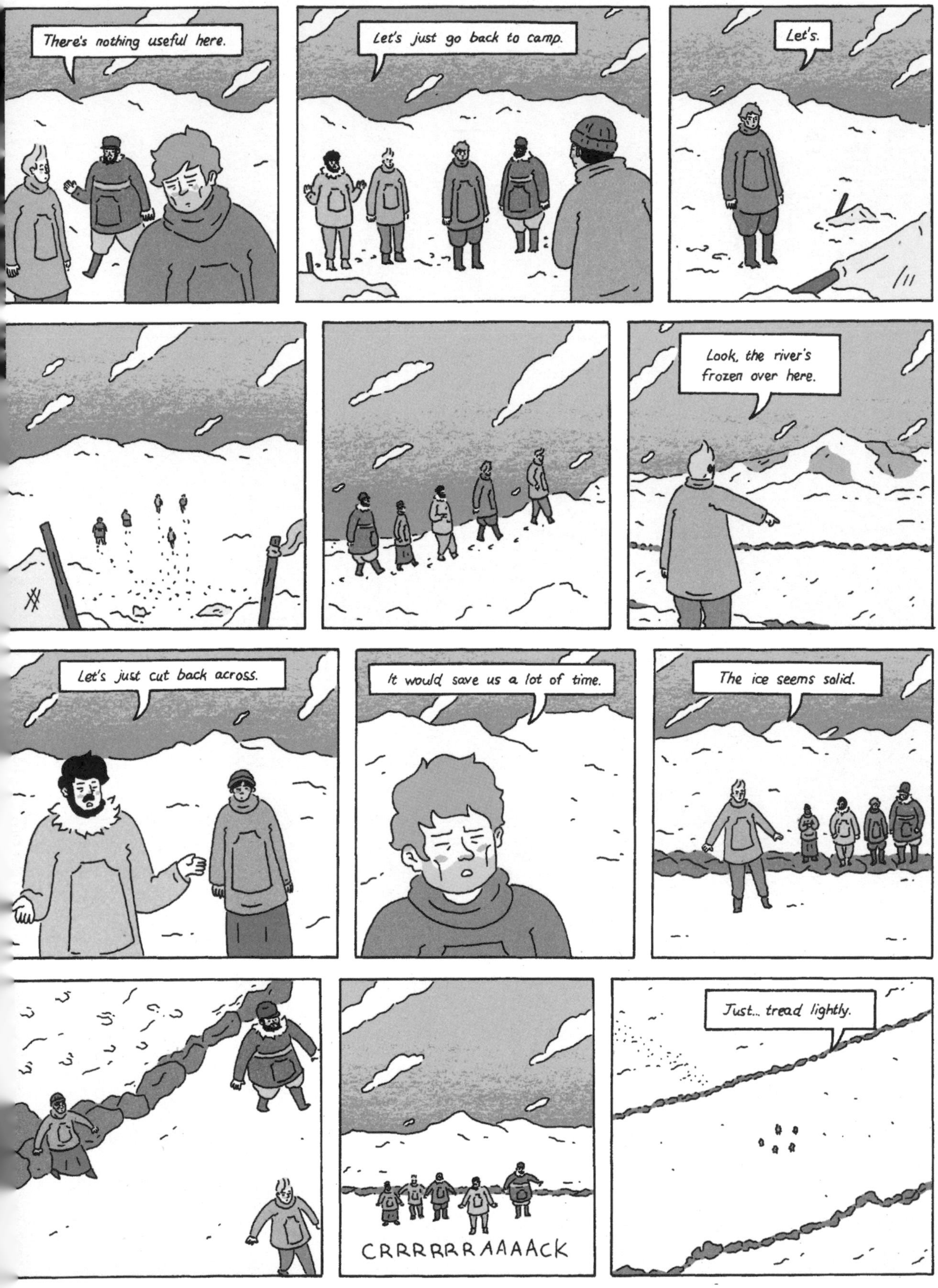

There's nothing useful here.
Let's just go back to camp.
Let's.
Look, the river's frozen over here.
Let's just cut back across.
It would save us a lot of time.
The ice seems solid.
CRRRRRRAAAACK
Just... tread lightly.

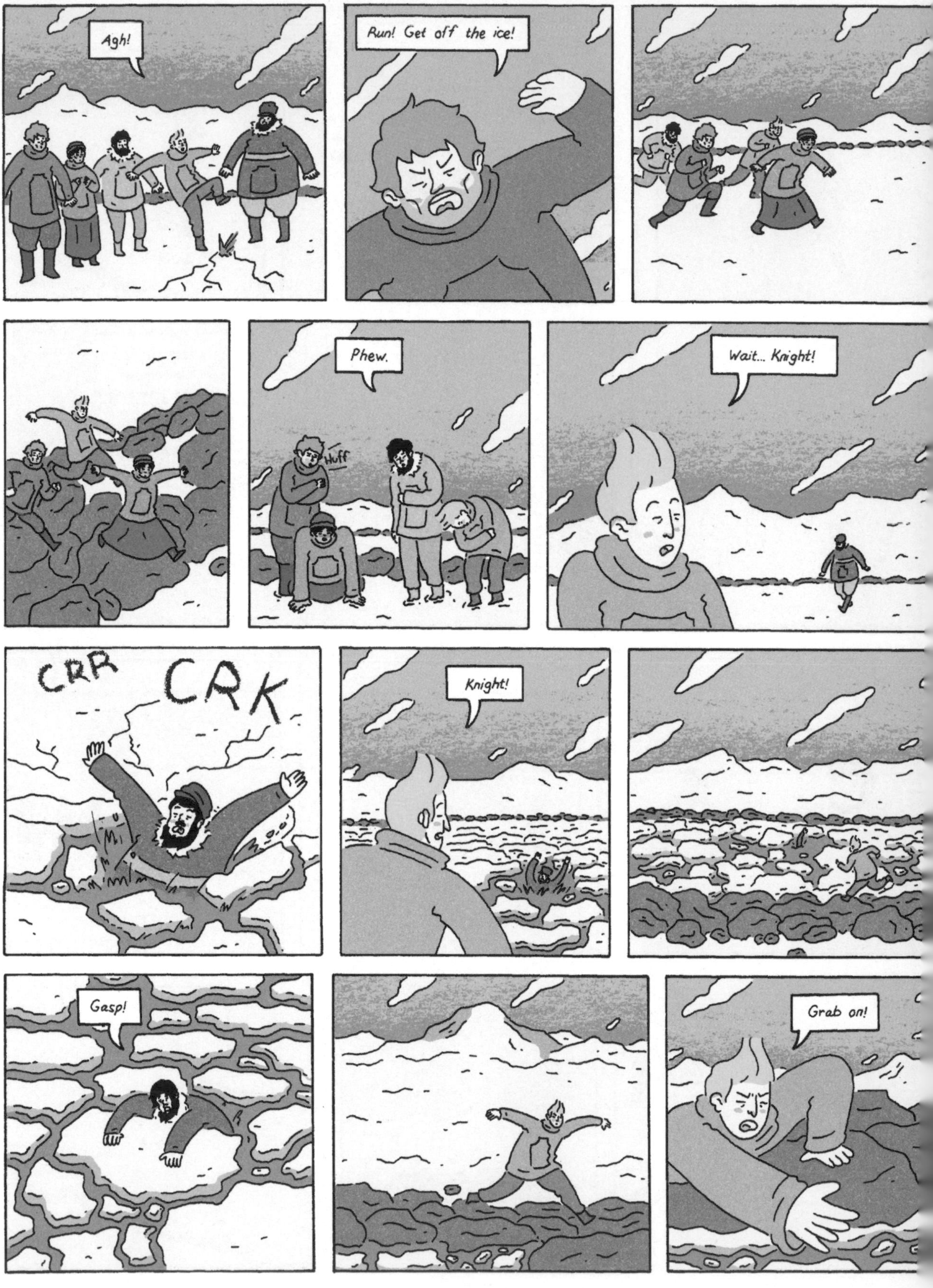
Agh!
Run! Get off the ice!
Phew.
Huff
Wait... Knight!
CRR
CRK
Knight!
Gasp!
Grab on!

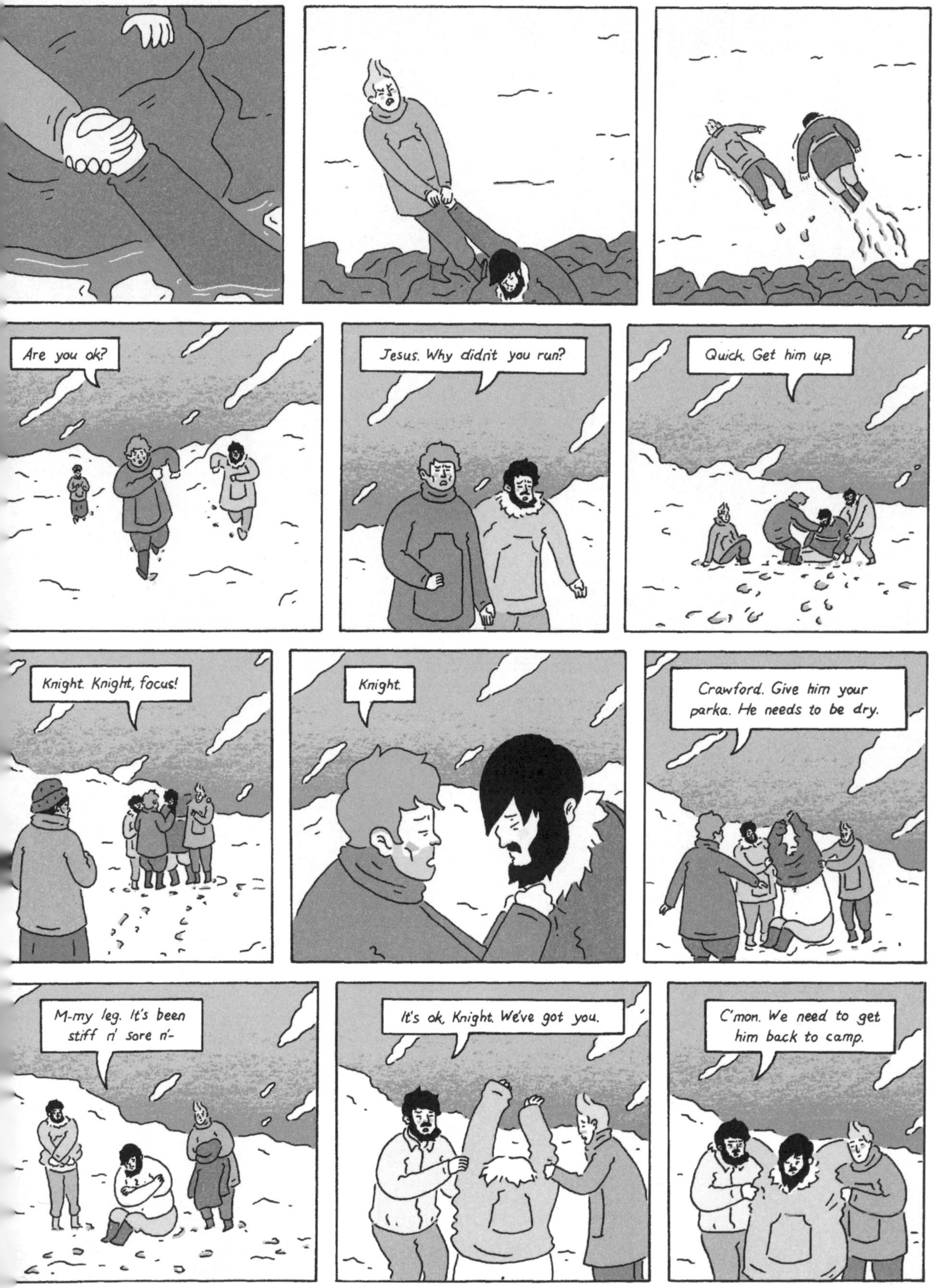
Are you ok?
Jesus. Why didn't you run?
Quick. Get him up.
Knight. Knight, focus!
Knight.
Crawford. Give him your parka. He needs to be dry.
M-my leg. It's been stiff n' sore n'-
It's ok, Knight. We've got you.
C'mon. We need to get him back to camp.

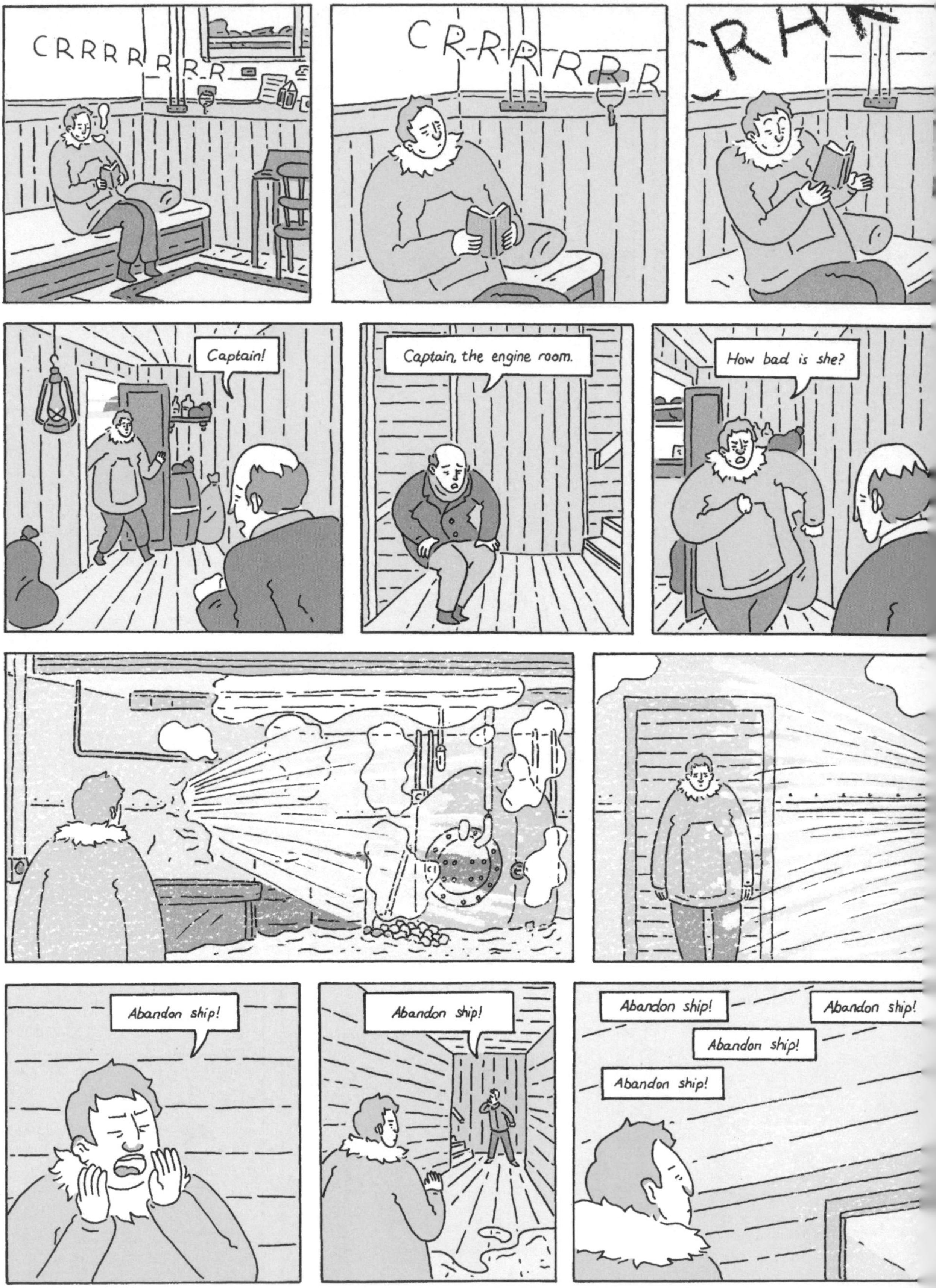
CRRRRRRR
CRRRRRRRR
CRAK
Captain!
Captain, the engine room.
How bad is she?
Abandon ship!
Abandon ship!
Abandon ship!
Abandon ship!
Abandon ship!
Abandon ship!

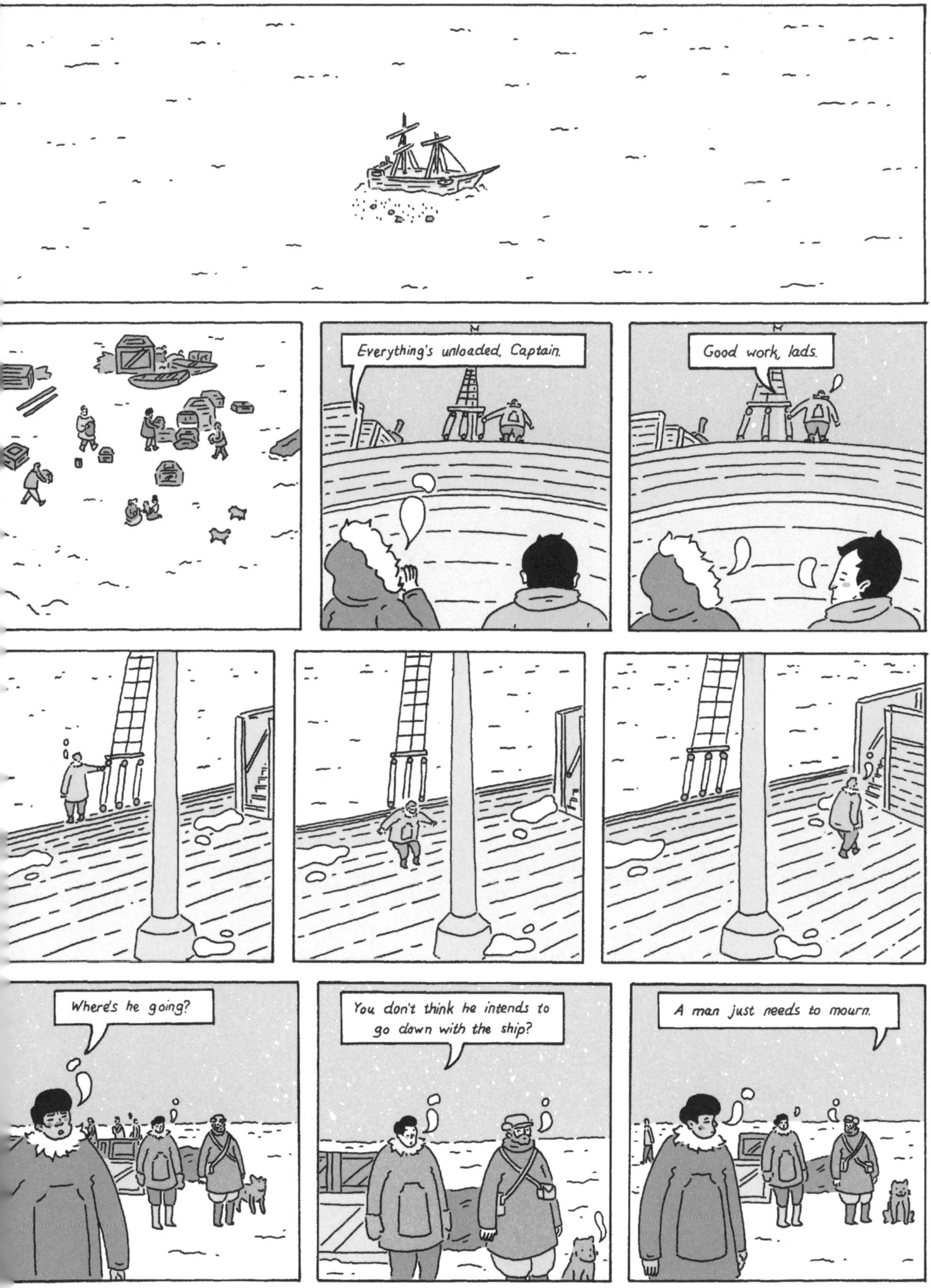
Everything's unloaded, Captain.
Good work, lads.
Where's he going?
You don't think he intends to go down with the ship?
A man just needs to mourn.

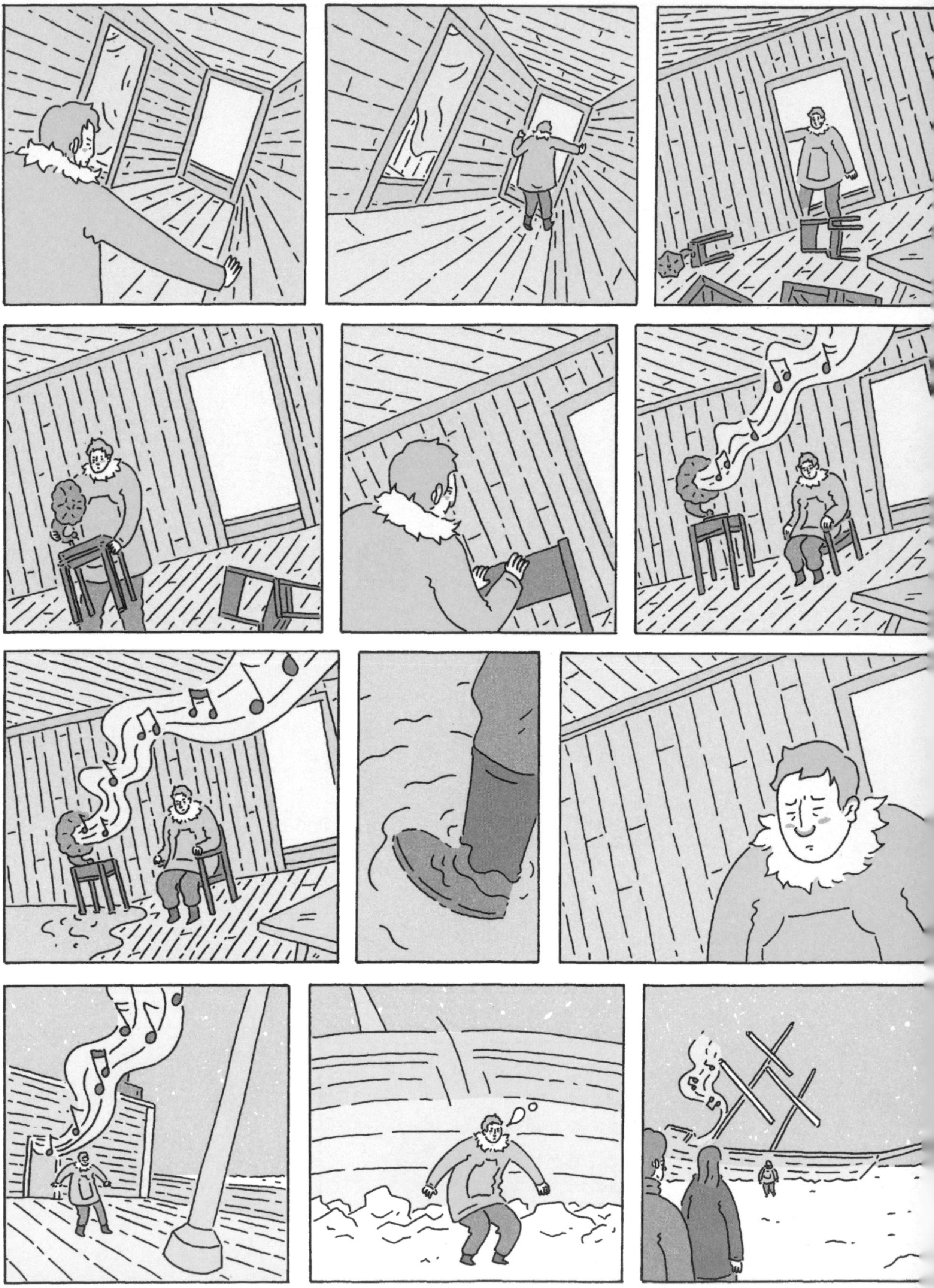

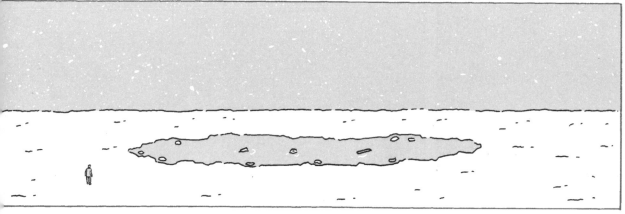

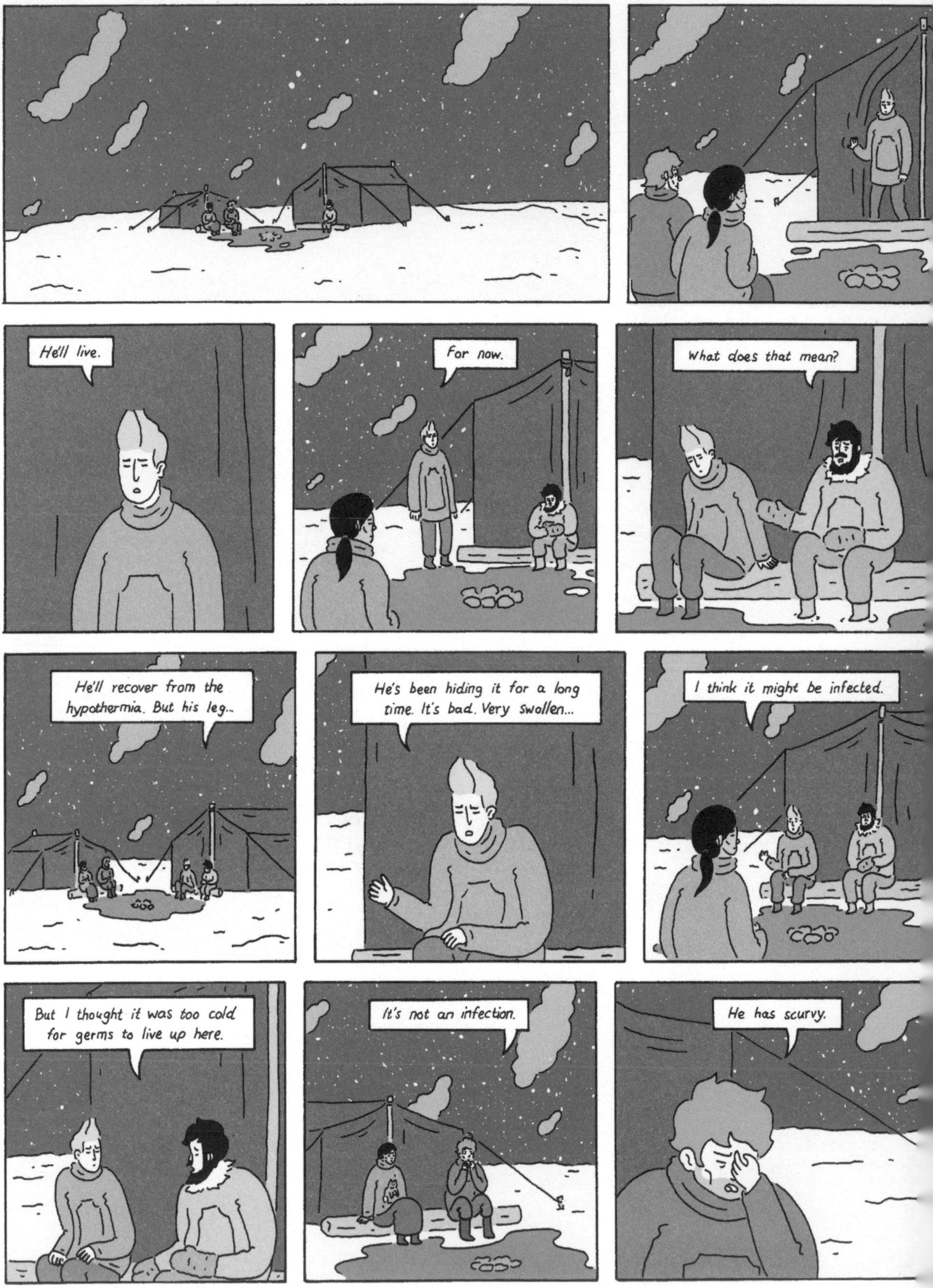
He'll live.
For now.
What does that mean?
He'll recover from the hypothermia. But his leg..
He's been hiding it for a long time. It's bad. Very swollen...
I think it might be infected.
But I thought it was too cold for germs to live up here.
It's not an infection.
He has scurvy.

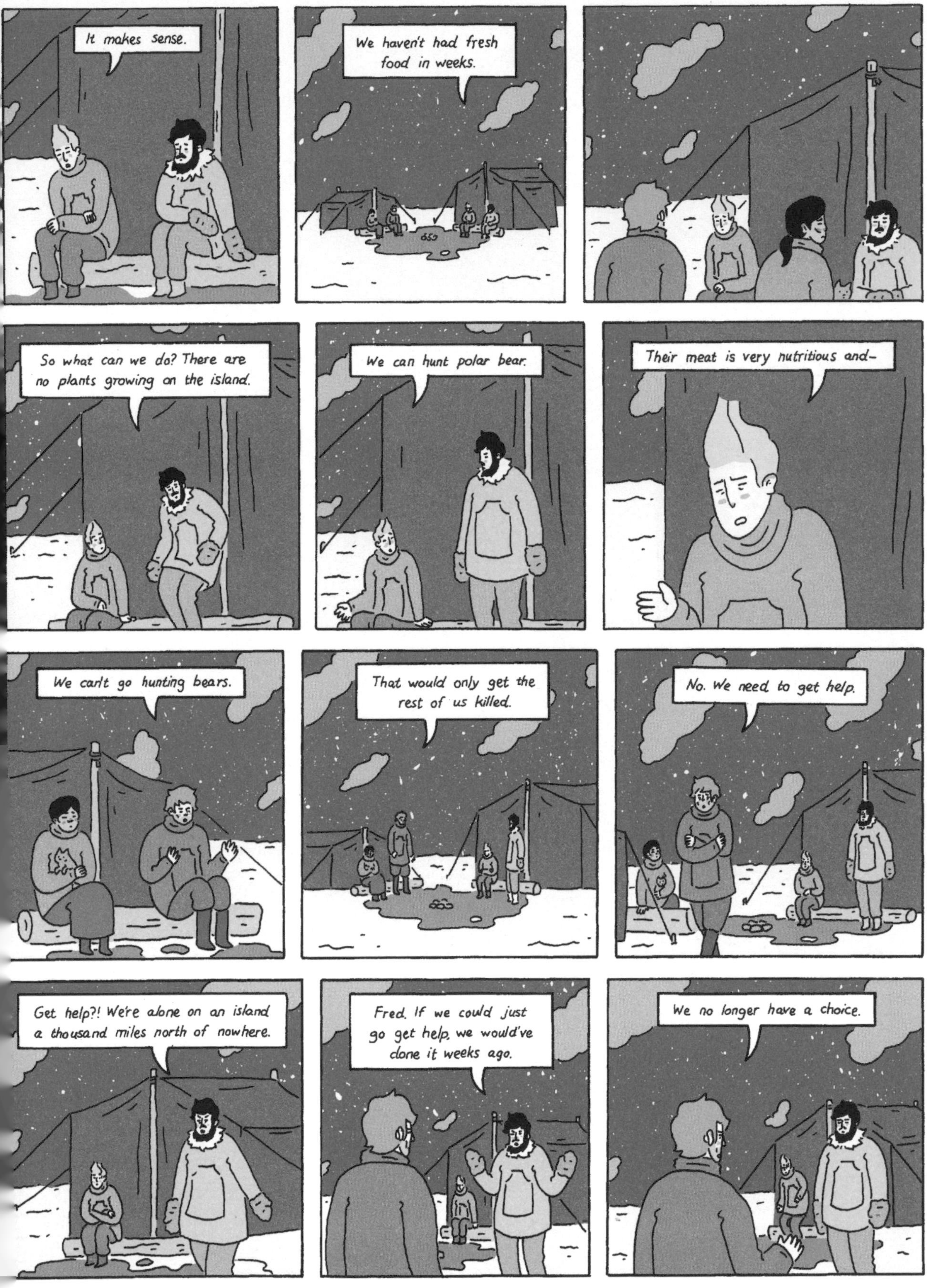

It makes sense.
We haven't had fresh food in weeks.
So what can we do? There are no plants growing on the island.
We can hunt polar bear.
Their meat is very nutritious and–
We can't go hunting bears.
That would only get the rest of us killed.
No. We need to get help.
Get help?! We're alone on an island a thousand miles north of nowhere.
Fred. If we could just go get help, we would've done it weeks ago.
We no longer have a choice.

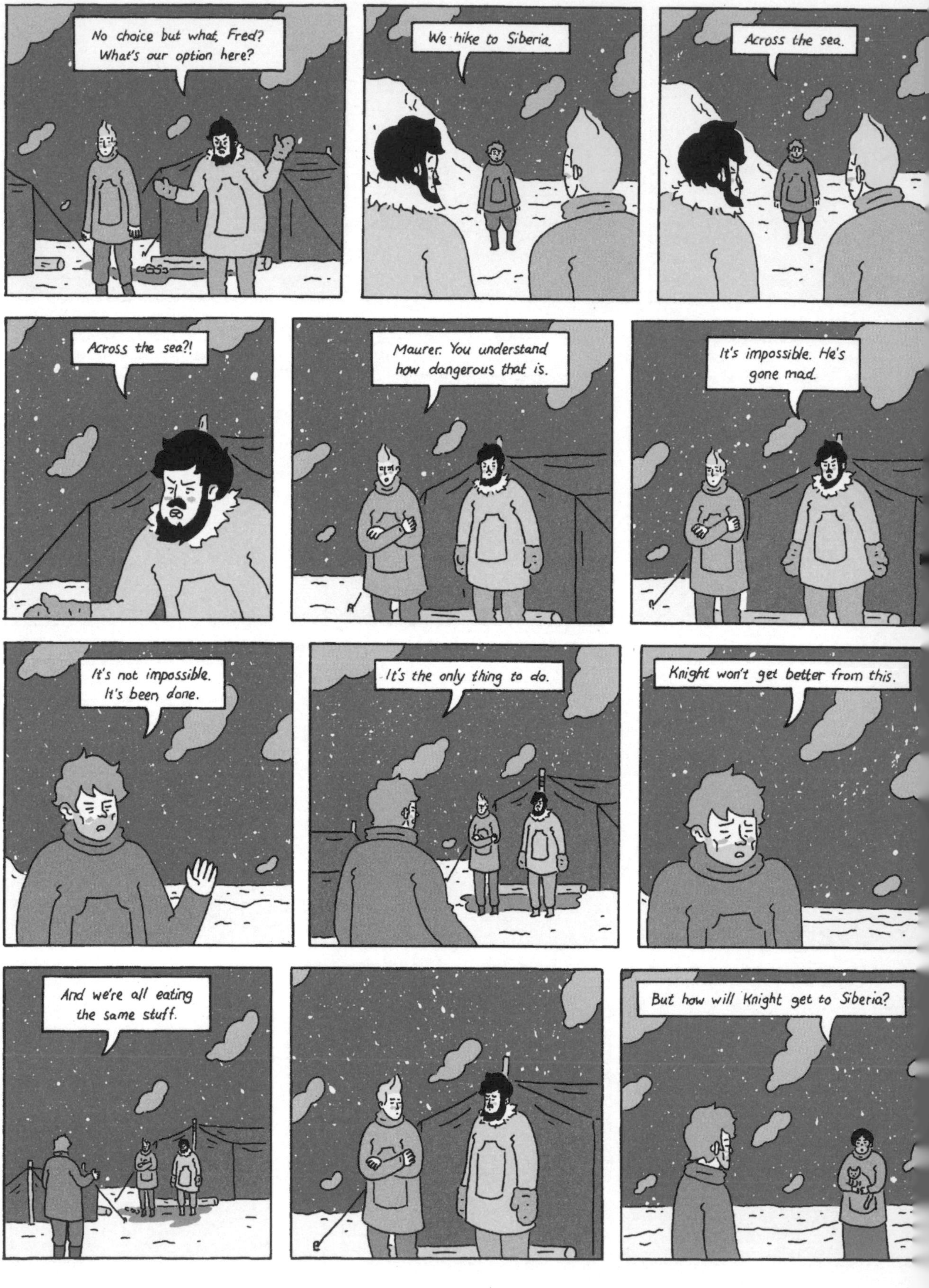
No choice but what, Fred? What's our option here?
We hike to Siberia.
Across the sea.
Across the sea?!
Maurer. You understand how dangerous that is.
It's impossible. He's gone mad.
It's not impossible. It's been done.
It's the only thing to do.
Knight won't get better from this.
And we're all eating the same stuff.
But how will Knight get to Siberia?

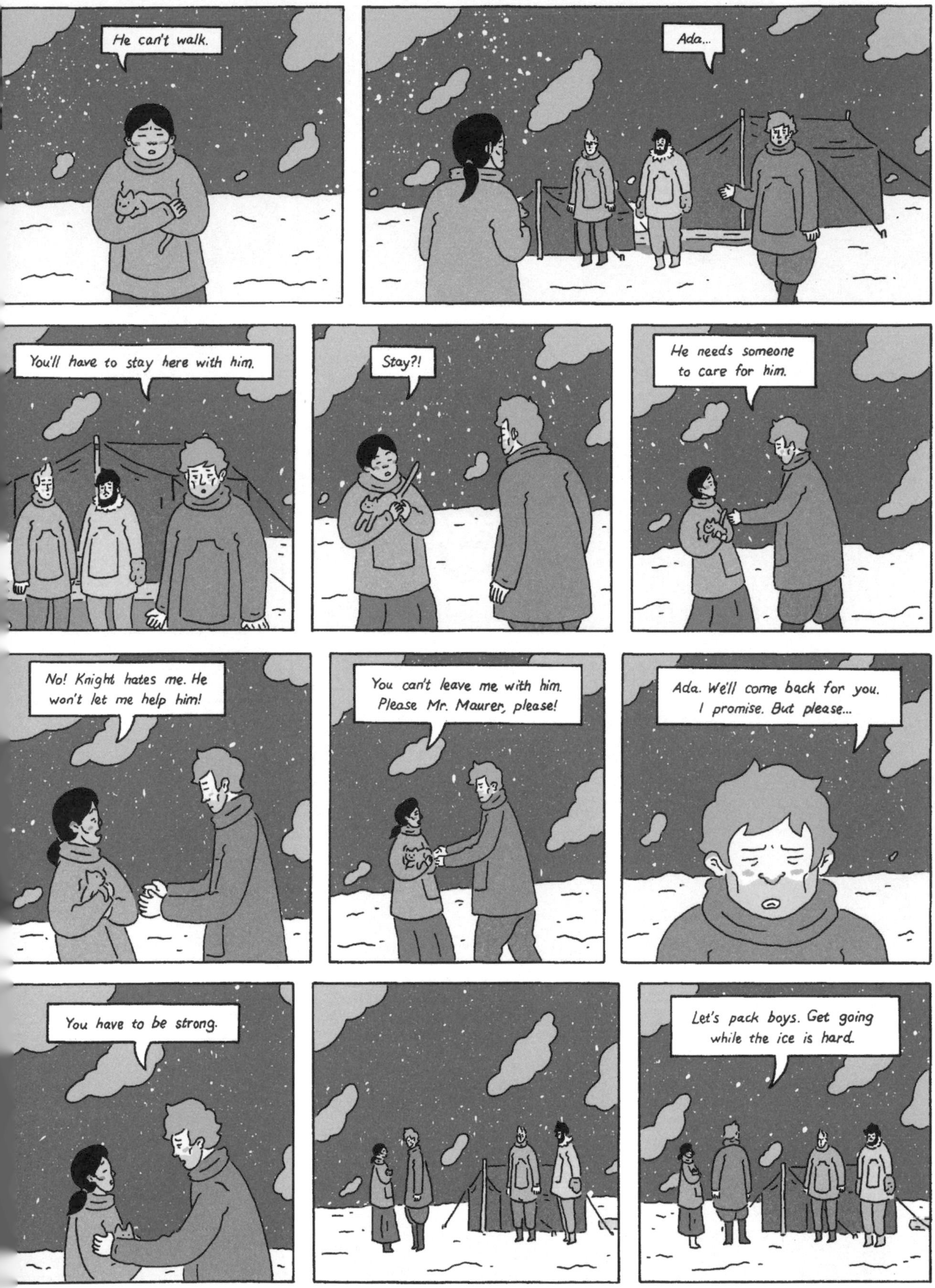
He can't walk.
Ada...
You'll have to stay here with him.
Stay?!
He needs someone to care for him.
No! Knight hates me. He won't let me help him!
You can't leave me with him. Please Mr. Maurer, please!
Ada. We'll come back for you. I promise. But please...
You have to be strong.
Let's pack boys. Get going while the ice is hard.

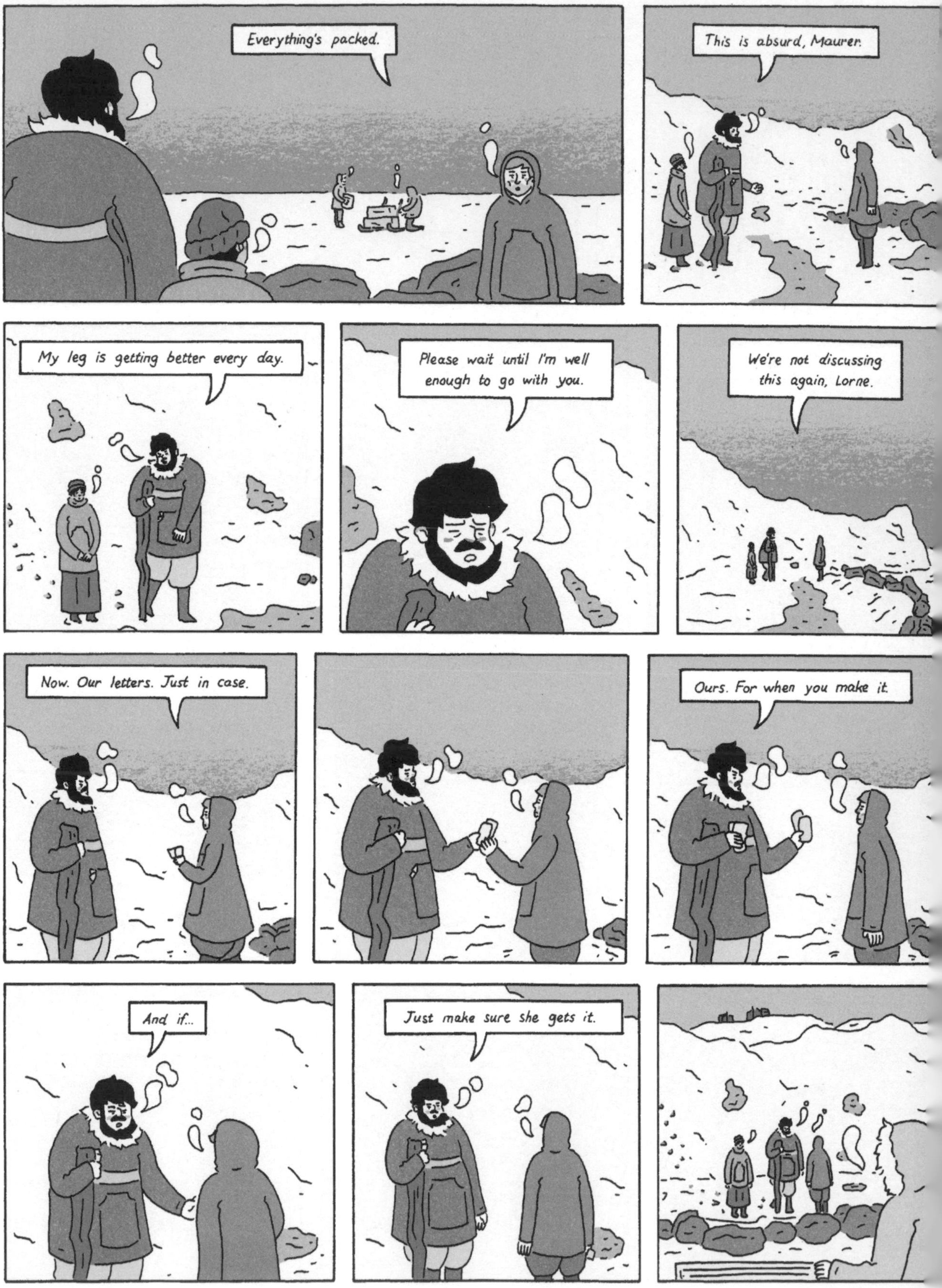
Everything's packed.
This is absurd, Maurer.
My leg is getting better every day.
Please wait until I'm well enough to go with you.
We're not discussing this again, Lorne.
Now. Our letters. Just in case.
Ours. For when you make it.
And if...
Just make sure she gets it.

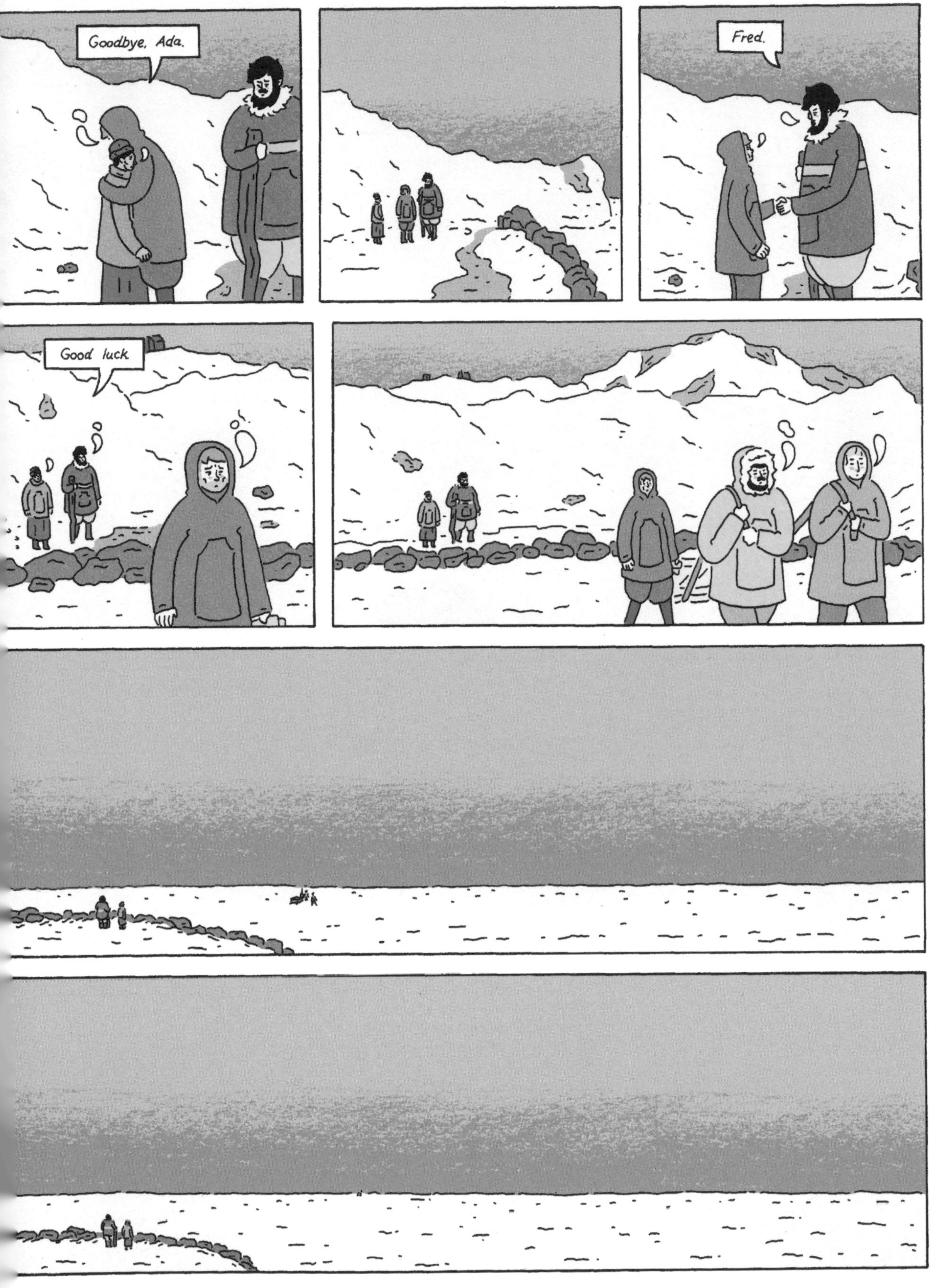
Goodbye, Ada.
Fred.
Good luck.

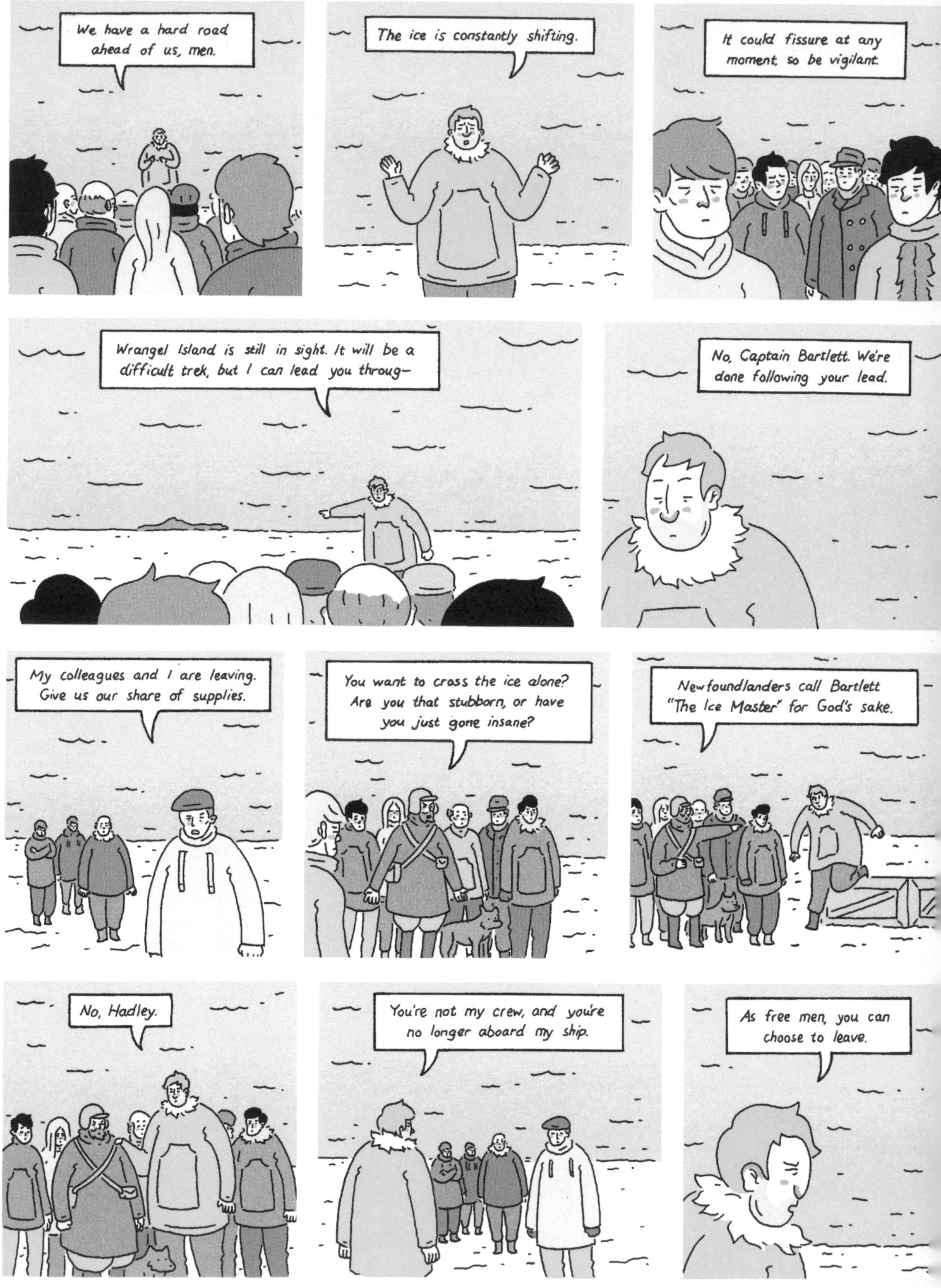
We have a hard road ahead of us, men.
The ice is constantly shifting.
It could fissure at any moment, so be vigilant.
Wrangel Island is still in sight. It will be a difficult trek, but I can lead you throug–
No, Captain Bartlett. We're done following your lead.
My colleagues and I are leaving. Give us our share of supplies.
You want to cross the ice alone? Are you that stubborn, or have you just gone insane?
Newfoundlanders call Bartlett "The Ice Master" for God's sake.
No, Hadley.
You're not my crew, and you're no longer aboard my ship.
As free men, you can choose to leave.

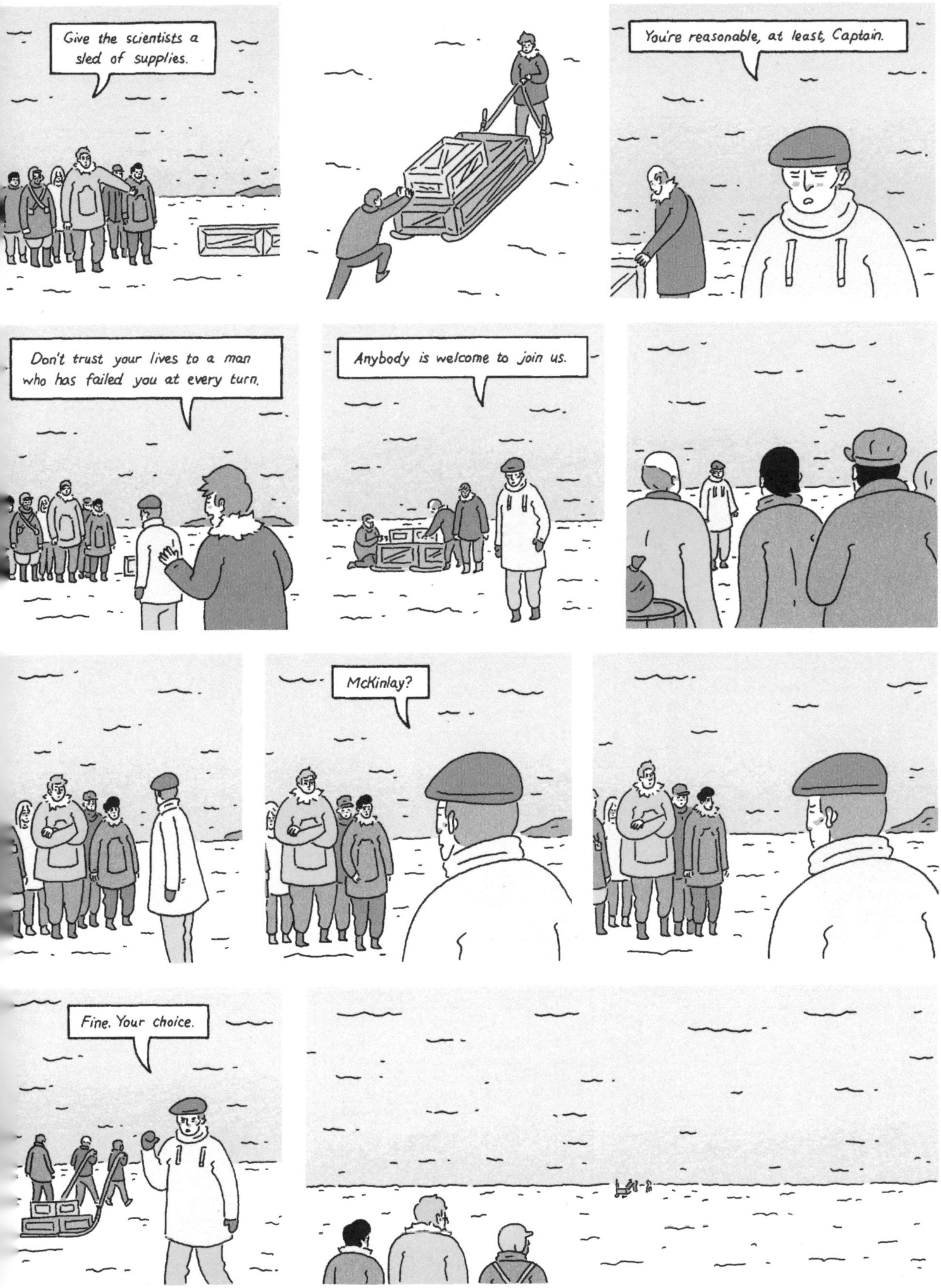

Give the scientists a sled of supplies.
You're reasonable, at least, Captain.
Don't trust your lives to a man who has failed you at every turn.
Anybody is welcome to join us.
McKinlay?
Fine. Your choice.

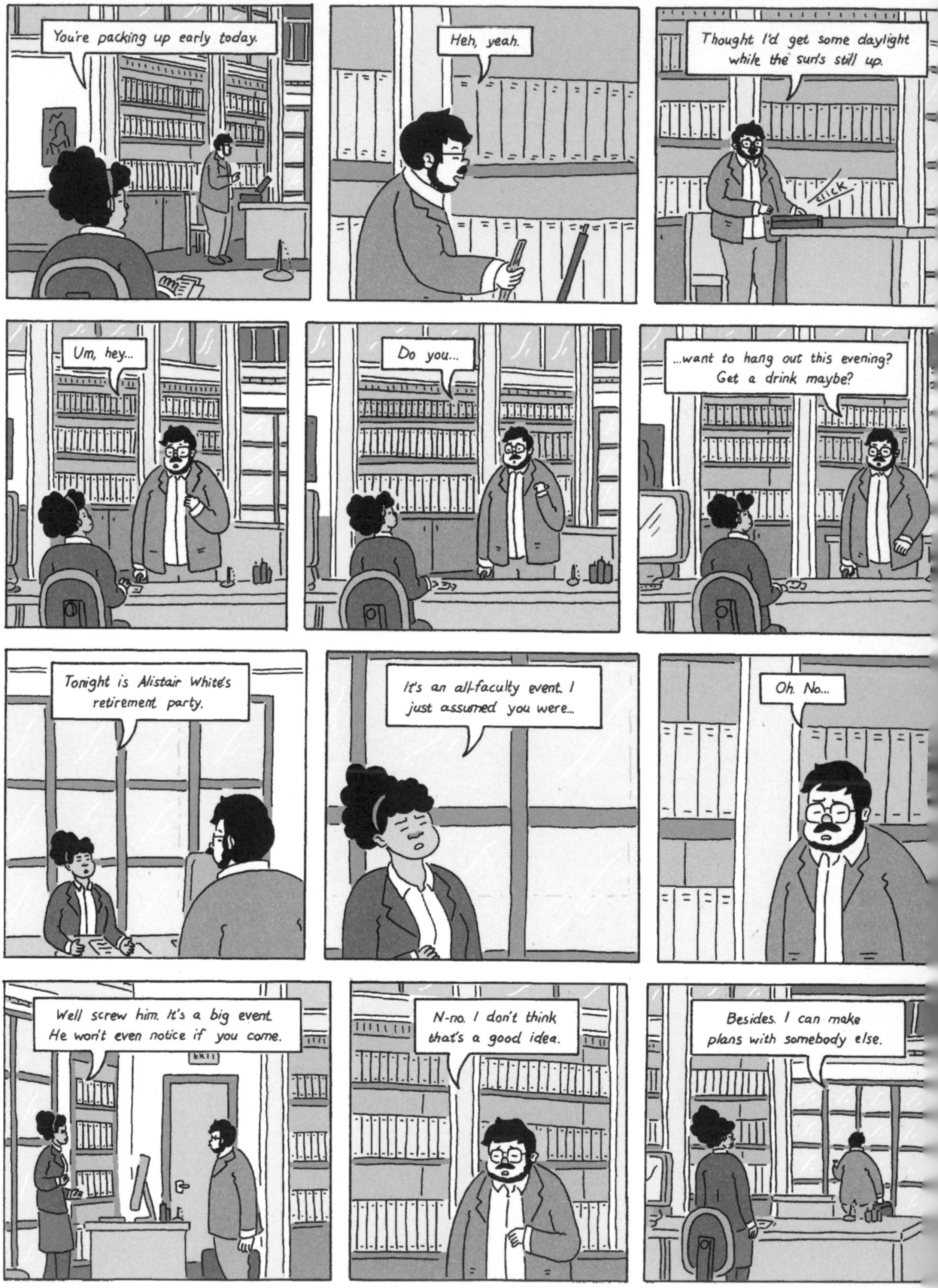
You're packing up early today.
Heh, yeah.
Thought I'd get some daylight while the sun's still up.
CLICK
Um, hey...
Do you...
...want to hang out this evening? Get a drink maybe?
Tonight is Alistair White's retirement party.
It's an all-faculty event. I just assumed you were...
Oh. No...
Well screw him. It's a big event. He won't even notice if you come.
EXIT
N-no. I don't think that's a good idea.
Besides. I can make plans with somebody else.

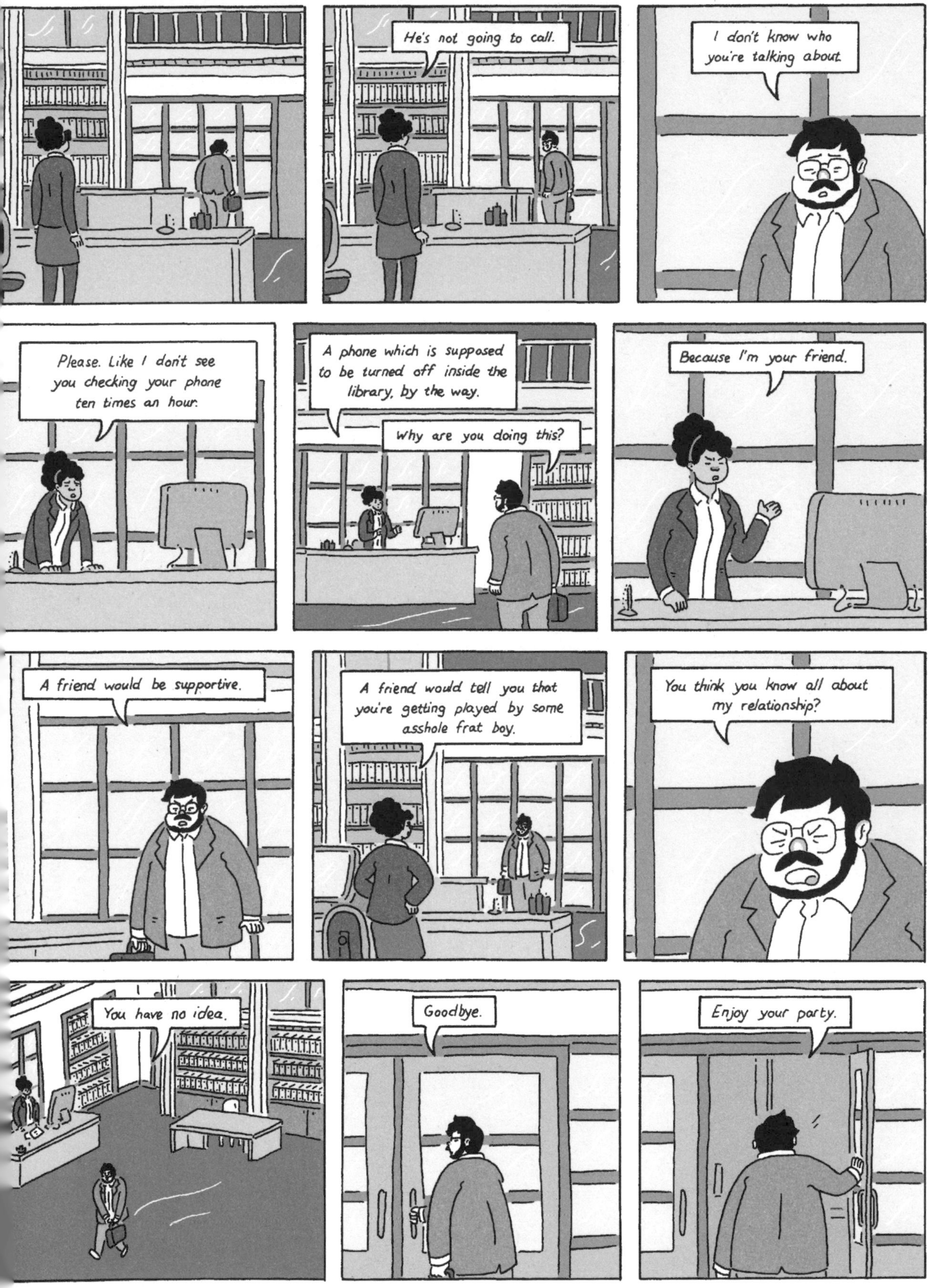
He's not going to call.
I don't know who you're talking about.
Please. Like I don't see you checking your phone ten times an hour.
A phone which is supposed to be turned off inside the library, by the way.
Why are you doing this?
Because I'm your friend.
A friend would be supportive.
A friend would tell you that you're getting played by some asshole frat boy.
You think you know all about my relationship?
You have no idea.
Goodbye.
Enjoy your party.

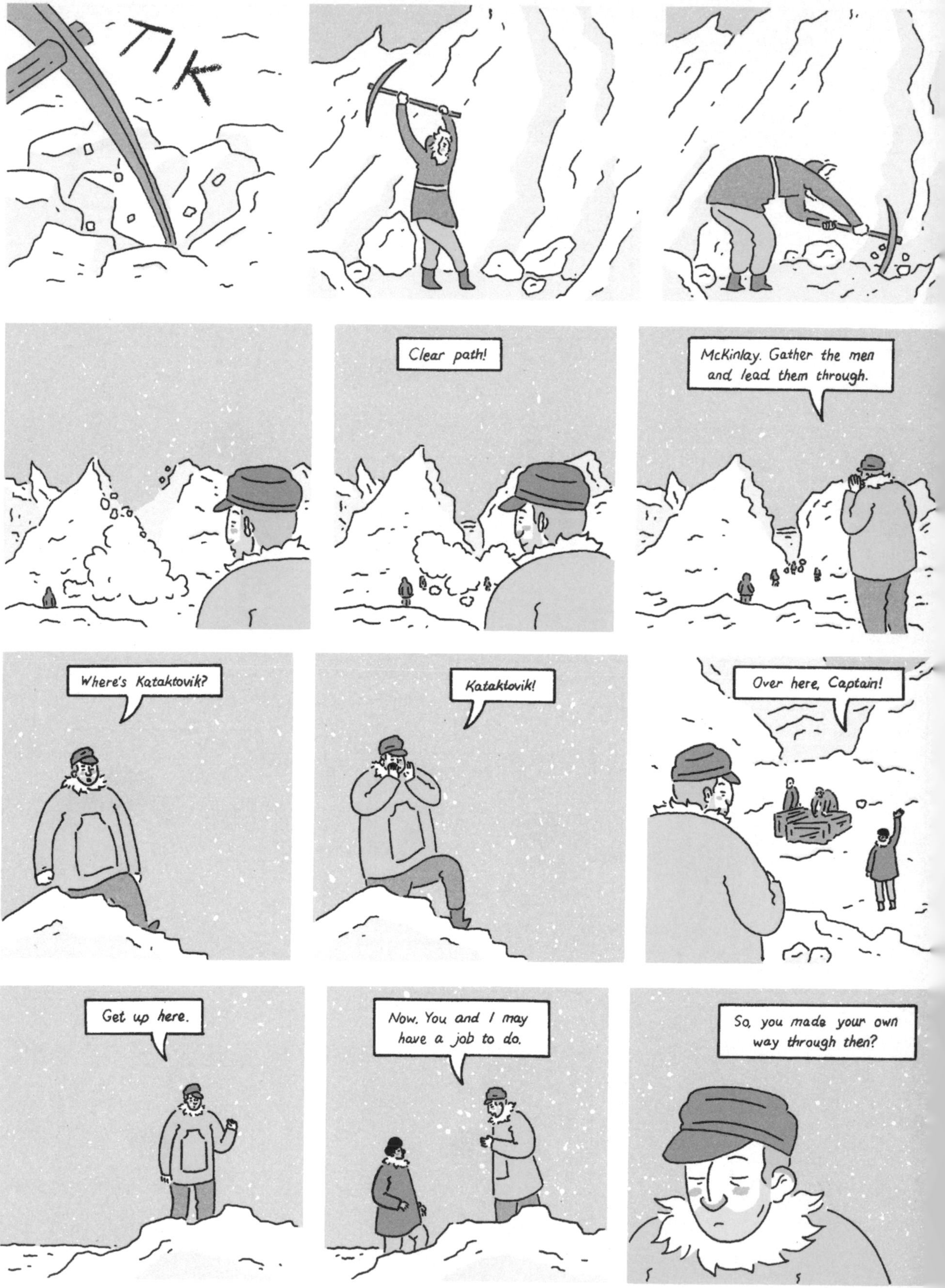
TIK
Clear path!
McKinlay. Gather the men and lead them through.
Where's Kataktovik?
Kataktovik!
Over here, Captain!
Get up here.
Now. You and I may have a job to do.
So, you made your own way through then?

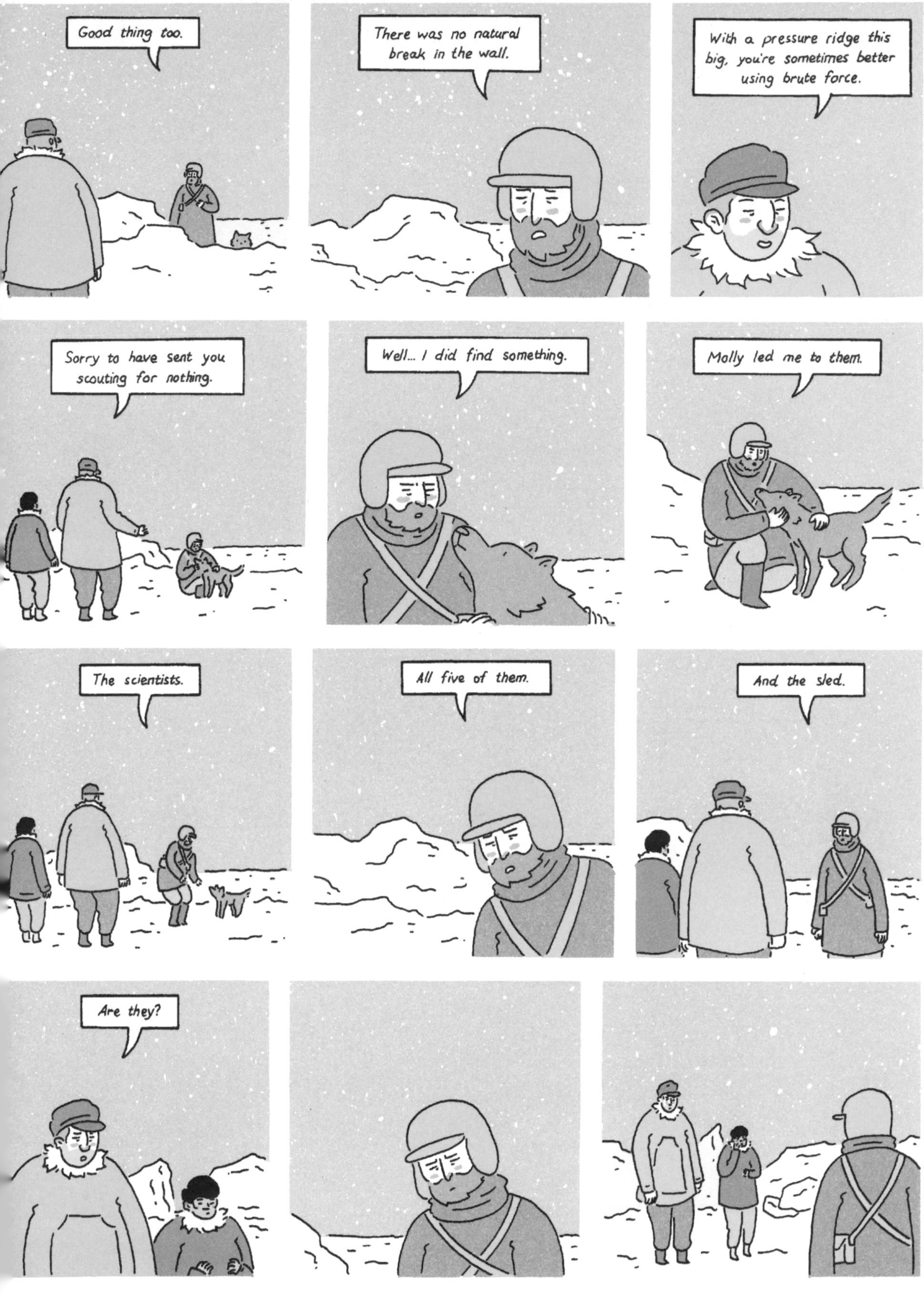
Good thing too.
There was no natural break in the wall.
With a pressure ridge this big, you're sometimes better using brute force.
Sorry to have sent you scouting for nothing.
Well... I did find something.
Molly led me to them.
The scientists.
All five of them.
And the sled.
Are they?

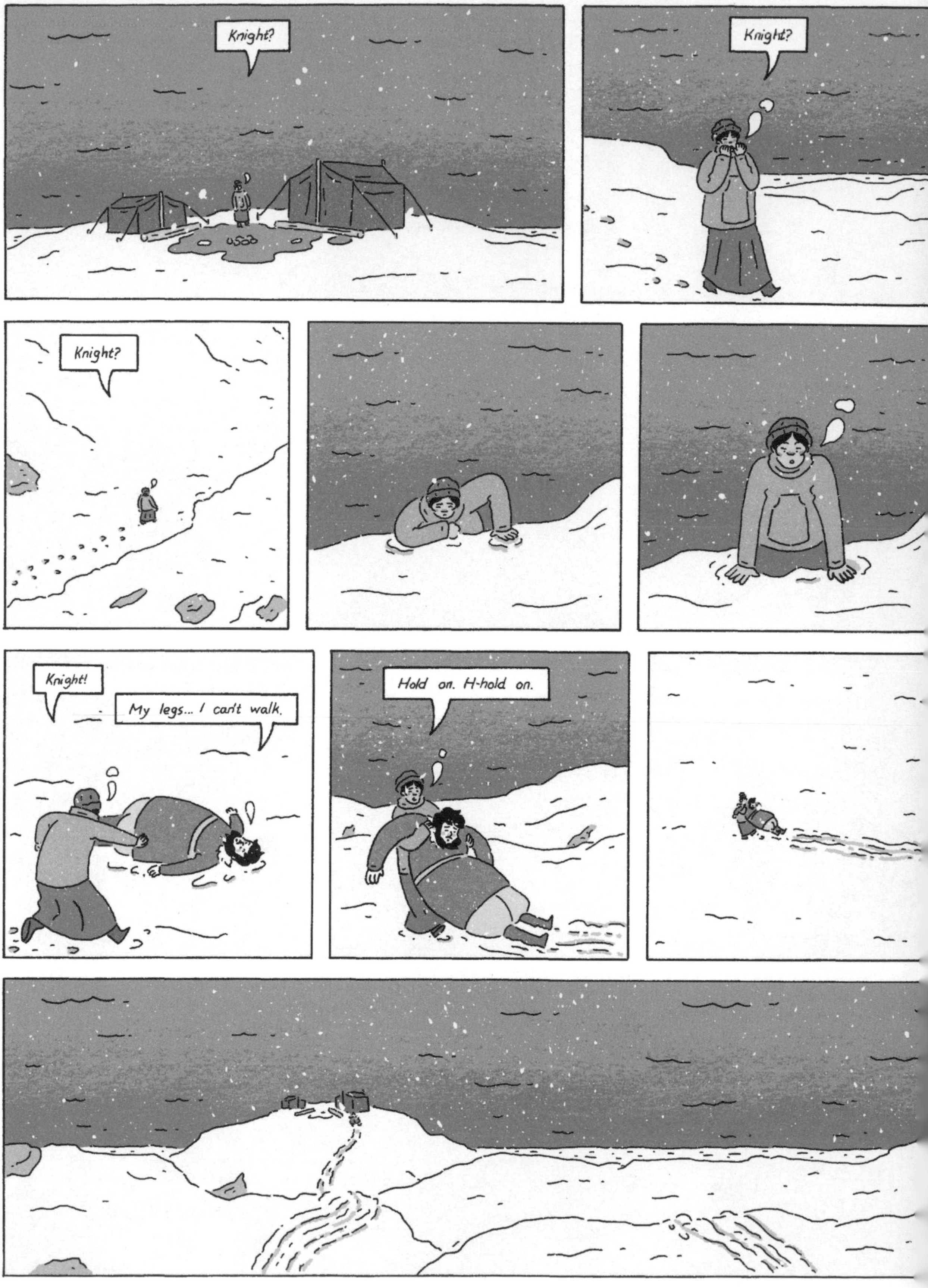
Knight?
Knight?
Knight?
Knight!
My legs... I can't walk.
Hold on. H-hold on.

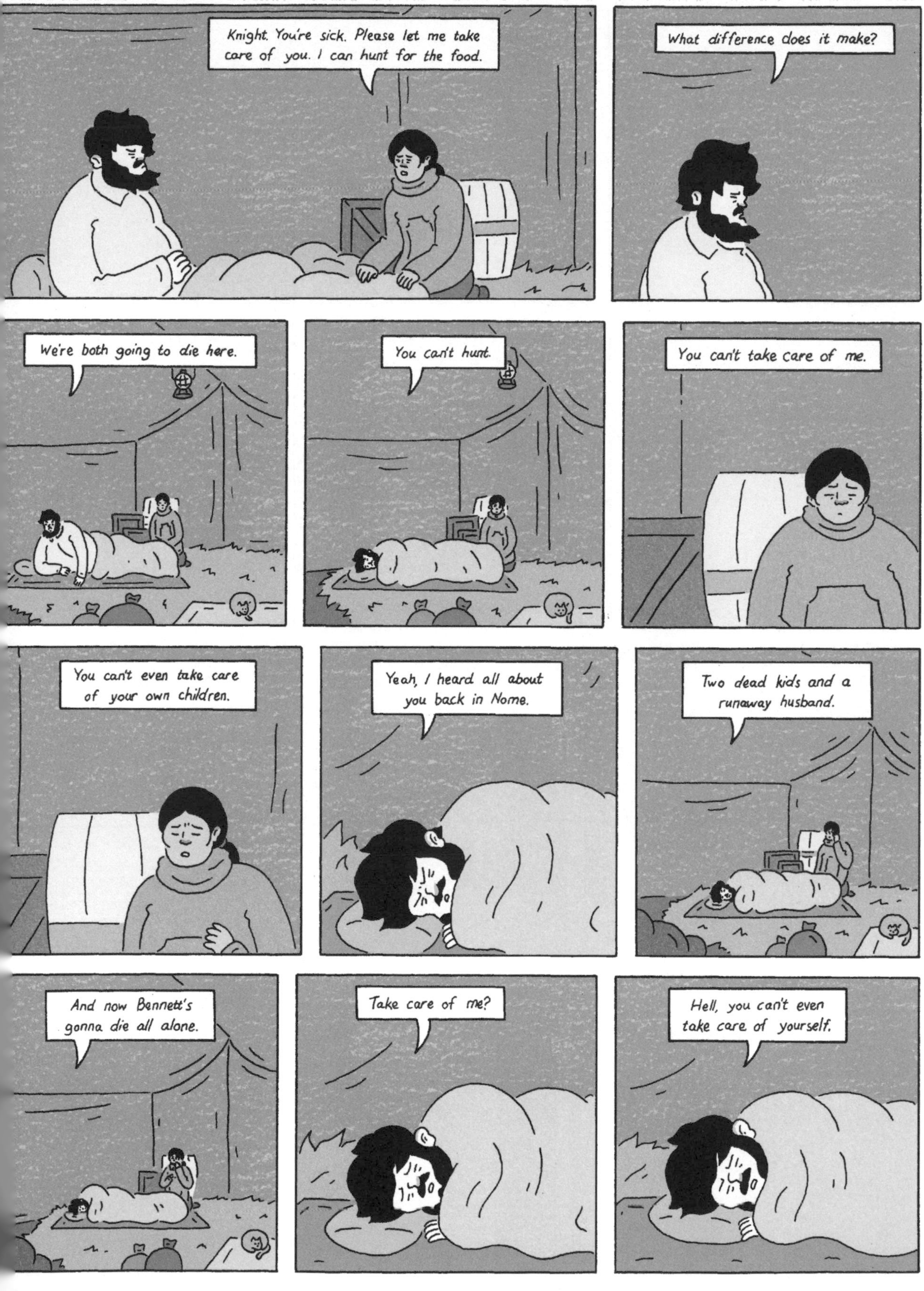
Knight. You're sick. Please let me take care of you. I can hunt for the food.
What difference does it make?
We're both going to die here.
You can't hunt.
You can't take care of me.
You can't even take care of your own children.
Yeah, I heard all about you back in Nome.
Two dead kids and a runaway husband.
And now Bennett's gonna die all alone.
Take care of me?
Hell, you can't even take care of yourself.

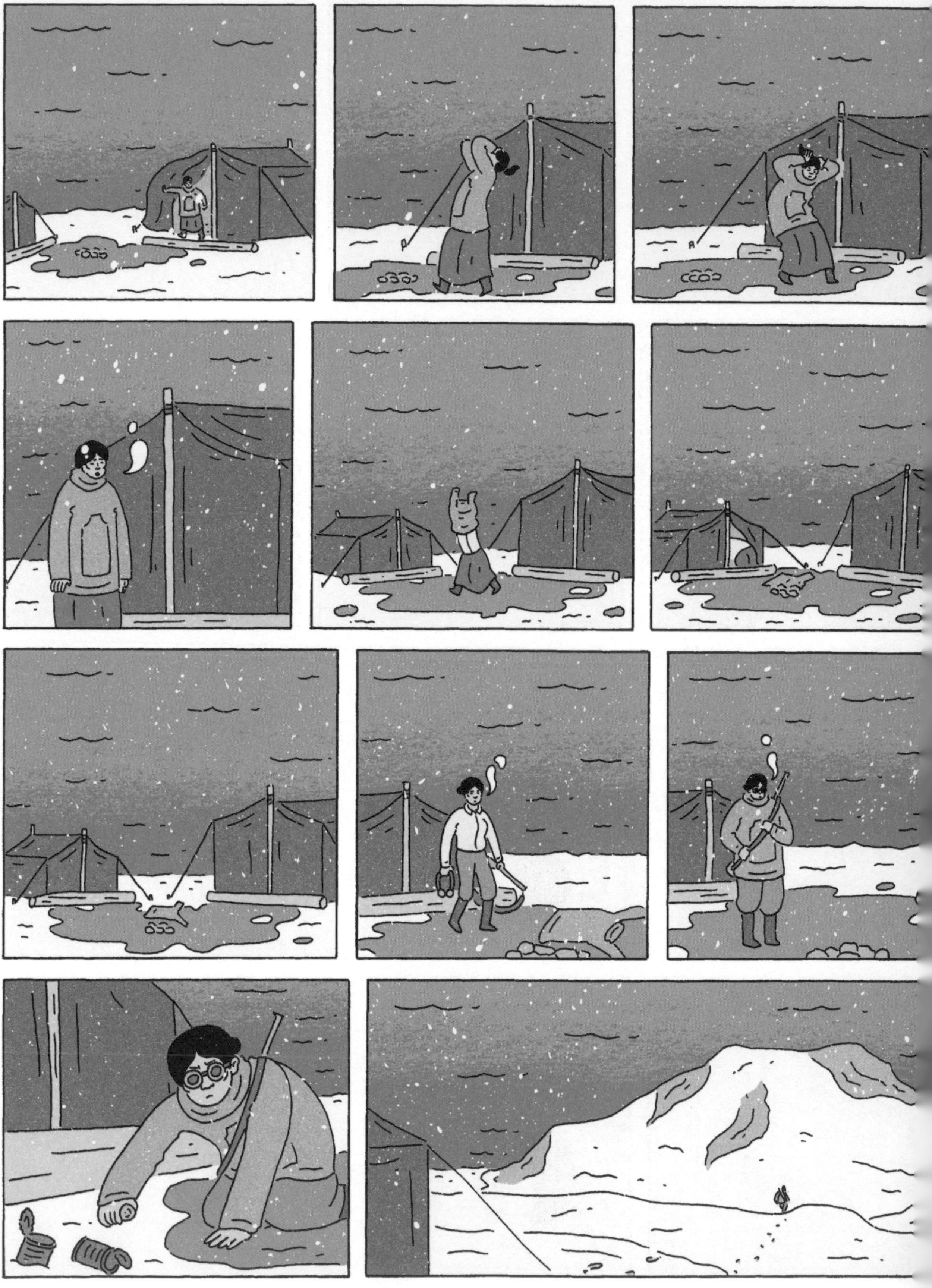

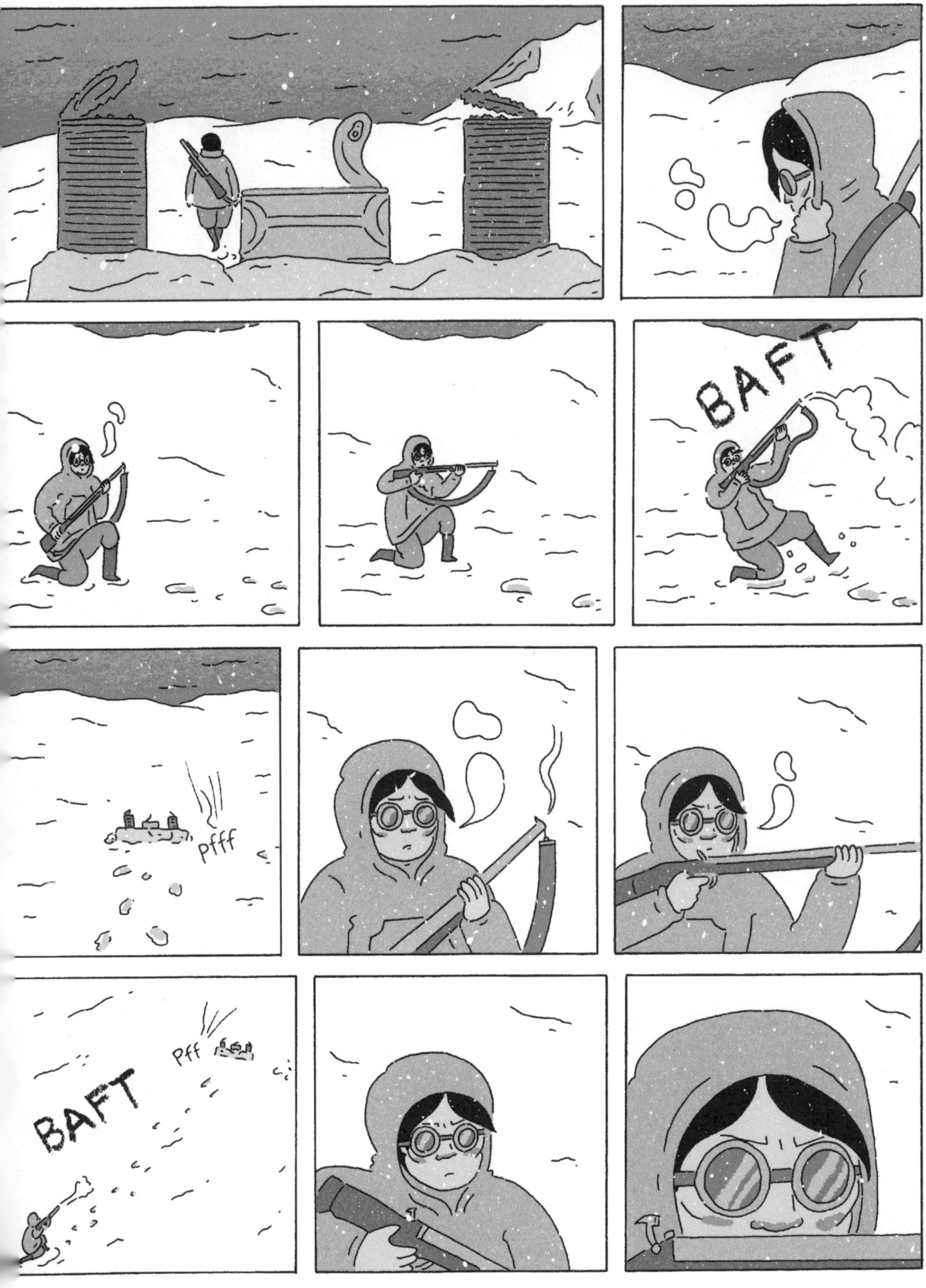
BAFT
pfff
BAFT
Pff

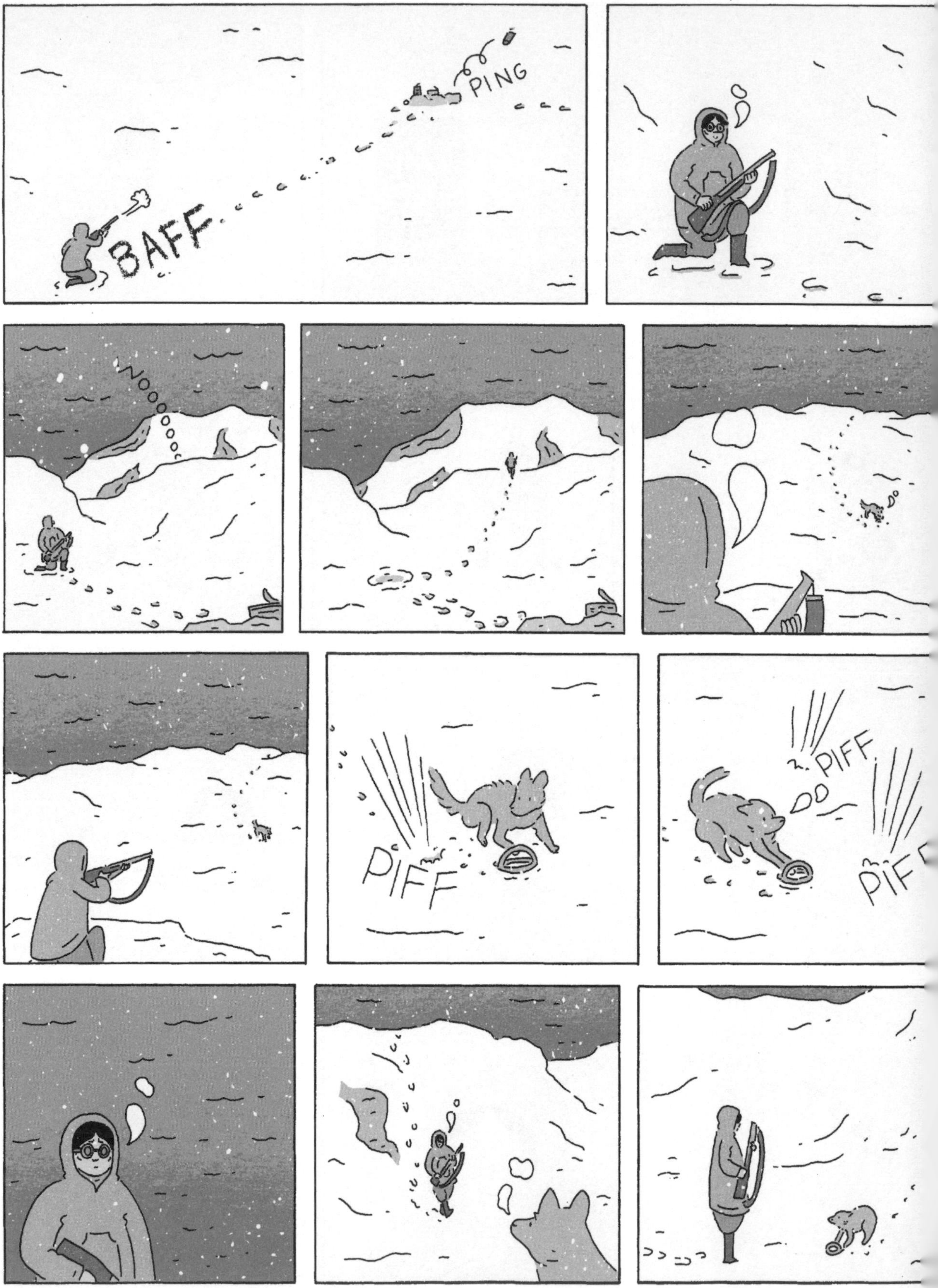
PING
BAFF
NOOOOOOO
PIFF
PIFF
PIFF

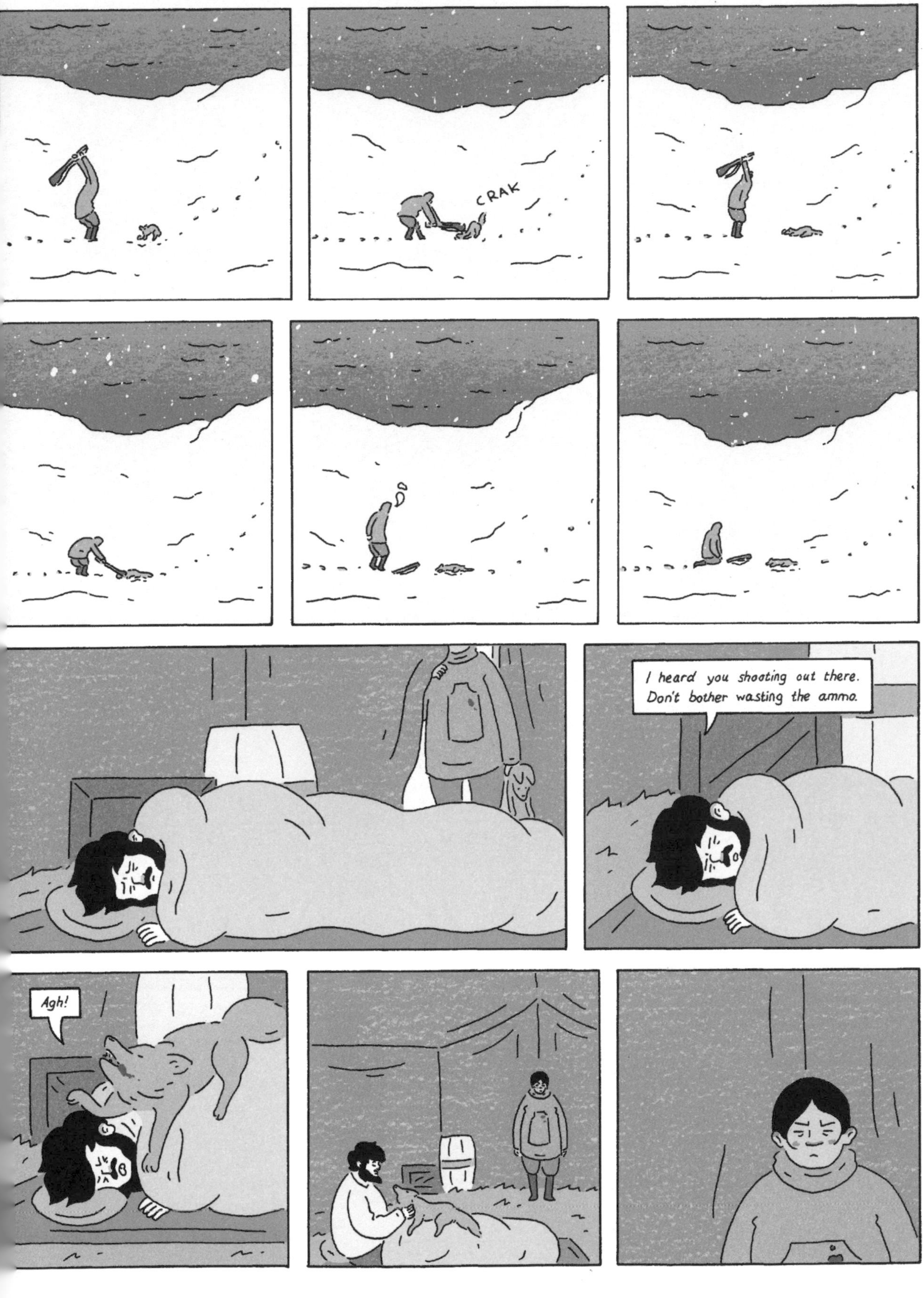
CRAK
I heard you shooting out there. Don't bother wasting the ammo.
Agh!

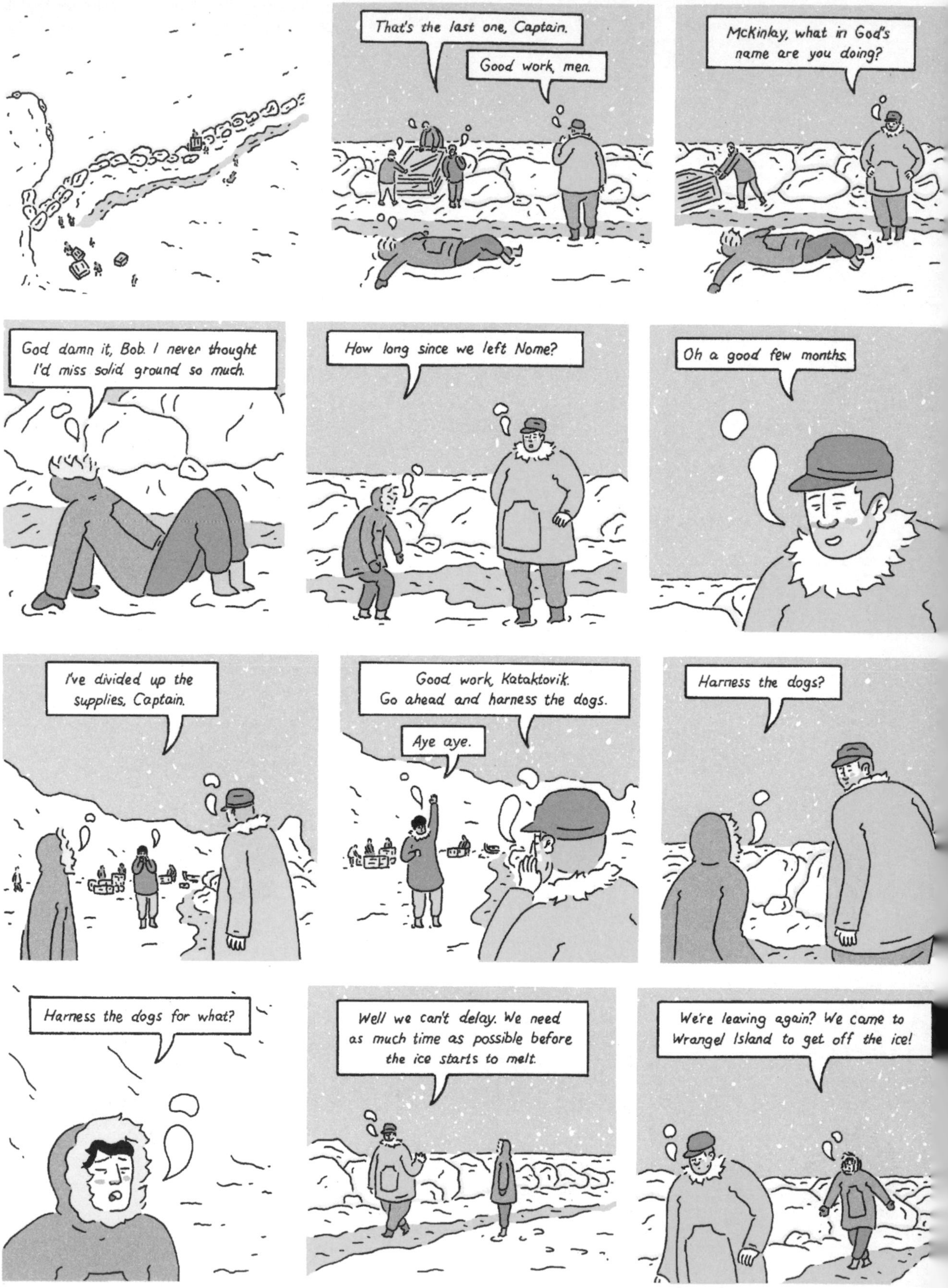

That's the last one, Captain.
Good work, men.
McKinlay, what in God's name are you doing?
God damn it, Bob. I never thought I'd miss solid ground so much.
How long since we left Nome?
Oh a good few months.
I've divided up the supplies, Captain.
Good work, Kataktovik. Go ahead and harness the dogs.
Aye aye.
Harness the dogs?
Harness the dogs for what?
Well we can't delay. We need as much time as possible before the ice starts to melt.
We're leaving again? We came to Wrangel Island to get off the ice!

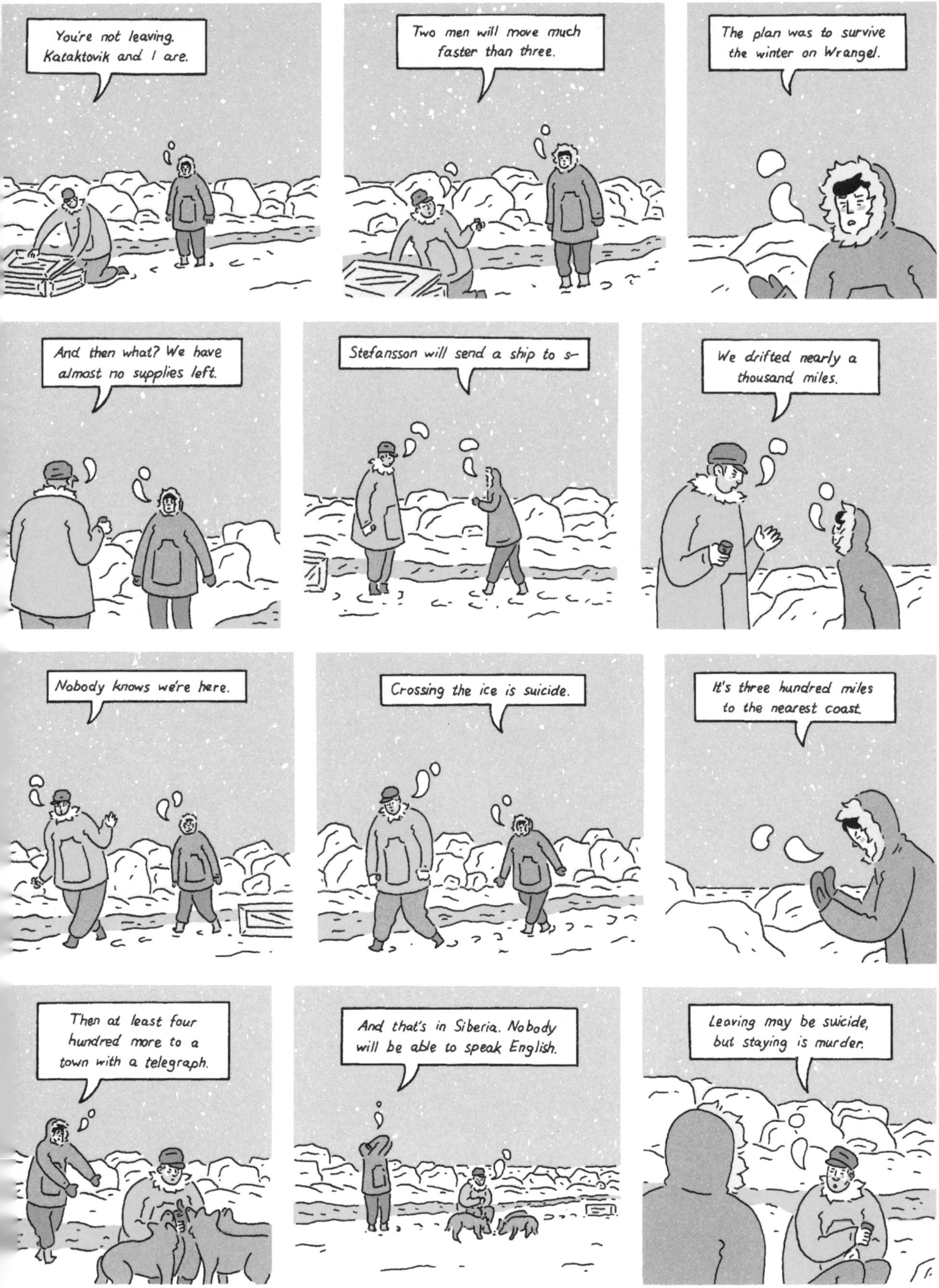
You're not leaving. Kataktovik and I are.
Two men will move much faster than three.
The plan was to survive the winter on Wrangel.
And then what? We have almost no supplies left.
Stefansson will send a ship to s-
We drifted nearly a thousand miles.
Nobody knows we're here.
Crossing the ice is suicide.
It's three hundred miles to the nearest coast.
Then at least four hundred more to a town with a telegraph.
And that's in Siberia. Nobody will be able to speak English.
Leaving may be suicide, but staying is murder.

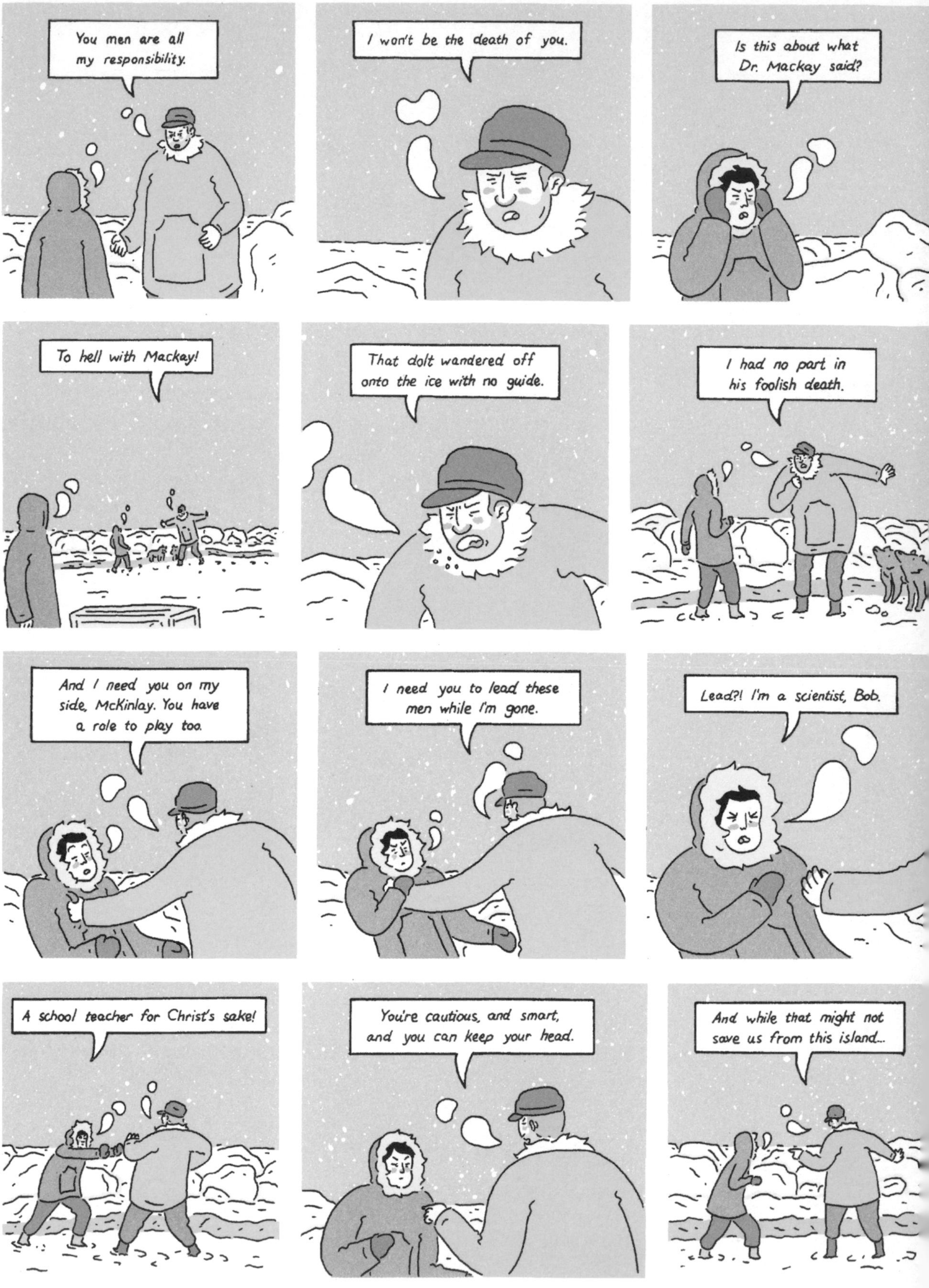
You men are all my responsibility.
I won't be the death of you.
Is this about what Dr. Mackay said?
To hell with Mackay!
That dolt wandered off onto the ice with no guide.
I had no part in his foolish death.
And I need you on my side, McKinlay. You have a role to play too.
I need you to lead these men while I'm gone.
Lead?! I'm a scientist, Bob.
A school teacher for Christ's sake!
You're cautious, and smart, and you can keep your head.
And while that might not save us from this island...

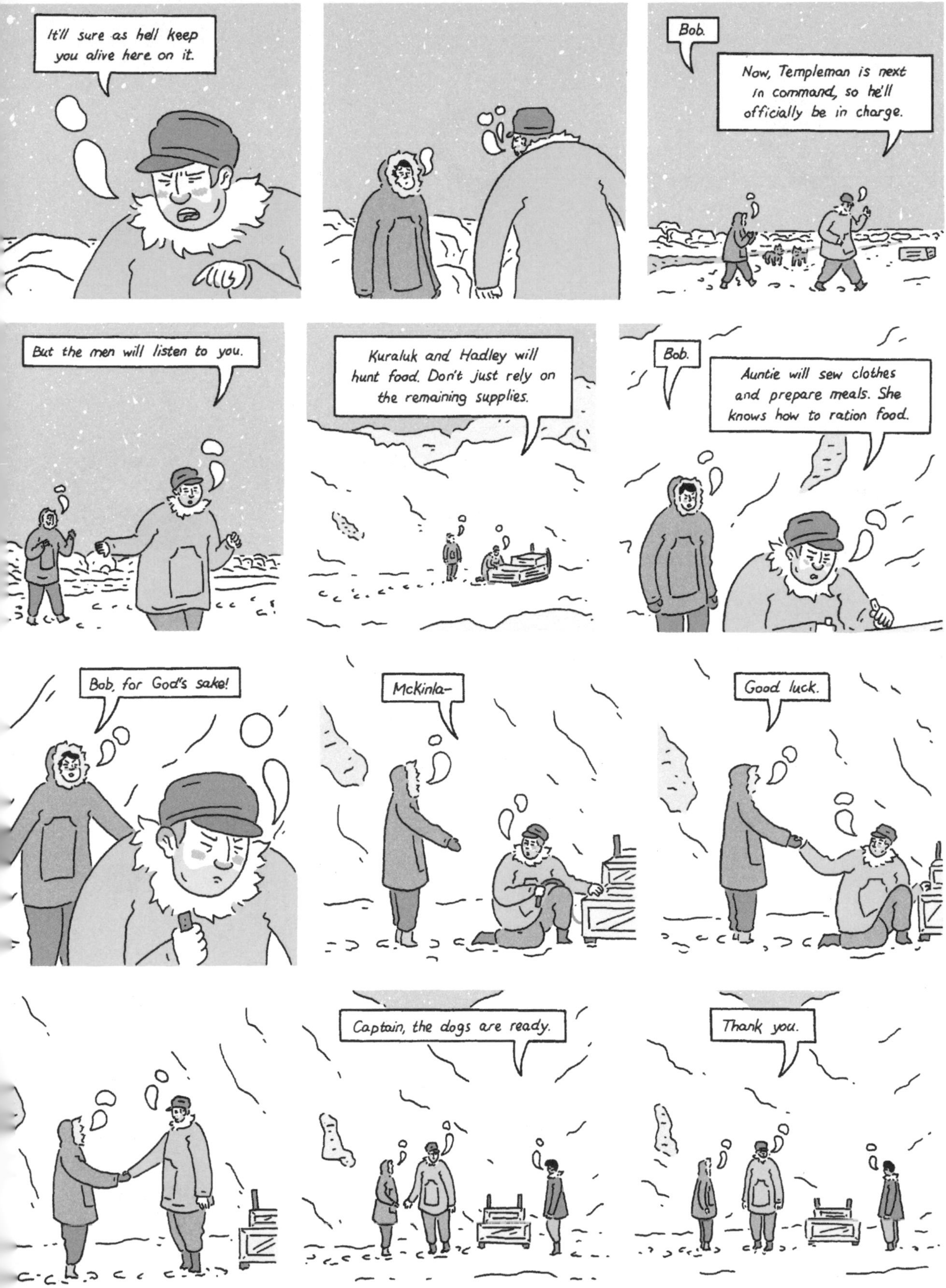

It'll sure as hell keep you alive here on it.
Bob.
Now, Templeman is next in command, so he'll officially be in charge.
But the men will listen to you.
Kuraluk and Hadley will hunt food. Don't just rely on the remaining supplies.
Bob.
Auntie will sew clothes and prepare meals. She knows how to ration food.
Bob, for God's sake!
McKinla-
Good luck.
Captain, the dogs are ready.
Thank you.

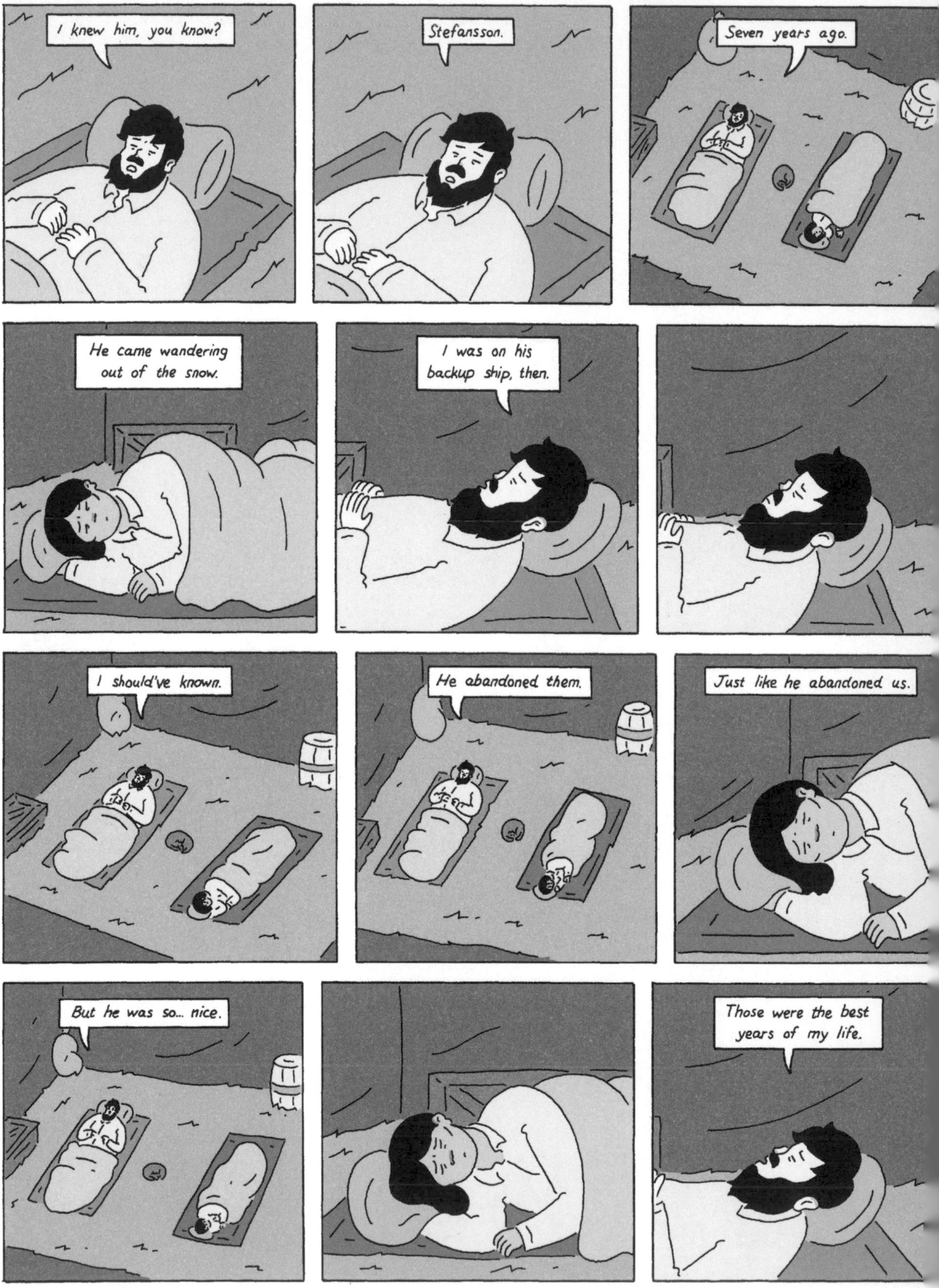

I knew him, you know?
Stefansson.
Seven years ago.
He came wandering out of the snow.
I was on his backup ship, then.
I should've known.
He abandoned them.
Just like he abandoned us.
But he was so... nice.
Those were the best years of my life.

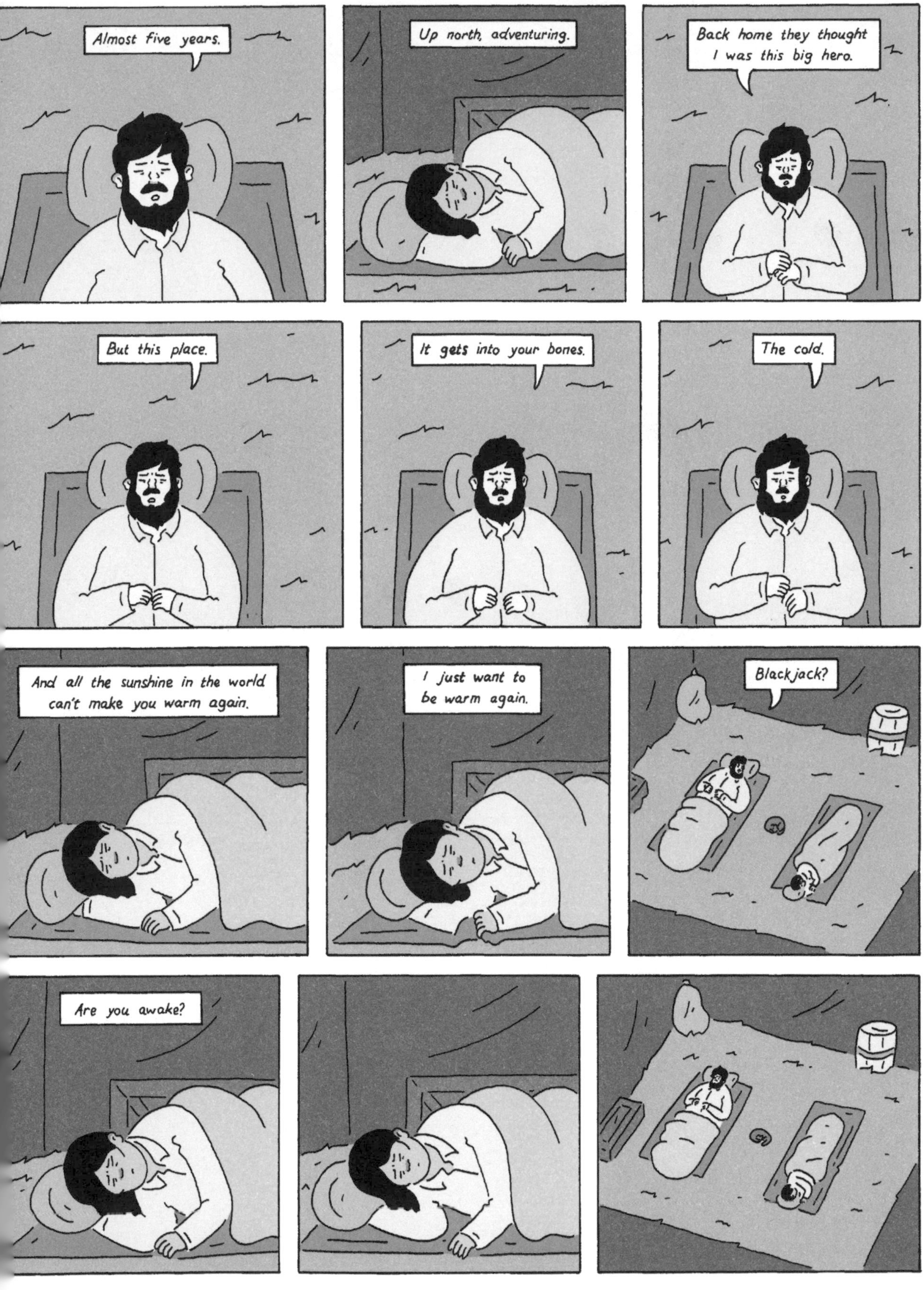
Almost five years.
Up north, adventuring.
Back home they thought I was this big hero.
But this place.
It gets into your bones.
The cold.
And all the sunshine in the world can't make you warm again.
I just want to be warm again.
Blackjack?
Are you awake?

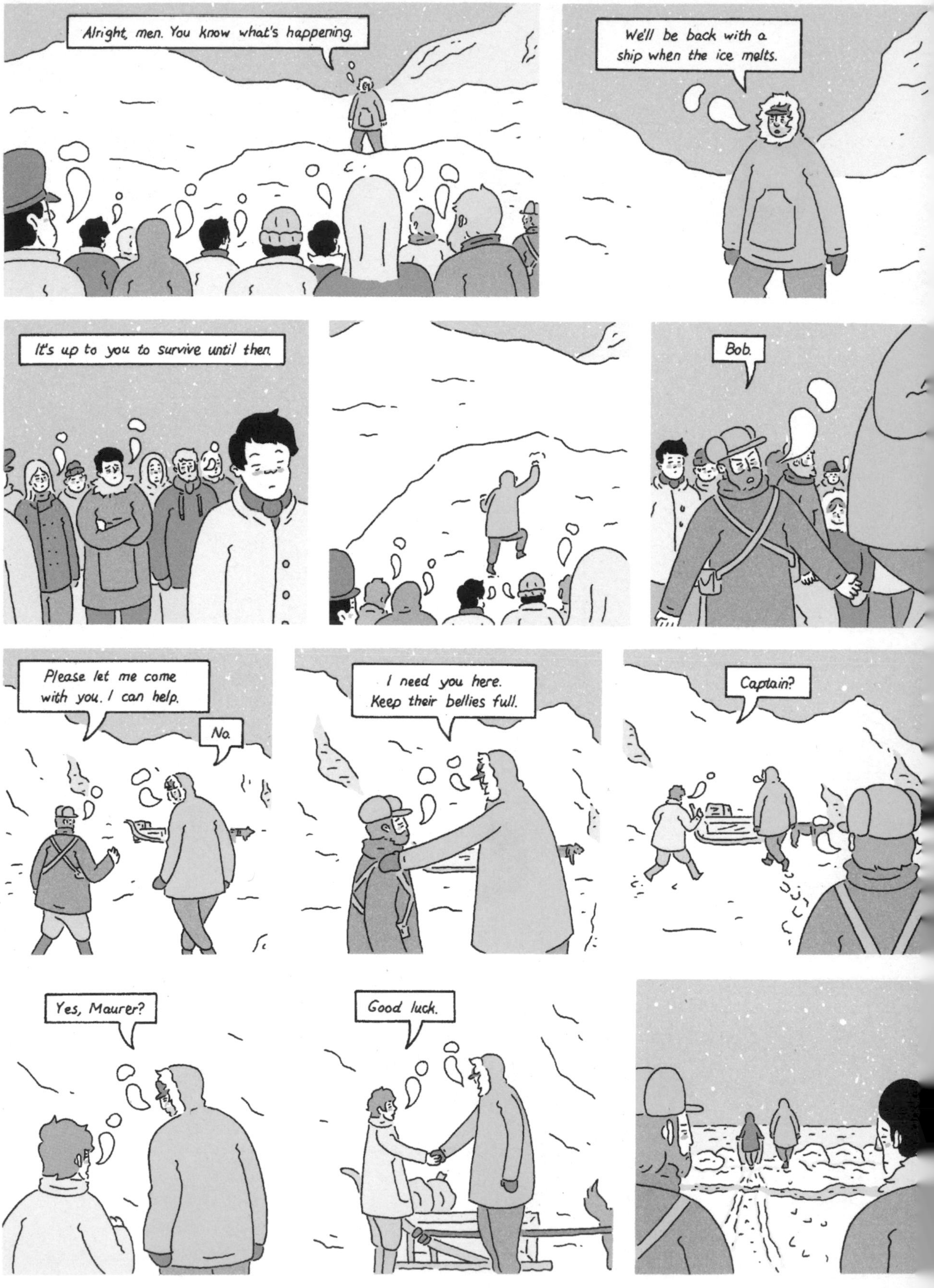
Alright, men. You know what's happening.
We'll be back with a ship when the ice melts.
It's up to you to survive until then.
Bob.
Please let me come with you. I can help.
No.
I need you here. Keep their bellies full.
Captain?
Yes, Maurer?
Good luck.

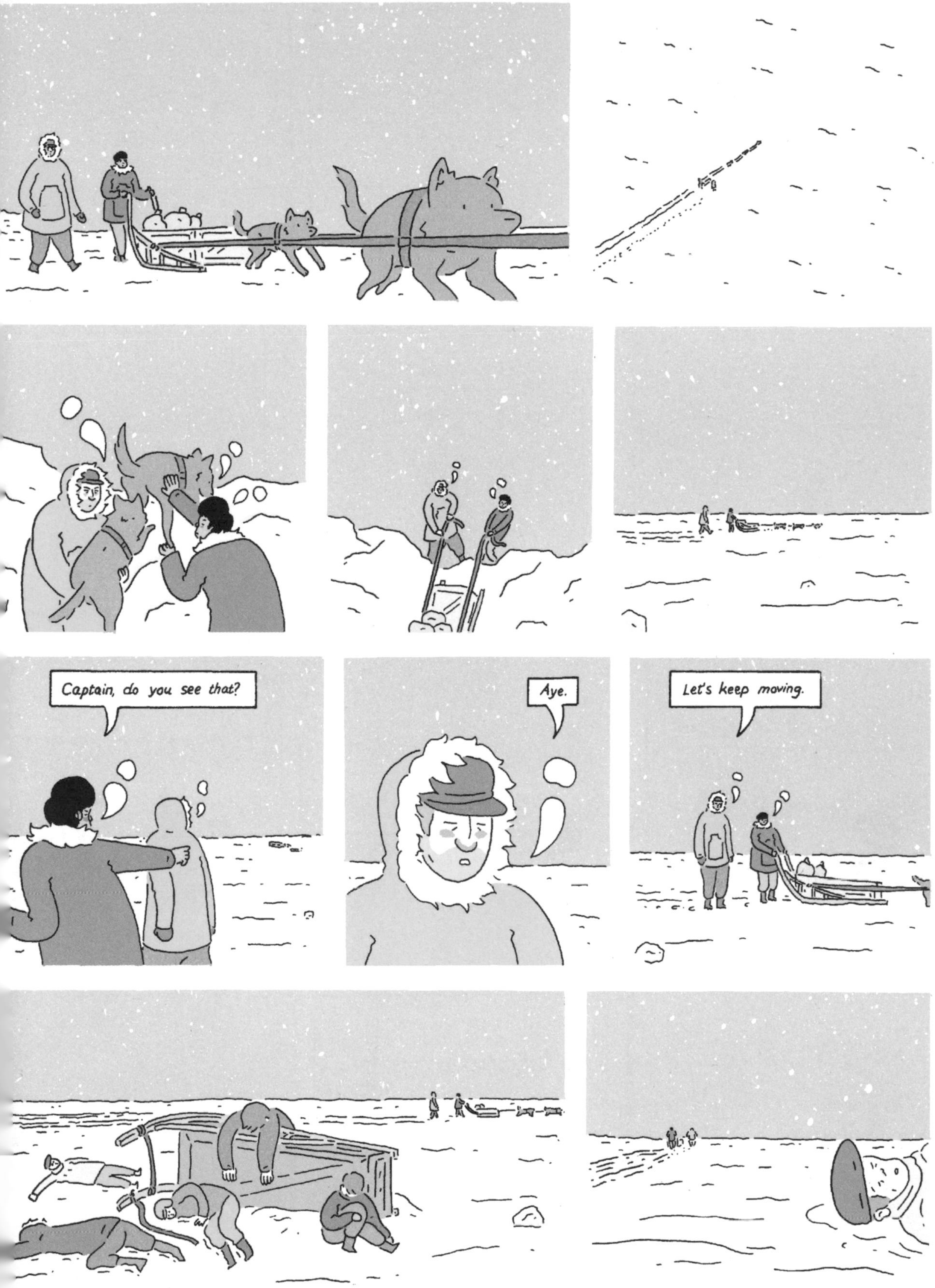
Captain, do you see that?
Aye.
Let's keep moving.

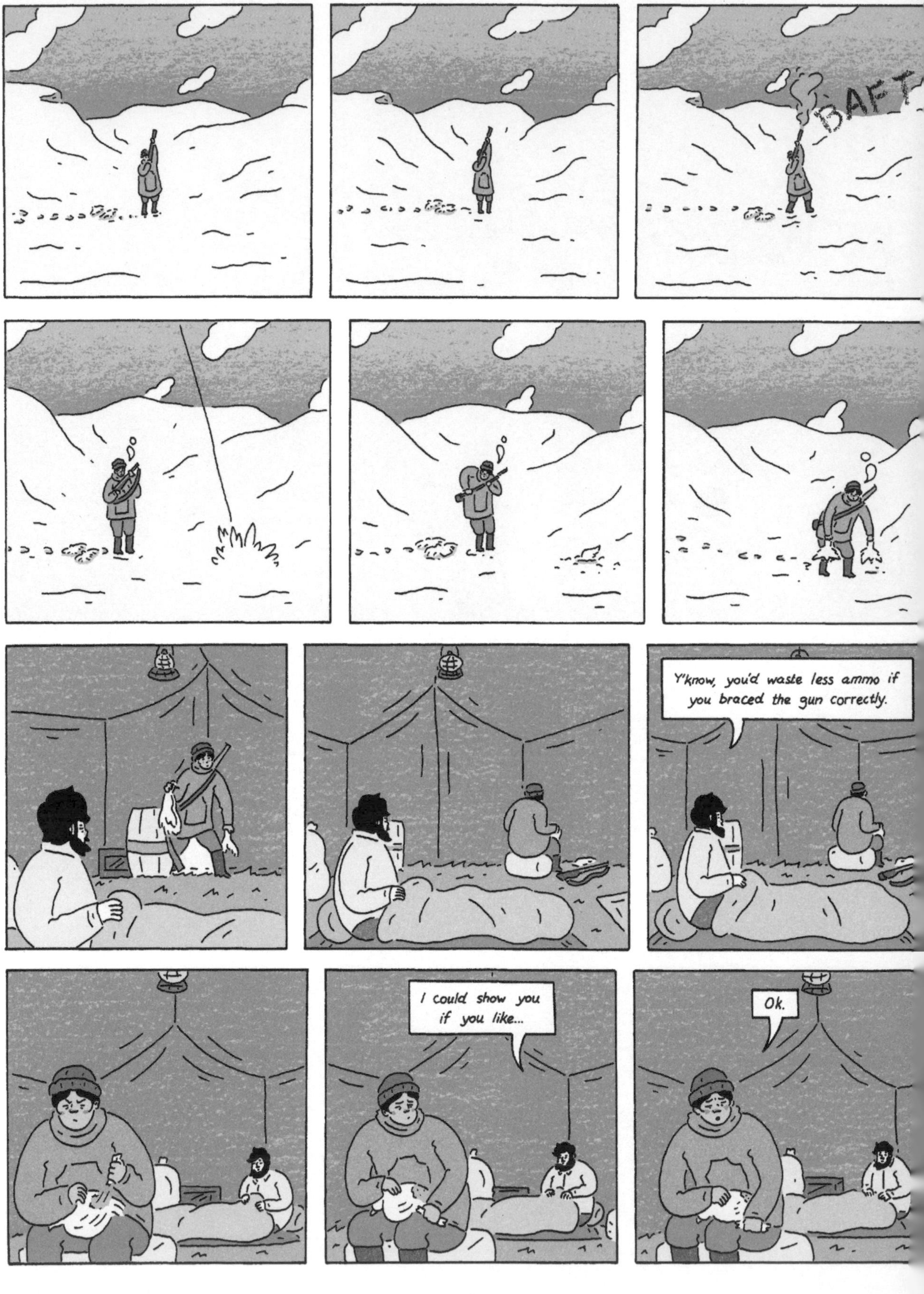
BAFT
Y'know, you'd waste less ammo if you braced the gun correctly.
I could show you if you like...
Ok.

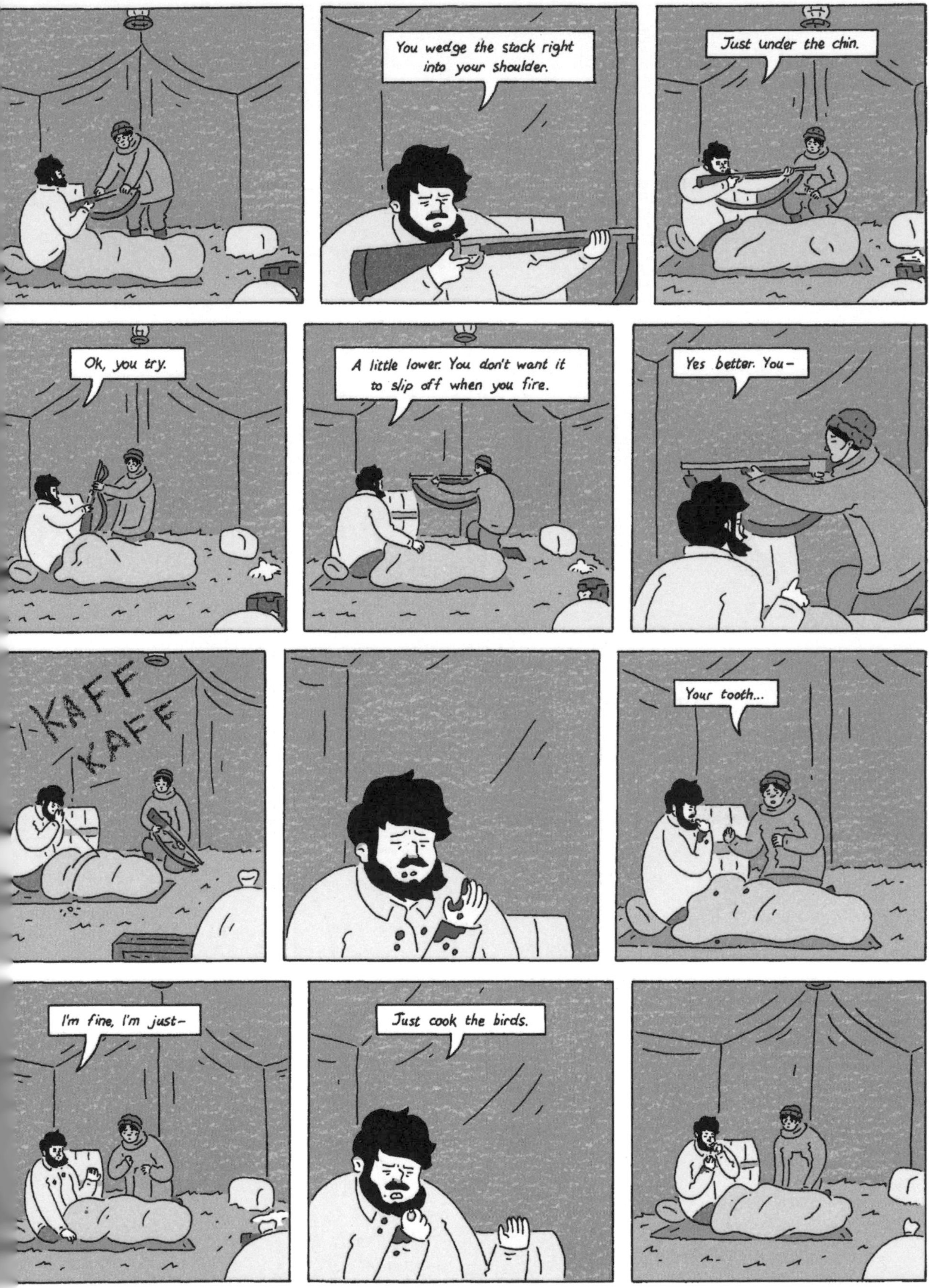
You wedge the stock right into your shoulder.
Just under the chin.
Ok, you try.
A little lower. You don't want it to slip off when you fire.
Yes better. You-
KAFF KAFF
Your tooth...
I'm fine, I'm just-
Just cook the birds.

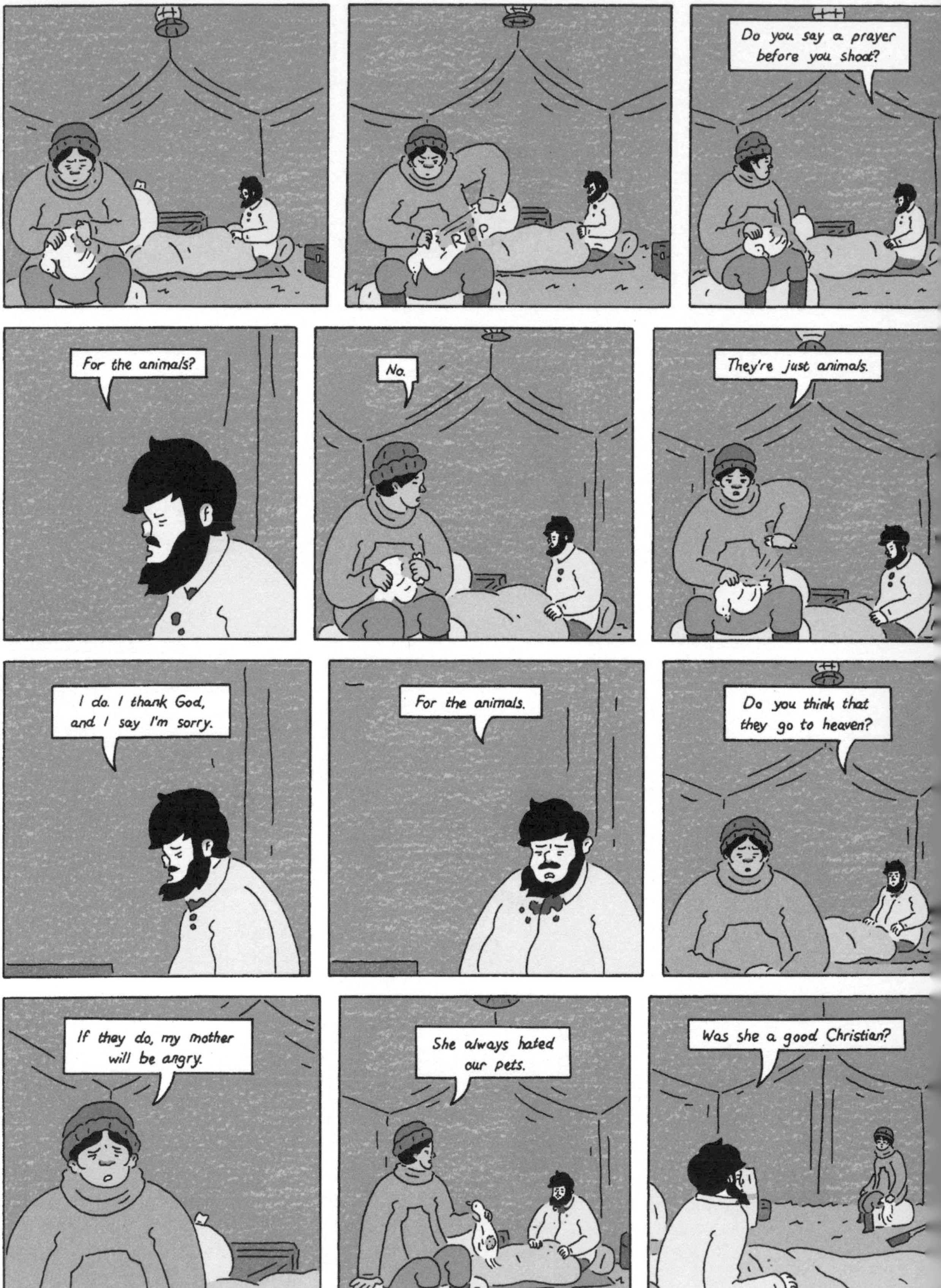
RIPP
Do you say a prayer before you shoot?
For the animals?
No.
They're just animals.
I do. I thank God, and I say I'm sorry.
For the animals.
Do you think that they go to heaven?
If they do, my mother will be angry.
She always hated our pets.
Was she a good Christian?

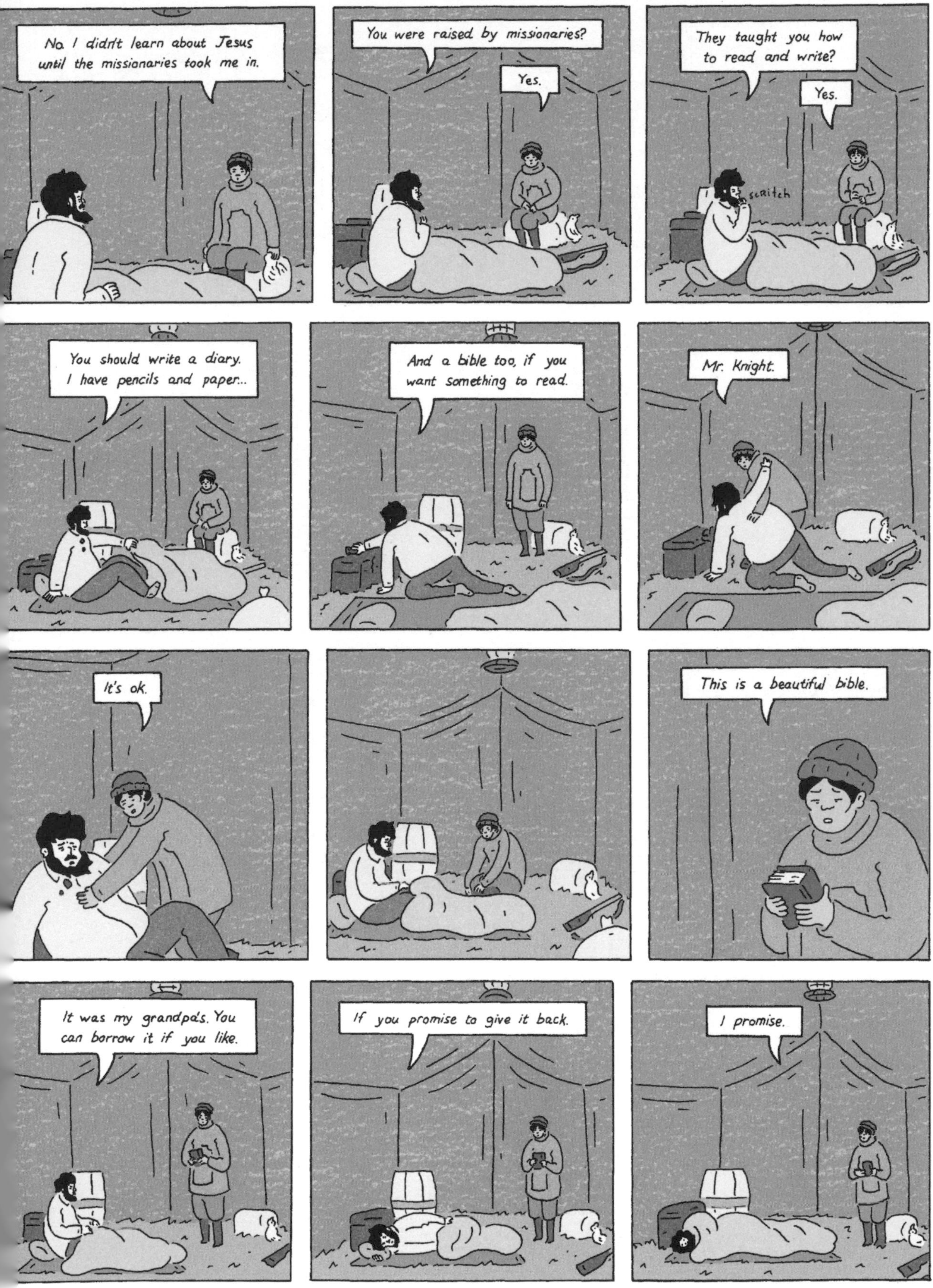
No. I didn't learn about Jesus until the missionaries took me in.
You were raised by missionaries?
Yes.
They taught you how to read and write?
Yes.
scritch
You should write a diary. I have pencils and paper...
And a bible too, if you want something to read.
Mr. Knight.
It's ok.
This is a beautiful bible.
It was my grandpa's. You can borrow it if you like.
If you promise to give it back.
I promise.

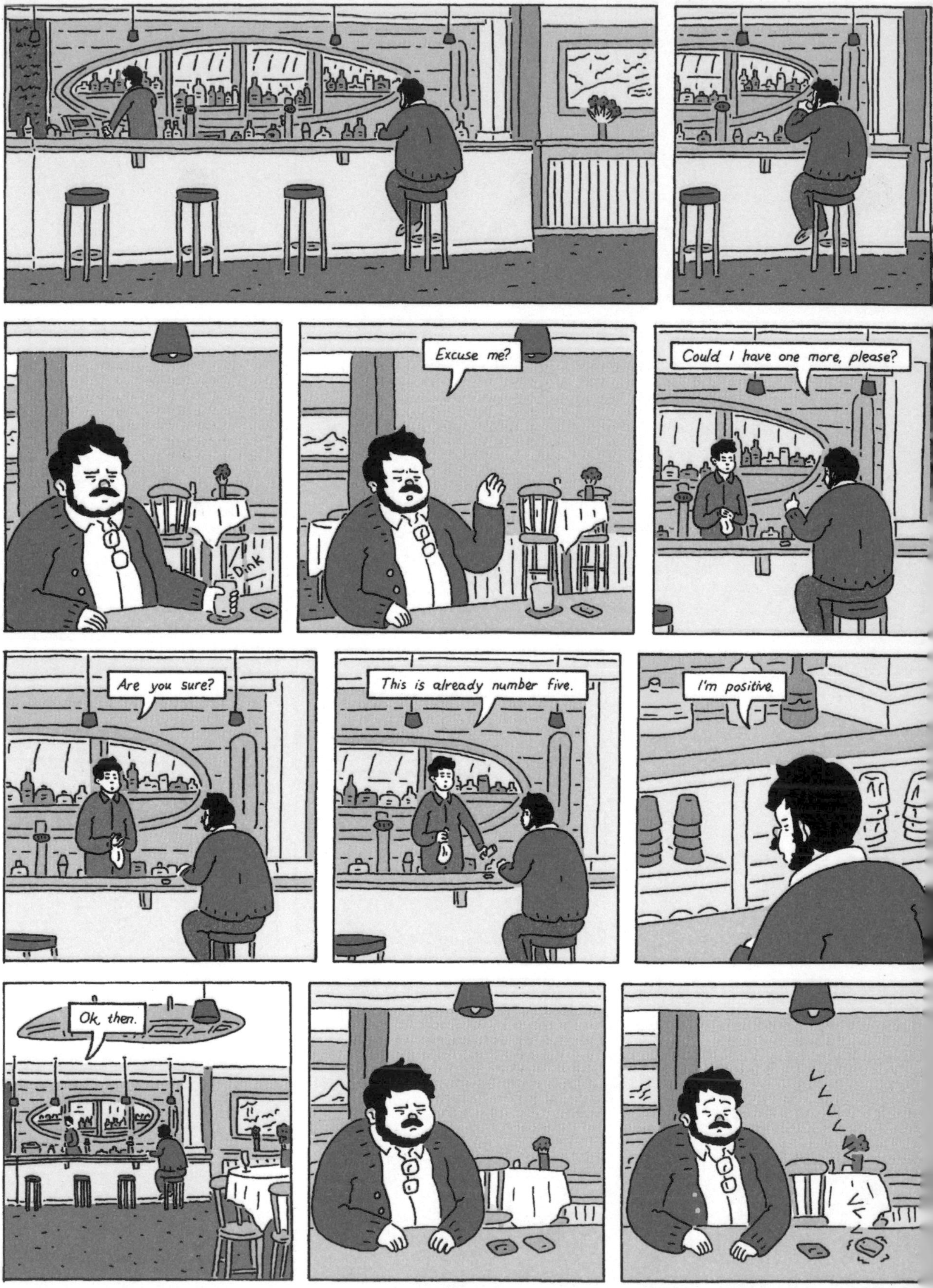
Dink
Excuse me?
Could I have one more, please?
Are you sure?
This is already number five.
I'm positive.
Ok, then.

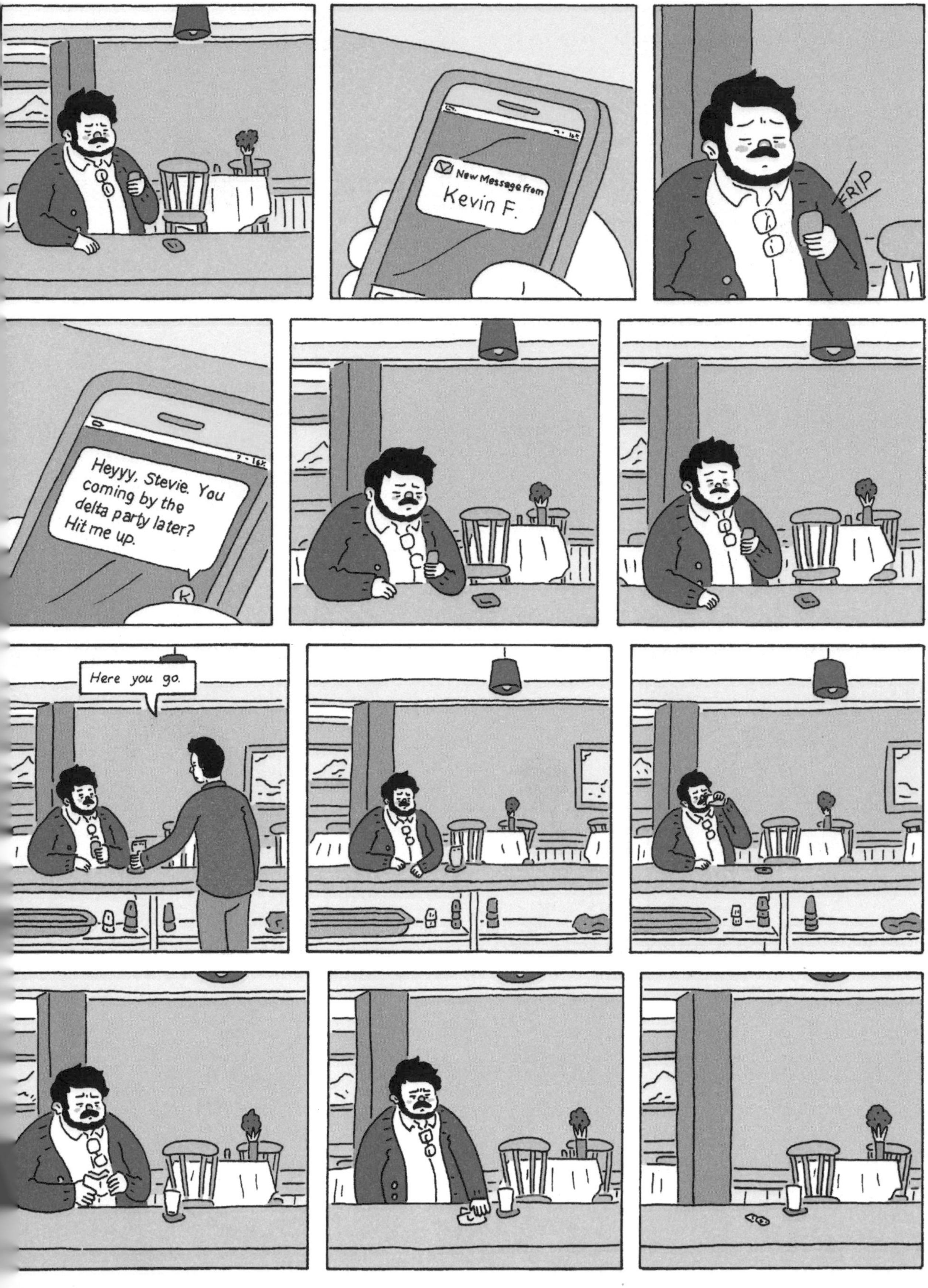
New Message from
Kevin F.
FRIP
Heyyy, Stevie. You coming by the delta party later? Hit me up.
Here you go.

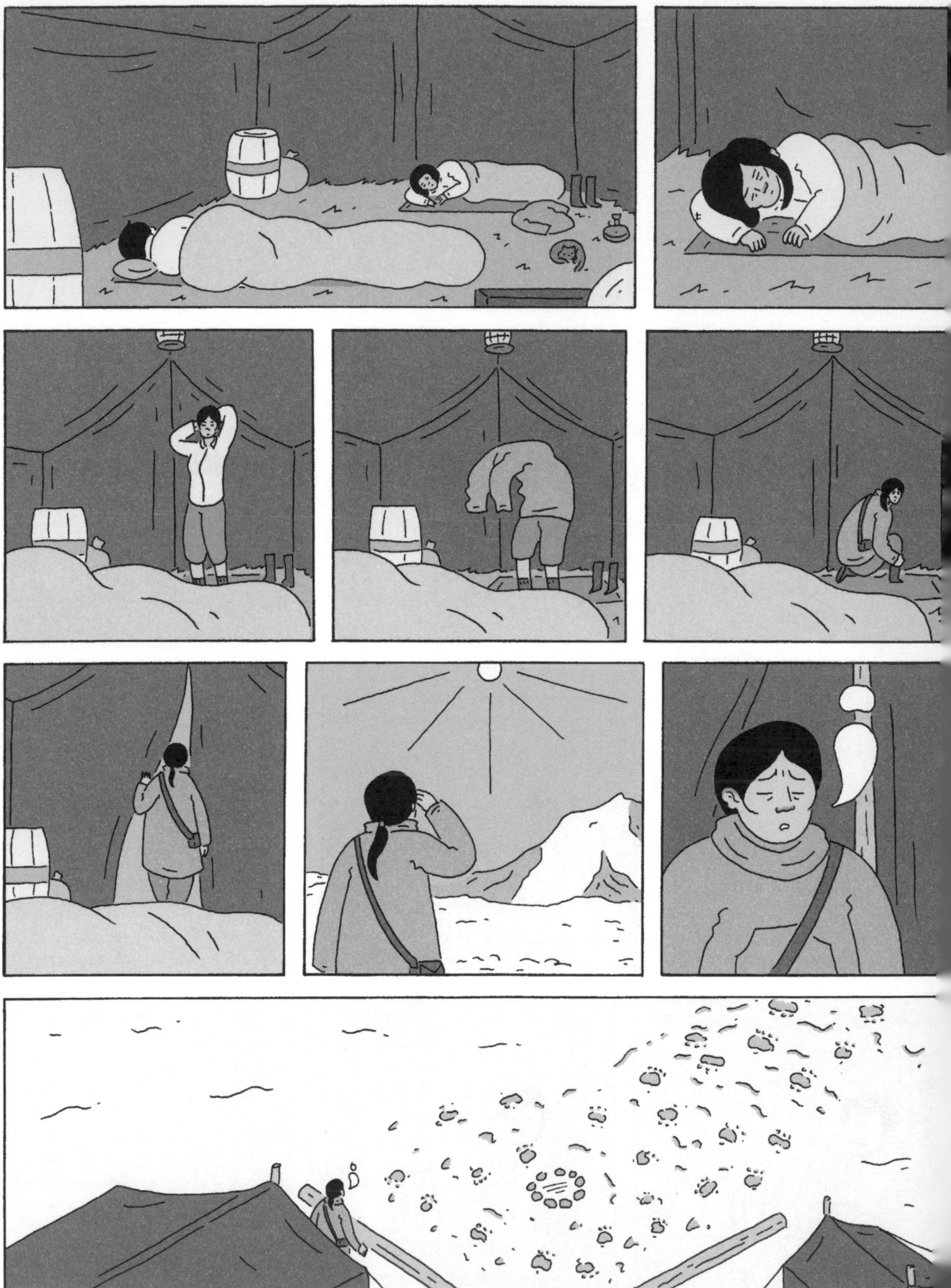

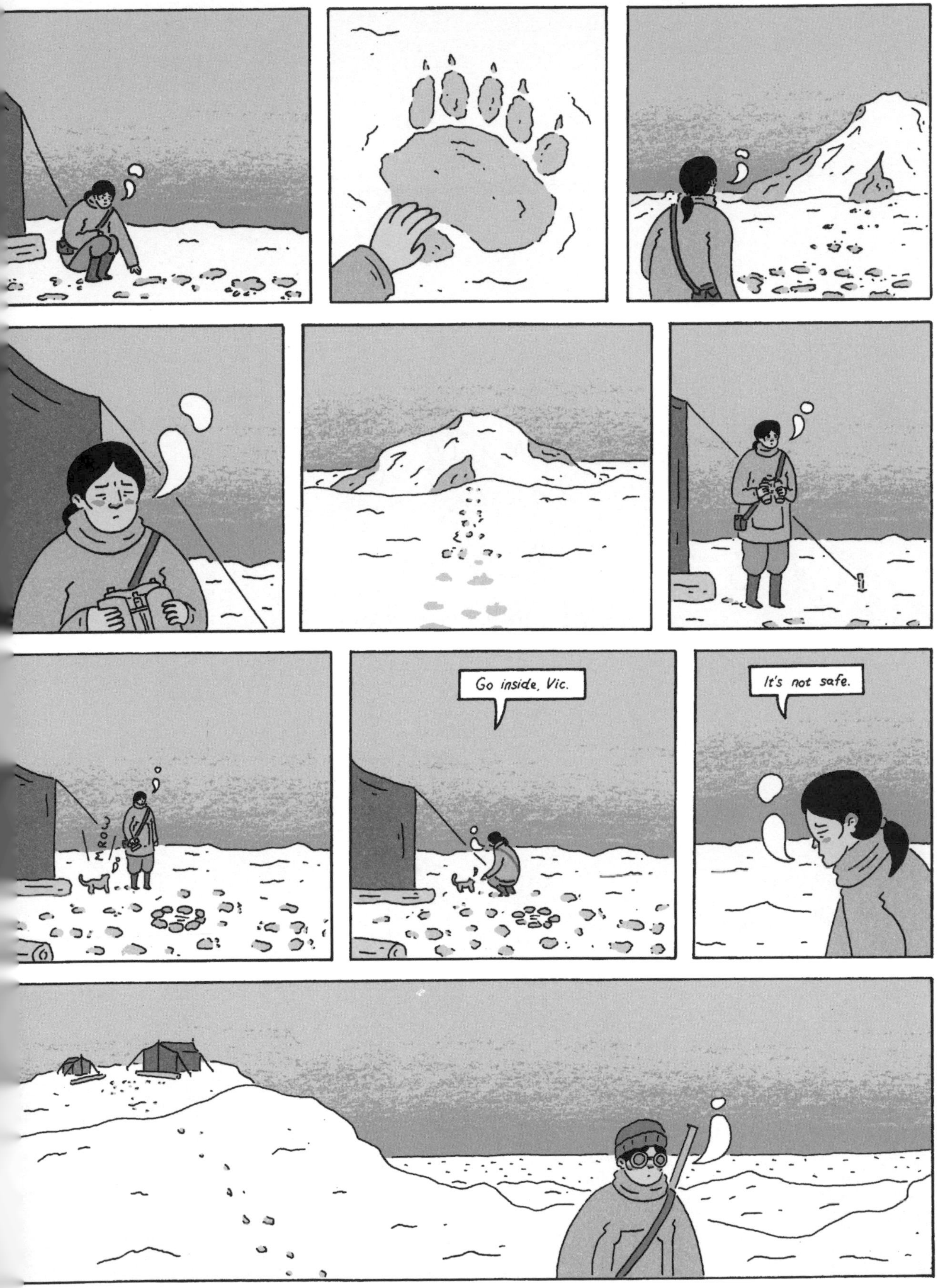
MROW
Go inside, Vic.
It's not safe.

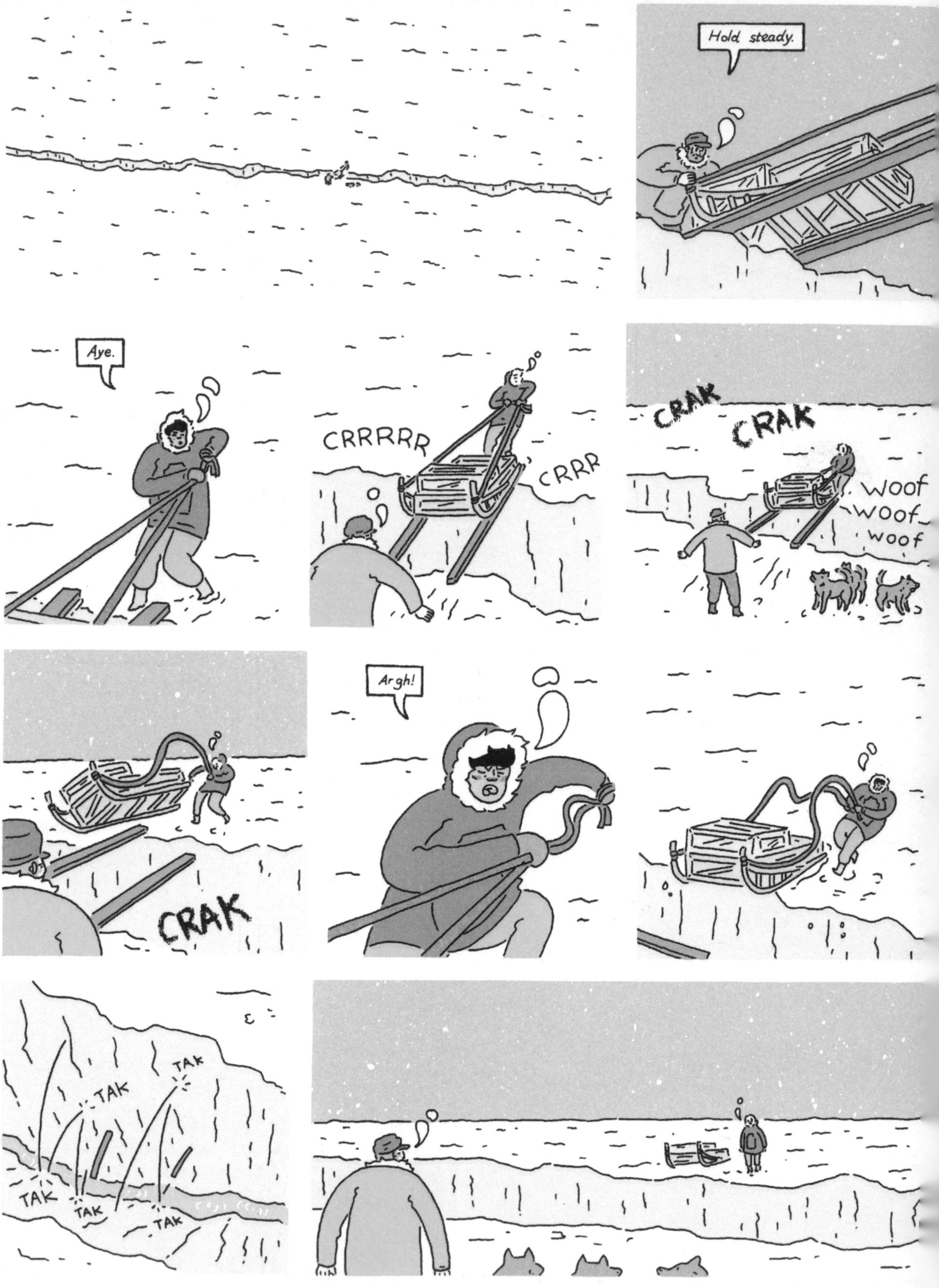
Hold steady.
Aye.
CRRRRR
CRRR
CRAK
CRAK
woof
woof
woof
CRAK
Argh!
TAK
TAK
TAK
TAK
TAK

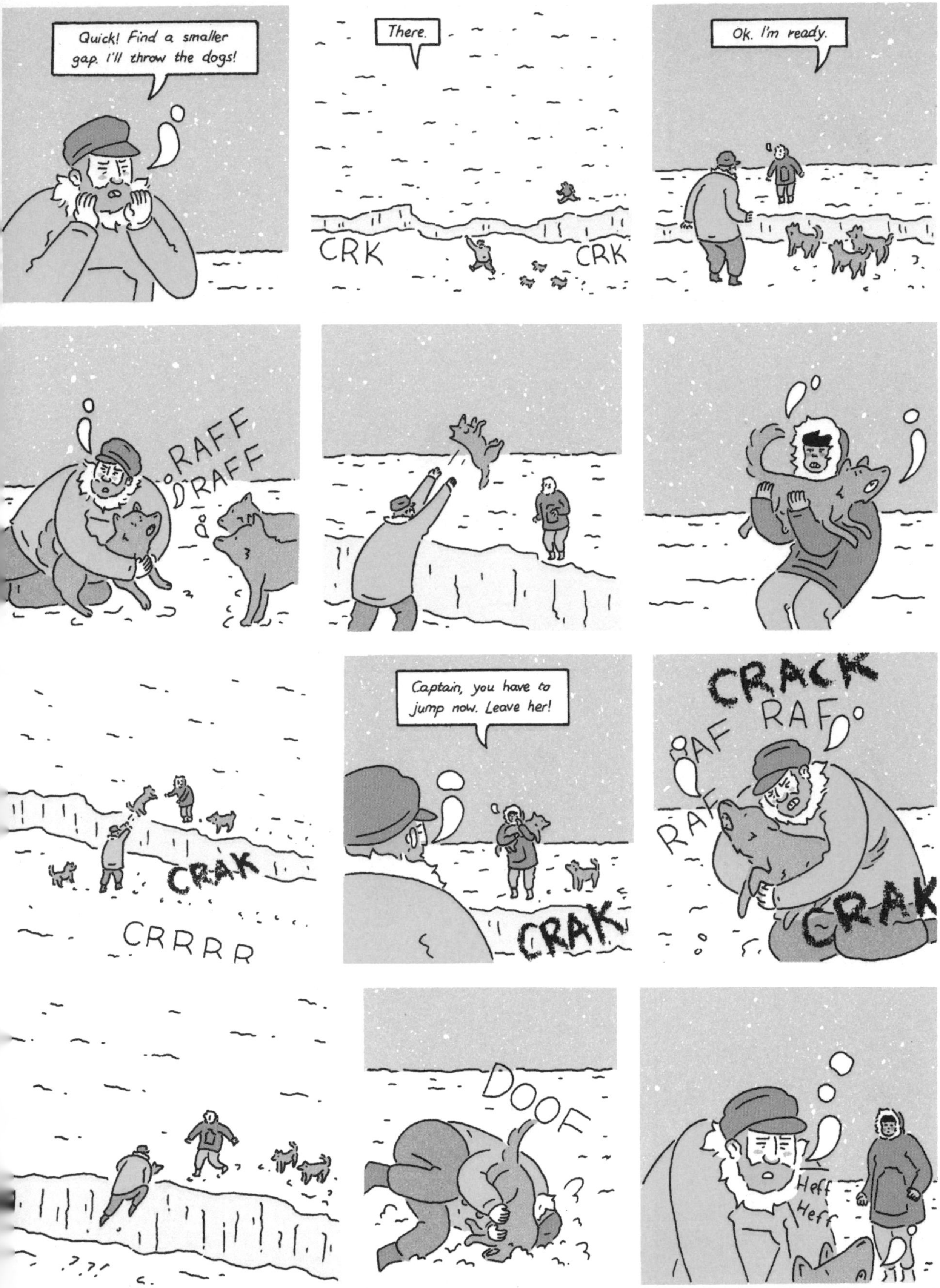
Quick! Find a smaller gap. I'll throw the dogs!
There.
CRK
CRK
Ok. I'm ready.
RAFF
RAFF
CRAK
CRRRR
Captain, you have to jump now. Leave her!
CRAK
CRACK
RAF
RAF
RAF
CRAK
DOOF
Heff
Heff

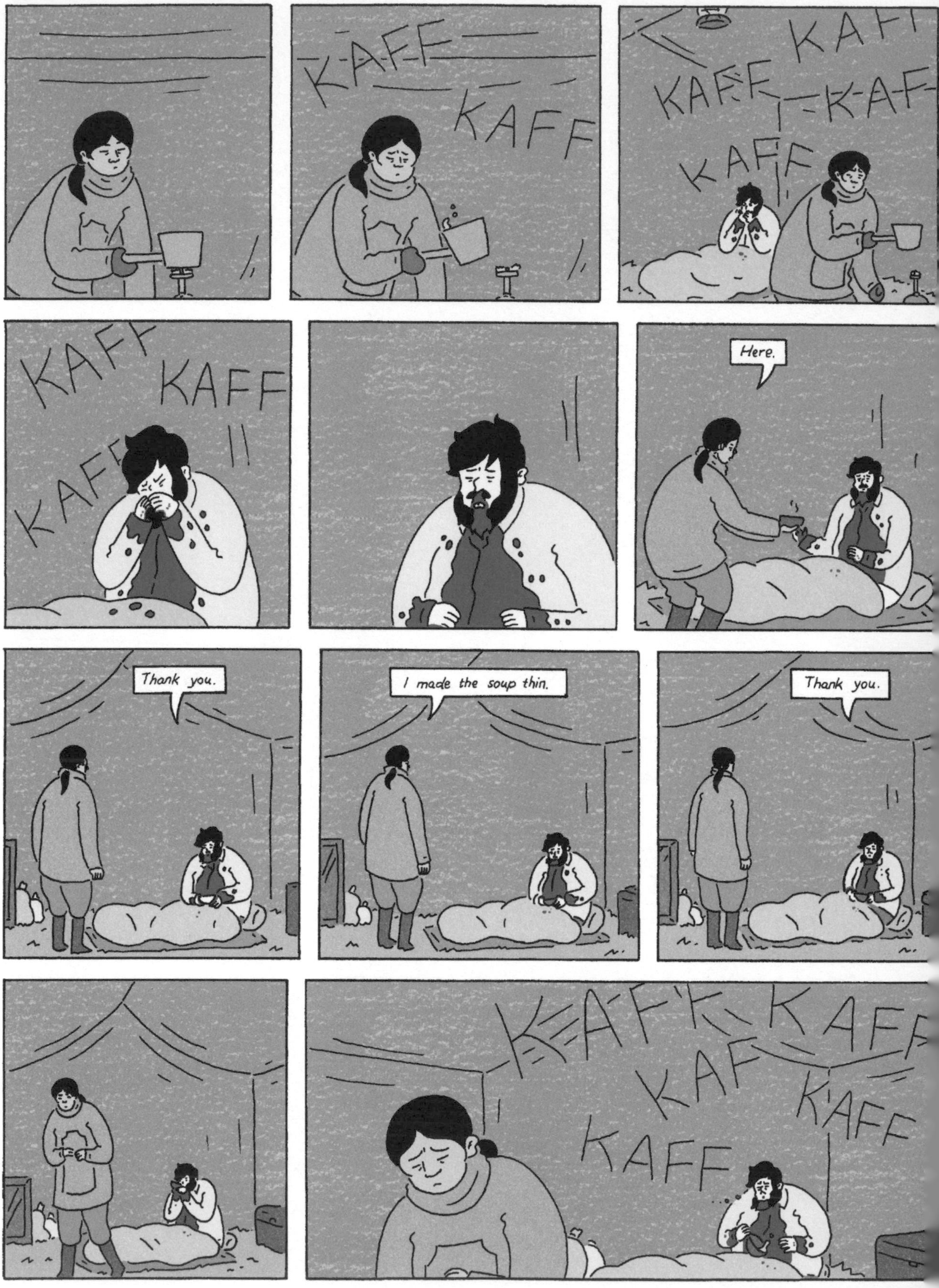
KAFF
KAFF
KAFF
KAFF
KAFF
KAFF
KAFF
KAFF
KAFF
Here.
Thank you.
I made the soup thin.
Thank you.
KAFF
KAFF
KAFF
KAFF
KAFF

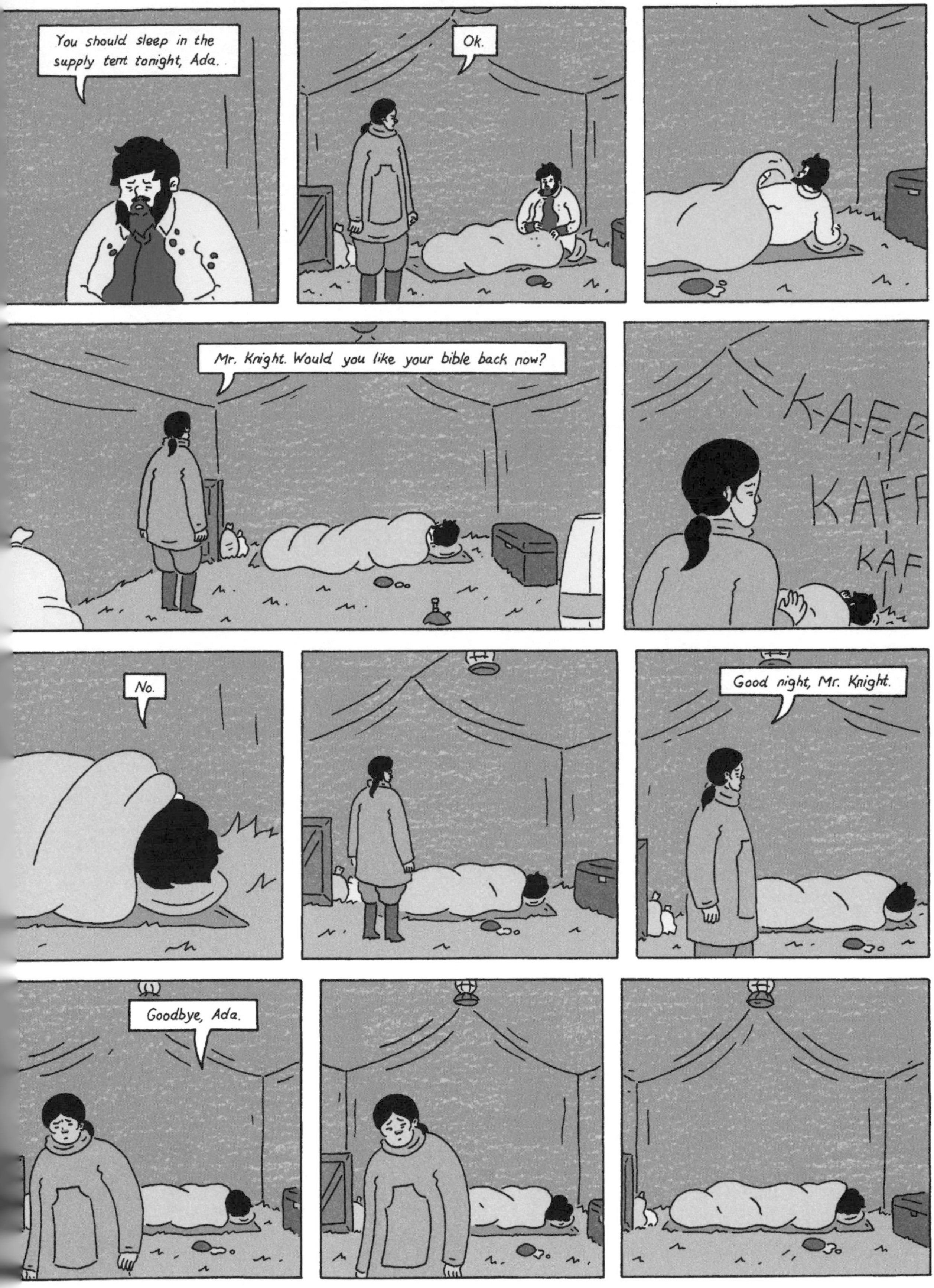
You should sleep in the supply tent tonight, Ada.
Ok.
Mr. Knight. Would you like your bible back now?
KAFF
KAFF
KAF
No.
Good night, Mr. Knight.
Goodbye, Ada.

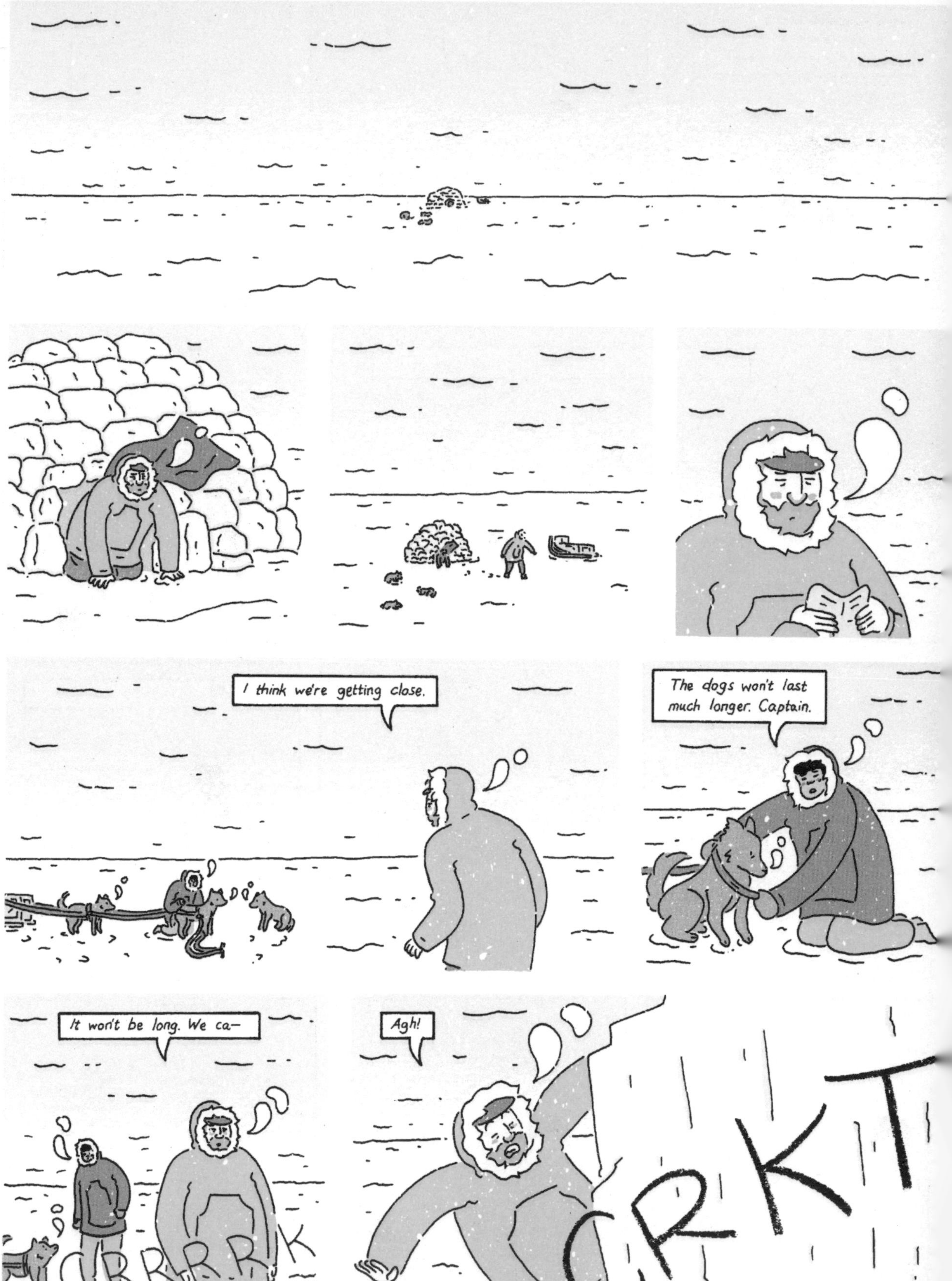

I think we're getting close.
The dogs won't last much longer. Captain.
It won't be long. We ca—
CRRRRK
Agh!
CRKT

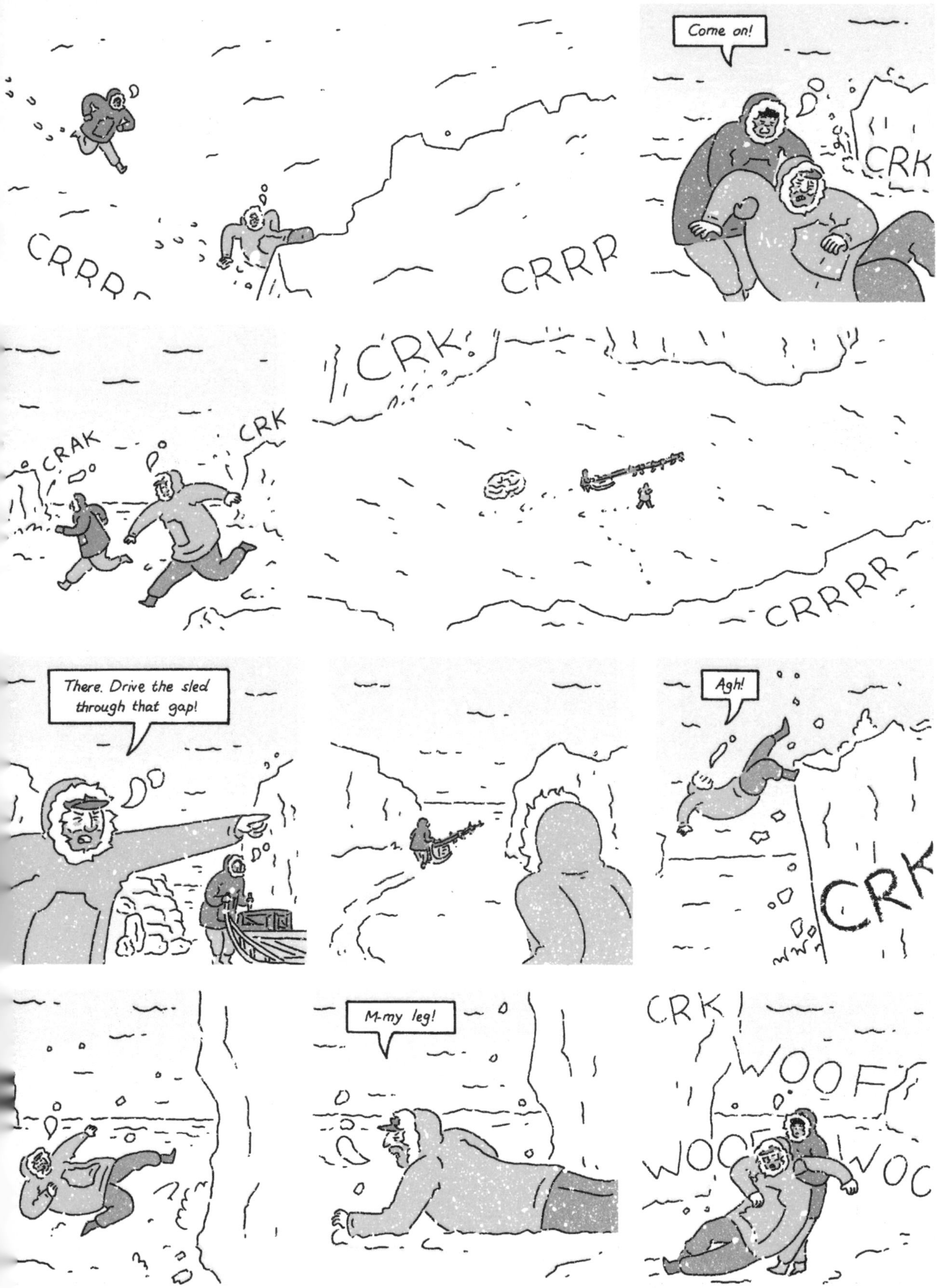
CRRRR
CRRR
Come on!
CRK
CRAK
CRK
CRK
CRRRR
There. Drive the sled through that gap!
Agh!
CRK
M-my leg!
CRK
WOOF
WOOF
WOO

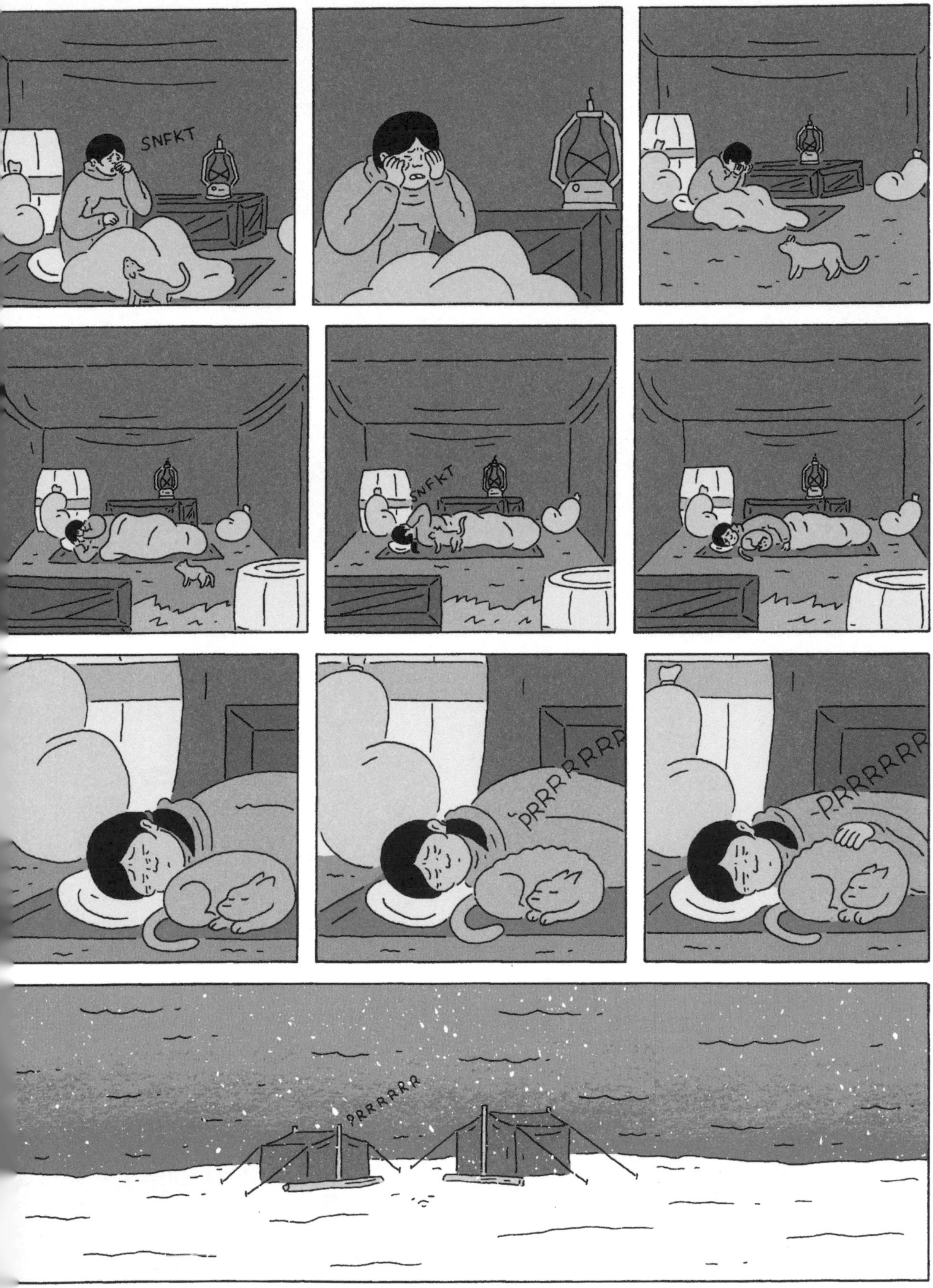
SNFKT
SNFKT
PRRRRRRR
PRRRRRR
PRRRRRR

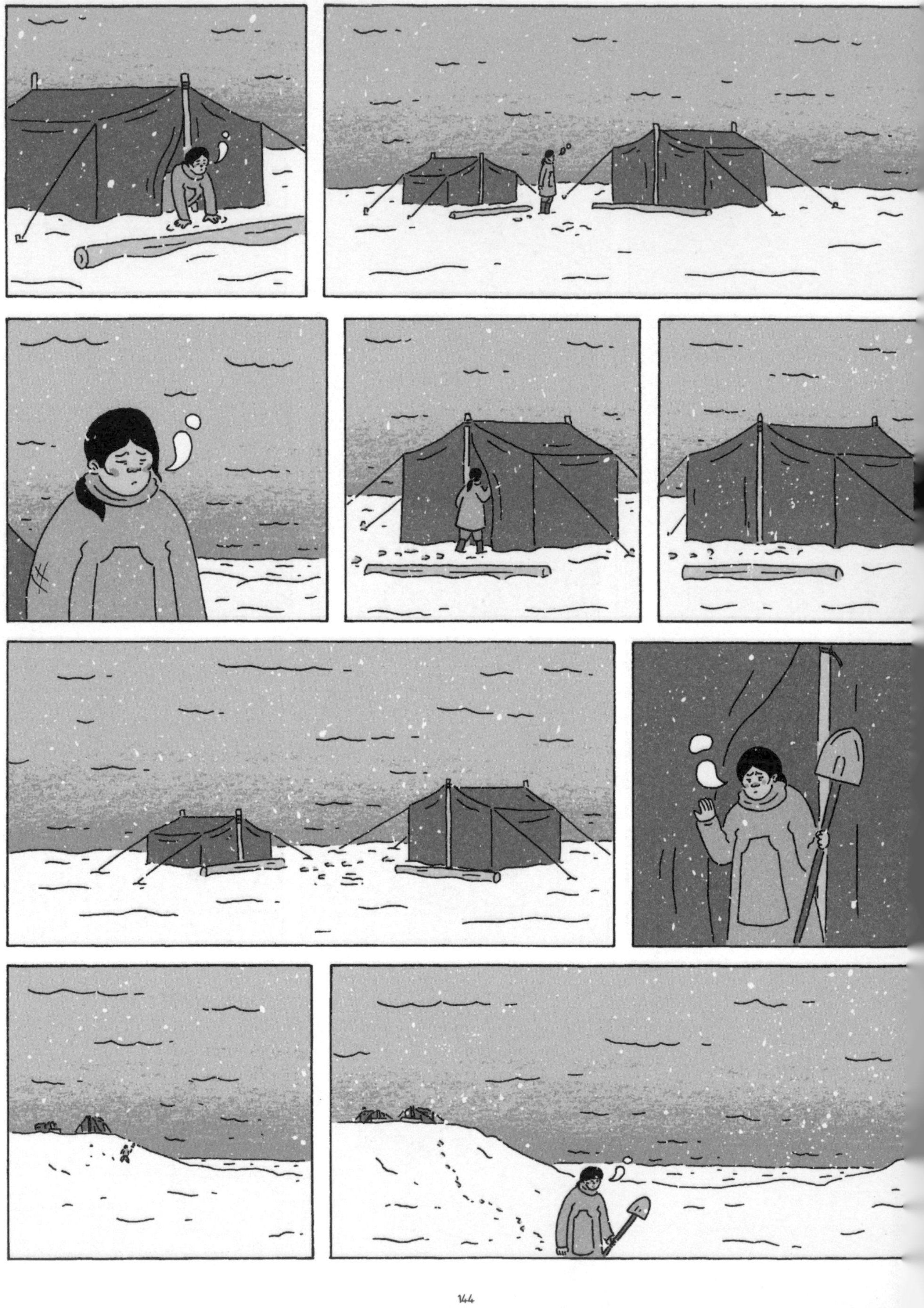

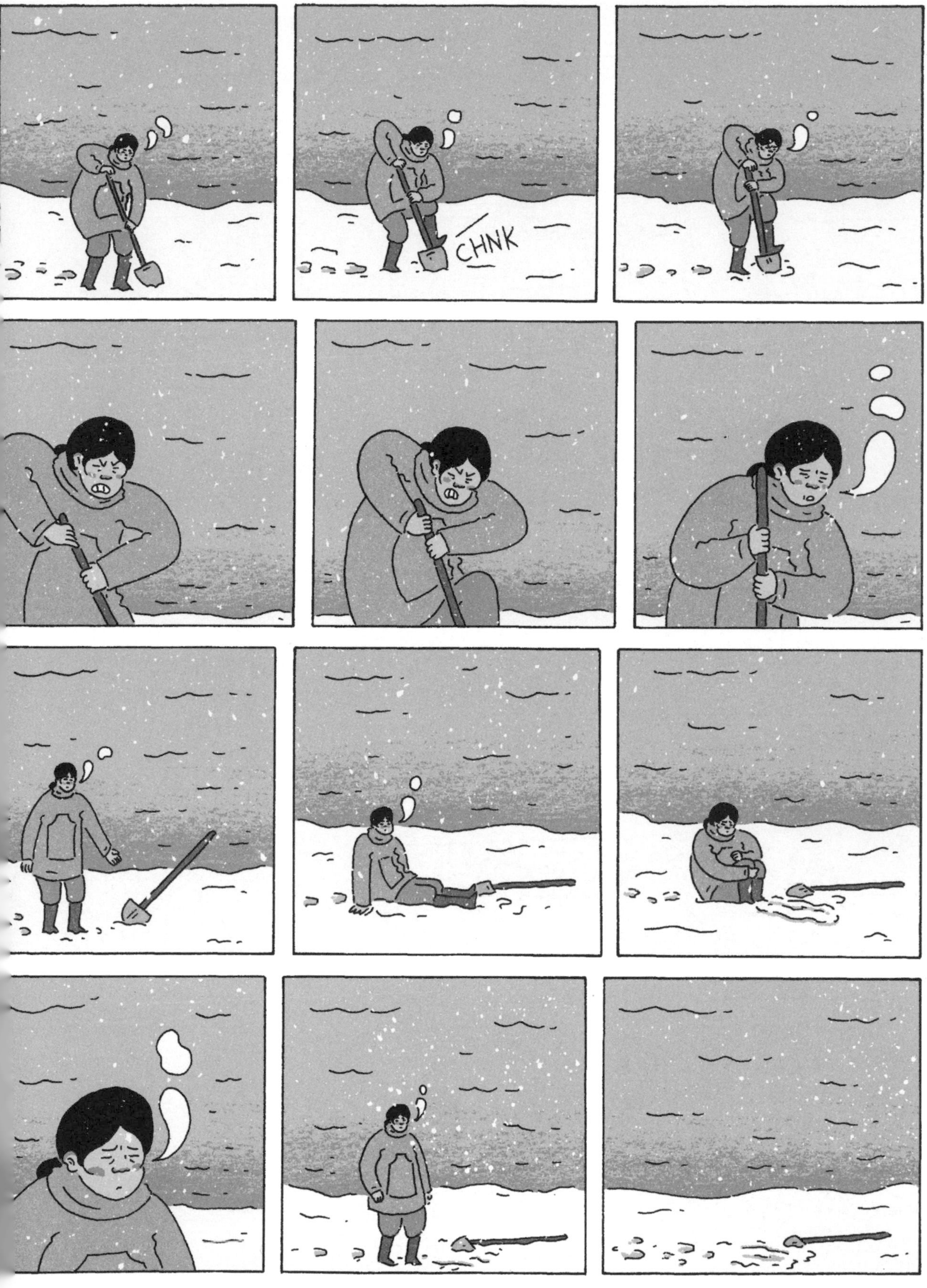
CHNK

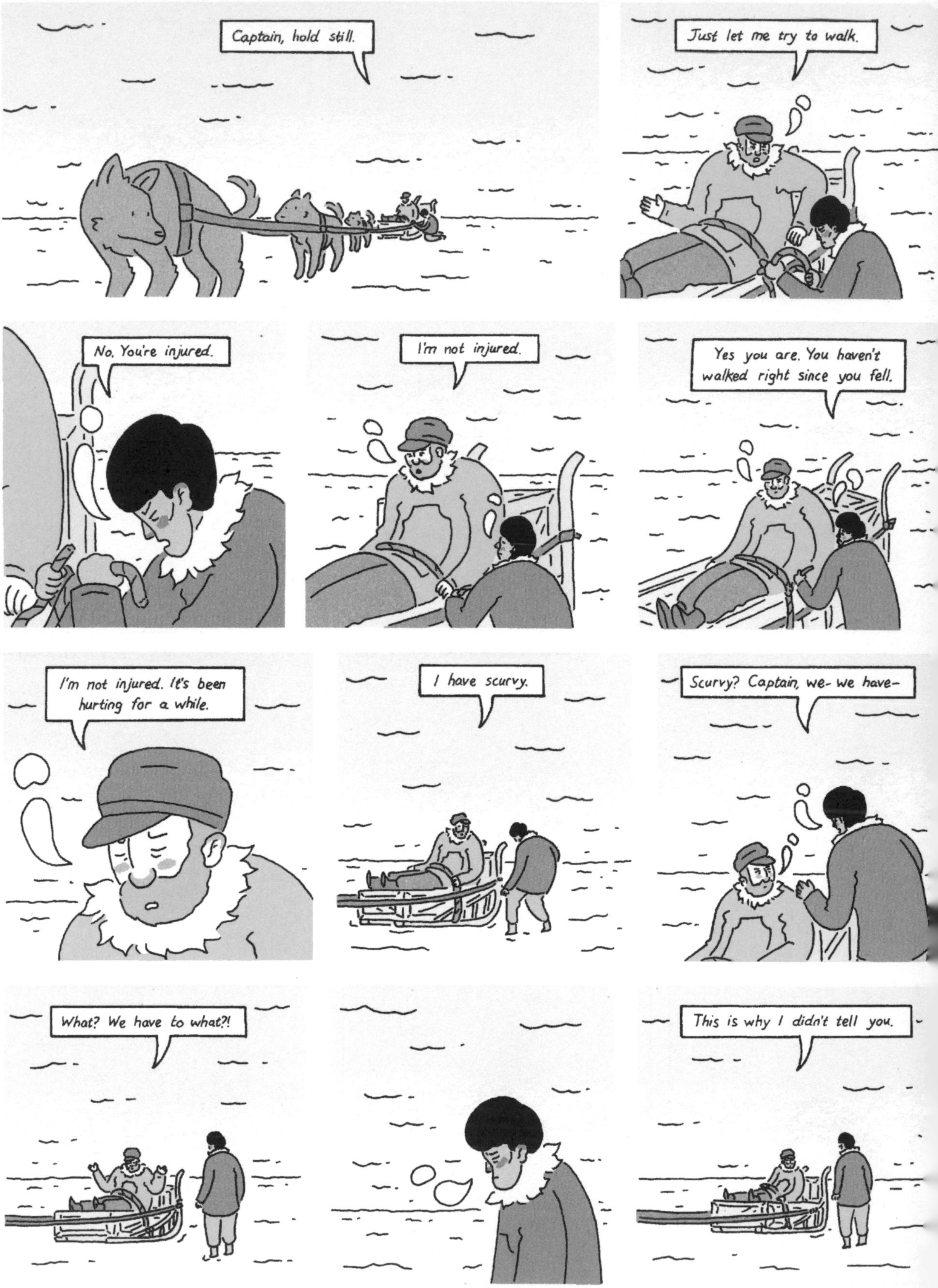

Captain, hold still.
Just let me try to walk.
No. You're injured.
I'm not injured.
Yes you are. You haven't walked right since you fell.
I'm not injured. It's been hurting for a while.
I have scurvy.
Scurvy? Captain, we- we have-
What? We have to what?!
This is why I didn't tell you.

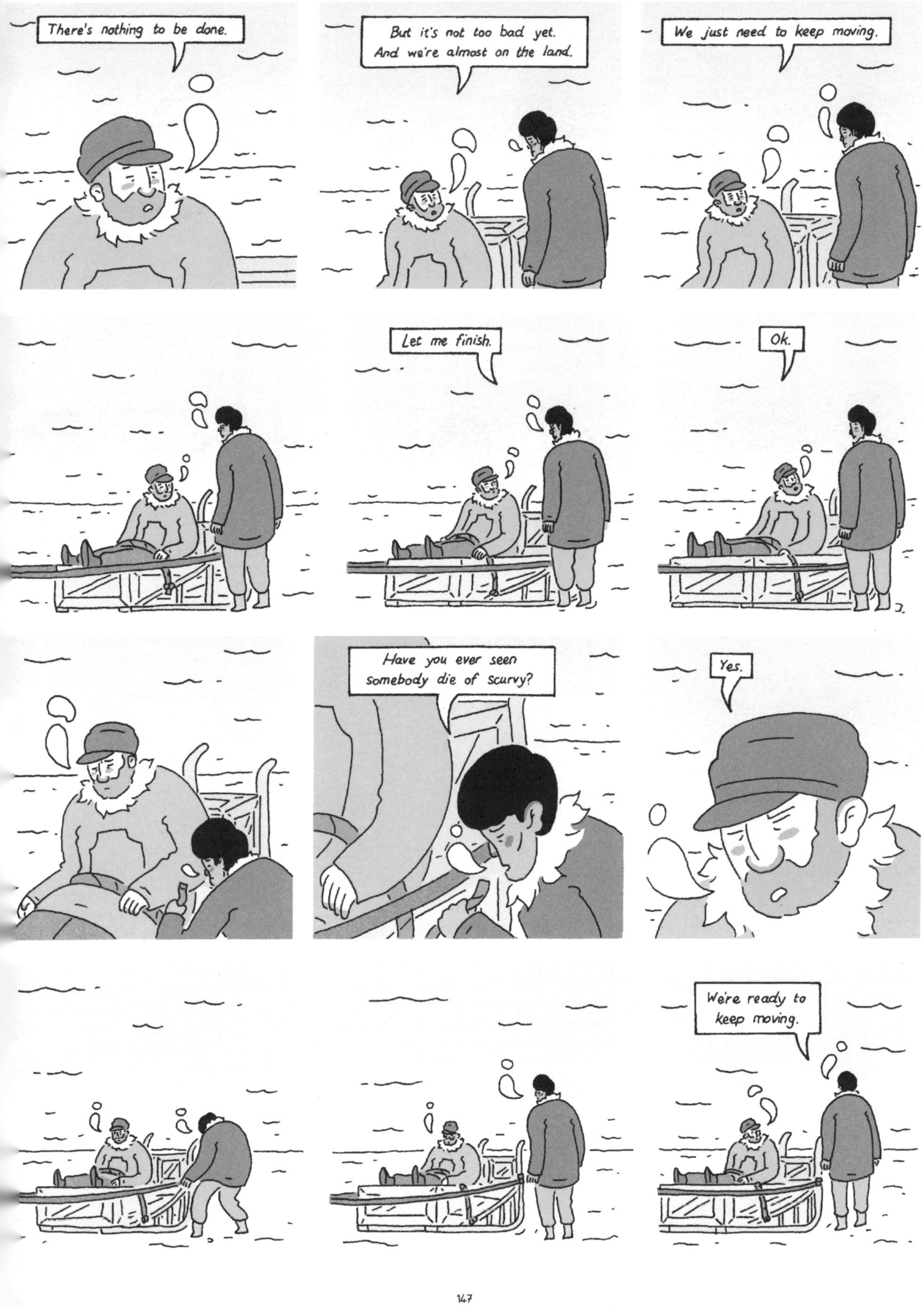
There's nothing to be done.
But it's not too bad yet. And we're almost on the land.
We just need to keep moving.
Let me finish.
Ok.
Have you ever seen somebody die of scurvy?
Yes.
We're ready to keep moving.

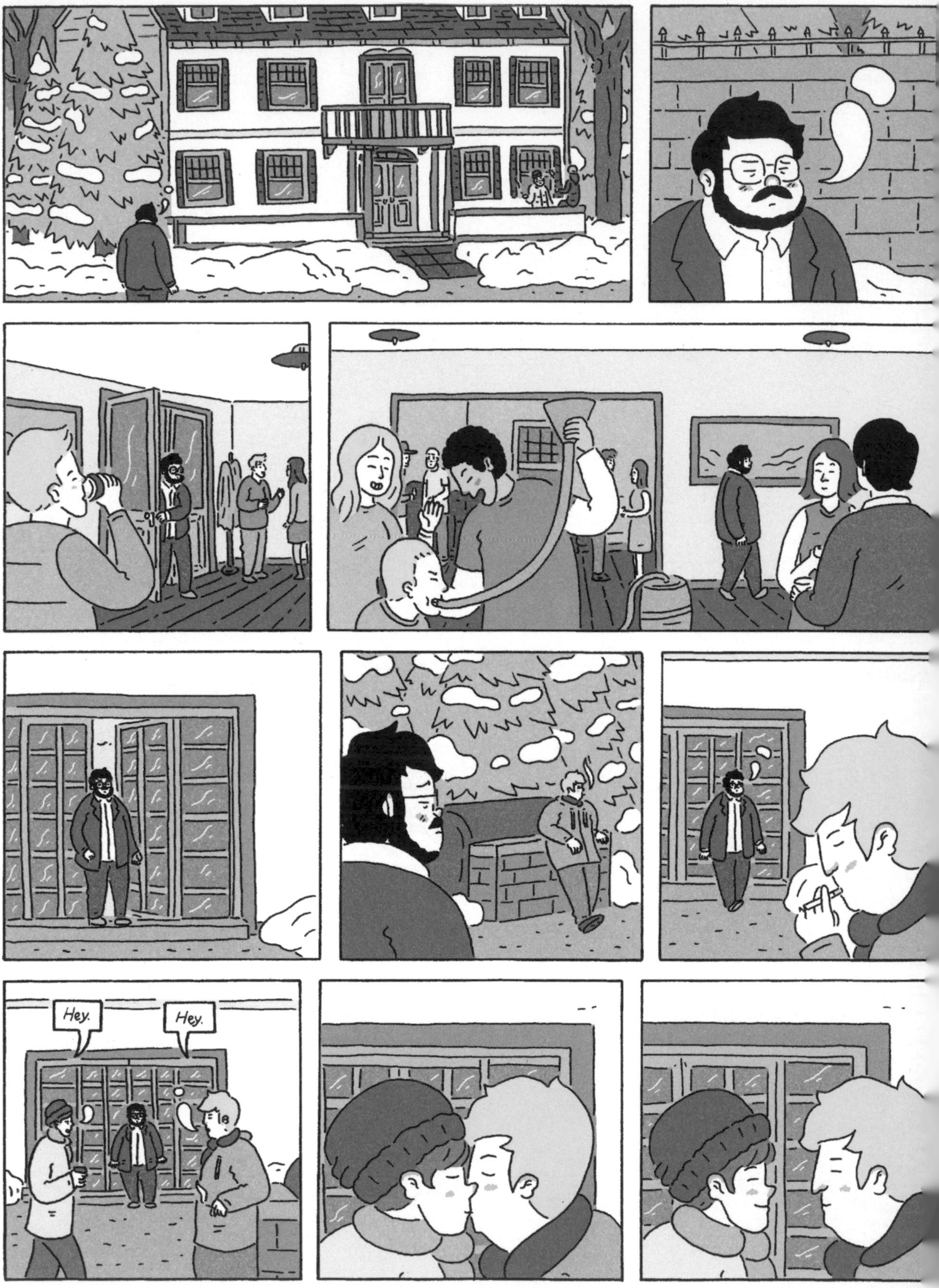
Hey.
Hey.

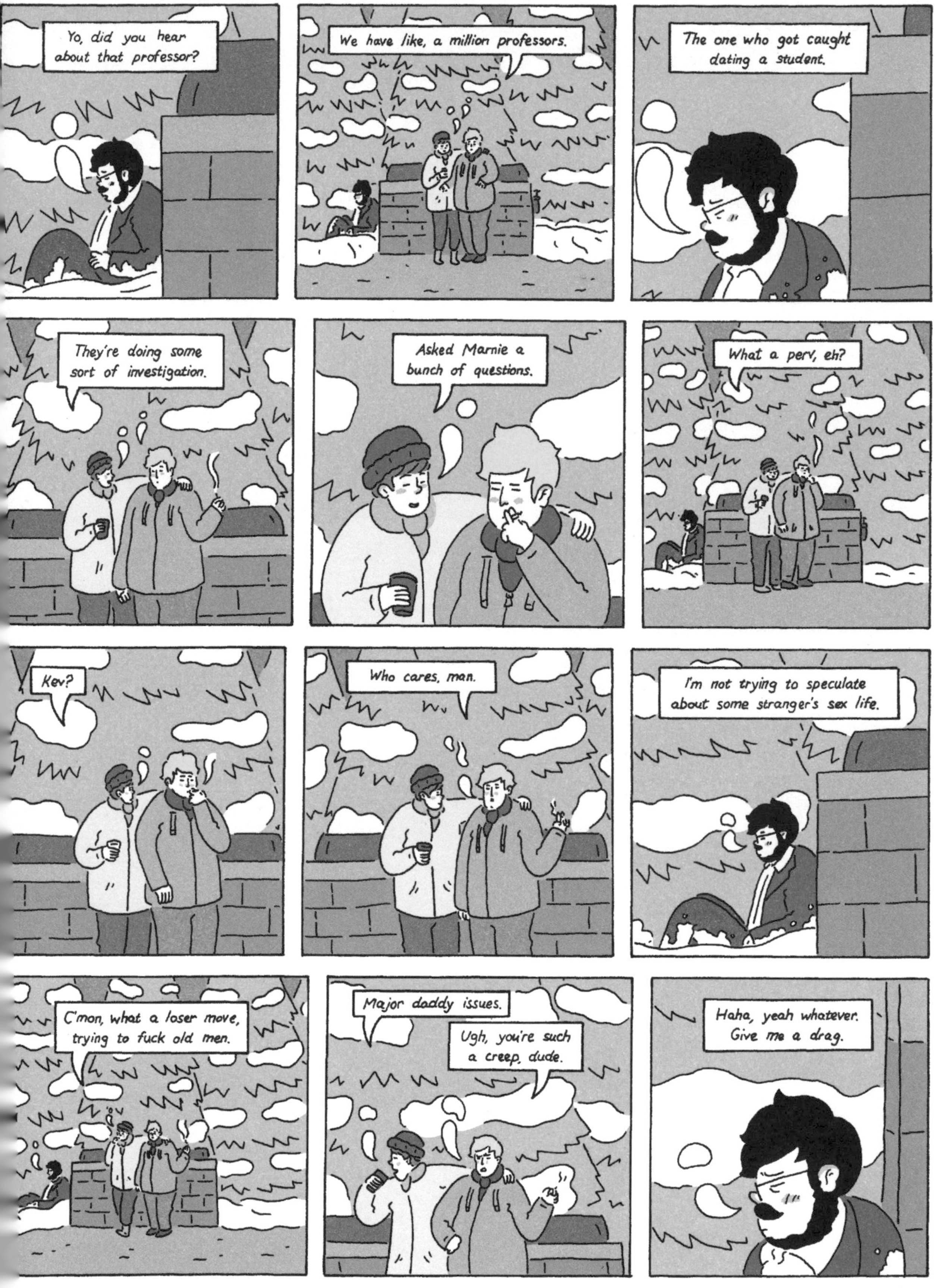
Yo, did you hear about that professor?
We have like, a million professors.
The one who got caught dating a student.
They're doing some sort of investigation.
Asked Marnie a bunch of questions.
What a perv, eh?
Kev?
Who cares, man.
I'm not trying to speculate about some stranger's sex life.
C'mon, what a loser move, trying to fuck old men.
Major daddy issues.
Ugh, you're such a creep, dude.
Haha, yeah whatever. Give me a drag.

Stay quiet, Vic.
MOW
SNAK
Yes!
MOAR
No.

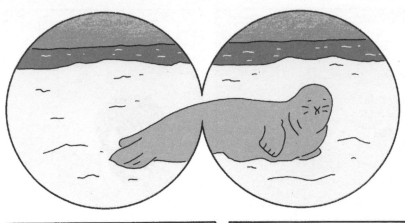

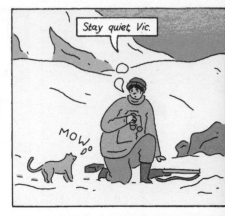

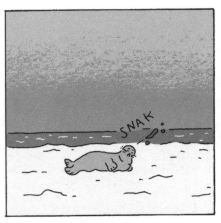

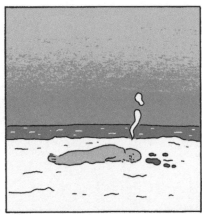

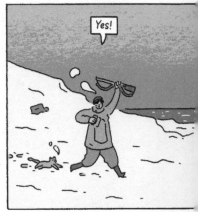

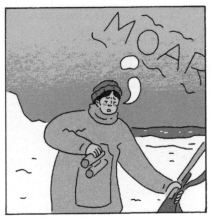

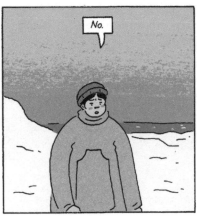

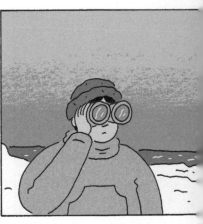

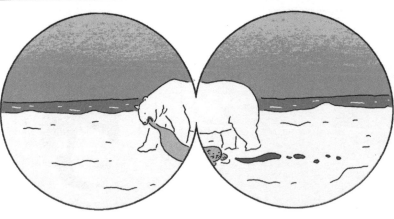

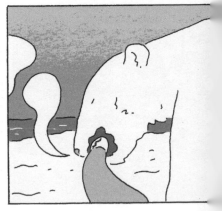

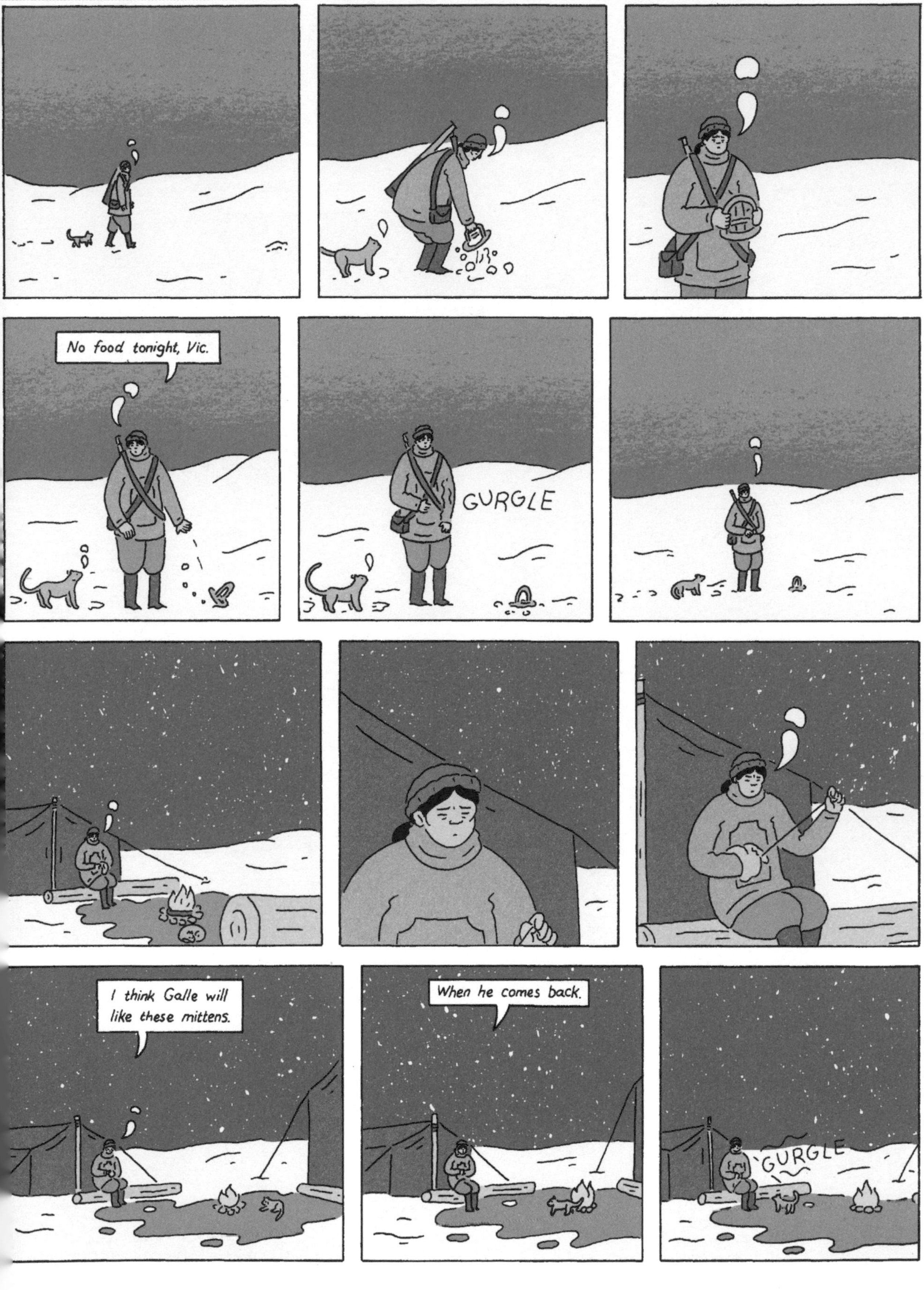
No food tonight, Vic.
GURGLE
I think Galle will like these mittens.
When he comes back.
GURGLE

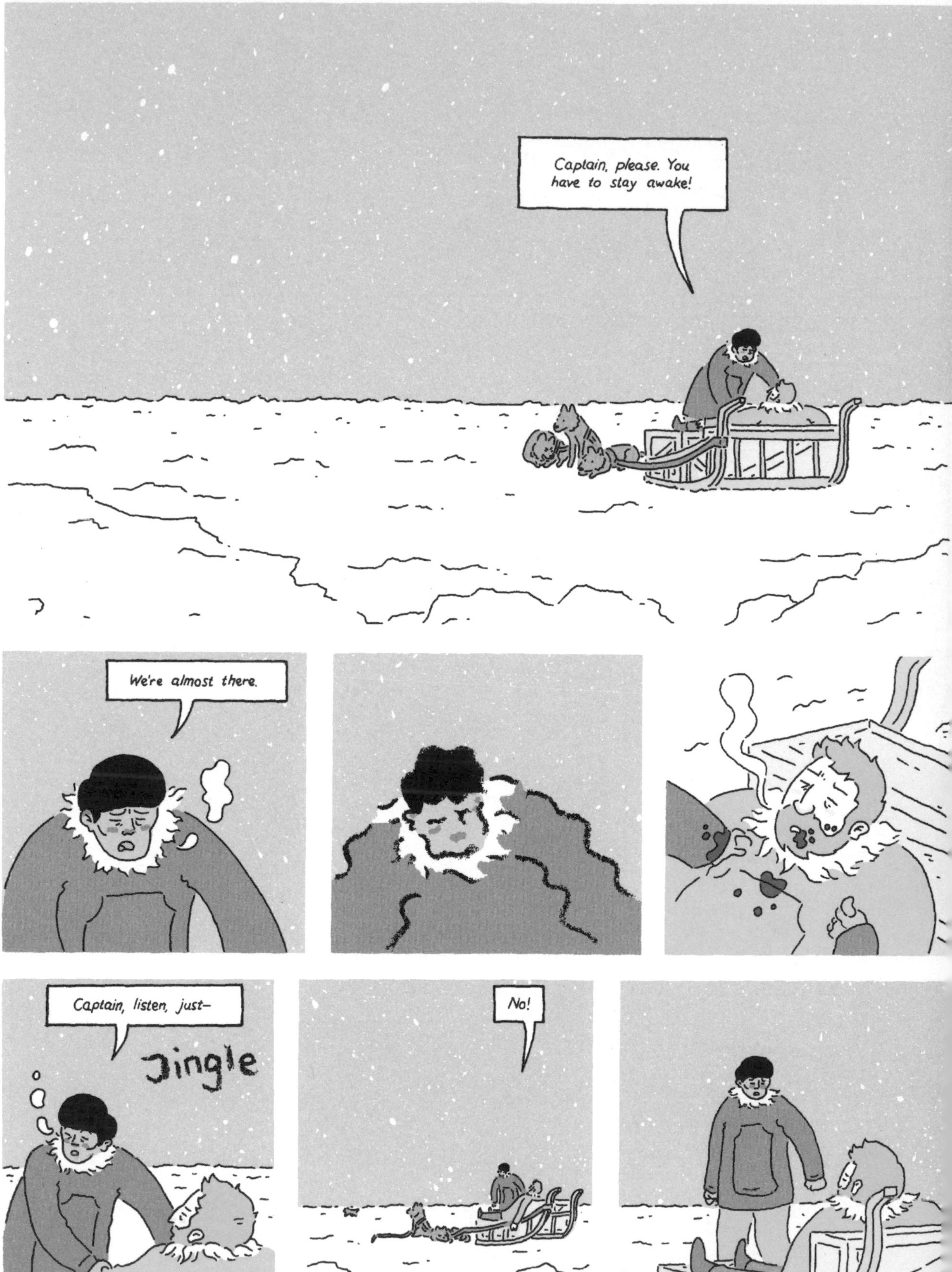
Captain, please. You have to stay awake!
We're almost there.
Captain, listen, just-
Jingle
No!

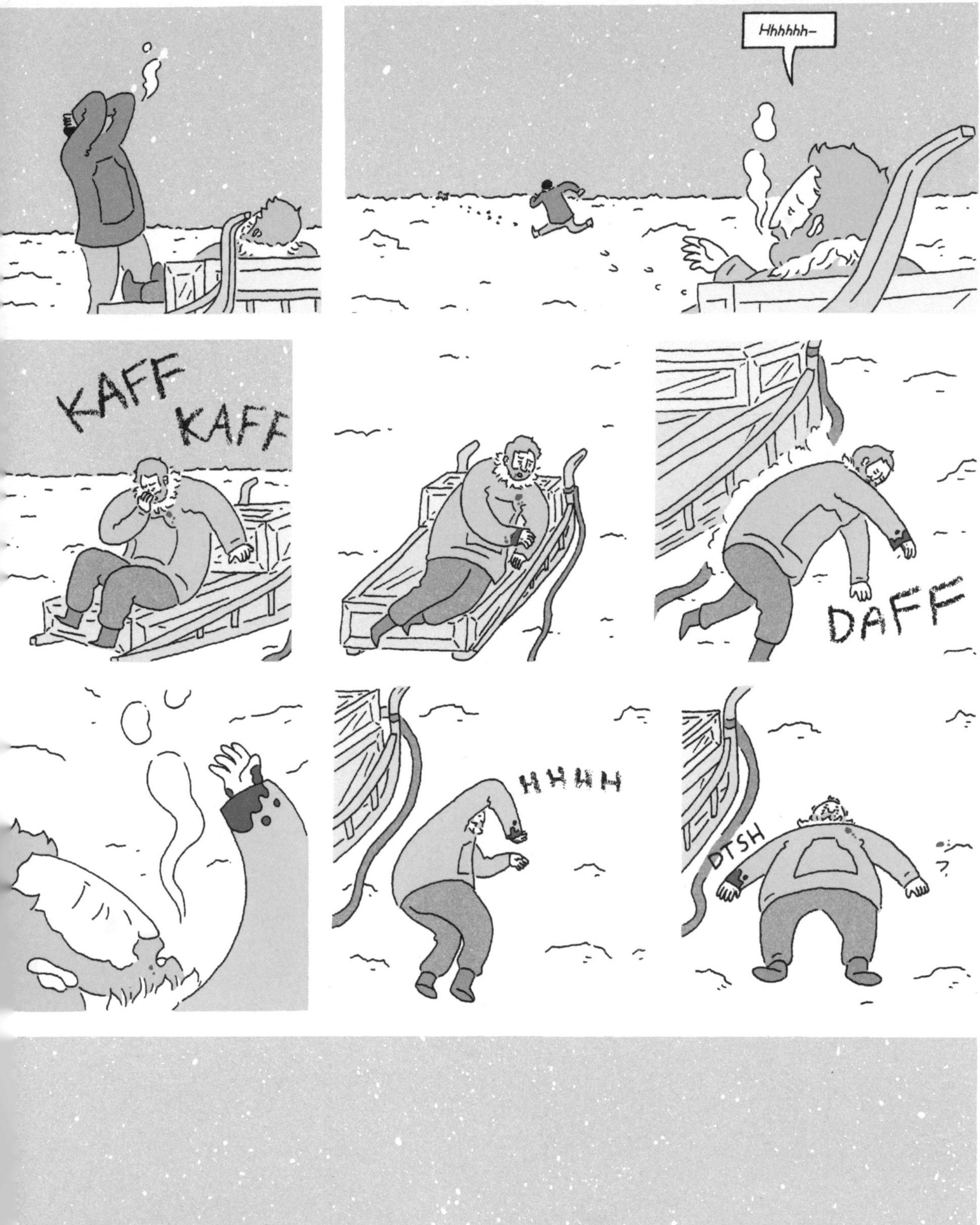
Hhhhhh-
KAFF
KAFF
DAFF
HHHH
DTSH

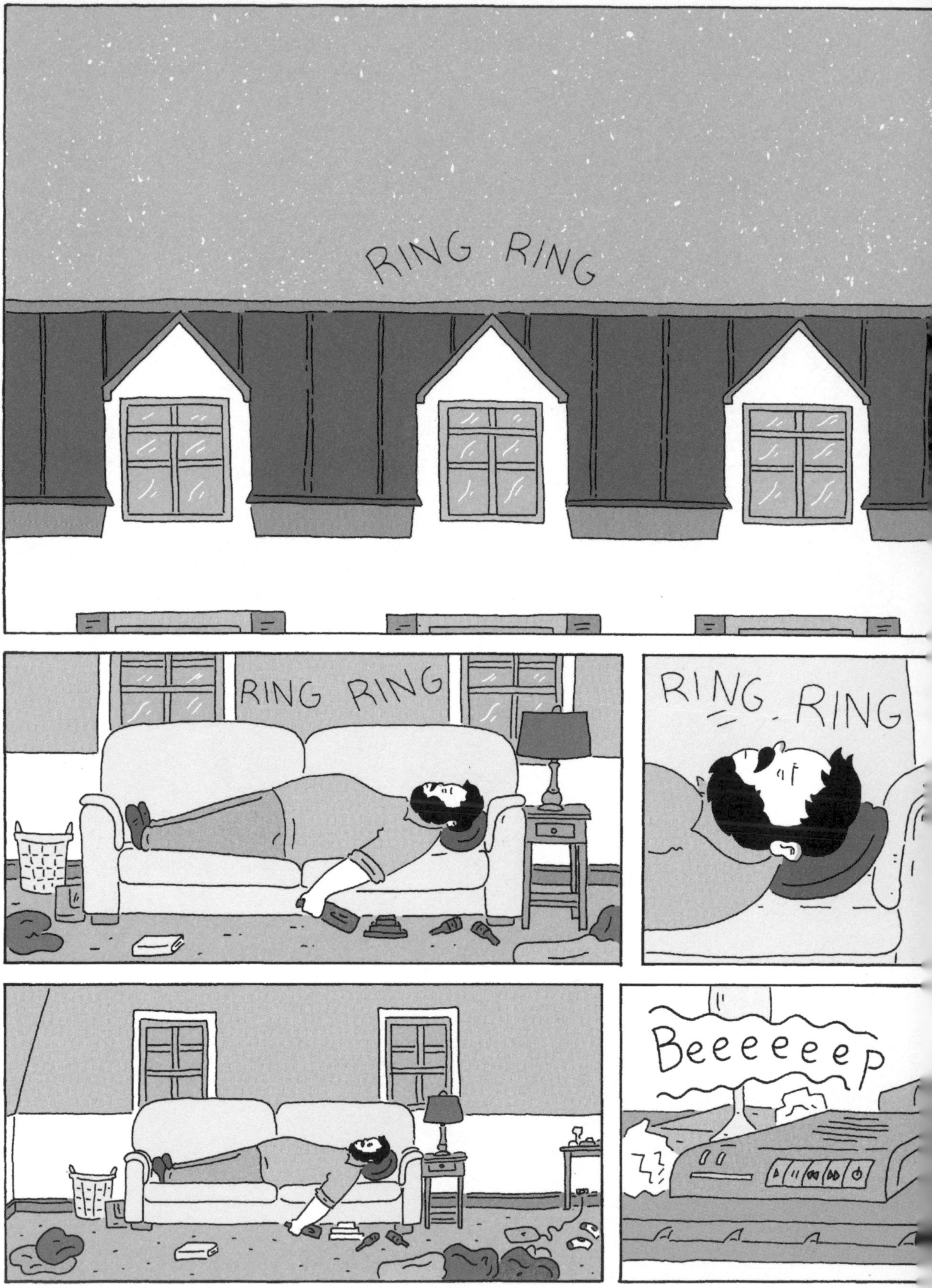
RING RING
RING RING
RING RING
Beeeeeep

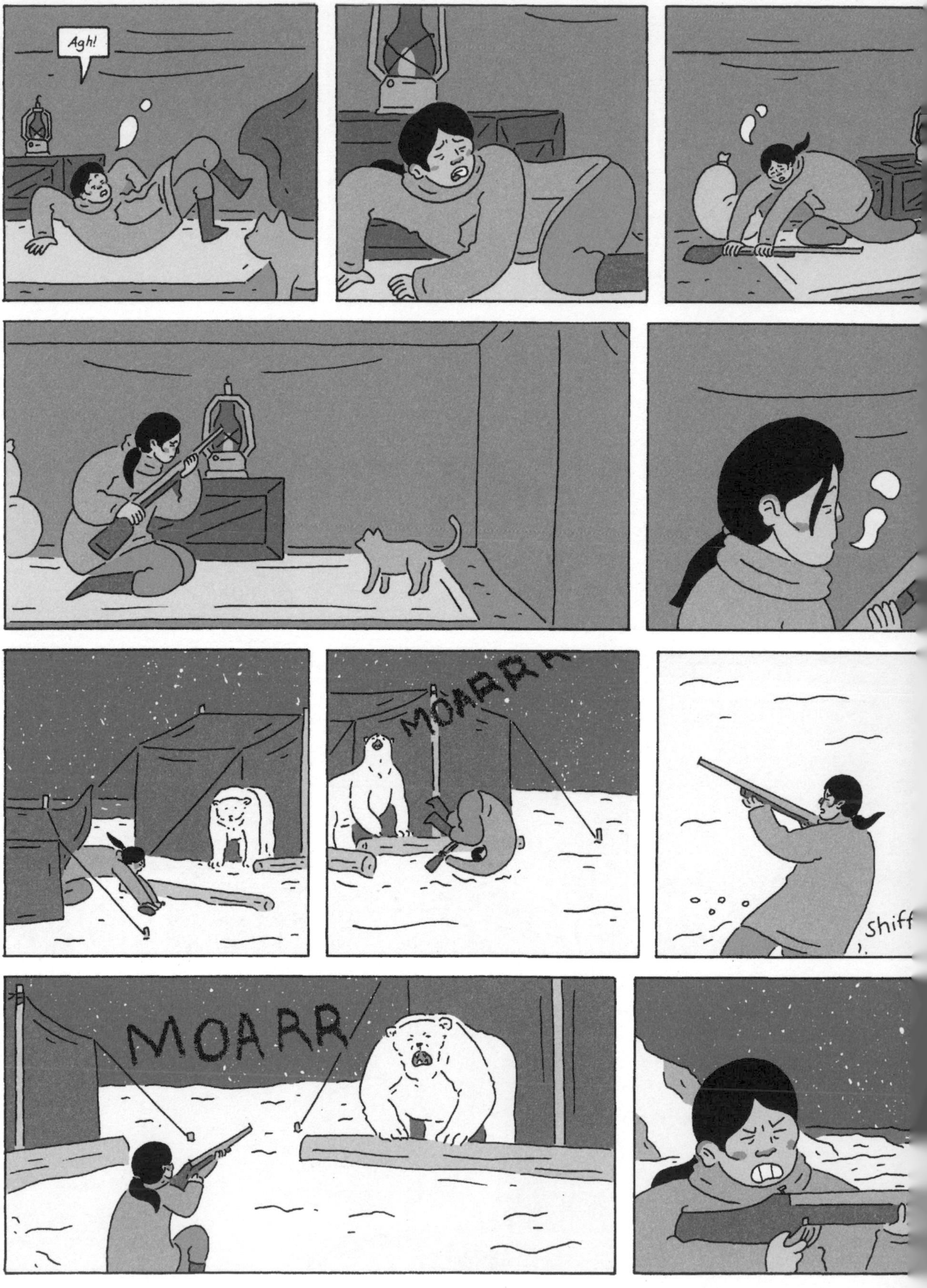
Agh!
MOARR
Shiff
MOARR

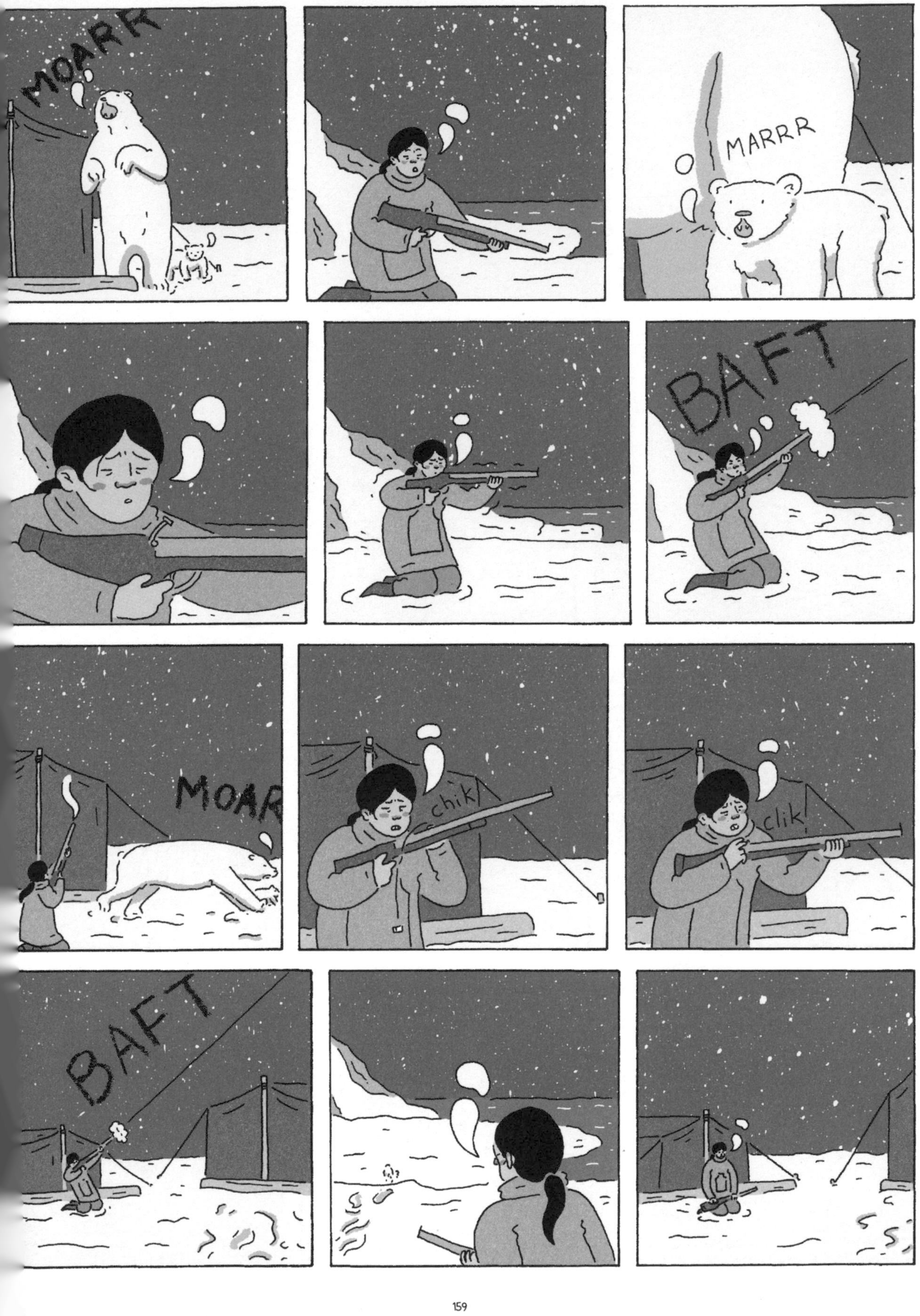
MOARR
MARRR
BAFT
MOAR
chik!
clik!
BAFT

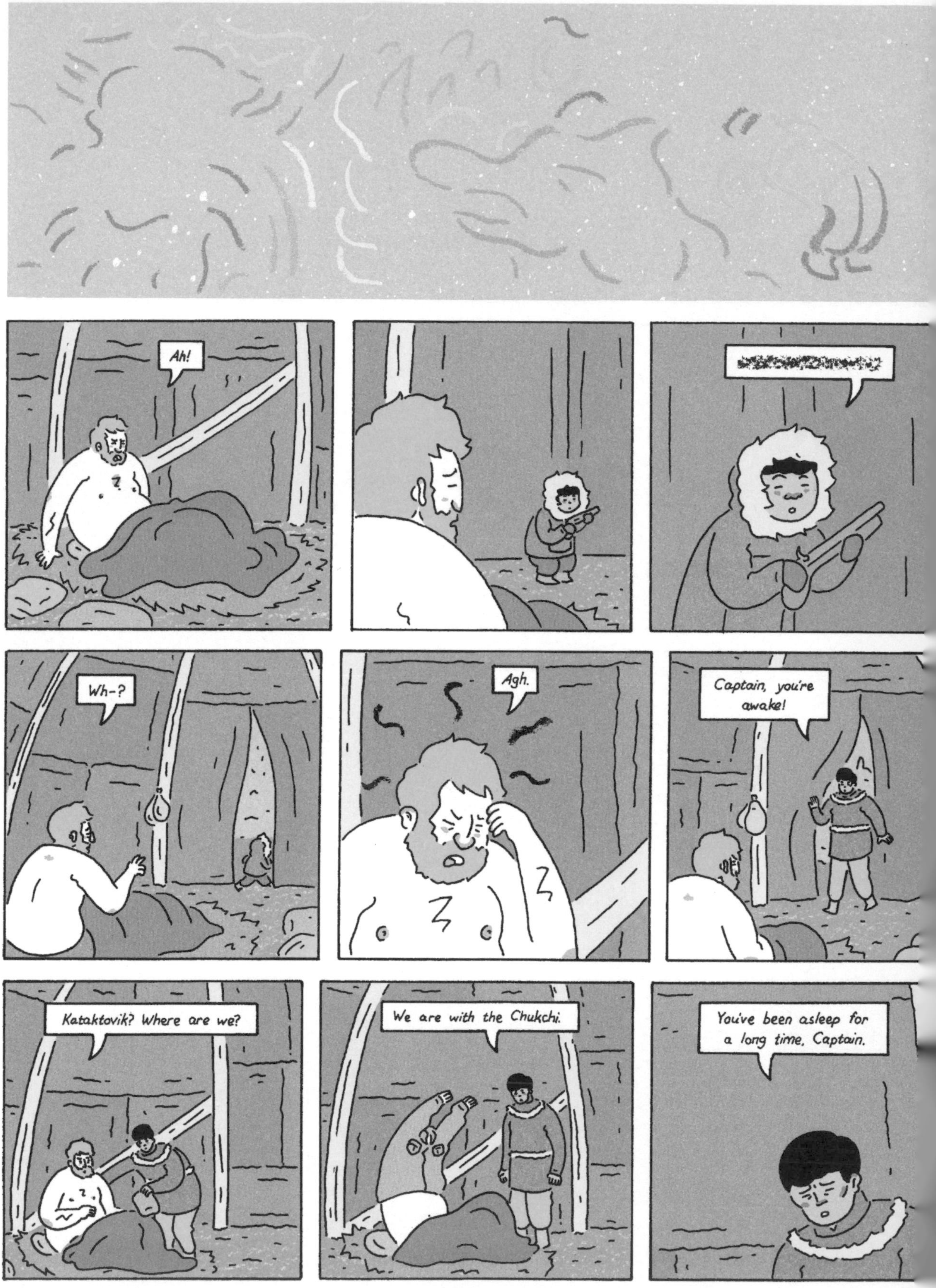
Ah!
Wh-?
Agh.
Captain, you're awake!
Kataktovik? Where are we?
We are with the Chukchi.
You've been asleep for a long time, Captain.

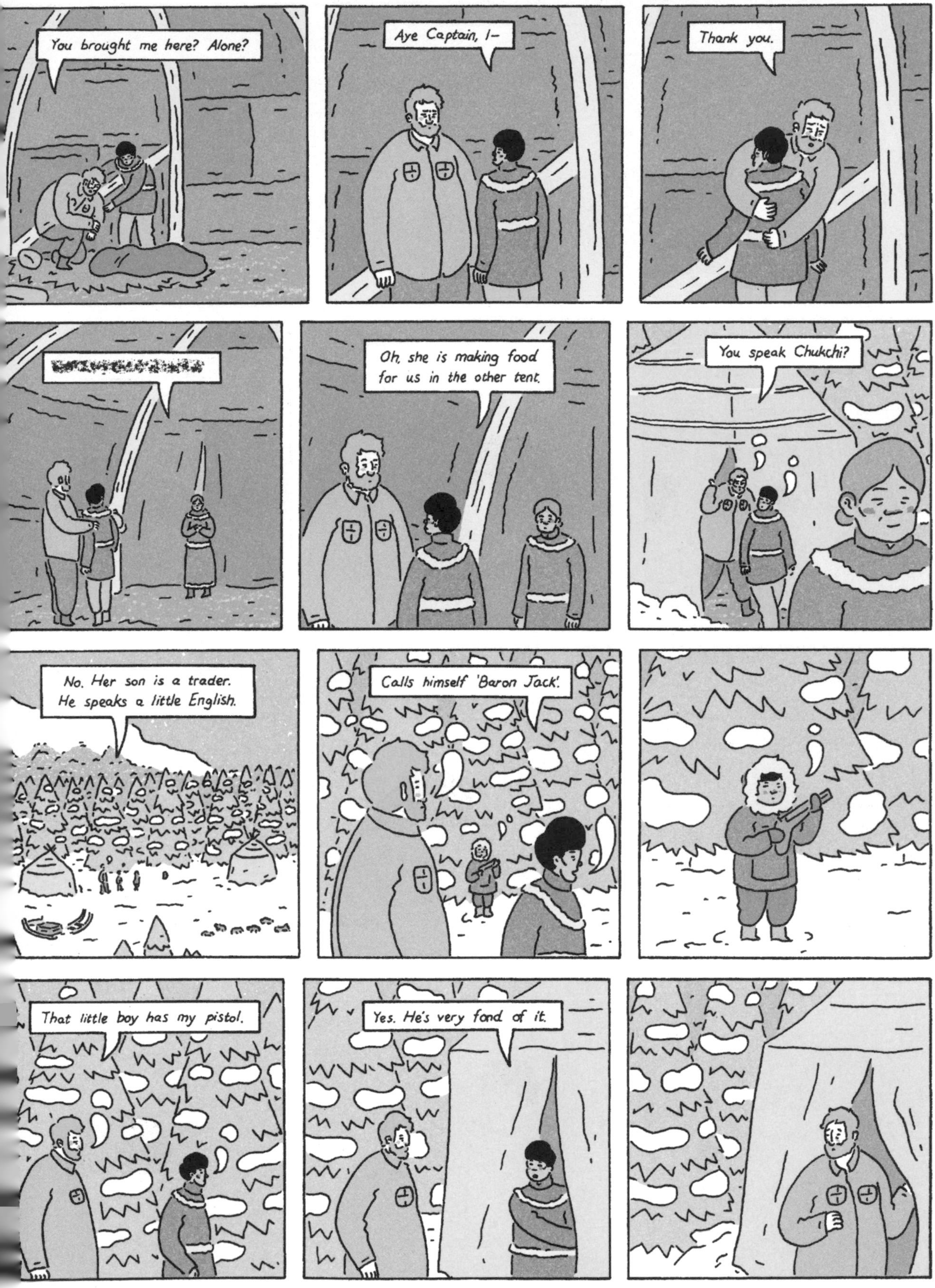
You brought me here? Alone?
Aye Captain, I-
Thank you.
Oh, she is making food for us in the other tent.
You speak Chukchi?
No. Her son is a trader. He speaks a little English.
Calls himself 'Baron Jack'.
That little boy has my pistol.
Yes. He's very fond of it.

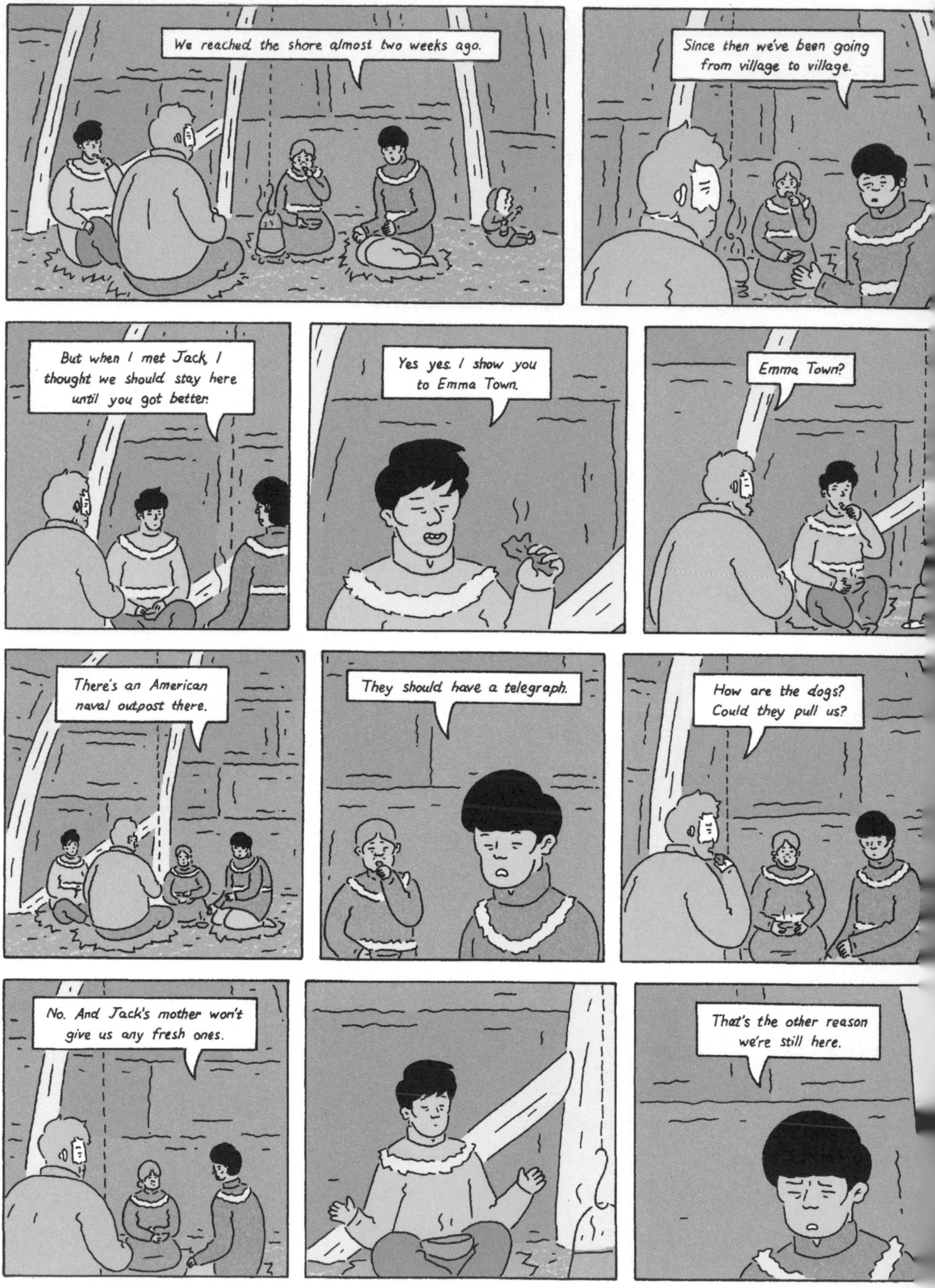
We reached the shore almost two weeks ago.
Since then we've been going from village to village.
But when I met Jack, I thought we should stay here until you got better.
Yes yes. I show you to Emma Town.
Emma Town?
There's an American naval outpost there.
They should have a telegraph.
How are the dogs? Could they pull us?
No. And Jack's mother won't give us any fresh ones.
That's the other reason we're still here.

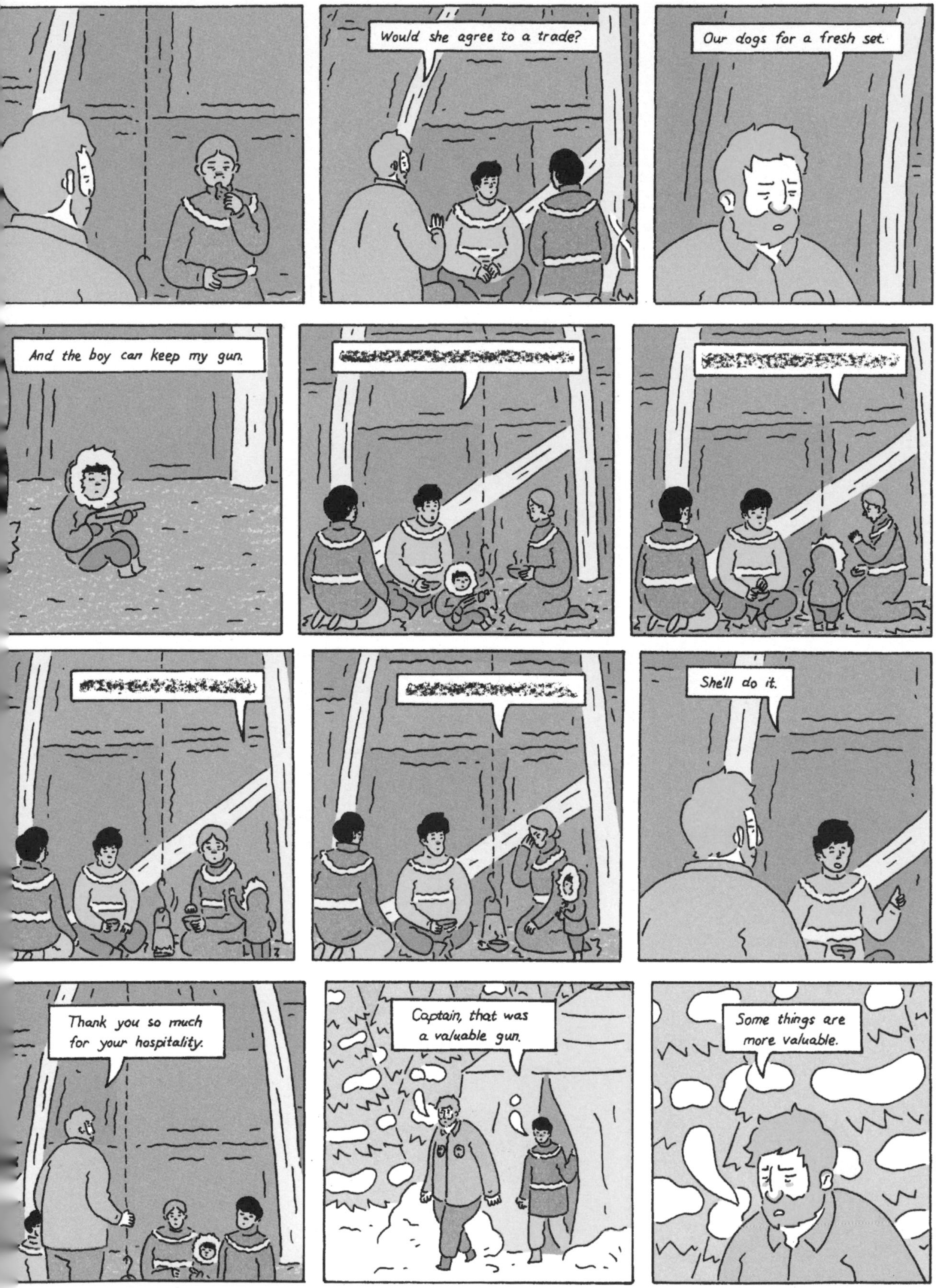
Would she agree to a trade?
Our dogs for a fresh set.
And the boy can keep my gun.
She'll do it.
Thank you so much for your hospitality.
Captain, that was a valuable gun.
Some things are more valuable.

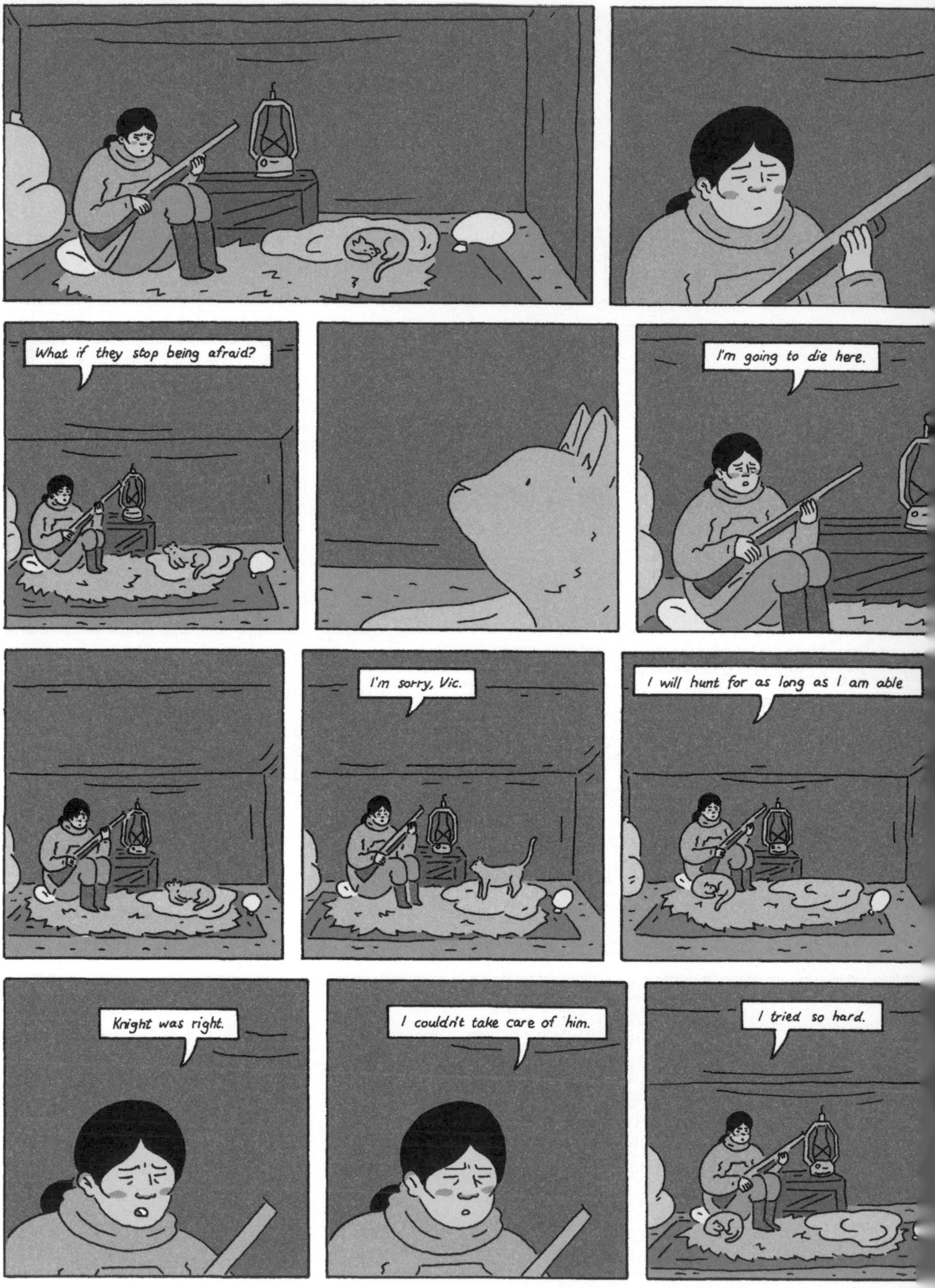
What if they stop being afraid?
I'm going to die here.
I'm sorry, Vic.
I will hunt for as long as I am able
Knight was right.
I couldn't take care of him.
I tried so hard.

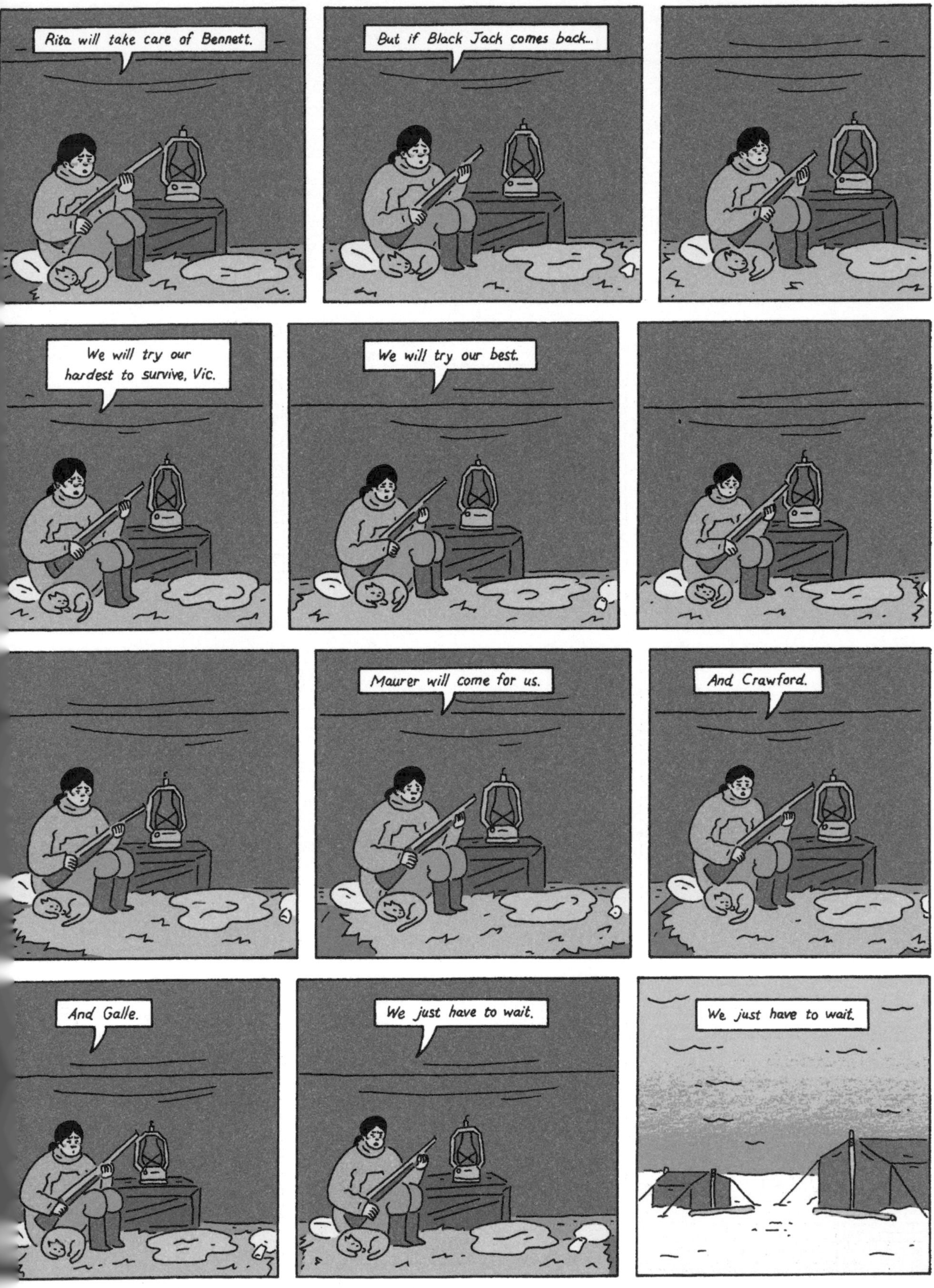
Rita will take care of Bennett.
But if Black Jack comes back...
We will try our hardest to survive, Vic.
We will try our best.
Maurer will come for us.
And Crawford.
And Galle.
We just have to wait.
We just have to wait.

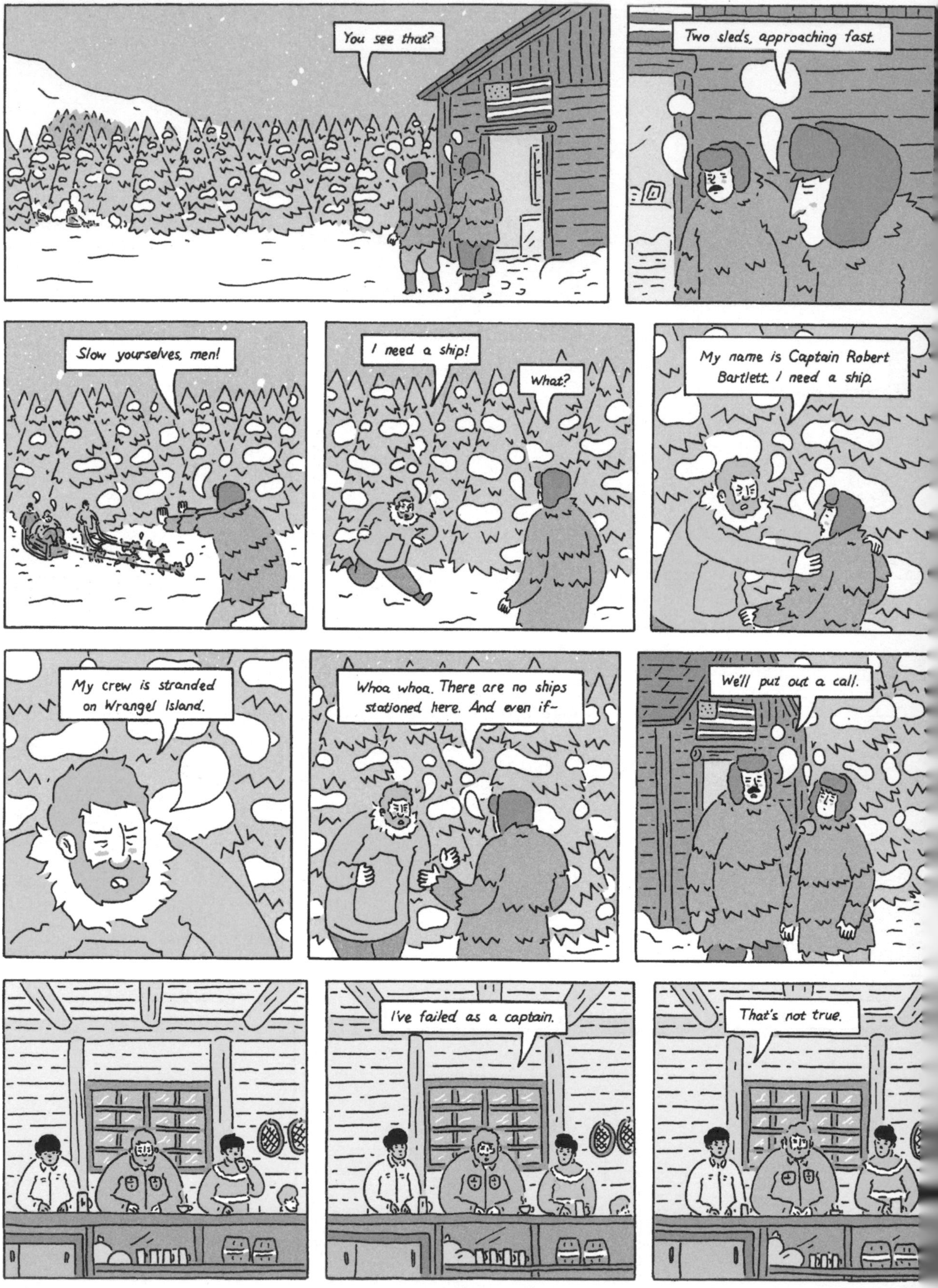
You see that?
Two sleds, approaching fast.
Slow yourselves, men!
I need a ship!
What?
My name is Captain Robert Bartlett. I need a ship.
My crew is stranded on Wrangel Island.
Whoa whoa. There are no ships stationed here. And even if–
We'll put out a call.
I've failed as a captain.
That's not true.

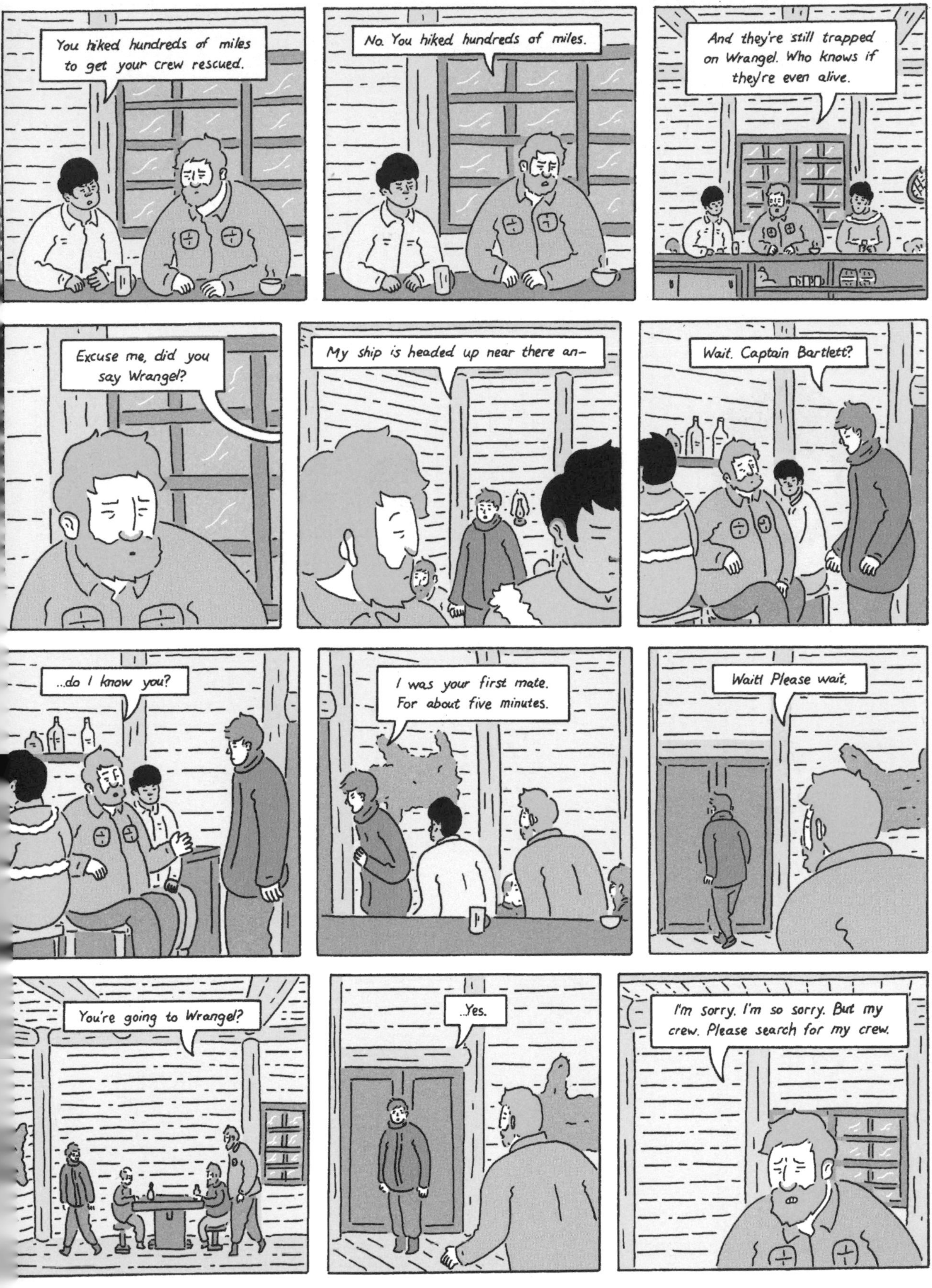
You hiked hundreds of miles to get your crew rescued.
No. You hiked hundreds of miles.
And they're still trapped on Wrangel. Who knows if they're even alive.
Excuse me, did you say Wrangel?
My ship is headed up near there an-
Wait. Captain Bartlett?
...do I know you?
I was your first mate. For about five minutes.
Wait! Please wait.
You're going to Wrangel?
...Yes.
I'm sorry. I'm so sorry. But my crew. Please search for my crew.

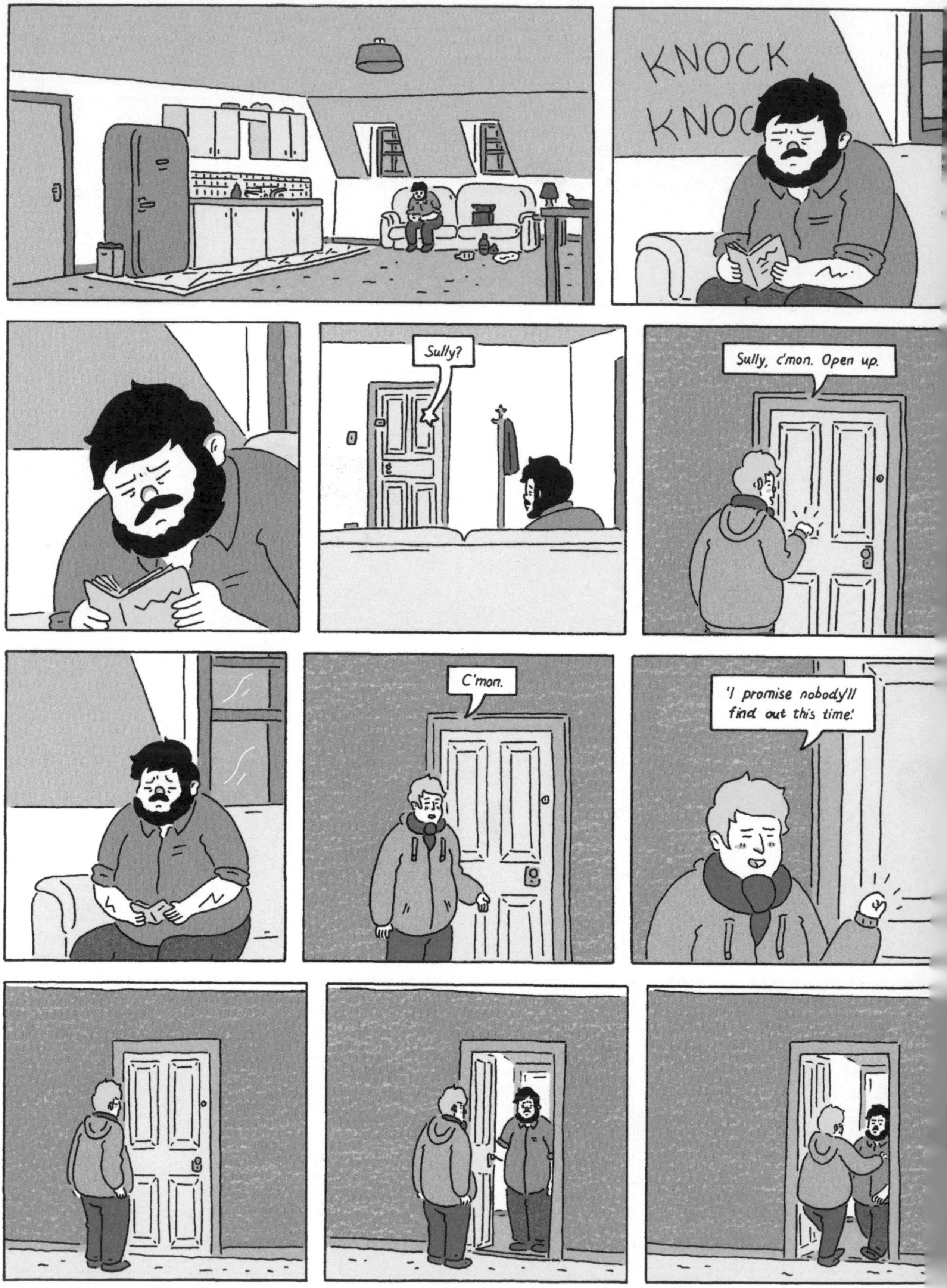
KNOCK
KNOC
Sully?
Sully, c'mon. Open up.
C'mon.
'I promise nobody'll find out this time.'

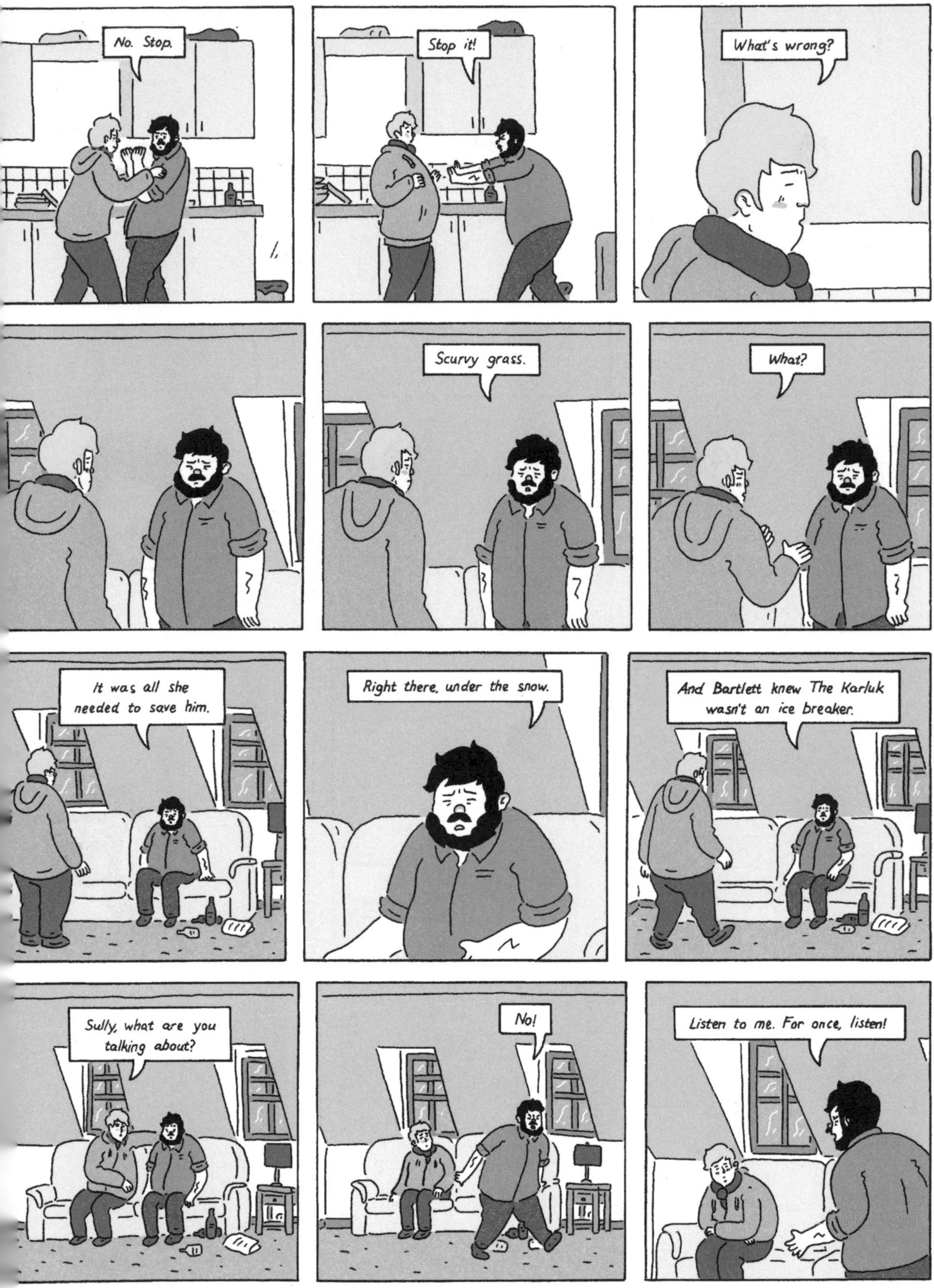
No. Stop.
Stop it!
What's wrong?
Scurvy grass.
What?
It was all she needed to save him.
Right there, under the snow.
And Bartlett knew The Karluk wasn't an ice breaker.
Sully, what are you talking about?
No!
Listen to me. For once, listen!

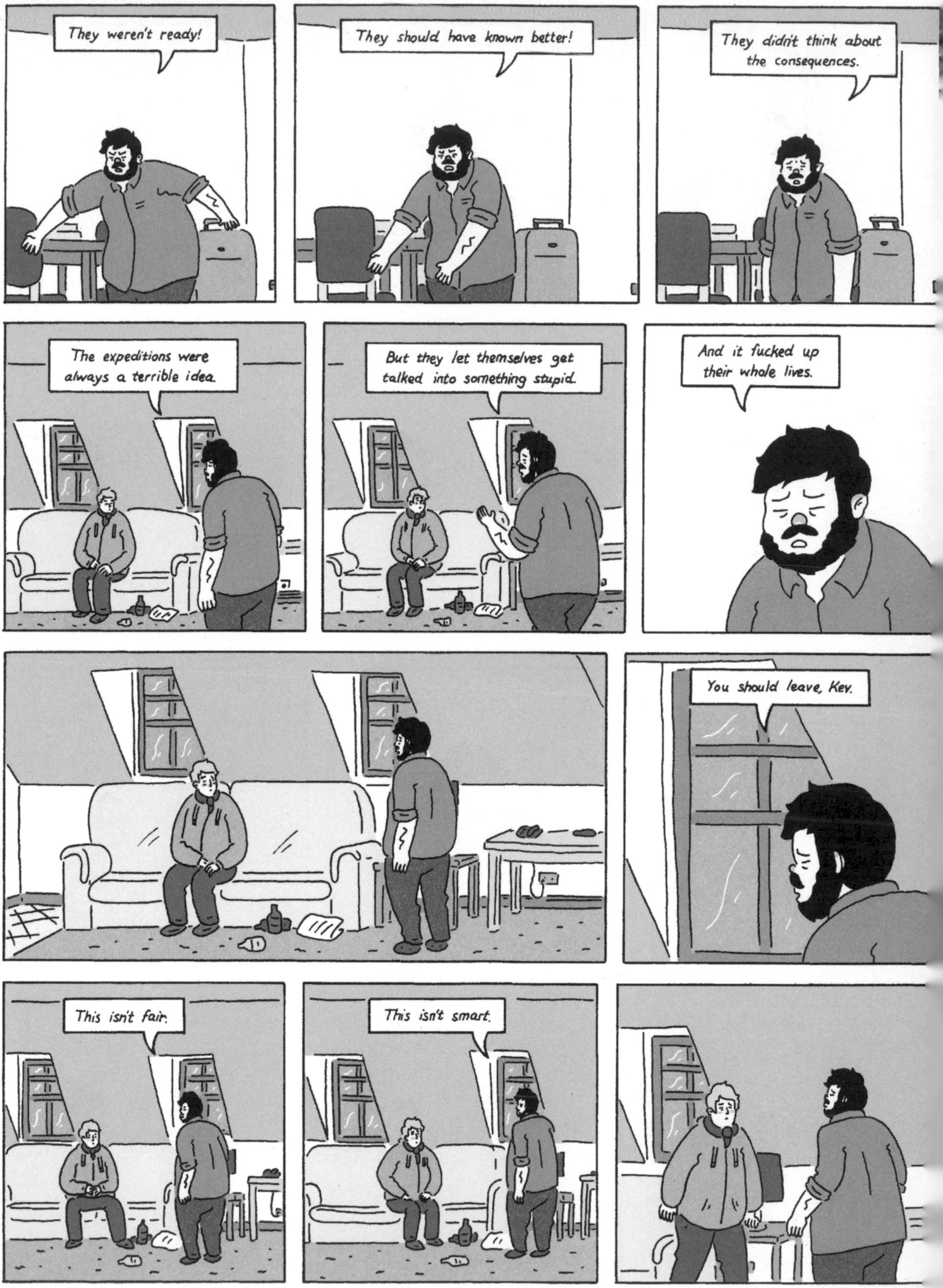
They weren't ready!
They should have known better!
They didn't think about the consequences.
The expeditions were always a terrible idea.
But they let themselves get talked into something stupid.
And it fucked up their whole lives.
You should leave, Kev.
This isn't fair.
This isn't smart.

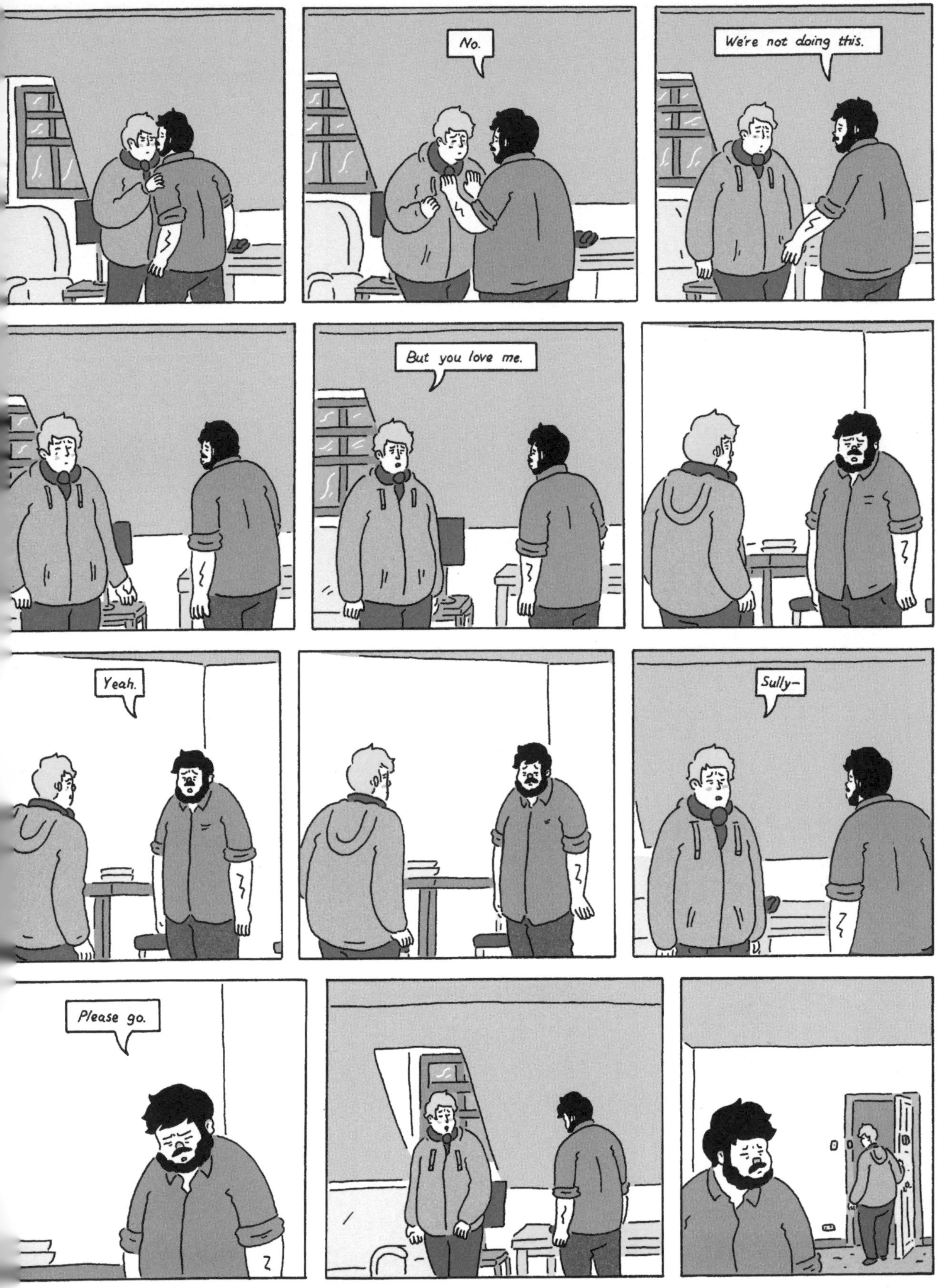
No.
We're not doing this.
But you love me.
Yeah.
Sully—
Please go.

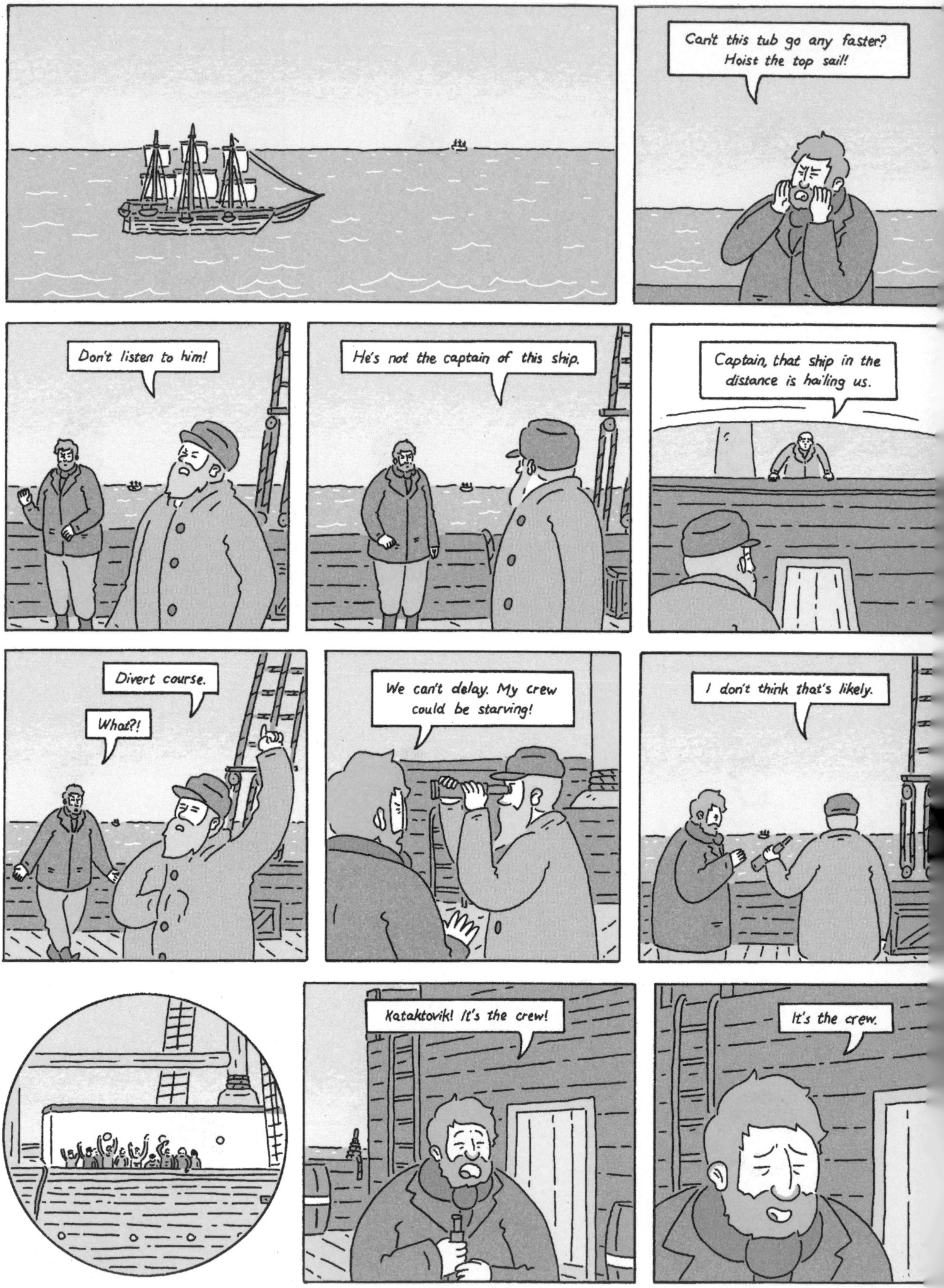
Can't this tub go any faster? Hoist the top sail!
Don't listen to him!
He's not the captain of this ship.
Captain, that ship in the distance is hailing us.
Divert course.
What?!
We can't delay. My crew could be starving!
I don't think that's likely.
Kataktovik! It's the crew!
It's the crew.

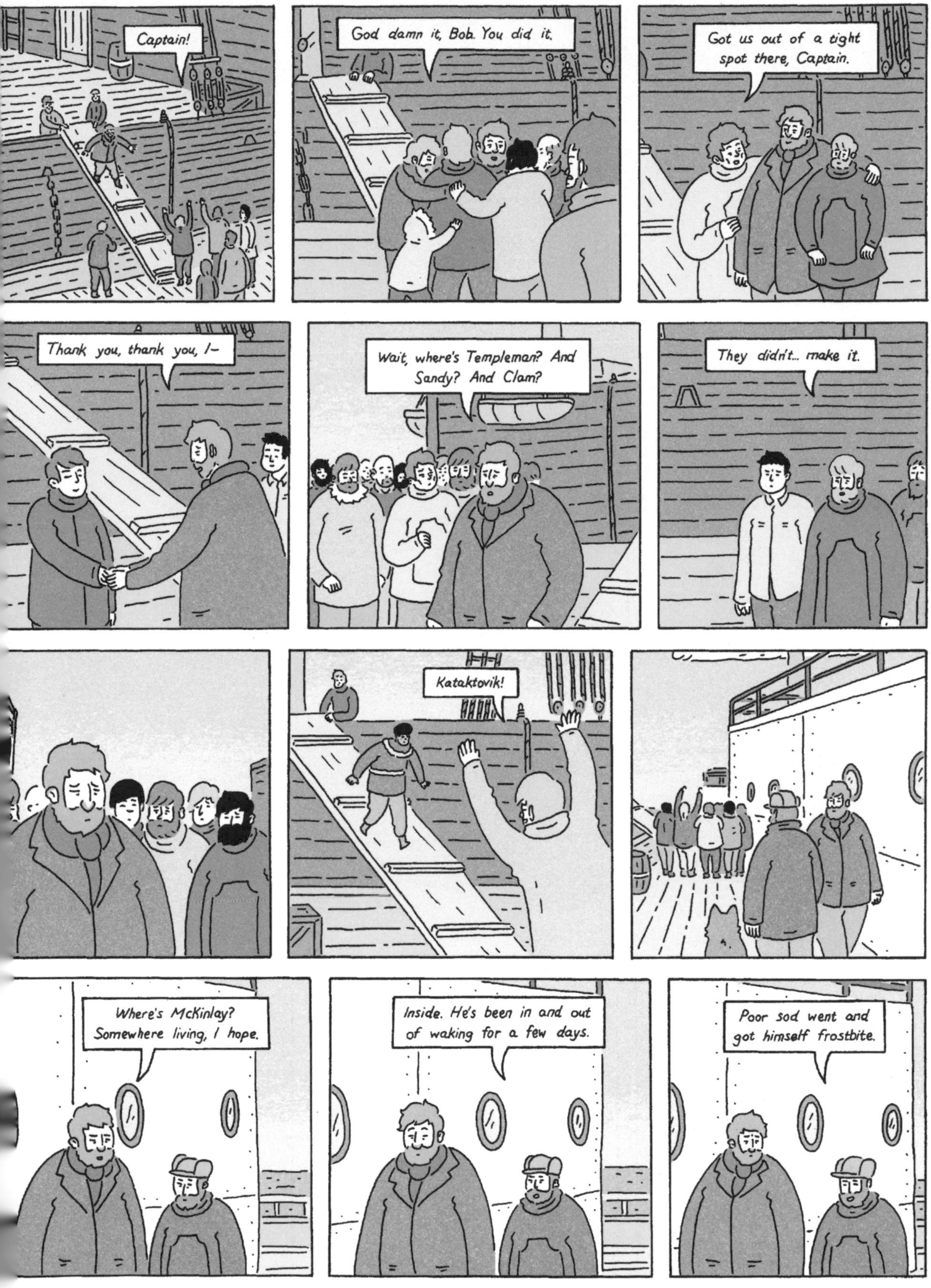
Captain!
God damn it, Bob. You did it.
Got us out of a tight spot there, Captain.
Thank you, thank you, I–
Wait, where's Templeman? And Sandy? And Clam?
They didn't... make it.
Kataktovik!
Where's McKinlay? Somewhere living, I hope.
Inside. He's been in and out of waking for a few days.
Poor sod went and got himself frostbite.

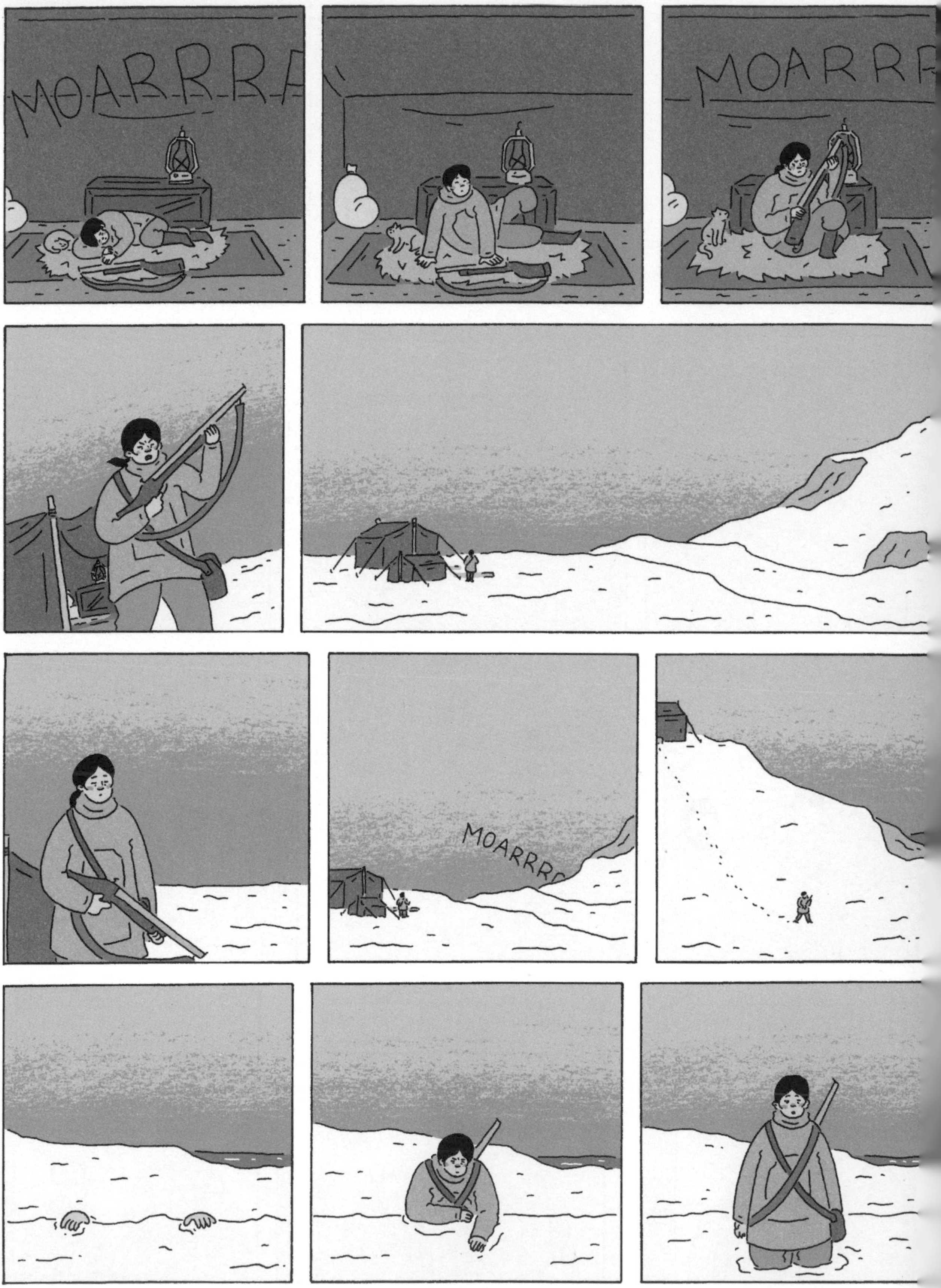
MOARRRA
MOARRR
MOARRRR

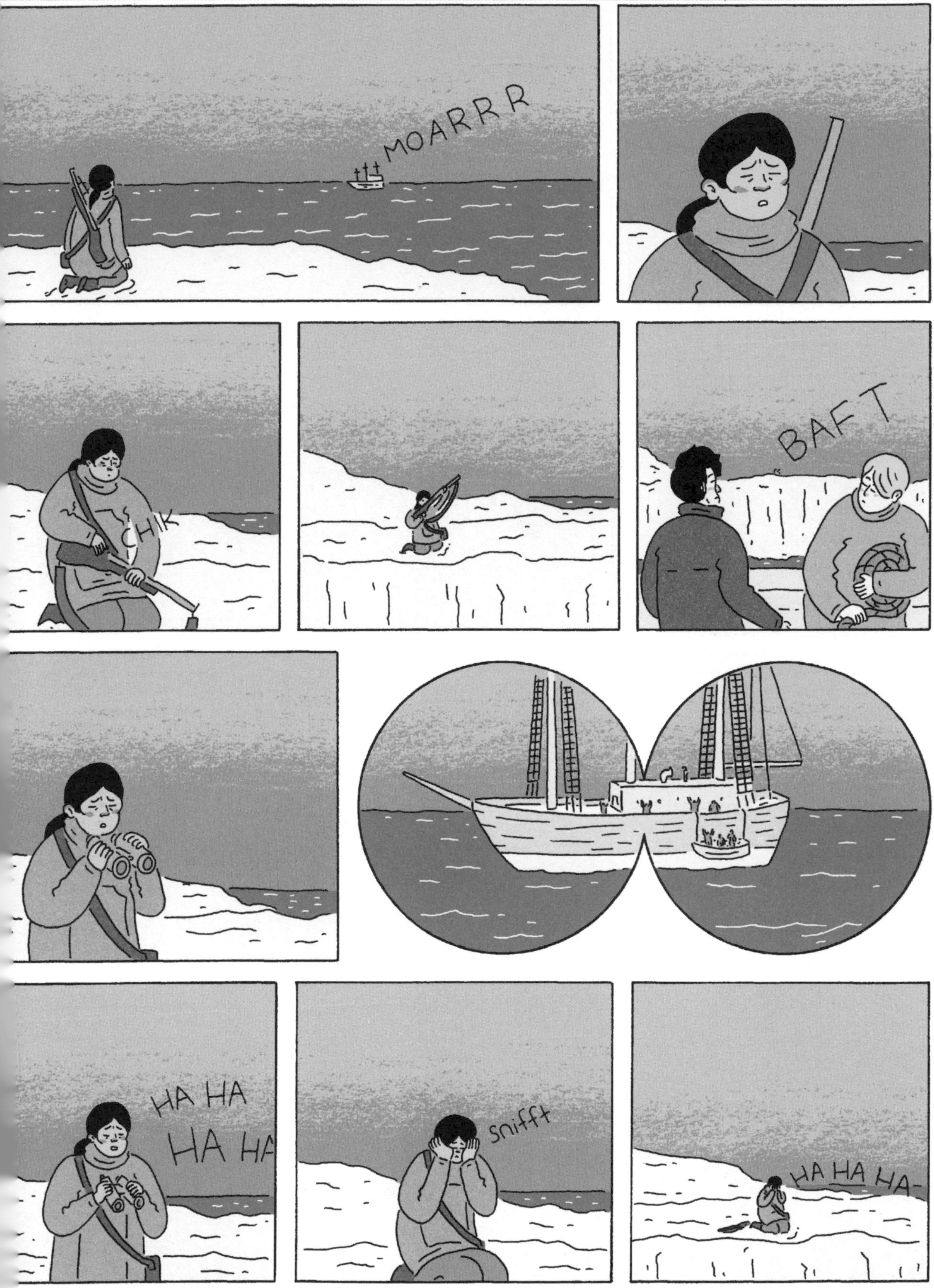
MOARRR
CHIK
BAFT
HA HA
HA HA
Snifft
HA HA HA-

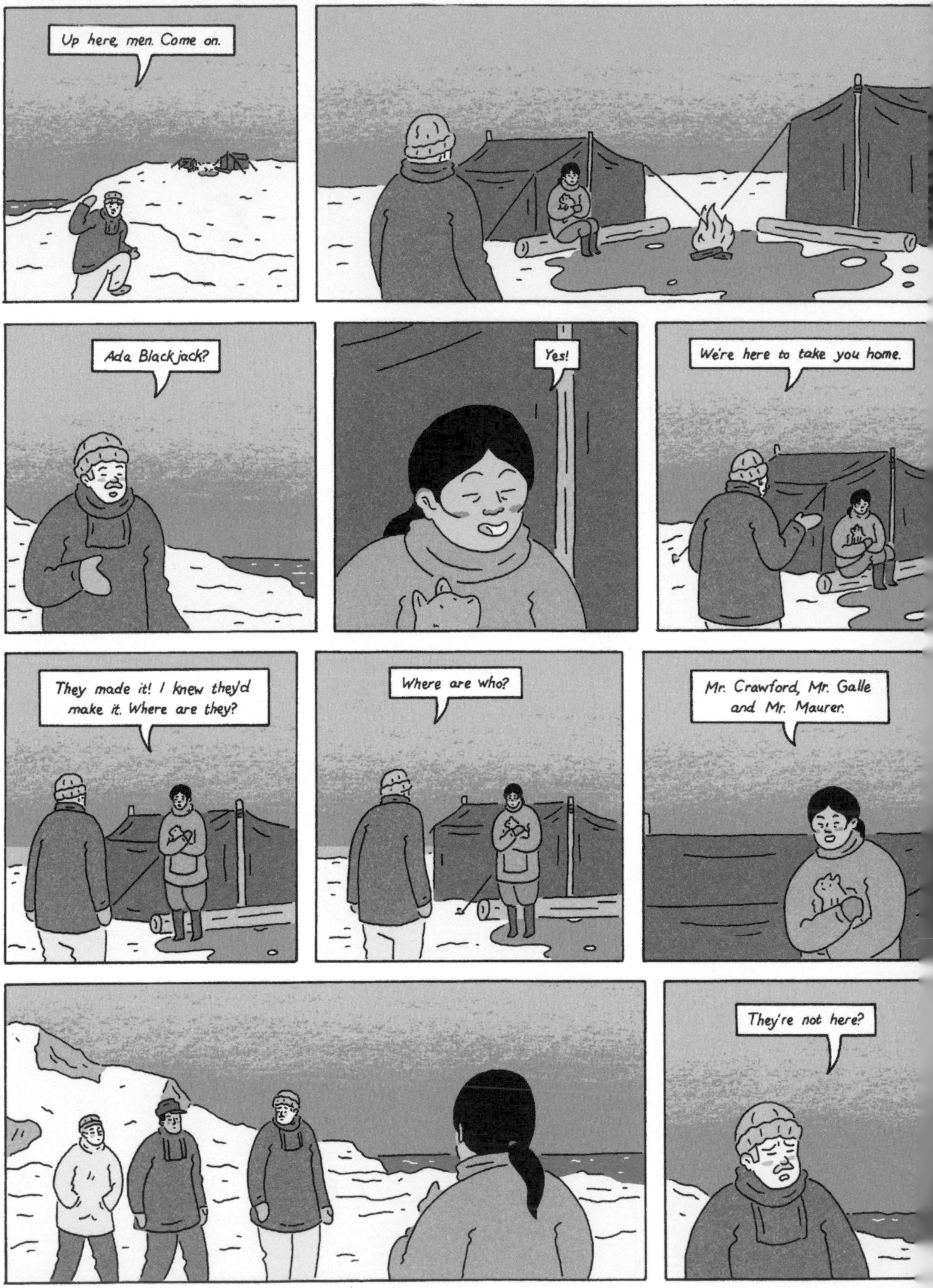
Up here, men. Come on.
Ada Blackjack?
Yes!
We're here to take you home.
They made it! I knew they'd make it. Where are they?
Where are who?
Mr. Crawford, Mr. Galle and Mr. Maurer.
They're not here?

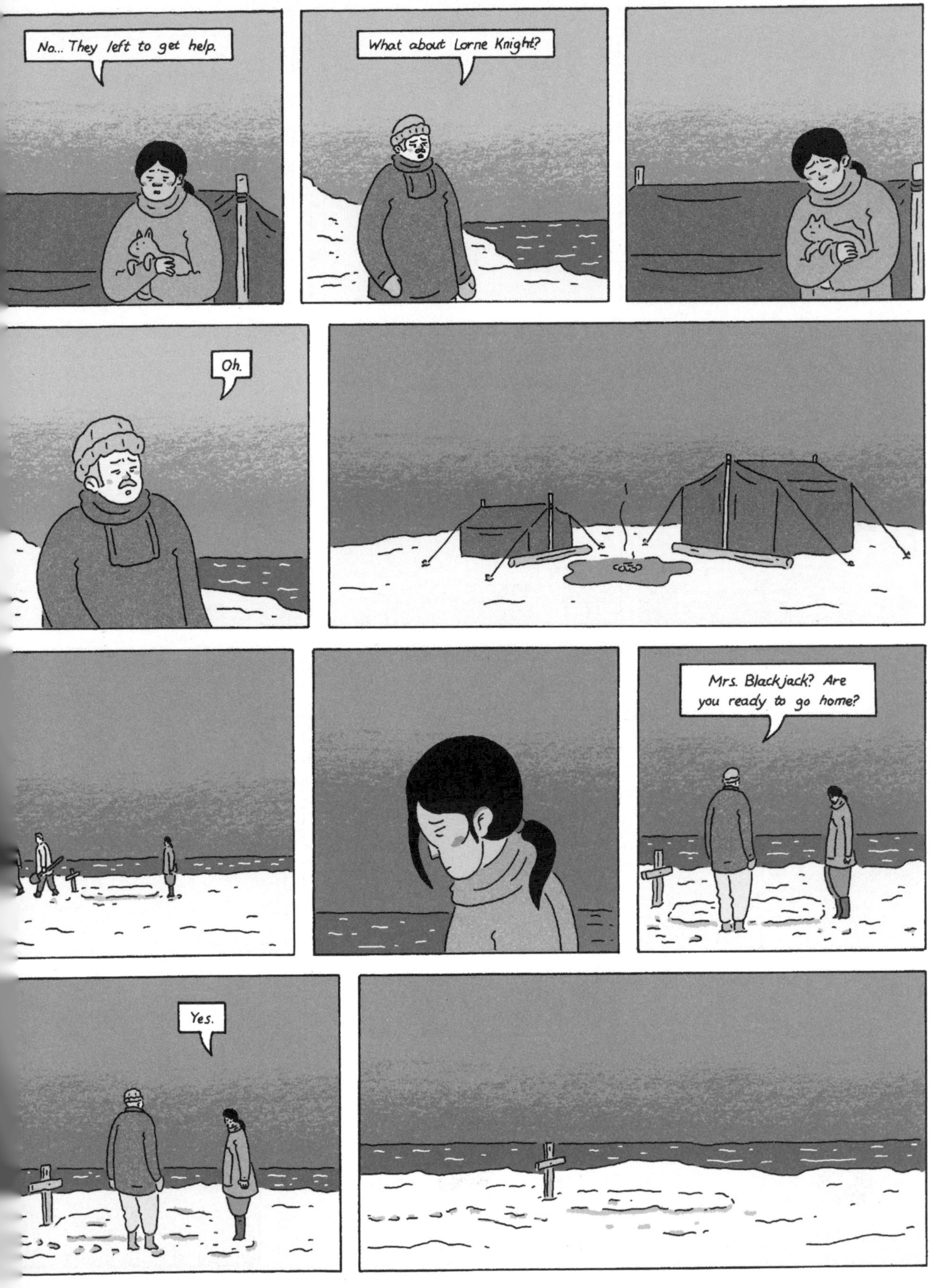

No... They left to get help.
What about Lorne Knight?
Oh.
Mrs. Blackjack? Are you ready to go home?
Yes.

Bob?
McKinlay, good of you to join us.
Stay down boyo.
DUFF
The ship. It came but you weren't on it.
Aye. I sent someone on ahead. Couldn't have you waiting for me.
So we made it? We're finally safe?
Aye McKinlay, you're safe.
PAT PAT
FFF
Less a few toes, but safe.
A cane will make you look distinguished, anyway.
You're an auld bastard, Bob Bartlett You know that?
Aye McKinlay. I know.

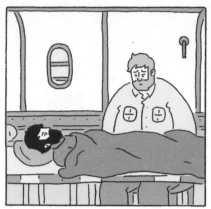

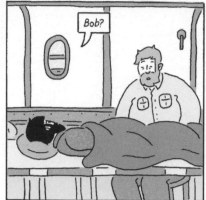

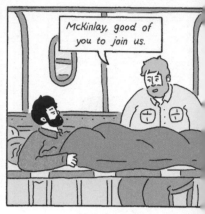

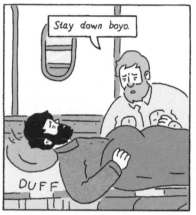

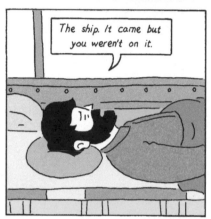

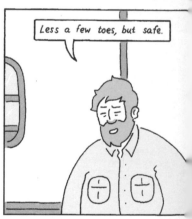

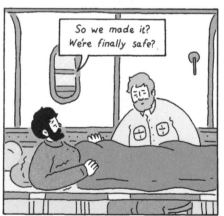

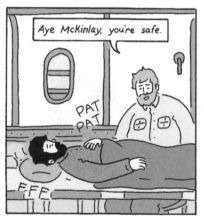

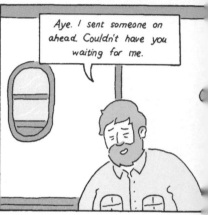

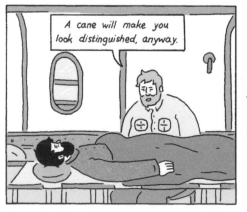

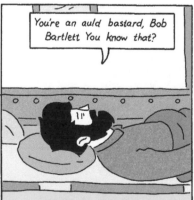

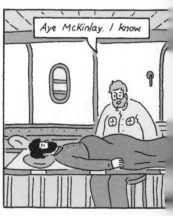

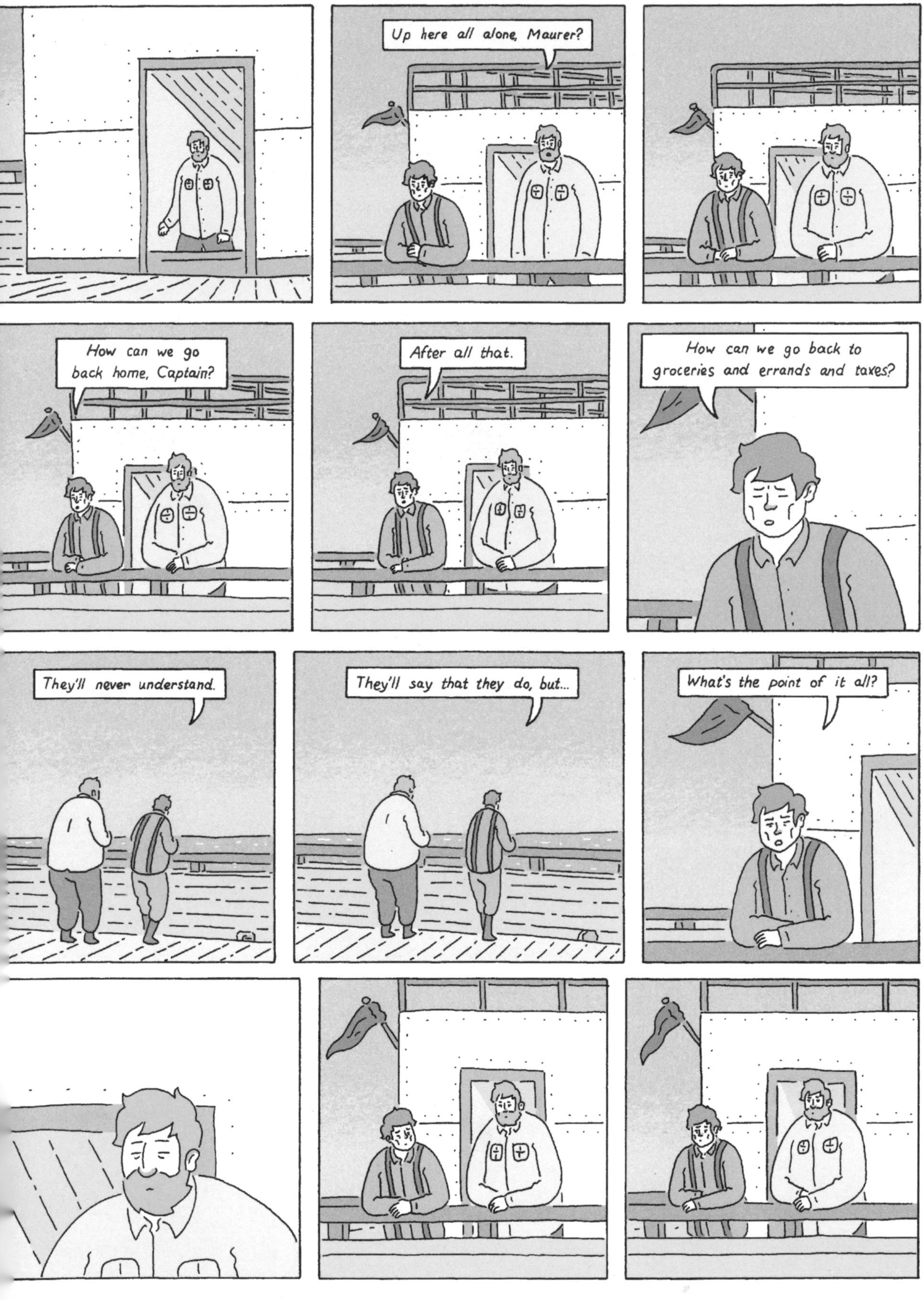

Up here all alone, Maurer?
How can we go back home, Captain?
After all that.
How can we go back to groceries and errands and taxes?
They'll never understand.
They'll say that they do, but...
What's the point of it all?

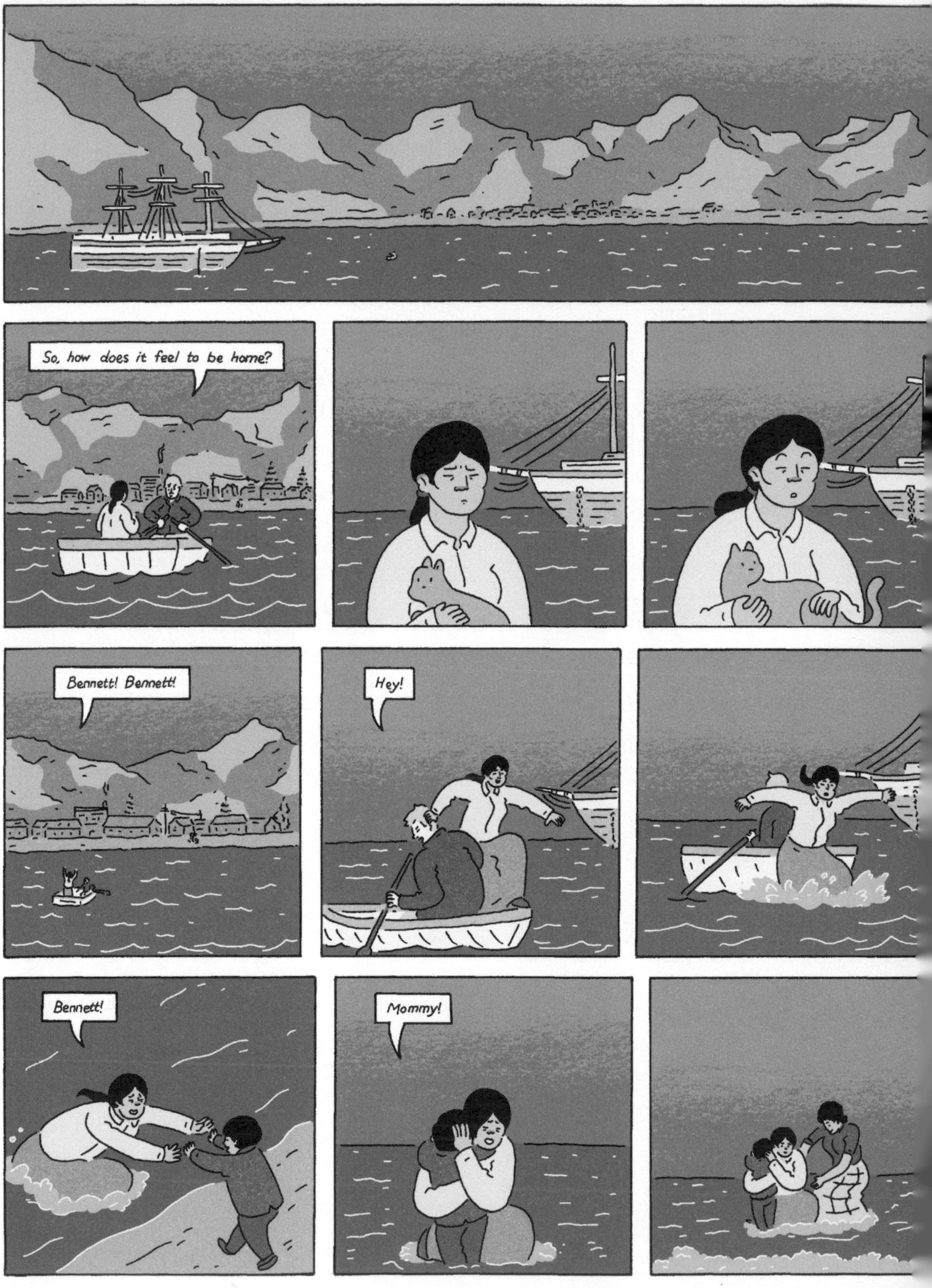
So, how does it feel to be home?
Bennett! Bennett!
Hey!
Bennett!
Mommy!

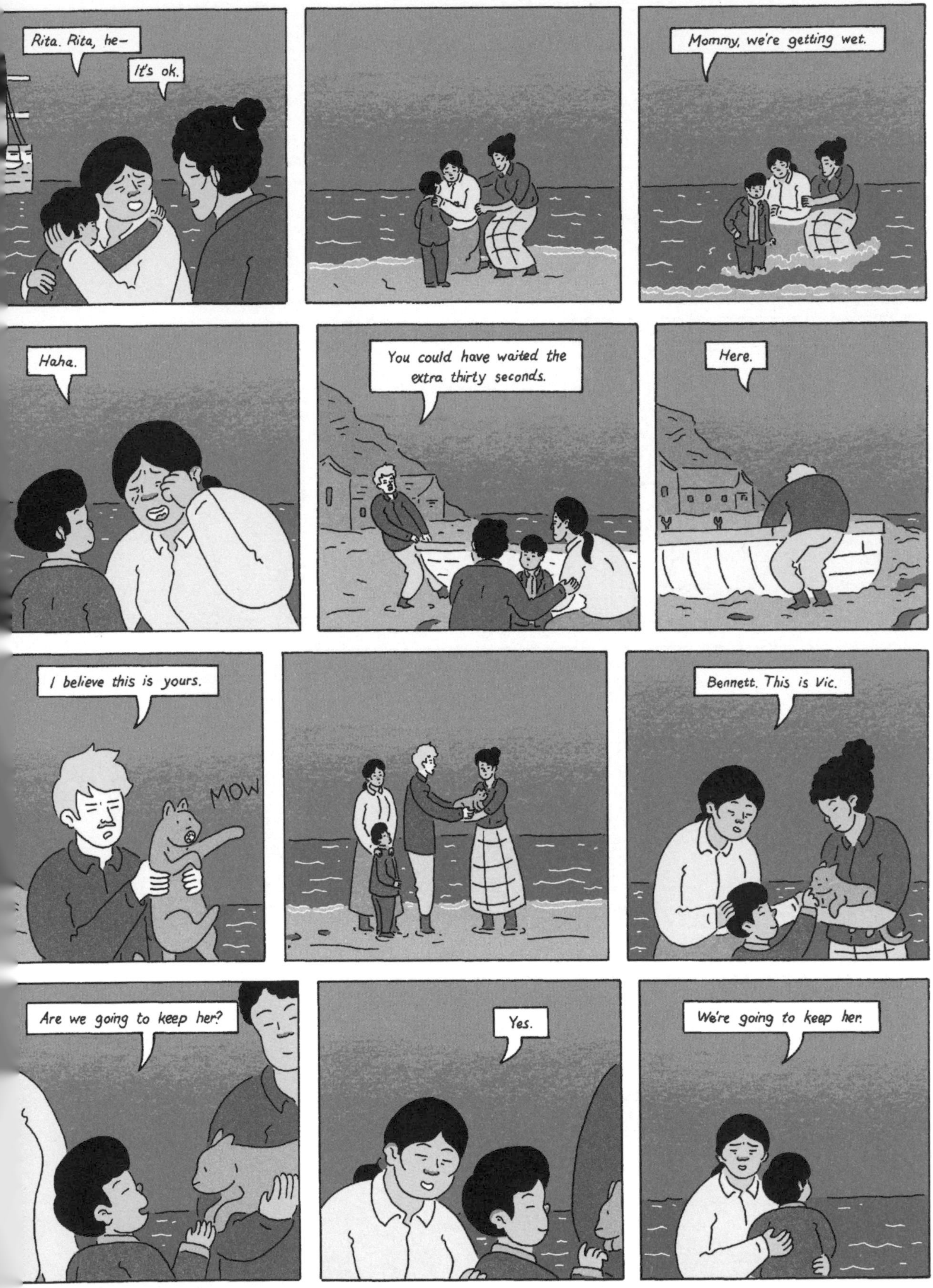
Rita. Rita, he–
It's ok.
Mommy, we're getting wet.
Haha.
You could have waited the extra thirty seconds.
Here.
I believe this is yours.
MOW
Bennett. This is Vic.
Are we going to keep her?
Yes.
We're going to keep her.

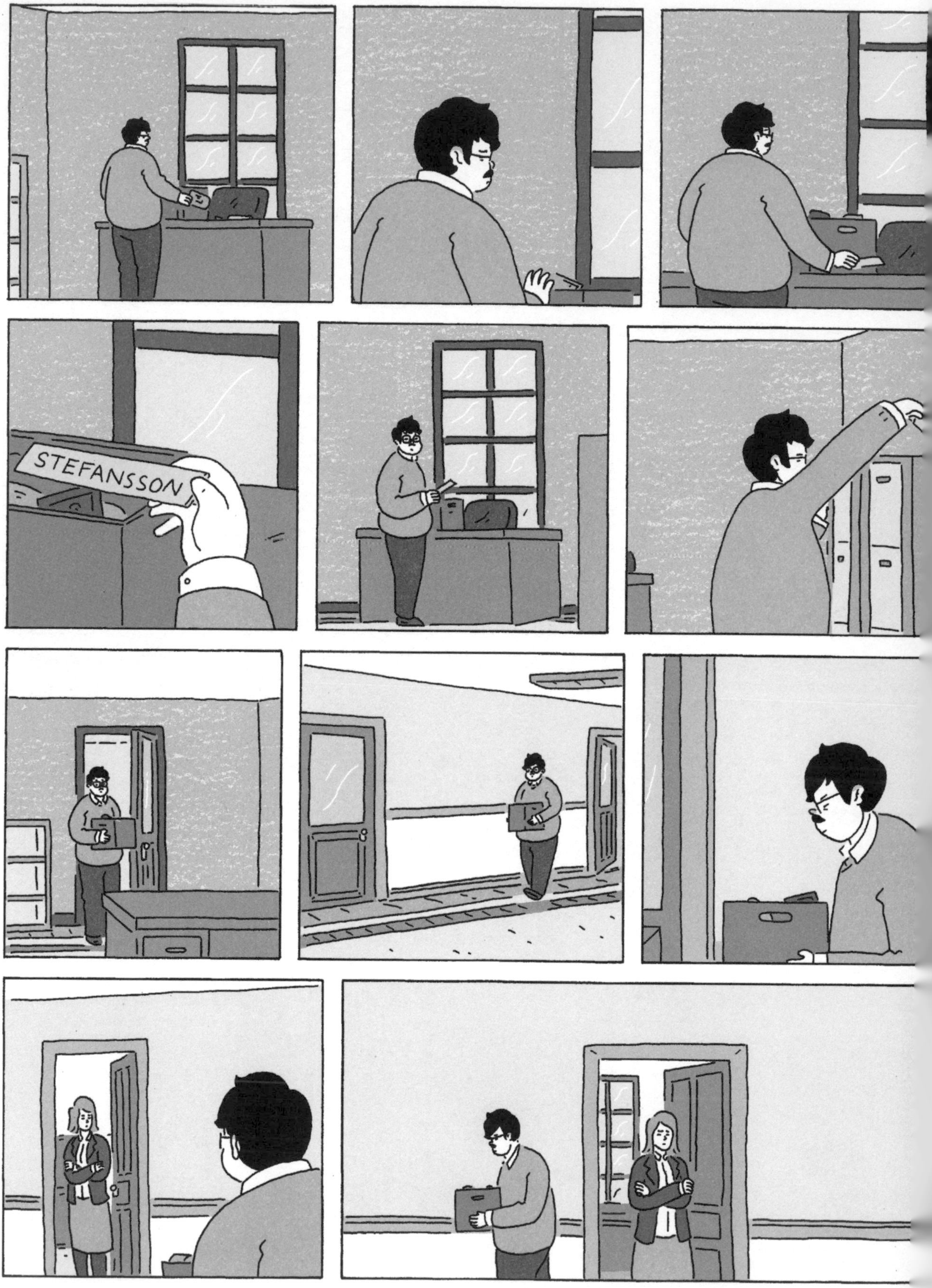
STEFANSSON

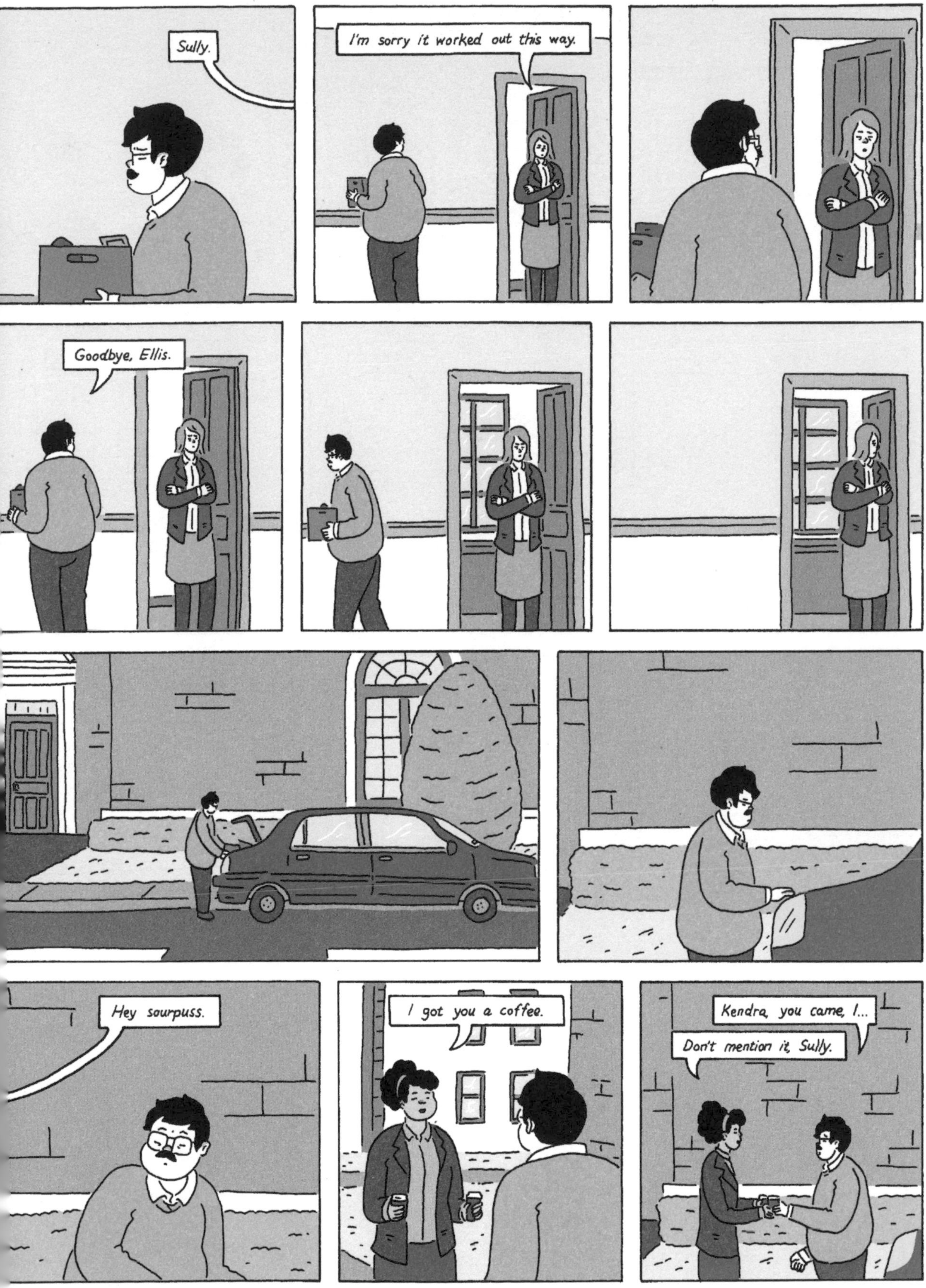

Sully.
I'm sorry it worked out this way.
Goodbye, Ellis.
Hey sourpuss.
I got you a coffee.
Kendra, you came, I...
Don't mention it, Sully.

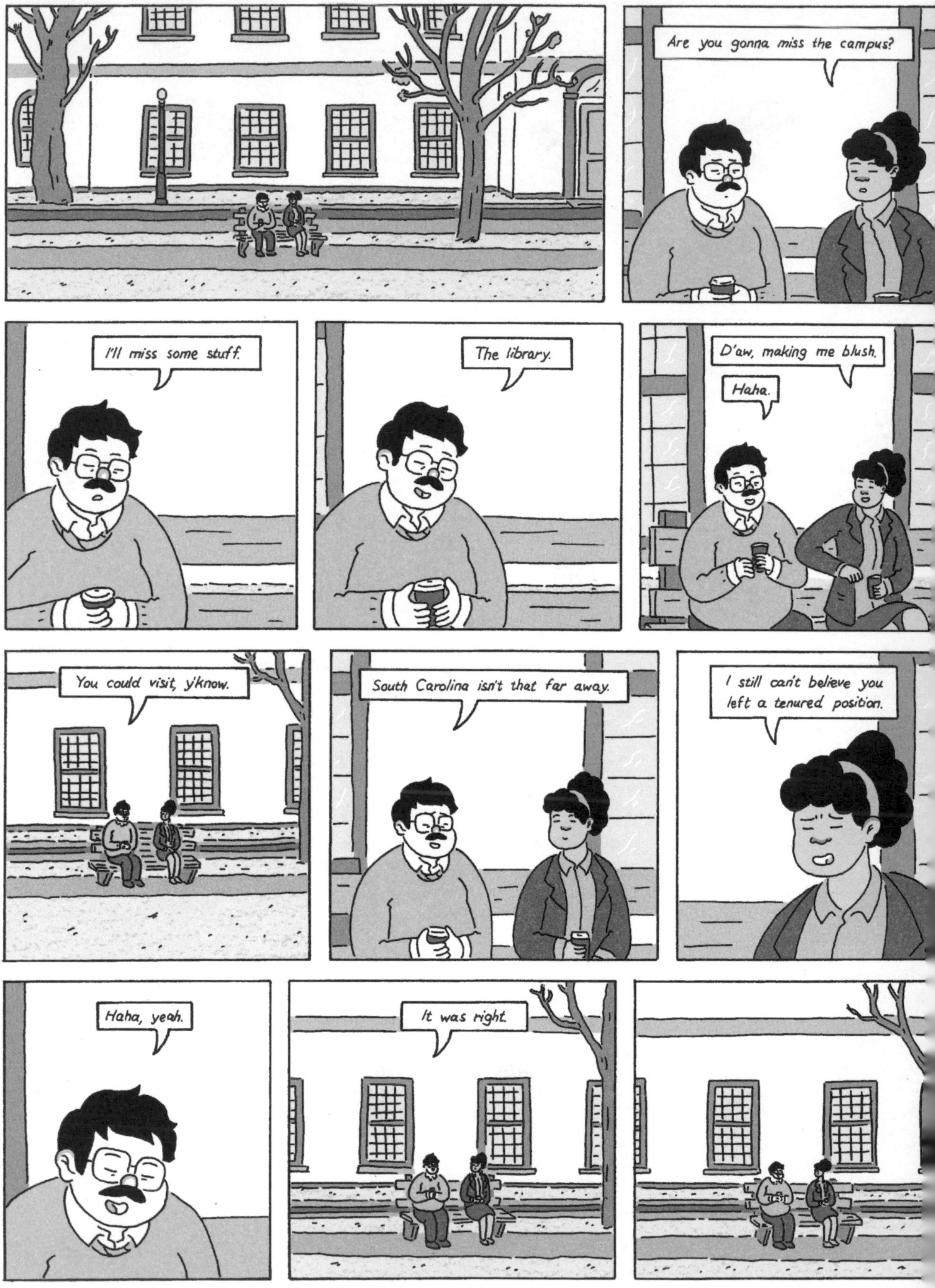

Are you gonna miss the campus?
I'll miss some stuff.
The library.
D'aw, making me blush.
Haha.
You could visit, y'know.
South Carolina isn't that far away.
I still can't believe you left a tenured position.
Haha, yeah.
It was right.

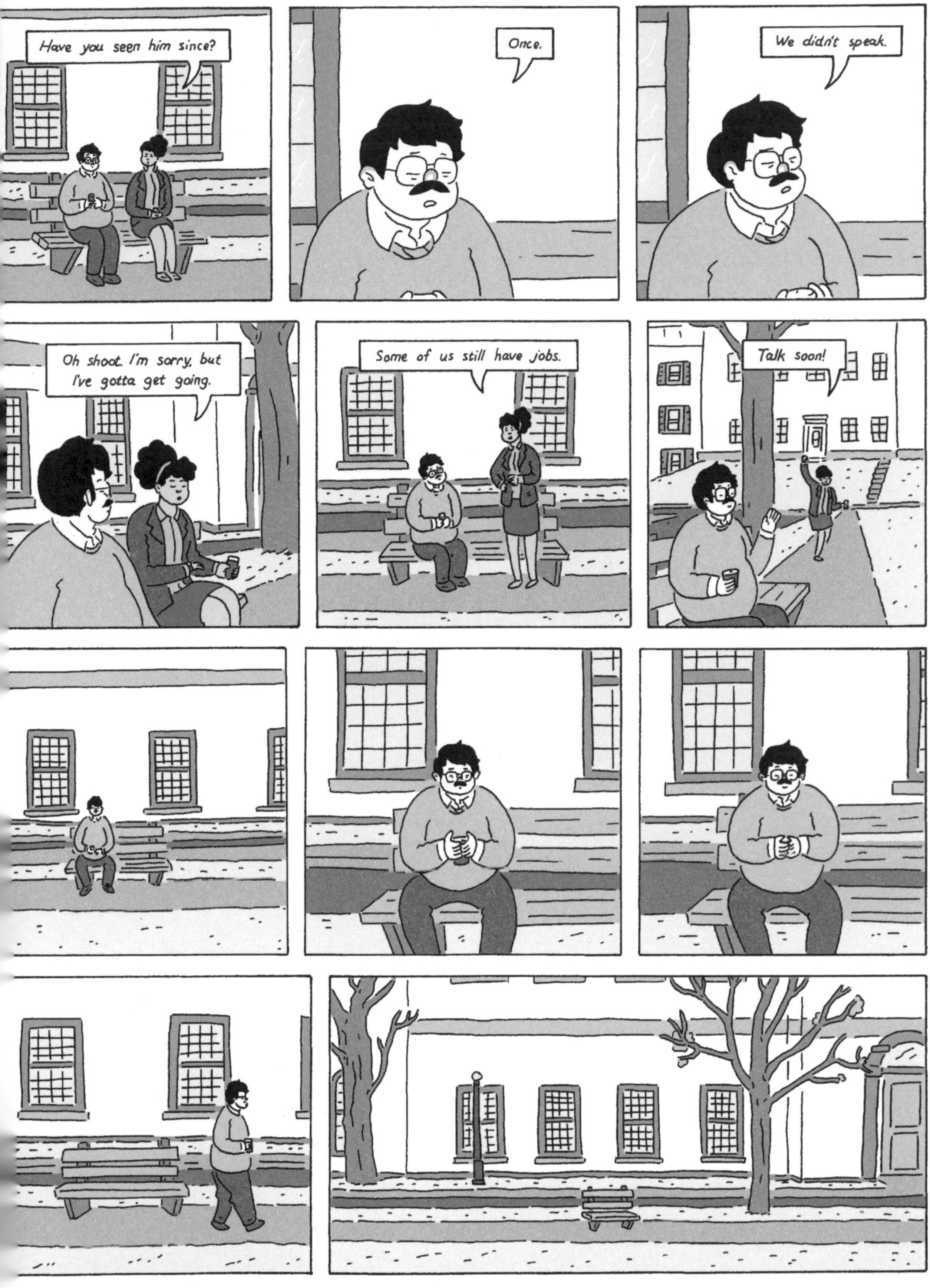
Have you seen him since?
Once.
We didn't speak.
Oh shoot. I'm sorry, but I've gotta get going.
Some of us still have jobs.
Talk soon!

Epilogue

From PECHUCK by Richard G. Montgomery, a reconstruction of Lorne Knight's diaries.

"Would you do it again, Knight?" asked Stefansson as he saw me off.

"Just try me," I said, gripping his hand. "But wait a couple of years if you don't mind. I want to get thoroughly warm and thoroughly clean again before I start out. It'll take that long at least !"

In the smoking compartment of my Pullman, I slumped down to enjoy the unrivaled scenery of the Canadian Rockies. Through my mind, in a muddled procession, raced the events of four and a half years. The stern tutelage of the Arctic had transformed me from a boy into a man.

For four and a half long years the North had been a stern and superior teacher. As we traversed giant mountains and rushing streams, I began to think more clearly of the old home I had left so long ago and of the new one toward which I was speeding. Mother and Dad—how startled they'd be when I hopped off the train at McMinnville! [...]

Thoughts, thoughts, thoughts, —and the miles flew by. Leaving the mountains behind, we dropped down into a beautiful farming country. Outside the car window, a light rain was falling. With my eyes half closed, it required only a slight stretch of the imagination to picture the green meadow as a wide expanse of ice, the haystacks as ice hummocks and the falling rain as driving snow ! How long ago it seemed—all of that !

Four traveling salesmen were playing bridge across from me. A fifth chap, somewhat pompous, read a newspaper.

"Been glancin' over this account of Stefansson's trip to the Arctic," he said, looking at me. "Great stuff, ain't it?"
"Think so?"
"Think so?" he thundered. "Why, I know so. Take a young chap like you, for instance. You ought to go up there. It'd make a man of you !"
"Well, now, maybe I will some day," I said, "you never can tell."

Very suddenly, I decided to bury my nose in the Saturday Evening Post. The Arctic was just a pleasant dream or a terrible nightmare—I wasn't sure which. A warm coziness covered me like a great soft cloak. Each click of the rails was bringing me closer to Oregon and home !

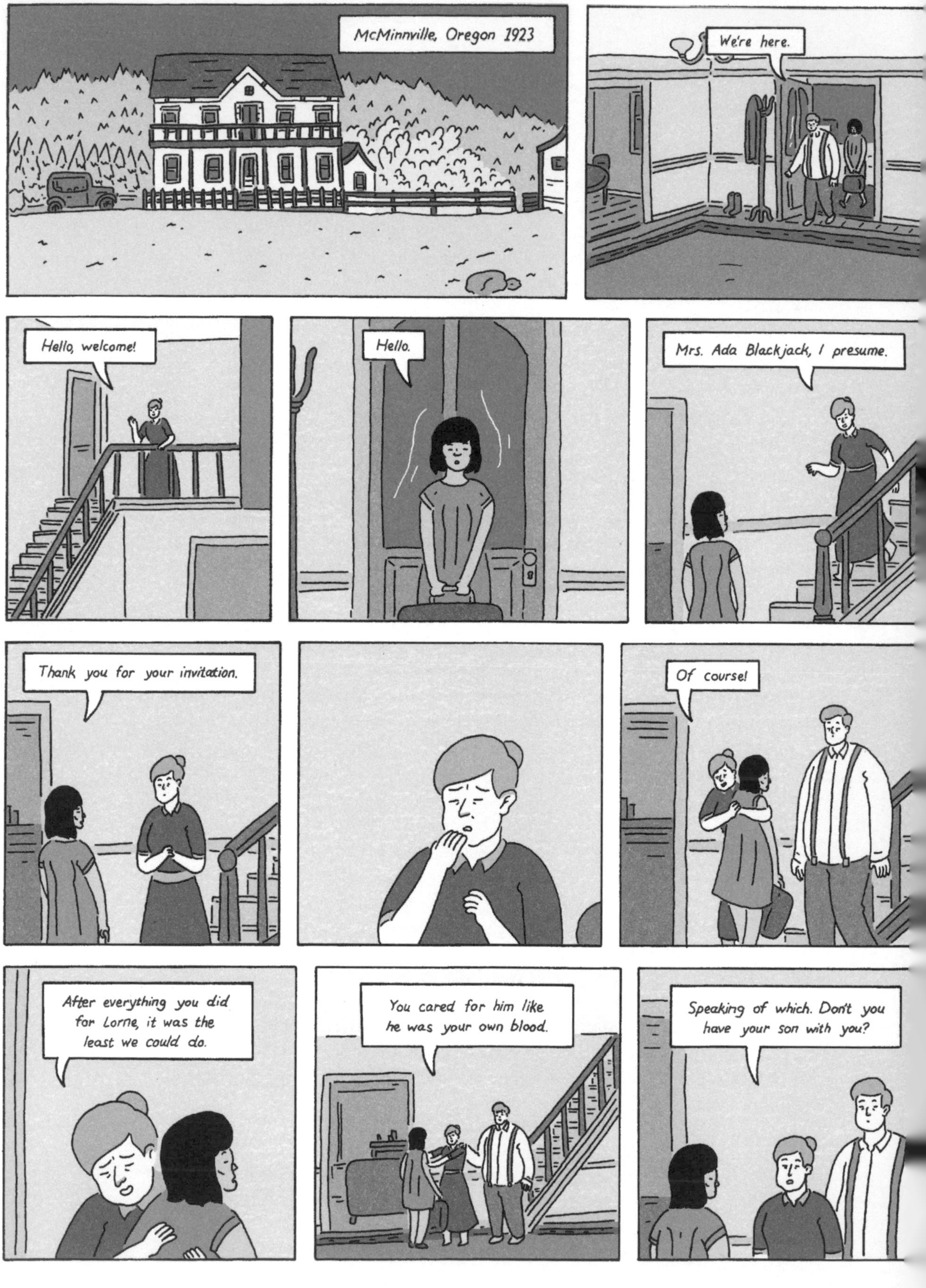
McMinnville, Oregon 1923
We're here.
Hello, welcome!
Hello.
Mrs. Ada Blackjack, I presume.
Thank you for your invitation.
Of course!
After everything you did for Lorne, it was the least we could do.
You cared for him like he was your own blood.
Speaking of which. Don't you have your son with you?

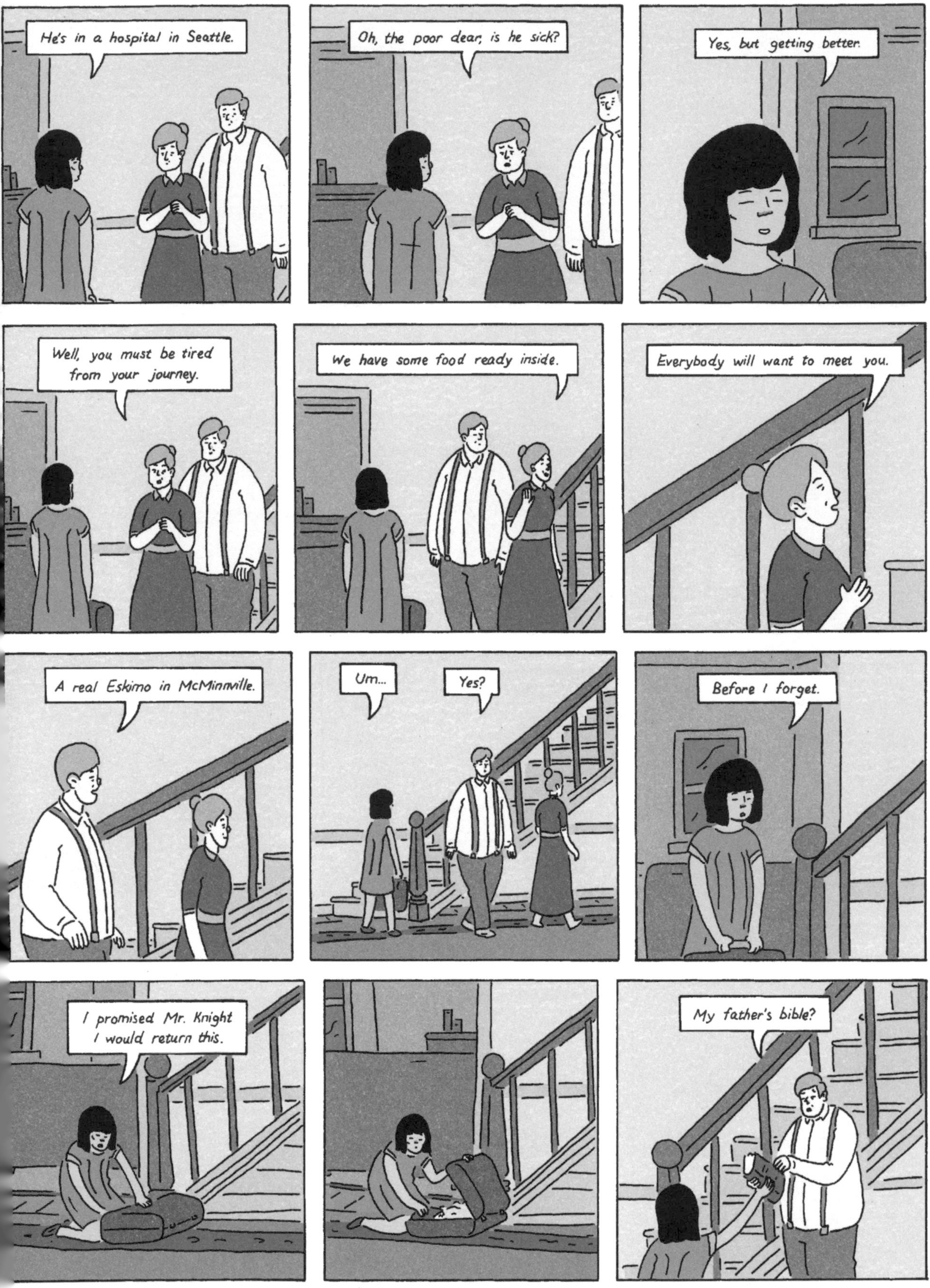
He's in a hospital in Seattle.
Oh, the poor dear, is he sick?
Yes, but getting better.
Well, you must be tired from your journey.
We have some food ready inside.
Everybody will want to meet you.
A real Eskimo in McMinnville.
Um...
Yes?
Before I forget.
I promised Mr. Knight I would return this.
My father's bible?

Thank you.

Um, let me help you put your bag upstairs.

Everyone really is excited to meet you.

Especially Lorne's fiancée.

Here's the room.

I'll see you downstairs.

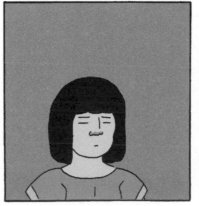

It was no-one's fault but my own that I
went up there for no one would have
forced me to go but I wanted to go and
thought I would never have another
chance to go so I took it.

Very respectfully,

Mrs Ada Black Jack

After the Expeditions

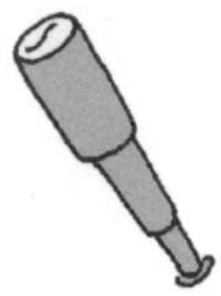

Robert Bartlett received the highest award from the Royal Geographical Society for his heroism in rescuing 11 members of the Karluk's crew from Wrangel Island. Only 3 years later Bartlett rescued the crew of another ill-fated expedition, who had been stuck in the ice for over 4 years.

From 1925-1945 he captained his own ship, the Effie M. Morrissey, which he led on many successful scientific expeditions into the Arctic.

He died in New York City on the 28th of April 1946 from pneumonia, aged 70. He is remembered in many pieces of writing, including his own memoirs, and has been commemorated for his outstanding career in a myriad of ways. In 2009, his picture appeared on a Canadian postage stamp.

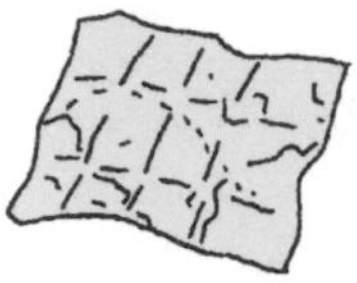

William McKinlay returned to his native Scotland, where he lived to the age of 95, eventually becoming the headmaster of his school. Every so often he would receive letters from Bartlett, whom he considered a true friend.

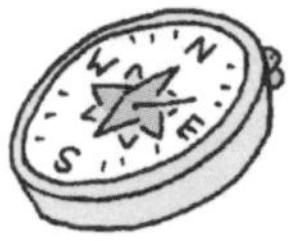
N
S
E

The last time Bartlett saw Kataktovik he learned that the young hunter was happily engaged to be married at the age of 20.

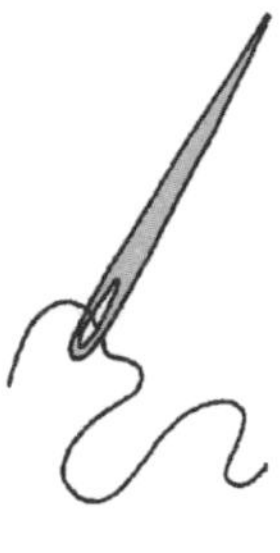

Unfortunately, Ada's life after Wrangel Island was not easy. Upon her return, she was a media sensation across the United States. The press alternately heroised and vilified her. Harold Noice, the man who had rescued her from Wrangel, publicly blamed her for Lorne Knight's death, a sentiment that was quashed only when Lorne's father issued a statement of his own: "I still maintain that Ada Blackjack is a real heroine, and that there is nothing to justify me in the faintest belief that she did not do for Lorne all that she was able to do..."

Ada used the small salary she had earned on the expedition, as well as some money from selling the furs she had trapped on Wrangel, to bring her son Bennett to Seattle where doctors cured his tuberculosis. She remarried and had another son, Billy Blackjack Johnson, but divorced quickly. Eventually she settled back in Alaska, where she spent her remaining days.

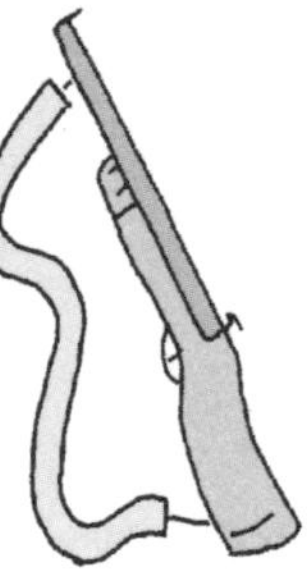

Ada died in a nursing home on May 9th 1983, at the age of 85. One month after her death, following a letter from her son Billy, the Alaska Legislature officially honoured Ada for her bravery and heroism

Fred Maurer, Alan Crawford and Milton Galle were never seen again after leaving Wrangel Island. Their fate remains unknown, though it is almost certain that they perished while attempting to cross the sea ice to Siberia.

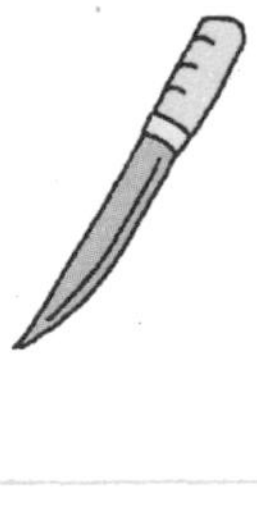

Lorne Knight is commemorated by monuments in McMinnville, Oregon and on Wrangel Island. After his death, his diaries were published by his friend Richard G. Montgomery under the name PECHUCK:. Lorne Knight's Adventures in the Arctic.

Stefansson, despite this book's perhaps dim view of him, went on to contribute significantly to the field of Arctic science. He received many honours over the course of his career. He died on August 26th 1962 at the age of 81.

Sullivan Barnaby, as noted, is not a real person. Though if he was, I think he'd probably be at least 5% closer to having his life together by now.

A Note on the Historical Accuracy of the Text

The 1913 and 1921 stories in this book are based closely on the true events of the Canadian Arctic, and Wrangel Island Expeditions respectively.

Certain events and characters in these true stories were omitted, combined or edited for the sake of clarity. Additionally, the research for this book included subjective first-hand accounts of the events, some of which are more factually correct than others. I believe that the stories remain essentially true, and that the changes do not overly affect the integrity of the book's relationship to reality. However, to call this book a work of non-fiction would be dishonest. For these and other reasons (not least of which is the interweaving of a third, fictional narrative) it is best described as being "based on the true stories" of Robert Bartlett and Ada Blackjack.

All events taking place in the 2013 storyline of this book are entirely fictional, and any similarities to actual people or events are completely coincidental.

I also understand that the word "Eskimo" is largely considered to be a pejorative term. My apologies for any hurt or offence its inclusion in this book may have caused. I chose to include it purely for the sake of historical accuracy.

This book is dedicated to Mary and Fergus.

Special thanks to: Jon C. Jason L. Steve B. James S. Nicole G. Valerie F. Sarah S.T. Paul K. Joyana M. Eleri H. Tom B. Mathew N. Juan F. Simon R. April M. Harriet B. Cefn R. Sam A. and Alex S.

Luke Healy is a cartoonist from Dublin, Ireland.
After finishing work on How to Survive in the North,
he was so tired of sitting indoors drawing pictures
that he went hiking for five months.

THIS IS A FIRST PAPERBACK EDITION PUBLISHED IN 2017 BY
NOBROW LTD. 27 WESTGATE STREET, LONDON E8 3RL.

EDITED BY CEFN RIDOUT.

2 4 6 8 10 9 7 5 3 1

PUBLISHED IN THE US BY NOBROW (US) INC.
PRINTED IN POLAND ON FSC® CERTIFIED PAPER.

MIX
Paper from responsible sources
FSC® C001693

ISBN: 978-1-910620-32-8
ORDER FROM WWW.NOBROW.NET